STATE DOCUMENTS ON
FEDERAL RELATIONS

Da Capo Press Reprints in

AMERICAN CONSTITUTIONAL AND LEGAL HISTORY

GENERAL EDITOR: LEONARD W. LEVY
Brandeis University

STATE DOCUMENTS ON FEDERAL RELATIONS

The States and The United States

Edited with notes by
HERMAN V. AMES

DA CAPO PRESS • NEW YORK • 1970

A Da Capo Press Reprint Edition

This Da Capo Press edition of *State Documents on Federal Relations* is an unabridged republication of the first edition published in
Philadelphia between 1900 and 1906. It is reprinted from copies of
that edition owned by the Cornell University Library and the
Ohio State University Library.

Library of Congress Catalog Card Number 78-77697
SBN 306-71335-7

Published by Da Capo Press
A Division of Plenum Publishing Corporation
227 West 17th Street, New York, N. Y. 10011

Manufactured in the United States of America

CONTENTS

INTERPRETATION OF THE CONSTITUTION DURING THE FIRST TWO DECADES OF ITS HISTORY. 1789–1809.

STATE RIGHTS
AND THE WAR OF 1812. 1809–1815.

THE RESERVED RIGHTS OF THE STATES
AND THE
JURISDICTION OF FEDERAL COURTS, 1819–1832.

THE TARIFF AND NULLIFICATION, 1820–1833.

SLAVERY AND THE CONSTITUTION, 1789–1845.

SLAVERY AND THE UNION, 1845–1861.

STATE DOCUMENTS ON
FEDERAL RELATIONS

INTERPRETATION OF THE CONSTITUTION DURING THE FIRST TWO DECADES OF ITS HISTORY. 1789–1809.

---

1. Memorial from the State of Rhode Island and Providence Plantations.

September Session, 1789.

In June of 1789, the Rhode Island Assembly for the sixth time defeated a proposition to call a convention to consider the ratification of the Federal Constitution, but hoping to avert hostile tariff legislation by Congress, it had passed in May an impost law providing for the collection of the same duties on imports as Congress might lay upon imports into the Union. In September, after re-enacting the law passed by Congress (July 31, 1 *U. S. Stat. at Large*, 48), they sent the following memorial, an overture for a commercial union. Congress, anticipating the receipt of the memorial, passed an act suspending the impost law in favor of Rhode Island and North Carolina until January 15, 1790. (Sept. 15, 1 *U. S. Stat. at Large*, 100. Memorial received, Sept. 26, *Senate Journal*, 1 *Cong.*, 89 (ed. 1820).) Finally the Rhode Island Assembly called a convention for March 1, 1790, and requested a further suspension of the revenue laws. Congress granted an extension until April 1. The convention, however, adjourned without completing its work to May 24. In consequence of its action, the Senate on May 18 passed a bill prohibiting all commercial intercourse with Rhode Island after the 1st of July next, and authorizing the government to demand of that State the payment of its portion of the continental debt without delay. (*Annals of Cong.*, 1, 976; *S. J.*, 1 *Cong.*, 142.) This attitude of the Senate, together with the open threats of coercion in the public press, apparently had an important influence on the convention. That body ratified the constitution, May 29, 1790, by a vote of 34 to 32, also proposing a series of amendments.

References: The text is from *Rhode Island Colonial Records*, X, 356, also slightly changed in *American State Papers, Miscellaneous*, I, 10. For the history, of prime importance is F. G. Bates, *Rhode Island and the Formation of the Union*, Chaps. V, VI (N. Y., 1898); cf. Arnold's *Rhode Island*, II, 536–564 (4th ed.); Curtis, *Constitution*, II, 598–604 (ed. 1860), or I, 692–697 (ed. 1897); Elliot's *Debates*, I, 336, 337.

To the President, Senate and House of Representatives of the eleven United States of America, in Congress assembled :

The critical situation in which the people of this state are placed, engage us to make these assurances, in the behalf of their attachment and friendship to their sister states, and of their disposition to cultivate mutual harmony and friendly intercourse. They know themselves to be a handful, comparatively viewed, and although they now stand as it were, alone, they have not separated themselves, or departed from the principles of that Confederation which was formed by the sister states, in their struggle for freedom and in the hour of danger. They seek by this *memorial* to call to your remembrance the hazard which we have run, the hardships we have endured, the treasures we have spent, and the *blood* we have lost together in one common cause, and especially the object we had in view—the preservation of our *liberty*—wherein ability considered they may truly say, they were equal in exertions with the foremost. The effects whereof in great embarrassments and other distresses, consequent thereon, we have since experienced with severity, which common sufferings and common danger we hope and trust will yet form a bond of union and friendship not easily to be broken. Our not having acceded to or adopted the new system of government found and adopted by most of our sister states, we doubt not have given uneasiness to them. That we have not seen our way clear to do it, consistent with our idea of the principle upon which we all embarked together, has also given *pain* to us; we have not doubted but we might thereby avoid present difficulties, but we have apprehended future mischief. The people of this state from its first settlement have been accustomed and strongly attached to a democratical form of government. They have read in the constitution an approach toward that form of government from which we have lately dissolved our connection at so much hazard of expense of life and treasure,—they have seen with pleasure the administration thereof, from the most important trusts downward, committed to men who have highly merited, and in whom the people of the United States place *unbounded confidence*. Yet, even on this circumstance, in itself so fortunate, they have apprehended danger by way of precedent. Can it be thought strange then, that with these impressions, they should wait to see the proposed system organized and in operation, to see what further checks and securities would be agreed to, etc. [and] established by way of *amendments* before they would adopt it as a constitution of government for themselves and their posterity?

These amendments we believe have already afforded some relief and satisfaction to the minds of the people of this state: And we earnestly look for the time, when they may with clearness and safety, be again united with their sister states under a con-stitution and form of government so well poised, as neither to need alteration or be liable thereto by a majority only of nine states out of *thirteen*, a circumstance which may possibly take place against the sense of a majority of the people of the United States. We are sensible of the extremes to which democratical government is sometimes liable; something of which we have lately experienced, but we esteem them temporary and partial evils compared with the loss of liberty and the rights of a free people. Neither do we apprehend they will be marked with severity by our sister states, when it is considered that during the late trouble, the whole United States, notwithstanding their joint wisdom and efforts, fell into the like misfortune. That from our extraordinary exertions, this state was left in a situation nearly as embarrassing at that during the war. That in the measures which were adopted, government unfortunately had not the aid and support from the monied interest, which our sister states of New York and the Carolinas experienced under similar circumstances, and especially when it is considered that upon some abatement of that fermentation in the minds of the people which is so common in the collision of sentiments and of parties, a disposition appears to provide a remedy for the difficulties we have labored under on that account.

We are induced to hope that we shall not be altogether considered as foreigners, having no particular affinity or connection with the United States.   But that trade and commerce upon which the prosperity of this state much depends, will be preserved as free and open between this and the *United* States as our different situations at present can possibly admit.   Earnestly desiring and proposing to adopt such commercial regulations on our part as shall not tend to defeat the collection of the revenue of the United States, but rather to act in conformity to, or corporate [co-operate] therewith, and desiring also to give the strongest assurances that we shall during our present situation use our utmost endeavors to be in preparation, from time to time, to answer our proportion of such part of the interest or principal of the foreign and domestic debt, as the United States shall judge expedient to pay and discharge.

We feel ourselves attached by the strongest ties of friendship, kindred and of interest with our sister states, and we cannot without the greatest reluctance look to any other quarter for those advantages of commercial intercourse which we conceve to be more natural and recprocal between them and us.[1]

---

2. Virginia on the Assumption of State Debts.

December 23, 1790.

Virginia especially was opposed to the act for the assumption of State debts, as she had already paid off the greater portion of her revolutionary debt. Jefferson, nearly a month prior to the adoption of this memorial, wrote Morris: "The States of Virginia and North Carolina are peculiarly dissatisfied with this measure.   I believe, however, that it is harped on by many to mask their disaffection to the government on other grounds.   Its great foe in Virginia is an implacable one." (Patrick Henry.)   Jefferson's *Works*, (ed. 1854), III, 198; *Writings* (Ford's ed.), V, 250.

In addition to this memorial, the Legislature of Virginia also passed resolutions, Dec. 21, 1790, one of which pronounced the law in question " repugnant to the Constitution of the United States, as it goes to the exercise of a power not expressly granted to the general government."   Hening's *Statutes*, XIII, 234.   As soon as this resolution had passed the House of Delegates, Hamilton wrote to Chief Justice Jay: "This is the first symptom of a spirit which must either be killed or will kill the Constitution of the United States.

---

[1] The formal indorsement is omitted, which practice will be followed usually.

I send the resolution to you that it may be considered what ought to be done. Ought not the collective weight of the different parts of the Government to be employed in exploding the principles they contain?" *Correspondence and Public Papers of John Jay*, III, 405. (N. Y., 1891.) Jay replied: "To treat them as very important might render them more so than I think they are. * * * The assumption will do its own work; it will justify itself, and not want advocates. Every indecent interference of State assemblies will diminish their influence; the national government has only to do what is right and, if possible, be silent. If compelled to speak, it should be in a few words strongly evinced of temper, dignity, and self-respect." *Ibid.*, 410.

These resolutions were presented to the Senate by Monroe on January 13, 1791, and to the House by Madison on the following day, and communicated by the President on January 17, but Congress took no important action thereon.

In Maryland resolutions pronouncing assumption as dangerous to the independent existence of the State government were defeated by the casting vote of the Speaker of the House. North Carolina likewise condemned the measure in vigorous language.

References: Text in Hening's *Statutes*, XIII, 237–239 (Phila., 1823); also in *Amer. State Papers, Finance*, I, 90, 91. For comments, see Jefferson's *Works*, III, 152, 166, 167, 198; Jay's *Correspondence and Public Papers*, III, 405, 410; Hamilton's *History of the Republic*, IV, 479, 480; McMaster's *United States*, I, 593. For references on the previous opposition to funding in Congress, see MacDonald's *Documents*, 47; Channing and Hart's *Guide*, § 158.

IN THE HOUSE OF DELEGATES, ⎱
THURSDAY, THE 16TH OF DECEMBER, 1790. ⎰
*The General Assembly of the Commonwealth of Virginia to the
United States in Congress assembled.*

Represent,

That it is with great concern they find themselves compelled, from a sense of duty, to call the attention of Congress to an act of their last session, intitled "An act making provision for the debt of the United States," which the General Assembly conceive neither policy, justice nor the constitution warrants. Republican policy in the opinion of your memorialists could scarcely have suggested those clauses in the aforesaid act, which limit the right of the United States, in their redemption of the public debt. On the contrary they discern a striking resemblance between this system and that which was introduced into England, at the revolution; a system which has perpetuated upon that nation an enormous debt, and has moreover insinuated into the hands of the executive, an unbounded influence, which pervading every branch of the government, bears down all opposition, and daily threatens the destruction of everything that appertains to English liberty. The same causes produce the same effects! In an agricultural country like this, therefore to erect, and concentrate, and perpetuate a large monied interest, is a measure which your memorialists apprehend must in the course of human events produce one or other of two evils, the prostration of agriculture at the feet of commerce, or a change in the present form of foederal government, fatal to the existence of American liberty.

The General Assembly pass by various other parts of the said act which they apprehend will have a dangerous and impolitic tendency, and proceed to show the injustice of it as it applies to this Commonwealth. * * * Your memorialists turn away from the impolicy and injustice of the said act, and view it in another light, in which to them it appears still more odious and deformed.

During the whole discussion of the foederal constitution by the convention of Virginia, your memorialists were taught to believe ' That every power not granted was retained," under this impression and upon this positive condition, declared in the instrument of ratification, the said government was adopted by the people of this Commonwealth; but your memorialists can find no clause in the constitution authorizing Congress to assume the debts of the states! As the guardians then of the rights and interests of their constituents, as sentinels placed by them over the ministers of the foederal government, to shield it from their encroachments, or at least to sound the alarm when it is threatened with invasion, they can never reconcile it to their consciences, silently to acquiesce in a measure, which violates that hallowed maxim : a maxim on the truth and sacredness of which the foederal government depended for its adoption in this Commonwealth. But this injudicious act not only deserves the censure of the General Assembly, because it is not warranted by the constitution of the United States, but because it is repugnant to an express provision of that constitution ; this provision is " That all debts contracted and engagements entered into, before the adoption of this constitution, shall be as valid against the United States under this constitution as under the confederation," which amounts to a constitutional ratification of the contracts respecting the state debts in the situation in which they existed under the confederation, and resorting to that standard there can be no doubt that in the present question the rights of states as contracting with the United States must be considered as sacred.

The General Assembly of the Commonwealth of Virginia confide so fully in the justice and wisdom of Congress upon the present occasion, as to hope that they will revise and amend the aforesaid act generally, and repeal in particular, so much of it as relates to the assumption of the state debts.

December the 23d, 1790. Agreed to by the Senate.

Georgia and the Federal Judiciary.

1792, 1793.

A suit instituted by Chisholm against the State of Georgia came up for a hearing before the Supreme Court in the August term of 1792, but the case was postponed to the February term of the next year, in order that the State of Georgia might have time to deliberate on the measures she ought to adopt. A resolution was introduced into the Georgia House of Representatives, December 14, 1792, declaring that this suit " if acquiesced in by this State would not only involve the same in numberless law-suits for papers issued from the Treasury thereof to supply the armies of the United States, and perplex the citizens of Georgia with perpetual taxes, in addition to those the injustice of the funding system of the United States hath already imposed upon them, but would effectually destroy the retained sovereignty of the States, and would actually tend in its operation to annihilate the very shadow of State government, and to render them but tributary corporations to the government of the United States," therefore the State of Georgia would not be bound by the decision of the Supreme Court in such cases, but would regard it " as unconstitutional and extra-judicial." It further recommended " an explanatory amendment " to the constitution. Apparently the resolution was not adopted, but it represents the policy which the State followed. At the February term of the Supreme Court a written remonstrance on behalf of the State was presented, but otherwise the State declined to appear. The opinion of the Court was rendered February 18, 1793. It was ordered that unless Georgia should appear, or show cause by the first day of the next term, judgment by default should be entered against the State. At the opening of the next session of the Legislature of Georgia, in November, 1793, the Governor called attention to the case in his message as given below. The House of Representatives adopted a report authorizing the preparation of an address to the Legislatures of the several

States, "requesting their concurrence in a proposal for an explanatory amend-ment to the Constitution of the United States, in the second section of the third article," and they also passed a bill, "*Declaratory of the retained sovereignty of the State*," an extract from which follows. Apparently this measure did not pass the Senate, as the present Secretary of States writes that an examination of the manuscript laws for 1793 fails to disclose it.

State sovereignty was aroused elsewhere; two days after the decision of the Court was pronounced a proposed amendment, containing the exact language of the present eleventh amendment, was introduced in Congress by Senator Sedgwick of Massachusetts, against which State a similar suit was pending. The Legislatures of Massachusetts, Connecticut and Virginia each proposed an amendment; the former declaring that the power claimed by the Supreme Court was " dangerous to the peace, safety and independence of the several States and repugnant to the first principles of a Federal Government." Virginia pronounced " the decision of the Supreme Federal Court incompatible with and dangerous to the Sovereignty and Independence of the Individual States, as the same tends to a general consolidation of these confederated Republicks." Congress sent the proposed amendment to the States March 5, 1794, and its ratification was announced by a message of the President, January 8, 1798. At the February term of the Supreme Court 1794, judgment was rendered for the plaintiff, and a " Writ of Enquiry " awarded, but never executed, as the adoption of the eleventh amendment prevented the threatened conflict of authority.

References: The Texts are in *The Augusta Chronicle and Gazette of the State*, *December* 22, 1792; *November* 9, 16, 23, and *December* 7, 1793. This paper contains the House Journal.[1] Massachusetts resolutions, *Resolves of Mass.* (MS.), IX, 108; Copy of Connecticut and Virginia resolutions in *Massachusetts Archives*. In Hollingsworth *v.* Virginia (1798), 3 *Dallas*, 378, it was held that the XI Amendment applied to prior cases. Chisholm *v.* Georgia, 2 *Dallas*, 419, 479, 480. For history of this case and the amendment, see *Cohen v. Virginia*, 6 Wheaton, 406; Ames, *Proposed Amendments, Amer. Hist. Assoc. Report*, 1896, II, 156, 157, 322; McMaster, II, 182–186; V, 402; Story, *Commentaries*, II, 481, 482. Thorpe, *Const. History* I, 176-178.

3. Extracts from the Message of Governor Edward Telfair, Dated November 4, 1793.

The Augusta Chronicle and Gazette of the State, Saturday, November 9, 1793.

*　　　*　　　*　　　*　　　*　　　*　　　*

Notwithstanding certain amendments have taken place in the Federal Constitution, it still rests with the State Legislatures to

---

[1] I am indebted to Mr. William Harden, Librarian Georgia Historical Society, for transcripts of these texts and examination of newspaper files.

act thereon as circumstances may dictate. A process from the Supreme Court of the United States, at the instance of Chisholm, Executor of Farquhar, has been served on me and the Attorney General. I declined entering any appearance, as this would have introduced a precedent replete with danger to the Republic, and would have involved this state in complicated difficulties abstracted from the infractions it would have made on her retained sovereignty. The singular predicament to which she has been reduced by savage inroads has caused an emission of paper upwards of one hundred and fifty thousand pounds since the close of the late war, a considerable part of which is yet outstanding, and which in good faith and upon constitutional principles is the debt of the United States. I say were action admissible under such grievous circumstances, an annihilation of her political existence must follow. To guard against civil discord as well as the impending danger, permit me most ardently to request your most serious attention to the measure of recommending to the Legislatures of the several States that they effect a remedy in the premises by an amendment to the constitution; and that to give further weight to this matter the delegation of this state in Congress be required to urge that body to propose such an amendment to the said several Legislatures. * * *

4. Act Declaratory of the Retained Sovereignty of the State.

Extracts from the Journal of the House of Representatives, Tuesday, November 19, 1793.

The Augusta Chronicle and Gazette of the State, Saturday, November 23, and December 7, 1793.

The House proceeded to resolve itself into a committee of the whole, to take under consideration a bill to be entitled an act declaratory of certain parts of the retained sovereignty of the State of Georgia—Mr. Speaker left the chair.

Mr. McNeil took the chair of the committee—and some time being spent therein, Mr. Speaker resumed the chair, and Mr. McNeil from the committee of the whole reported that the committee had taken the said bill under consideration, had gone through the same, and had made several amendments thereto, which he reported.

And the bill as reported amended, being read, a motion was made by Mr. Waldburger to strike out the following section therein :

And be it further enacted, That any Federal Marshal, or any other person or persons levying, or attempting to levy, on the territory of this State, or any part thereof, or on the Treasury, or any other property belonging to the said State, or on the property of the Governor or Attorney-General, or any of the people thereof, under or by virtue of any execution or other compulsory process issuing out of or by authority of the Supreme Court of the United States, or any other Court having jurisdiction under their authority, or which may at any period hereafter under the constitution of the said United States, as it now stands, be constituted, for, or in behalf of the before mentioned Alexander Chrisholm, Executor of Robert Farquhar, or for, or in behalf of, any other person or persons whatsoever, for the payment or recovery of any debt, or pretended debt, or claim, against the said State of Georgia, shall be, and he or they attempting to levy as aforesaid are hereby declared to be guilty of felony, and shall suffer death, without the benefit of clergy, by being hanged.

And on the question for striking out as aforesaid, the yeas and nays being required, are as follows :

Yeas. Messrs. Barnett, Burnett, Carnes, Fort, R. Jones, J. Jones of Chatham, Waldburger, and Winn—8.

Nays. Messrs. Barrow, Early, Greer, Howell, Hardin, Harris, J. Jones of Burke, G. Jones, Jack, Kemp, Lanier, M'Neil, Rutherford, Simms, Stuart, Walker, Watkins, Worsham, and Wilkinson—19. So the motion was lost.

Ordered, That the bill be engrossed for a third reading.

Extracts from the Journal of the House of Representatives, Thursday, November 21, 1793 :

* * * A bill to be entitled an act declaratory of certain parts of the retained sovereignty of the state of Georgia was read the third time.

And on motion made—*Resolved,* That the bill be inserted at full length on the journals of this House.

Resolved, That the bill do pass under the title of "An act declaratory of certain parts of the retained sovereignty of the State of Georgia."

Ordered, That the clerk do carry the same to the Senate and desire their concurrence.

New Hampshire and the Federal Judiciary.

1794, 1795.

The first of the following remonstrances was due to a decision rendered by the United States Circuit Court for the District of New Hampshire, October 24, 1793, enforcing the decree of the Court of Appeals in Cases of Capture, in a case growing out of the capture of the brigantine " *Susannah* " by the privateer the " *McClary* " in October, 1777. The latter vessel was owned and manned by citizens of New Hampshire, but was acting under the commission and authority of Congress. The Courts of New Hampshire condemned the " *Susannah* " and her cargo as lawful prize, and refused to grant an appeal to Congress as contrary to the law of the State. A petition for an appeal in this case (*Treadwell and Penhallow v. brig Susannah*) was, however, sent to Congress, and its prayer granted by the Court of Commissioners, June 26, 1779, by virtue of the Resolves of Congress of November 25, 1775 (*Journal of Congress* [ed. 1800], I, 241, 242.) The case came up for trial before the legal successors of this body, the newly erected Court of Appeals in Cases of Capture (Resolves of January 15, 1780, *Jour. of Cong.*, VI, 10) in September, 1783. This Court reversed the decision of the New Hampshire Courts. Here the case rested until Elisha Doane, one of the appellants, finally brought proceedings in the Federal Circuit Court of New Hampshire in 1793, with the result as indicated above. On a writ of error the case was brought before the Supreme Court of the United States, and judgment was given, February 24, 1795, in the case of *Penhallow et al., v. Doane's Administrators*, maintaining the jurisdiction of the United States Courts, and confirming the decision of the inferior courts. The second of these remonstrances was presented to Congress three days later.

References: Texts: *Amer. State Papers, Misc.*, I, 79, 123, 124. See the case of *Penhallow v. Doane*, 3 *Dallas*, 54, for full facts in the case. For history of the United States Courts prior to the adoption of the Constitution, and incidentally of this case, see J. F. Jameson, *The Predecessor of the Supreme Court*, in *Essays in Const. History*, ch. 1; J. C. Bancroft Davis, *Courts of Appeal in Prize Cases*, 131 *United States Reports*, Appx. xxix–xxxiv.

5. First Remonstrance of the Legislature, February 20, 1794.

State of New Hampshire:

To the Senate and House of Representatives of the United States in Congress assembled: The remonstrance of the Legislature of the State of New Hampshire, showeth :—

That the citizens of the State of New Hampshire adopted the federal constitution of the United States under the full conviction that more extensive general powers were necessary to be vested in Congress than they ever possessed or pretended that they possessed, when they were entirely dependent on the good-will or the resolves of the several States. But by this adoption they did not then intend, nor does their Legislature now choose to admit, that the confederation was in force prior to March, 1781, or that the federal constitution existed with respect to New Hampshire before June, 1788. That a question respecting the powers of Congress and the powers of the several States previous to the constitution or the confederation has been determined in the circuit court for the district of New Hampshire, held at Exeter on the 24th day of October, 1793, in which the foundation of the action was, whether this State, prior to an express grant to Congress, had a right to pass a law final in every way concerning the capture of vessels by this State, or citizens thereof, from the British, the enemy we were then engaged with in war. That the determination of this circuit court was, that the State of New Hampshire had no such power; but that Congress, or a court commissioned by them, could nullify the laws of any particular State; could control their several courts; and that in fact, the constitution of 1789 was unnecessary to be adopted, as it contained no new grant of powers, but only a confirmation of old ones.

*   *   *   *   *   *   *

The states are forbidden by the federal constitution to make any retrospective laws. The Legislature conceived that Congress was under the same obligations; and that their courts could not rejudge cases that were finally adjudged by courts existing prior to its adoption. In fact, the Legislature conceive, and feel no inclination to relinquish the idea, that Congress, in its origin, was merely an advisory body, chosen by the several States to consult upon measures for the general good of the whole; that the adoption of measures recommended by them was entirely in the breast of the several States or their Legislatures; that no measure could be carried into effect in any State without its agreement thereto; that the subsequent powers of Congress entirely depended upon the express grants of the State Legislatures; that the Legislature of this State, so far from agreeing to the exercise of the power by Congress or its courts, now determined by the circuit court to have belonged to them, on request from Congress, did not grant, but denied it; that the declaration of independence received effect from its being acceded to by the Legislatures of the several States; and that the confederation was the first act binding upon the States which was not expressly agreed to by them individually; that a declaration by any body whatever contrary thereto is subversive of the principles of the revolution; unsettling all the proceedings of the State Governments prior to the existence of the constitution; and will inevitably involve the States, and this State in particular, in confusion, and will weaken, if not perhaps destroy, the National Government; the true principles of which the State of New Hampshire has, and will always endeavor to maintain.

The Legislature of New Hampshire, therefore, again protest and remonstrate against the exercise of any such powers by Congress, or any court or body of men appointed by them, and request that measures may be taken to prevent and annihilate such illegal acts of power.

6. Second Remonstrance of the Legislature, January 16, 1795.

To the Senate and House of Representatives of the United States in Congress assembled: The Memorial of the Legislature of New Hampshire, showeth:

That impelled by a firm attachment to the first principles of a free Government, and the accumulated distresses of a number of their citizens, they again remonstrate to Congress against a violation of State independence and an unwarrantable encroachment in the courts of the United States.

[Here follows a statement of the case as they view it.]

That this State had a right to oppose the British usurpation in the way it thought best ; could make laws as it chose, with respect to every transaction where it had not explicitly granted the power to Congress ; that the formation of courts for carrying those laws into execution belonged only to the several States ; that Congress might advise and recommend, but the States only could enact and carry into execution ; and that the attempts repeatedly made to render the laws of this State in this respect null and void is a flagrant insult to the principle of the revolution ; is establishing a Government they hoped to be a blessing on the uniform plea of arbitrary power, on an implication of grants of jurisdiction not intended to be included, nor even in contemplation.

Can the rage for annihilating all the power of the States, and reducing this extensive and flourishing country to one domination, make the administrators blind to the danger of violating all the principles of our former Government, to the hazard of convulsions in endeavoring to eradicate every trace of State power, except in the resentment of the people? Can the constitutional exercise of the power of Congress in future be in no other way established than by the belief that the former Congress always possessed the same? Can the remembrance of the manner of our opposition to tyranny, and the gradual adoption of federal ideas, be so painful as to exclude (unless forced into view) the knowledge that Congress, in its origin, was merely an advisory body ; that it entirely depended upon the will of the several Legislatures to enforce any measure they might recommend ; that the inconveniences of this principle produced the confederation ; and, even at that late day, it was declared that powers not expressly delegated to Congress are reserved to the States, or the people, respectively ; that the experience of years, of the inefficacy of thirteen Legislatures to provide for the wants and to procure the happiness of the American people, caused the adoption of the present constitution—an adoption totally unnecessary, in point of principle, if the claims of former Congressional power are established.

Forced by events, the Legislature of New Hampshire have made the foregoing statements ; and while they cheerfully acknowledge the power of Congress in cases arising under the constitution, they equally resolve not to submit the laws, made before the existence of the present government by this (then independent State) to the adjudication of any power on earth, while the freedom of the Federal Government shall afford any constitutional means of redress

Impressed with the singular merits of the present case, and deprecating the many and complicated evils which must be the necessary consequence of establishing the power claimed by the courts of the United States, and its tendency to produce disaffection to our Government, the Legislature of New Hampshire rest assured that a speedy and just decision will be had, and that the rights of State Governments and the interests of their citizens will be secured against the exercise of a power of a court, or any body of men under Congress, of carrying into effect an unconstitutional decree of a court instituted by a former Congress, and which, in its effects, would unsettle property and tear up the laws of the several states.

Kentucky and Virginia Resolutions.

1798, 1799.

It has been deemed unnecessary to reprint these resolutions in this series, as this has already been done in various publications. Among the most accessible and convenient of such reprints may be mentioned the following:

American History Leaflets, No. 15. (10c. A. Lovell & Co., New York, 1894.) William MacDonald, Editor. *Select Documents, illustrative of the History of the United States*, 148–160. (The Macmillan Co., New York, 1898.) Howard W. Preston, *Documents, illustrative of American History*, 283–295. (Putnam's, New York, 1886.) *The Federalist* (Ford's ed., New York, 1898), Appx. 679–686. Elliot's *Debates*, 528–532, 540–545 (ed. 1861). For a facsimile of a copy of the Kentucky resolutions of 1798, as sent to the other States, cf. *Writings of Jefferson* (Ford's ed., New York, 1896), VII, inserted between pages 288 and 289. Jefferson's draft is to be found in his *Writings* (Ford's ed.), VII, 289–309; *Works* (ed. 1856), IX, 464–471. Also important portions in *Am. History Leaflets, No. 15*, 17–21. For history of the same, cf. E. D. Warfield, *Kentucky Resolutions of 1798* (New York, 1887). For additional bibliography, cf. Channing and Hart, *Guide to American History*, § 165.

Replies of the States.

Copies of the Virginia and Kentucky resolutions were sent to the " Co-States."   Replies were made to Virginia by the legislatures of New Hampshire, Vermont, Massachusetts, Rhode Island, Connecticut, New York (different replies from the Senate and the House), Delaware, Pennsylvania (the House) and Maryland.   Replies to Kentucky were adopted by the following: New Hampshire (same as to Virginia), Vermont, Rhode Island (similar as to Virginia), Connecticut, New York (the House, same as to Virginia), Pennsylvania, Delaware (similar as to Virginia), Maryland (the House).   No State seems to have adopted resolutions at this time approving of the Kentucky and Virginia resolutions.   It was in answer to these replies that the second set of Kentucky resolutions (Nov. 22, 1799) and Madison's Report for the Virginia Legislature (1800) were adopted.

The minority in the Virginia Legislature issued an " *Address containing a Vindication of the Constitutionality of the Alien and Sedition Laws.*"

References: The replies to Virginia from the New England States, the Senate of New York, and from Delaware are in Elliot's *Debates* (ed. 1861), IV, 532–539; also in a pamphlet entitled *The Virginia and Kentucky Resolutions*, etc., published by Jonathan Elliot (Washington, May, MDCCCXXXII), 9–15; additional replies are in *The American Historical Review*, V, 244–252, supplementing an important article by F. M. Anderson, on *Contemporary Opinion of the Virginia and Kentucky Resolutions, ibid.*, 45–63, 225–244. The most important of the replies from eight of the States, either because of the previous or subsequent attitude of these States toward the Federal Government, or because of the declaration in regard to the function of the Federal Judiciary, are here re-printed.

7. Delaware to Virginia.[1]

IN THE HOUSE OF REPRESENTATIVES, *February* 1, 1799.

Resolved, By the Senate and House of Representatives of the state of Delaware, in General Assembly met, that they consider the resolutions from the state of Virginia, as a very unjustifiable interference with the General Government and constituted authorities of the United States, and of dangerous tendency, and therefore not fit subject for the further consideration of the General Assembly.

ISAAC DAVIS, *Speaker of the Senate.*

STEPHEN LEWIS, *Speaker of the House of Representatives.*

Test, JOHN FISHER, *C. S.*   JOHN CALDWELL, *C. H. R.*[2]

[Elliot's *Va. and Ky. Res.*, etc., 9].

[1] Similar reply sent to Kentucky.

[2] The formal indorsements are omitted in the other cases.

8. The State of Rhode Island and Providence Plantations to Virginia.[1]

IN GENERAL ASSEMBLY, *February*, *A. D.* 1799.

Certain resolutions of the Legislature of Virginia, passed on the 21st of December last, being communicated to the Assembly,—

1. *Resolved*, That, in the opinion of this legislature, the second section of the third article of the Constitution of the United States, in these words, to wit,—" The judicial power shall extend to all cases arising under the laws of the United States,"—vests in the Federal Courts, exclusively, and in the Supreme Court of the United States, ultimately, the authority of deciding on the constitutionality of any act or law of the Congress of the United States.

2. *Resolved*, That for any state legislature to assume that authority would be—

1st. Blending together legislative and judicial powers;

2d. Hazarding an interruption of the peace of the states by civil discord, in case of a diversity of opinions among the state legislatures; each state having, in that case, no resort, for vindicating its own opinions, but the strength of its own arm;

3d. Submitting most important questions of law to less competent tribunals; and,

4th. An infraction of the Constitution of the United States, expressed in plain terms.

3. *Resolved*, That, although, for the above reasons, this legislature, in their public capacity, do not feel themselves authorized to consider and decide on the constitutionality of the Sedition and Alien laws, (so called,) yet they are called upon, by the exigency of this occasion, to declare that, in their private opinions, these laws are within the powers delegated to Congress, and promotive of the welfare of the United States.

4. *Resolved*, That the governor communicate these resolutions to the supreme executive of the state of Virginia, and at the same time express to him that this legislature cannot contemplate, without extreme concern and regret, the many evil and fatal consequences which may flow from the very unwarrantable resolutions aforesaid, of the legislature of Virginia, passed on the twenty-first day of December last.

[Elliot's *Va. and Ky. Res.*, 9, 10.]

[1] Similar reply sent to Kentucky.

9. Massachusetts to Virginia.

IN SENATE, *February* 9, 1799.

The legislature of Massachusetts, having taken into serious consideration the resolutions of the state of Virginia, passed the 21st
day of December last, and communicated by his excellency the
governor, relative to certain supposed infractions of the Constitution of the United States, by the government thereof; and being
convinced that the Federal Constitution is calculated to promote
the happiness, prosperity, and safety, of the people of these
United States, and to maintain that union of the several states, so
essential to the welfare of the whole; and being bound by solemn
oath to support and defend that Constitution, feel it unnecessary
to make any professions of their attachment to it, or of their firm
determination to support it against every aggression, foreign or
domestic.

But they deem it their duty solemnly to declare that, while
they hold sacred the principle, that consent of the people is the
only pure source of just and legitimate power, they cannot admit
the right of the state legislatures to denounce the administration
of that government to which the people themselves, by a solemn
compact, have exclusively committed their national concerns.
That, although a liberal and enlightened vigilance among the
people is always to be cherished, yet an unreasonable jealousy of
the men of their choice, and a recurrence to measures of extremity, upon groundless or trivial pretexts, have a strong tendency to destroy all rational liberty at home, and to deprive the
United States of the most essential advantages in relations abroad.
That this legislature are persuaded that the decision of all cases
in law and equity arising under the Constitution of the United
States, and the construction of all laws made in pursuance thereof,
are exclusively vested by the people in the judicial courts of the
United States.

That the people, in the solemn compact, which is declared to
be the supreme law of the land, have not constituted the state
legislatures the judges of the acts or measures of the Federal Gov
ernment, but have confided to them, the power of proposing such
amendments of the Constitution, as shall appear to them necessary

to the interests, or conformable to the wishes, of the people whom they represent.

That, by this construction of the Constitution, an amicable and dispassionate remedy is pointed out for any evil which experience may prove to exist, and the peace and prosperity of the United States may be preserved without interruption.

But, should the respectable state of Virginia persist in the assumption of the right to declare the acts of the National Government unconstitutional, and should she oppose successfuliy her force and will to those of the nation, the Constitution would be reduced to a mere cypher, to the form and pageantry of authority, without the energy of power. Every act of the Federal Government which thwarted the views or checked the ambitious projects of a particular state, or of its leading and influential members, would be the object of opposition and of remonstrance; while the people, convulsed and confused by the conflict between two hostile jurisdictions, enjoying the protection of neither, would be wearied into a submission to some bold leader, who would establish himself on the ruins of both.

The legislature of Massachusetts, although they do not themselves claim the right, nor admit the authority, of any of the state governments, to decide upon the constitutionality of the acts of the Federal Government, still, lest their silence should be construed into disapprobation, or at best into a doubt as to the constitutionality of the acts referred to by the state of Virginia; and as the General Assembly of Virginia has called for an expression of their sentiments, do explicitly declare, that they consider the acts of Congress, commonly called " the Alien and Sedition Acts," not only constitutional, but expedient and necessary. [Here follows a discussion of these acts.]   *   *   *

The legislature further declare, that in the foregoing sentiments they have expressed the general opinion of their constituents, who have not only acquiesced wthout complaint in those particular measures of the Federal Government, but have given their explicit approbation by re-electing those men who voted for the adoption of them. Nor is it apprehended, that the citizens of this state will be accused of supineness, or of an indifference to their constitutional rights; for while, on the one hand, they regard with due vigilance the conduct of the government, on the other, their freedom, safety, and happiness require that they should defend that government and its constitutional measures against the open or insidious attacks of any foe, whether foreign or domestic.

And, lastly, that the legislature of Massachusetts feel a strong conviction that the several United States are connected by a common interest, which ought to render their union indissoluble ; and that this state will always coöperate with its confederate states in rendering that union productive of mutual security, freedom, and happiness.

In the House of Representatives, February 13,1799. Read and concurred.

[Elliot's *Va. and Ky. Res.*, 10-13.]

10. Resolutions of the House of Representatives of Pennsylvania to Kentucky, February 9, 1799.

Resolved, That in the opinion of this House the people of the United States have vested in their President and Congress, as well the right and power of determining on the intent and construction of the constitution, as on the ordinary subjects of legislation, and the defence of the Union ; and have committed to the supreme judiciary of the nation the high authority of ultimately and conclusively deciding upon the constitutionality of all legislative acts. The constitution does not contemplate, as vested or residing in the Legislatures of the several states, any right or power of declaring that any act of the general government " is not law, but is altogether void, and of no effect ;" and this House considers such declaration as a revolutionary measure, destructive of the purest principles of our State and national compacts.

That it is with deep concern this House observes, in any section of our country, a disposition so hostile to her peace and dignity, as that which appears to have dictated the resolutions of the Legislature of Kentucky. Questions of so much delicacy and magnitude might have been agitated in a manner more conformable to the character of an enlightened people, flourishing under a government adopted by themselves, and administered by the men of their choice.

That this House view, as particularly inauspicious to the general principles of liberty and good government, the formal declaration by a legislative body, " that confidence is everywhere the parent of despotism, and that free governments are founded in jealousy." The prevalence of such an opinion cuts asunder all the endearing relations in life, and renews, in the field of science and amity, the savage scenes of darker ages. Governments truly republican and free are eminently founded on opinion and confidence ; their execution is committed to representatives, selected by voluntary preference, and exalted by a knowledge of their virtues and their talents. No portion of the people can assume the province of the whole, nor resist the expression of its combined will. This House therefore protests against principles, calculated only to check the spirit of confidence, and overwhelm with dismay the lovers of peace, liberty and order.

That this House consider the laws of the United States, which are the subjects of so much complaint, as just rules of civil conduct, and as component parts of a system of defence against the aggressions of a nation, aiming at the dominion of the world— conducting her attacks more by the arts of intrigue, than by her skill in arms—never striking, until she has deeply wounded or destroyed the confidence of the people in their government— and, in fact, subduing more by the infamous aids of seduction, than by the strength of her numerous legions. The sedition and alien acts this House conceive contain nothing terrifying, but to the flagitious and designing. Under the former, no criminality can be infered or punishment inflicted, but for writing, printing, uttering, or publishing false, scandalous and malicious aspersions against the government, either House of Congress, or the President of the United States, with an intent to defame and bring them into contempt. Under the latter, the citizens of the United States have not anything more to fear, inasmuch as its operation will only remove foreigners, whose views and conduct are inimical to a government, instituted only for the protection and benefit of the citizens of the United States, and others, whose quiet and submission give them some claim to the blessing. Yet these laws are subjects of loud complaint. But this House forbears an examination into the cause, and only expresses its surprise that such an opposition to them exists ! Our country's dearest interest demands everywhere unanimity and harmony in her councils, and this House is unable to discover any means more favourable to those important objects, than confidence in the wise and honest labours of those, in whose hands is reposed the sacred charge of preserving her peace and independence. The voice of the greater number the constitution declares shall pronounce the national will; but in the opinion of this House the provision is vain, unless it be followed by the unfeigned and practical acquiescence of the minor part. Loud and concerted appeals to the passions of the community are calculated to produce discussions more boisterous than wise, and effects more violent than useful. Our prayer therefore is, that our country may be saved from foreign war and domestic strife.

That it is the opinion of this House, that it ought not to concur in the design of the resolutions of the Legislature of Kentucky.

On motion of Mr. Kelly, seconded by Mr. Strickler,

Resolved, That the foregoing resolution be signed by the Speaker, and that the Governor be requested to transmit the same to the Governor of Kentucky.

[Journal of the House of Representatives of the Commonwealth of Pennsylvania, ix, 198-200. (Philadelphia, 1799.)]

11. Resolutions of the House of Representatives of Pennsylvania to Virginia, March 11, 1799.

Resolved, That as it is the opinion of this House that the principles contained in the resolutions of the Legislature of Virginia, relative to certain measures of the general government, are calculated to excite unwarrantable discontents, and to destroy the very existence of our government, they ought to be, and are hereby, rejected.

[Journal of House of Representatives, ix, 289.]

12. Senate of New York to Virginia and Kentucky.[1]

IN SENATE, *March* 5, 1799.

Whereas, the people of the United States have established for themselves a free and independent national government: And

[1] For reply of the House of Representatives, cf. *Amer. Hist. Review,* v, 248, 249.

whereas it is essential to the existence of every government, that it have authority to defend and preserve its constitutional powers inviolate, inasmuch as every infringement thereof tends to its subversion : And whereas the judicial power extends expressly to all cases of law and equity arising under the Constitution and the laws of the United States, whereby the interference of the legislatures of the particular states in those cases is manifestly excluded : And, whereas, our peace, prosperity, and happiness, eminently depend upon the preservation of the Union, in order to which a reasonable confidence in the constituted authorities and chosen representatives of the people is indispensable : And, whereas, every measure calculated to weaken that confidence has a tendency to destroy the usefulness of our public functionaries, and to excite jealousies equally hostile to rational liberty, and the principles of a good republican government : And, whereas, the Senate, not perceiving that the rights of the particular states have been violated, nor any unconstitutional powers assumed by the general government, cannot forbear to express the anxiety and regret with which they observe the inflammatory and pernicious sentiments and doctrines which are contained in the resolutions of the legislatures of Virginia and Kentucky—sentiments and doctrines no less repugnant to the Constitution of the United States, and the principles of their union, than destructive to the Federal Government, and unjust to those whom the people have elected to administer it ; wherefore,

Resolved, That while the Senate feel themselves constrained to bear unequivocal testimony against such sentiments and doctrines, they deem it a duty no less indispensable, explicitly to declare their incompetency, as a branch of the legislature of this state, to supervise the acts of the General Government.

Resolved, That his excellency, the governor, be, and he is hereby requested to transmit a copy of the foregoing resolution to the executives of the states of Viringia and Kentucky, to the end that the same may be communicated to the legislatures thereof.

[Elliot's *Va. and Ky. Res.*, 13, 14.]

13. Connecticut to Virginia,[1] May, 1799.

At a General Assembly of the State of Connecticut, holden at Hartford, in the said State, on the second Thursday of May, Anno Domini 1799, his excellency, the Governor, having communicated to this Assembly sundry resolutions of the Legislature of Virginia, adopted in December, 1798, which relate to the measures of the general government, and the said resolutions having been considered, it is

Resolved, That this Assembly views with deep regret, and explicitly disavows, the principles contained in the aforesaid resolutions, and particularly the opposition to the "Alien and Sedition Acts "—acts which the Constitution authorized, which the exigency of the country rendered necessary, which the constituted authorities have enacted, and which merit the entire approbation of this Assembly. They, therefore, decidedly refuse to concur with the legislature of Virginia in promoting any of the objects attempted in the aforesaid resolutions.

And it is further resolved, That his excellency, the Governor, be requested to transmit a copy of the foregoing resolutions to the Governor of Virginia, that it may be communicated to the Legislature of that State.

[Passed both branches unanimously; Elliot's *Va. and Ky. Res.*, 14.]

14. New Hampshire to Virginia and Kentucky, June 15, 1799.

IN THE HOUSE OF REPRESENTATIVES, *June* 14, 1799.

The committee to take into consideration the resolutions of the General Assembly of Virginia, dated December 21, 1798; also certain resolutions of the Legislature of Kentucky, of the 10th November, 1798, report as follows :

The Legislature of New Hampshire, having taken into consideration certain resolutions of the General Assembly of Virginia, dated December 21, 1798; also certain resolutions of the Legislature of Kentucky, of the 10th of November, 1798 :

Resolved, That the Legislature of New Hampshire unequivocally express a firm resolution to maintain and defend the Constitution of the United States, and the Constitution of this State, against

[1] For reply to Kentucky, cf. *Amer. Hist. Review*, v, 247, 248.

every aggression, either foreign or domestic, and that they will support the government of the United States in all measures warranted by the former.

That the State Legislatures are not the proper tribunals to determine the constitutionality of the laws of the general government; that the duty of such decision is properly and exclusively confided to the judicial department.

That, if the Legislature of New Hampshire, for mere speculative purposes, were to express an opinion on the acts of the general government, commonly called " the Alien and Sedition Bills," that opinion would unreservedly be, that those acts are constitutional, and, in the present critical situation of our country, highly expedient.

That the constitutionality and expediency of the acts aforesaid, have been very ably advocated and clearly demonstrated by many citizens of the United States, more especially by the minority of the General Assembly of Virginia. The Legislature of New Hampshire, therefore, deem it unnecessary, by any train of arguments, to attempt further illustration of the propositions, the truth of which, it is confidently believed, at this day, is very generally seen and acknowledged.

Which report, being read and considered, was unanimously received and accepted, one hundred and thirty-seven members being present.

In Senate, same day, read and concurred unanimously.

[Elliot's *Va. and Ky. Res.*, 14, 15.]

15. Vermont to Virginia,[1] October 30, 1799.

IN THE HOUSE OF REPRESENTATIVES, *October* 30, A. D. 1799.

The House proceeded to take under their consideration the resolutions of the General Assembly of Virginia, relative to certain measures of the general government, transmitted to the Legislature of this State, for their consideration : Whereupon,

Resolved, That the General Assembly of the State of Vermont do highly disapprove of the resolutions of the General Assembly of Virginia, as being unconstitutional in their nature, and dan-

---

[1] For protest of the minority, cf. *Amer. Hist. Review*, V, 249–252.

gerous in their tendency. It belongs not to State Legislatures to decide on the constitutionality of laws made by the general government; this power being exclusively vested in the judiciary courts of the Union. That his excellency, the governor, be requested to transmit a copy of this resolution to the executive of Virginia, to be communicated to the General Assembly of that State: And that the same be sent to the Governor and Council for their concurrence.

In Council, October 30, 1799. Read and concurred unanimously.

[Elliot's *Va. and Ky. Res.*, 15.]

The General Court of Massachusetts on the Embargo.

1808, 1809.

The embargo act, passed December 22, 1807 (*U. S. Stat. at Large*, II, 451–453), was at first acquiesced in by the majority of the people in New England, and the Democratic-Republican party being in control of the State government of Massachusetts, the General Court passed a resolution, February 8, 1808, declaring that " we consider the imposing of embargo a wise and highly expedient measure, and from its impartial nature calculated to secure to us the blessings of peace." (*Resolves of Mass.*, 1808, 89, 90.) As the distress resulting from the embargo increased, resistance began to show itself, and gradually political power returned to the party in opposition. The Federalists carried both branches of the legislature by a small majority in the spring of 1808, although the Republican Governor, James Sullivan, was re-elected. The change in the legislature is at once apparent in their " Answers " to the Governor's " Speech," June 9, 1808, in which the embargo is denounced and its constitutionality questioned. (*Resolves of Mass.*, 1808, 164–173; see also Barry's *Mass.*, III, 359, 360, note.) A similar spirit is shown in the November session (*Ibid.*, 207), and on November 18, 1808, the legislature instructed the State's delegation in Congress to procure the repeal of the embargo laws. (*Amer. State Papers, Commerce and Navigation*, I, 728–729.) But Congress, instead of repealing the obnoxious laws, passed a stringent enforcement act, which became a law January 9, 1809. (*U. S. Stat. at Large*, II, 506–511.) This called forth the pent-up anger and indignation of the Federalists. The protests and resolutions of the various towns in the State vied with each other in their vehemence, and there were ominous whisperings of secession. (Adams, *United States*, IV, 408–419.) Such was the situation when the General Court re-assembled, January 26, 1809. The Lieutenant-Governor, Levi Lincoln, an ardent supporter of Jefferson, succeeded to the duties of the

executive office, owing to the death of the Governor.   In his "Speech" to
the legislature, he deprecated the agitation against the laws of the land, condemned the action of the town meetings as seditious and uncalled for, and
suggested further restraints upon the licentiousness of the press as desirable.
(*Resolves of Mass.*, 1809, 221–229.) Both branches of the legislature
"answered" with spirit, as the extracts given below show. They also adopted
a Report and Resolutions on the petitions of the town-meetings, extracts from
which follow; dispatched a Memorial and Remonstrance to Congress (*Amer.
State Papers, Commerce*, etc., I, 776–778) issued an Address to the People of
the Commonwealth, suggesting as "indispensable amendments" to the Federal Constitution, one abolishing the three-fifths representation for slaves,[1] and
another "to secure commerce and navigation from a repetition of destructive
and insidious theories," and declaring that "nothing less than a perfect union
and intelligence among the Eastern States can preserve to them any share of
influence in the national government" (*Patriotic Proceedings*, 126–130;
Hildreth, VI, 151–154); denounced the acts of the Lieutenant-Governor in
detaching State militia to aid in carrying out the Enforcement Act "as irregu-
lar, illegal and inconsistent with the principles of the constitution;" passed a
bill "agatnst unreasonable, arbitrary and unconstitutional searches," which
was intended to prevent the execution of the Enforcement Act, but which was
vetoed by the Governor; and finally, set apart a "Day of Humiliation and
Prayer."

The threatening attitude of Massachusetts and several of the other New England States led the federal administration to consent to the repeal of the Embargo, and the substitution of a non-intercourse act. (March 1, 1809, *U. S. Stat.
at Large*, II, 528–533.) The recent experience of the State led Governor Gore
to suggest, and the Legislature to propose, June 20, 1809, an amendment to
the Constitution, placing a limit on the duration of an embargo to "thirty days
from the commencement of the session of Congress next succeeding that session
in which said law shall have been enacted." (*Resolves of Mass.*, 1809, 312,
313, 356, 357.) This recommendation appears to have received only the approval of Connecticut, but was disapproved of by the legislatures of at least
eight States. (Ames, *Proposed Amendments*, 264, 329.)

References: In addition to the above, the texts of the important measures
are given in *The Patriotick Proceedings of the Legislature of Massachusetts*,
[Boston, 1809]; several are found in *The American Register*, 1809, Part II,
183–209 [Phila., 1809]; The Memorial to Congress is also given in *Amer.
State Papers, Commerce*, etc., I, 776–778; *Annals of Congress*, 10 *Cong.*, 2
Sess., 444–450; for debate on same and refusal to print in House of Rep.,
Annals, 538, 539; for history, see Adams, *United States*, IV, esp. 398–453;
Hildreth, VI, esp. 75–79, 108–117,*9*151–154; McMaster, III, esp. 321–331;
Barry, *Massachusetts*, III, 352–364; Adams, *New Eng. Federalism*, esp.

---

[1] Such an amendment had been proposed by the Legislature in 1804 as a protest against
the annexation of Louisiana; for this, and the replies of the other States, see McMaster, III,
44–47; Ames, *Proposed Amendments*, 45, 46, 326.

372–379; Lodge, *Cabot*, 366–407 in passim; Quincy, *Life of Josiah Quincy*, 120–130, 138–165, 171–186; *Writings of Jefferson* [Ford's ed.], IX, 202, 227, 235–239, 244, 248–250; X, 352–354, 356; consult Channing and Hart's *Guide*, § 171; MacDonald's *Documents*, 176, 177.

16. Extract from the Answer of the Senate, January, 1809.

Resolves of Massachusetts (1809), 231–235.

MAY IT PLEASE YOUR HONOUR,

*   *   *   *   *   *   *

The people of New England perfectly understand the distinction between the Constitution and the Administration. They are as sincerely attached to the former as any section of the United States. They may be put under the ban of the empire, but they have no intention of abandoning the Union. And we have the pleasure explicitly to declare our full concurrence with your Honour, " that such suggestions are not less a libel upon the great body of the New England people, than on their patriotism."

As the government of the Union is a confederation of equal and independent states with limited powers, we agree with your Honour " that it is not unbecoming any member of the Union with firmness and moderation to question the justness or policy of measures while they are pending and ripening for adoption," and we learn with concern from your Honour, " that there are stages when questions "—without even excepting questions involving unalienable rights—" can be no longer open to controversy and opposition "—" stages when an end must be put to debate and a decision thence resulting be respected by its prompt and faithful execution, or government loses its existence and the people are ruined." * * * We owe it to ourselves and to the people distinctly to deny this doctrine, at once novel and pernicious.

*   *   *   *   *   *   *

We beg leave to observe, that those rights, which the people have not chosen to part with, should be exercised by them with delicacy—only in times of great danger—not with " distraction and confusion "—not to oppose the laws, but to prevent acts being respected as laws, which are unwarranted by the commission given to their rulers. On such occasions, passive submission, would, on the part of the people, be a breach of their allegiance, and on our part treachery and perjury. For the people are bound by their allegiance, and we are additionally bound by our oaths to support the Constitution of the State—and we are responsible to the people, and to our God, for the faithful execution of the trust.

But your Honour is pleased to observe, that " the union have their favorite projects—states, towns and individuals have theirs " and to inquire whether " thus jarring with augmented resentments we are to rush together in ruinous collisions."

Can it be necessary to remind your Honour that the aggressor is responsible for all the consequences, which you have been pleased so pathetically to describe? That the people have not sent us here to surrender their rights but to maintain and defend them?—and, that we have no authority to dispense with the duties thus solemnly imposed :

* * * * * * *

We most heartily concur with your Honour, " that there is a point in national sensibility, as in the feelings of men, where patience and submission end." And when that crisis shall arrive your Honour may rest assured that the people of New England " will (as you have been pleased to say) rally round the national constitution." But, Sir they will not " cling " to an administration which has brought them to the brink of destruction—they will not " keep their hold in the extremity of its exit," nor " sink with it into the frightful abyss." No, Sir ! The people of Massachusetts will not willingly become the victims of fruitless experiment.

17. Extracts from the Answer of the House.

Resolves of Massachusetts (1809), 236-242.

MAY IT PLEASE YOUR HONOUR,

* * * * * * *

We are unwilling to believe that any division of sentiment can exist among the New England States or their inhabitants as to the obvious infringement of rights secured to them by the Constitution of the United States ; and still more so that any man can be weak or wicked enough to construe a disposition to support that Constitution and preserve the union by a temperate and firm opposition to acts which are repugnant to the first principles and purposes of both, into a wish to recede from the other states. If a secession has been conceived by the states or people referred to in your Honour's communication, it is unknown to the House of Representatives, who absolutely disclaim any participation therein, or having afforded the least colour for such a charge. If ever such suspicions existed they can have arisen only in the minds of those who must be sensible that they had adopted and were persisting in, measures which had driven the people to desperation, by infringing rights which the citizens of Massachusetts conceive to be unalienable, and which they fondly hoped had been inviolably secured to them by the federal compact.

The Legislature and people of Massachusetts ever have been and now are firmly and sincerely attached to the union of the States, and there is no sacrifice they have not been, and are not now, willing to submit to, in order to preserve the same, according to its original purpose. Of this truth your Honour must be conceived.

      *   *   *   *   *   *   *

That the regulation of our commercial intercourse and our national defence, is most wisely confided to the general government, is a truth so plain and palpable, that we should hold it unnecessary to be repeated here, were it not for the purpose of concurring with your Honour in the justice of the sentiment; but the liberty of discussing the measures of our general government with freedom and firmness, though with fairness and moderation, is a right the House of Representatives never will relinquish.

We cannot agree with your Honour that in a free country there is any stage at which the constitutionality of an act may no longer be open to discussion and debate; at least it is only upon the high road to despotism that such stages can be found.

At such a point the Government undertaking to extend its powers beyond the limits of the constitution, degenerates into tyranny. The people, if temperate and firm, will, we confidently rely, eventually triumph over such usurpations.

Were it true, that the measures of government once passed into

an act, the constitutionality of that act is stamped with the seal
of infallibility, and is no longer a subject for the deliberation or
remonstrance of the citizen, to what monstrous lengths might
not an arbitrary and tyrannical administration carry its power.
It has only to pass through rapid readings and mid-night sessions,
without allowing time for reflection and debate to the final
enacting of a bill and before the people are even informed of the
intentions of their rulers, their claims are riveted, and the right
of complaint denied them.   Were such doctrine sound, what
species of oppression might not be inflicted on the prostrate
liberties of our country.   If such a doctrine were true, our constitution would be nothing but a name—nay worse, a fatal instrument to sanctify oppression, and legalize the tyranny which
inflicts it.

Nothing but madness or imbecility could put at hazard the
existence of a " balanced government, capable of operating and
providing for the public good," unless the administration of that
Government, by its arbitrary impositions had endangered or
destroyed the very objects for the protection of whch it had
been instituted.

Should such a case ever occur, on the administration who
should usurp powers and violate such sacred obligations, must
rest the odium of having hazarded a government " so safe, so
reasonable and so beyond everything else essential to the liberty
and happiness of our fellow ctizens."

    *   *   *   *   *   *   *

It cannot be denied, that jealousy and distrust have arisen
among the people of Massachusetts, and much it is to be regretted,
that they have been so well founded.   A system of policy ruinous
to their interests, and uncongenial to their enterprising spirit—
a system for which the adminstration has yet, in our opinion,
assigned no adequate reason, has borne most heavily and unequally
on the northern and commercial States.   For relief from this
oppression the people fondly looked to the meeting of Congress—
but alas! how fatally have their hopes been blasted: Their
humble prayers have been answered by an act so arbitrary and
oppressive, that it violates the first principles of civil liberty, and
the fundamental provisions of the Constitution.   At such a

moment and under such a pressure, when everything which free-men hold dear, is at stake it cannot be expected and it ought not to be wished, that they should suffer in silence. The House of Representatives cannot admit that laws which operate un-equally are unavoidable. The government, in their opinion, has no right to sacrifice the interests of one section of the Union to the prejudices, partialities, or convenience, of another.

We perfectly agree with your Honour in the general principle that, in a free government, the majority must determine and decide upon all existing or projected measures. But it will be recollected, that the decision of that majority, to be binding, must be constitutional and just. Government is formed for the security of the citizen, and the protection of its rights. When-ever his liberty is infringed, his rights violated or unprotected, if not absolved from his allegiance, he may demand redress, and take all lawful measures to obtain it.

* * * * * * *

The early habits and constant practice of our fathers and ourselves have led us, on every great emergency, and on the pressure of political calamities, to resort to town meetings, wherein the general sense of the people might be collected. This practice, so wholesome and salutary, was one of the most influential means employed in bringing about the glorious revolution which established our independence. It was against these meetings, therefore, that the strong arm of royal power was elevated, in the year seventeen hundred and seventy-four, and they were prohibited under severe penalties. Had the British ministry of that day attended to the voice of the people so expressed, they would have avoided the evils which they had afterwards so much reason to deplore. The expression of the publick sentiment has become necessary to counteract the errours and misrepresentations of those who have falsely incul-cated upon the administration of the General Government a belief, that the measures they were pursuing were satisfactory to the people. From the suppression of these meetings would liberty have more to apprehend than from any other cause whatever. From such a cause should we most dread " the overturning the splendid edifice erected by the wisdom and valour of our fathers." A privilege so wisely secured by our constitution, we cannot hesitate to declare, the citizens of Massaachusetts will never resign.

* * * * * * *

In the description which your Honour has drawn of the situation of our country previous to the adoption of the federal constitution, we cannot but observe the very strong resemblance which it bears to the picture of the present times. " Our government humbled and inefficient, our Union a thread, our commerce unprotected, our revenue nothing, individuals embarrassed, grievances complained of, our rulers censured, town and county resolutions published, combinations formed, non-compliance with the laws announced, property sold for one-third its value, the insolvent imprisoned, and the courts of justice stopped ;" that this description applies to the present state of parts, if not the whole, of our country, we believe will not be denied.

Whence comes it that from a state of the most flourishing prosperity a few months should have produced a change so truly astonishing? It is not in the restless and unsteady habits of the people, till lately contented and happy, that we must look for the causes of these frightful calamities; it is in the pernicious and dreadful consequences of this shallow system of Embargo and Non Intercourse, that we shall find the fruitful sources of our country's ruin. We do most sincerely hope that neither Virginia or any other state may ever succeed in " dictating measures to Congress and by a convulsed state of things force their adoption." However, such an usurpation might from various causes endure for a time, the returning good sense of the people would eventually restore the equilibrium and effectually prevent those tempestuous scenes which your Honour has so eloquently described. " The importance and the interesting and perilous nature of the crisis," have excited the most alarming reflections in our minds, and we doubt not that every member of the Legislature will devote himself to the arduous yet necessary duty of " devising some reconciling expedient to quiet the agitated minds of our citizens," and relieve them from the weight of these unconstitutional restrictions.

* * * * * * *

18. Resolutions of the Enforcement Act, February 15, 1809.

The report and resolutions of the joint committee on petitions from the town meetings was made February 1, 1809. The same were adopted by the Senate, on the 11th inst, by a vote of 19 to 18. (*MS. Senate Journal*, 1808–09, vol. 29, pp. 196–209.) The House concurred, on the 15th inst., by a vote of 205 to 139. (*MS. House Journal*, May, 1808–March, 1809, pp. 278–282. The Report and Resolutions are also given in *Patriotick Proceedings*, pp. 41–53.

*   *   *   *   *   *   *

On viewing these provisions of the act under consideration, the committee do unequivocally declare their solemn conviction, that it is in many particulars, unjust, oppressive, and unconstitutional. They would by no means contend that this opinion, if confirmed and adopted by the legislature, would be decisive of the question. While the laws continue to have their free course, the judicial courts are competent to decide this question, and to them every citizen, when aggrieved, ought to apply for redress. It would be derogatory to the honour of the commonwealth to presume that it is unable to protect its subjects against all violations of their rights, by peaceable and legal remedies. While this state maintains its sovereignty and independence, all the citizens can find protection against outrage and injustice in the strong arm of the state government.

Any forcible resistance, therefore, by individuals, to the execution of this act of Congress, is not only unnecessary, but would be highly inexpedient and improper; it would endanger the public peace and tranquility, and tend essentially to injure and put at hazard that cause, on which nearly the whole people are now so zealously united. The committee are deeply sensible of the accumulated distress which has so long oppressed the whole community, and borne with aggravation on some particular parts of it. They cannot too highly applaud the unexampled patience and forbearance which has been already exhibited under this pressure of undeserved calamities. And they would earnestly recommend the exercise of the same forbearance, until all those peaceable and orderly means which the constitution and laws of our country will permit, and all those political expedients, which our habits and usages can suggest, shall have been exhausted in vain.

It is to be regretted that no immediate and efficacious remedy can now be proposed for these numerous and aggravated evils. The committee, however, consider it their duty to recommend, without loss of time, all such measures as have appeared to them to be now practicable, and calculated to remove or alleviate the publick distress; they therefore ask leave to

Report in part, A bill to secure the people of this commonwealth against unreasonable, arbitrary and unconstitutional searches in their dwelling houses—and also the following

Resolutions.

Resolved, That the act of the Congress of the United States passed on the ninth day of January in the present year, for enforcing the act laying an embargo, and the several acts supplementary thereto, is, in the opinion of the legislature, in many respects, unjust, oppressive and unconstitutional, and not legally binding on the citizens of this state. But notwithstanding this opinion, in order finally to secure a certain and permanent relief, it is earnestly recommended to all parties aggrieved by the operation of this act, to abstain from forcible resistance, and to apply for their remedy in a peaceable manner to the laws of the commonwealth.

Resolved, That a suitable remonstrance be prepared, and immediately forwarded to the Congress of the United States, from this legislature, expressing their opinions and feelings on the several subjects of complaint contained in the said petitions, and particularly urging the repeal of the said act of Congress, passed on the ninth of January last.

Resolved, That the legislature of this commonwealth will zealously co-operate with any of the other states, in all legal and constitutional measures, for procuring such amendments to the constitution of the United States, as shall be judged necessary to obtain protection and defence for commerce, and to give to the commercial states their fair and just consideration in the government of the Union; and for affording permanent security, as well as present relief, from the oppressive measures under which they now suffer.

Resolved, That the honourable the president of the Senate, and the honourable the speaker of the House of Representatives, be requested to transmit a copy of this report, and the resolutions thereon, to the legislatures of such of our sister states, as manifest a disposition to concur with us in measures to rescue our common country from impending ruin, and to preserve inviolate the union of the states.

---

19. Delaware and the Embargo.

January 30, 1809.

Delaware, the only Federalist State outside of New England, next showed its opposition to the embargo policy of the administration, through the adoption of the following resolutions by the House of Representatives. When these resolutions were presented to the Senate, February 1, a systematic attempt was made to defeat them, by motions to postpone, or to substitute other resolutions strongly indorsing the policy of the administration. These, however, were defeated, but several amendments modifying the language of the resolutions were agreed to, as follows: 1) Striking out the words in the the third resolution, "as a war measure worse than futile." 2) Striking out the fifth resolution. 3) Striking out the words "unwise and arbitrary laws" in the seventh resolution, and inserting in lieu therefor the words "laws however oppressive." 4) Causing the last part of the eighth resolution to read, "and that they will defend their country, when necessary, from the aggression of every foreign or domestic foe." Thus amended the resolutions were concurred in by the Senate by a vote of 5 yeas to 3 nays, but the House immediately refused to accept the Senate's amendments. The Senate thereupon reconsidered their amendments, adhering to all, except the one striking out the fifth resolution, from which it receded. Thus the two houses failed to agree. But in December the Legislature passed resolutions disapproving of the amendment to the Federal Constitution, proposed by Massachusetts, limiting the duration of an embargo.

References: Text:—*Journal of the House of Representatives*, 1808–1809, *January* 27 and 30, 1809, pp. 62, 63; *Journal of the Senate*, 1808–1809, *January* 31, and *February* 1, 1809, pp. 64, 65, 74–81. Dover, 1809. Resolutions disapproving amendment, *Annals*, 11 Congress, Part I, 658.

IN THE HOUSE OF REPRESENTATIVES, JANUARY 30, 1809.

Whereas, the measures pursued by the government of the United States, have justly excited considerable interest in the United States, and silence on our part might be construed into an approbation of those measures—

Therefore,

1. *Resolved,* By the Senate and House of Representatives of the State of Delaware, in General Assembly met, That we cannot approve the policy of those measures that have annihilated the commerce of the United States, and brought distress and ruin on our citizens, while at the same time they have done no injury to the enemies of our country; that we cannot approve the policy of an administration that does not act with impartiality and sincerity towards all foreign nations.

2. *Resolved,* That the people of the United States have a right freely to navigate the ocean, and to carry on a fair and honest commerce, and that we highly disapprove a policy that relinquishes those rights, or dares not defend them.

3. *Resolved,* That we consider the embargo, *as a war measure,* worse than futile, as a measure injurious to ourselves, destructive to the best interests of the country, and evidently intended to be partial in its operations against the belligerent nations; and that it becomes the United States, a great and gallant nation, to defend its rights in a manly, open, and efficient manner.

4. *Resolved,* That we consider the act to enforce, and make more effectual, an act, entitled, "An act laying an embargo on all ships and vessels in the ports and harbors of the United States," and the several acts supplementary thereto, approved on the ninth of January, one thousand eight hundred and nine, by the President of the United States, as an invasion of the liberty of the people, and the constitutional sovereignty of the State governments.

5. *Resolved,* That it will be dangerous to the freedom of these States, to place at the disposal of the President of the United States a standing army of fifty thousand volunteers.

6. *Resolved,* That, in our opinion, the present embarrassed and unhappy situation of our country might have been avoided, if the administration had pursued the wise and prudent policy of the *immortal* WASHINGTON.

7. *Resolved* nevertheless, that we have the fullest confidence, that the patriotism of the good people of the United States will induce them to submit to unwise and arbitrary laws, rather than resort to violence; and that they will use the remedy pointed out by the constitution for the evils under which they suffer, rather

than jeopardize the union of the States, and the independence of their country, by an open opposition to the laws.

8. *Resolved* also, That the legislature and people of the State of Delaware feel no foreign partiality, and that they will defend their country from the aggression of every foreign foe.

––––––––• •––––––––

Connecticut and the Enforcement Act.

February, 1809.

In Connecticut the Federalists had retained unbroken control of all departments of the State government, and the great majority of the people sympathized with Massachusetts in its opposition to the embargo. Naturally, therefore, upon receipt of the circular letter from the Secretary of War of January 18, 1809, requesting the governors to designate special officers of the militia, "of known respect for the laws," to aid in the enforcement of the embargo, Governor Trumbull replied, February 4, 1809, declining to take the "responsibility" of complying with the request, on the ground "that neither the constitution nor the statutes of this State," nor "the constitution or laws of the United States," authorized such an act, and also stating that "the great mass of the citizens of this State" regarded the enforcement act as "unconstitutional in many of its provisions, interfering with the State sovereignties, and subversive of the guaranteed rights, privileges and immunities of the citizens of the United States." The Governor then called a special session of the General Assembly, and addressed it in the famous speech given below. The legislature at once responded, passing, first, a resolution approving the action of the Governor in calling it together; next, a series of *Resolves* condemning the enforcement act and the attempts to carry it out, and finally issued an *Address to the People* in justification of the action taken.

Resolves: The texts of the *Resolutions* and the *Address* of the General Assembly were officially published. A rare pamphlet (16 pages, 8°) without title page or imprint, but containing the above-mentioned documents, as well as the Enforcement Act, is in the Library of the Connecticut Historical Society, Hartford;[1] the Governor's *Speech*, the *Correspondence* of the Secretary of War and the Governor, and the *Report* and *Resolutions* proposed by the Committee of the House of Representatives (nearly the same as later passed) are in *The American Register for 1809* (Phila., 1809), Part II, 176–181. The circular letter of the Secretary of War is also given in the *Writings of Jefferson* (*Ford's ed.*), IX, 237, 238. Consult the following general histories: Adams, IV, 417, 418, 455, 456; Hildreth, VI, 120, 121; McMaster, III, 331, 332; Schouler, II, 173, 193. See also references under *Massachusetts and the Embargo*.

[1] I am indebted to Mr. Albert C. Bates, Librarian, for directing my attention to this pamphlet.

20. Speech of Governor Jonathan Trumbull at the Opening
of the Special Session of the Legislature, February
23, 1809.

*Gentlemen of the Council, Mr. Speaker, and Gentlemen of the
House of Representatives.*

Impressed with the importance of the communications which
I have now to lay before you—prompted also by the concurrent
petitions of a number of the citizens of this State, conveyed to
me with their resolutions adopted in their several town meetings,
convoked for the purpose; and having had under my own consideration, the very alarming crisis of our national affairs, arising
from a variety of measures adopted and contemplated by our
national legislature, more especially from the permanency of the
embargo, with the means resorted to for its more rigorous enforcement, and particularly the late law of Congress, passed on
the 9th day of January last, containing many very extraordinary,
not to say unconstitutional provisions for its execution : I have
viewed the prospect so momentous and threatening, that I have
not hesitated to convene the Legislature of the State, at this unusual time, in order that they may have an opportunity to consider and deliberate on the extraordinary situation into which our
country seems about to be plunged, if not speedily prevented :
and to devise such constitutional measures as in their wisdom
may be judged proper to avert the threatening evil.

It will be useful for the Legislature to take a view of the various
measures of the national legislature, during their present and
preceding sessions, not only those which have immediate relation
to the embargo, but other acts which have been and are under
their consideration, affecting the rights, interests, welfare, and
even the peace of the Union.   Indeed, it would be useful for the
general good, if the State Legislatures were often to cast a watchful eye towards the general government, with a view, candidly to
consider, and judiciously discern, whether the powers delegated
to the United States are not exceeded, or are so exercised as not
to interfere with or counteract those which are reserved by the
people for their own management.   When under the direction of
a wise and prudent discernment, a temperate caution —not an

over jealous disposition, such an examination will always prove a wholesome measure.

On the present occasion, it will be unnecessary for me to enter into any particular statement of our private sufferings, or the threatening aspect of our public situation, in relation to the unprecedented acts of our General Government which are accumulating upon us. The individual feelings and experience of the members of this Legislature, now convened from all parts of the State, will speak the private distresses which have been produced by these acts: and your general information will give you, gentlemen, a correct view of the dangers which impend our public interests, liberty, rights and property, arising from the same source. Despairing of substantial relief from any other quarter, the people are now looking with anxious solicitude and hope, to the wisdom and direction of the Legislature of their own choice; and seem confident that some mode may be devised to remove the pressure under which they are at present suffering. To your collected wisdom and prudence they submit the task. And may it not be hoped, that, with our united efforts under a temperate, discreet and firm consideration of our situation and circumstances, we may be able by the influence of divine aid, to fulfil the just and reasonable expectations of our fellow citizens? Whenever our national legislature is led to overleap the prescribed bounds of their constitutional powers, on the State Legislatures, in great emergencies, devolves the arduous task—it is their right—it becomes their duty, to interpose their protecting shield between the right and liberty of the people, and the assumed power of the General Government. * * * * * * *

[*American Register*, 1809, Pt. II, 176, 177.]

21. Resolutions of the General Assembly.

At a special session of the General Assembly of the State of Connecticut, held at Hartford, on the twenty-third day of February, A. D. 1809.

This Assembly have attended with anxious concern, to the several acts of Congress interdicting foreign commerce, and more especially to an act, approved on the 9th day of January last, by the President of the United States, under the title of "An Act, to enforce and make more effectual an act laying an embargo on all ships and vessels in the ports and harbours of the United States."

After solemn deliberation and advisement thereon, the General Assembly are decided in the opinion, and do Resolve, that the acts aforesaid are a permanent system of measures, abandoning undeniable rights; interdicting the exercise of constitutional privileges, and unprecedented in the annals of nations; and do contain provisions for exercising arbitrary powers, grievous to the good people of this State, dangerous to their common liberties, incompatible with the constitution of the United States, and encroaching upon the immunities of this State.

Resolved, That to preserve the Union, and support the constitution of the United States, it becomes the duty of the Legislatures of the States, in such a crisis of affairs, vigilantly to watch over, and vigorously to maintain, the powers not delegated to the United States, but reserved to the States respectively, or to the people; and that a due regard to this duty, will not permit this Assembly to assist, or concur in giving effect to the aforesaid unconstitutional act, passed, to enforce the Embargo.

Resolved, That this Assembly highly approve of the conduct of his Excellency the Governor, in declining to designate persons to carry into effect, by the aid of *military power*, the act of the United States, enforcing the Embargo, and that his letter addressed to the Secretary for the Department of War, containing his refusal, to make such designation, be recorded in the public records of this State, as an example to persons, who may hold places of distinguished trust, in this free and independent republic.

Resolved, That the persons holding executive offices under this State, are restrained by the duties which they owe this State, from affording any official aid or co-operation in the execution of the act aforesaid; and that his Excellency the Governor be requested, as commander in chief of the military force of this State, to cause these resolutions to be published in general orders: And that the secretary of this State be and he is hereby directed to transmit copies of the same to the several sheriffs and town clerks.

Resolved, That his Excellency the Governor be requested to communicate the foregoing resolutions to the President of the United States, with an assurance that this Assembly regret that they are thus obliged under a sense of paramount public duty to assert the unquestionable right of this State to abstain from any agency in the execution of measures, which are unconstitutional and despotic.

Resolved, That this Assembly accord in sentiment, with the Senate and House of Representatives, of the commonwealth of Massachusetts, that it is expedient to effect certain alterations in the constitution of the United States; and will zealously co-operate with that commonwealth and any other of the States, in all legal and constitutional measures for procuring such amendments to the constitution of the United States as shall be judged necessary to obtain more effectual protection and defence for commerce; and to give to the commercial States their fair and just consideration in the Union, and for affording permanent security, as well as present relief, from the oppressive measures, under which they now suffer.

Resolved, That his Excellency the Governor be requested to transmit copies of the foregoing resolutions to the President of the Senate, and Speaker of the House of Representatives, in the commonwealth of Massachusetts, and to the Legislatures of such of our sister States, as manifest a disposition to concur, in restoring to commerce its former activity, and preventing the repetition of measures which have a tendency, not only to destroy it, but to dissolve the Union, which ought to be inviolate.

General Assembly, special session, February, 1809.

JOHN COTTON SMITH,
Speaker of the House of Representatives.
JONATHAN TRUMBULL, *Governor.*
Attest, SAMUEL WYLLYS, *Secretary.*
[Pamphlet containing Resolves, etc., 7, 8.]

---

22. Report and Resolutions of Rhode Island on the Embargo.

March 4, 1809.

The following resolutions were adopted by both branches of the General Assembly on March 4, 1809; in the Senate by a vote of 7 to 4, in the House, 35 to 28. Extracts from the report of the Committee which submitted the resolutions are also given. Rhode Island appears to have been the last State to take action condemning the embargo. In New Hampshire resolutions against the embargo were rejected by the House, December 23, 1808, by a vote of 25 to 101. (*National Intelligencer, Jan.* 6, 1809.) Many of the other States passed resolutions approving the policy of the administration, those of North Carolina, of December 5, 1808 (*Amer. State Papers*, Misc., I, 944, 945), and of Virginia, of February 7, 1809 (*Acts of the General Assembly of Virginia*, 1808-09, 99-104), may be taken as typical. The report accompanying the resolutions of Virginia is of considerable interest, as containing a reason for the failure of the embargo. It says: " If it has failed, in any degree, as a measure of constraint, your committee believe that it is not because our enemies have not felt its force, but because they believe we have felt it too sensibly; because the unfortunate opposition which the measure has met in some parts of the union, has inspired them with a fallacious hope, that we, ourselves, either could not or would not bear its privations."

The text of the resolutions of Rhode Island is from *Acts and Resolves of Rhode Island General Assembly held at E. Greenwich on the fourth Monday of February*, 1809, 32, 33.[1]

The State of Rhode Island and Providence Plantations.

The Committee to whom were referred the memorials, petitions and resolutions of the towns [here follow the names of twelve towns], beg leave to report * * * that it would be a paradox in the history of the human mind, if a people, who from the foundation of their government have ever manifested the most warm and zealous attachment to civil liberty, should regard with indifference its extinguishment. It would betray an ignorance of their true interests, if they did not esteem it the " more perfect union of these States," as it is declared and provided for in the federal constitution as the parent and perpetuator of their political prosperity.

That it would be a reflection on their discernment and sagacity, if they did not foresee that the dissolution of the Union may be more surely, and as speedily effected by the systematick oppression of the government, as by the inconsiderate disobedience of the people. That the people of this State, as one of the parties to the Federal compact, have a right to express their sense of any violation of its provisions and that it is the duty of this General Assembly as the organ of their sentiments and the depository of

---

[1] I am indebted to Mr. Clarence S. Brigham, Librarian of the Rhode Island Historical Society, for verifying the text of these resolutions.

their authority, to interpose for the purpose of protecting them from the ruinous inflictions of usurped and unconstitutional power.   *   *   *   *   *   *   *   *

Resolved, That the several acts of the Congress of the United States laying an embargo, by the permanent interdiction of foreign commerce, and by the numerous and vexatious restrictions upon the coasting trade, do, in the opinion of this General Assembly, infringe upon the undeniable rights and privileges of the good people of this State.

Resolved, That the act of Congress of the 9th of January last, enforcing the several embargo acts, is in many of its provisions unjust, oppressive, tyrannical and unconstitutional.

Resolved, That to preserve the Union and to support the constitution of the United States, it becomes the duty of this General Assembly, while it is cautious not to infringe upon the constitution and delegated powers and rights of the General Government, to be vigilant in guarding from usurpation and violation, those powers and rights which the good people of this State have expressly reserved to themselves, and have ever refused to delegate.

Resolved, That a committee be appointed and instructed to prepare a suitable remonstrance, addressed to the Congress of the United States, expressive of the feelings and opinions of this General Assembly on the several subjects of complaint in the aforesaid petitions, memorials and resolves; and praying the repeal of the aforesaid obnoxious and oppressive laws, and that Congress will in their wisdom devise efficacious measures for the preservation of the peace of the United States; and that said committee report the same at the next session of the General Assembly.

Resolved, That his Excellency the Governor be requested to transmit copies of the foregoing report and resolutions to the President of the Senate and the Speaker of the House of Representatives of the State of Massachusetts, and to the Governor of the State of Connecticut, and to the Legislatures of such other States as have manifested or may manifest a disposition to concur with us in the adoption of constitutional measures for the preservation of the Union of the States, and for the removal of the political evils under which we are now suffering.

STATE RIGHTS
AND THE WAR OF 1812. 1809–1815.

Pennsylvania and the Federal Judiciary.

The Olmstead Case.

1809.

The following resolutions present the final phase in a conflict, of more than thirty years duration, between the United States and the State of Pennsylvania over their respective jurisdictions. This conflict grew out of the appeal of Gideon Olmstead from the judgment of the Pennsylvania Court of Admiralty, in regard to the distribution of the prize money in the case of the sloop "*Active*," in 1778, to the Committee of Appeals of Congress.[1] This Committee reversed the decision, but their jurisdiction was denied by the Legislature and the other State authorities, and the enforcement of the decree was successfully withstood by the State until 1808. In that year the dispute was revived by the application of the Attorney General to the Supreme Court, in behalf of Olmstead, for a *writ of mandamus* commanding Judge Peters of the District Court to enforce the judgment previously given (1779). The application was granted by Chief Justice Marshall, February 23, 1809, in one of his most characteristic and important opinions, in which he solemnly declared, "If the legislatures of the several States may, at will, annul the judgments of the Courts of the United States, and destroy the rights acquired under those judgments, the constitution itself becomes a solemn mockery; and the nation is deprived of the means of enforcing its laws by the instrumentality of its own tribunals." (*U. S. v. Peters*, 5 Cranch, 136.) Judge Peters issued the writ, but the attempt of the United States Marshal to serve it was resisted by a brigade of the State militia, under the command of General Bright, which had been called out by Governor Snyder, February 27, 1809. The Marshal thereupon summoned a *posse-comitatus* of two thousand men, but in order to avoid bloodshed, fixed the day for the service of the warrant to three weeks ahead. In the mean time

[1] For action of New Hampshire in a similar case, cf. ante, pp. 11–15.

the Governor's appeal to President Madison to intervene was firmly declined. The Legislature, however, in justification of the action of the State, adopted an elaborate state rights report and the subjoined resolutions. The doctrines underlying these resolutions had been maintained by the Courts of the State in the opinions of Chief Justice McKean in 1792 in the case of *Ross et al. v. Rittenhouse* (2 Dallas, 160), a case growing out of the Olmstead case, and in 1798 in the case of *Res Publica v. Cobbett* (3 Dallas, 473, 474). When these resolutions were presented to Congress, June 9, 1809, the House of Representatives refused to print them by vote of 63 to 50. (*Annals*, 258–260.) For the action of the States on this proposal, see No. 24. The Legislature, however, at the same time, opened a way for retreat by placing at the disposal of the Governor a sum of money, equal to that in dispute, to be used as "might appear advisable and proper." On the 15th of April, the Marshal, eluding the vigilance of the militia, succeeded in executing his process, and two days later Chief Justice Tilghman, of the State Supreme Court, after presenting a forcible exposition of the rights of the State and of the United States (*Brightly's Reports, Penna.*, 14, 15; *Amer. Reg.* 1809, 171), issued the writ of *habeas corpus*, and the sum in dispute was finally turned over by the State authorities. Subsequently General Bright and others were tried for obstructing the process of the United States District Court in the Circuit Court, and were finally convicted and sentenced to fine and imprisonment, but were pardoned by the President on the ground that "they had acted under a mistaken sense of duty." A Committee of the State Senate, March 3, 1810, reported in favor of a bill donating a tract of two hundred acres of land to each of the condemned, "in consideration of their services and sufferings," but the measure failed. (*Journal of the Senate of Penna.* (1809–10), 382).

References: Sources. For message of Gov. Snyder, Report of the Committee and Resolutions, cf. *Journal of the Senate of Penna.*, 1808–09, 268, 269, 295–307; *Journal of the House*, 615–629, 692–697, 786–798; Resolutions and correspondence given in *Annals of Cong., 11 Cong., 2 Sess., Pt.* II, 2253–2269; Resolutions in *Pamphlet Laws of Penna.*, 1808–09, 200; *Amer. State Papers, Misc.* II, 2–7; *Annual Register*, 1809, 150–175, 168–174; *Niles' Register*, XLIII, *Sup.* 24. Two contemporary pamphlets: *The whole Proceedings in the Case of Olmstead v. Rittenhouse*, by Richard Peters, Jr. (Phila., 1809); *The Trial of General Bright in the Circuit Court of the United States for the District of Pennsylvania.* (Phila., 1809.) General accounts: H. L. Carson in *Penna. Mag.* XVI, 385–393; also in *The Green Bag*, VII, 17; Hildreth, VI, 155–164; McMaster, V, 403–406. Early history of the case set forth in *U. S. v. Peters*, 5 *Cranch*, 115. Davis in 131 *U. S. Reports, Appx. XXIX–XXXIV;* Jameson in *Essays in Const. History*, 17–23.

23. Resolution of the Legislature of Pennsylvania, April 3, 1809.

* * * * * * And whereas the causes and reasons which have produced this conflict between the general and state government

should be made known, not only that the state may be justified
to her sister states, who are equally interested in the preservation
of the state rights ; but to evince to the Government of the United
States that the Legislature, in resisting encroachments on their
rights, are not acting in a spirit of hostility to the legitimate
powers of the United States' courts ; but are actuated by a disposition to compromise, and to guard against future collisions of
power, by an amendment to the constitution : and that, whilst
they are contending for the rights of the State, that it will be at-
tributed to a desire of preserving the federal government itself,
the best features of which must depend upon keeping up a just
balance between the general and state governments, as guaranteed by the constitution.

Be it therefore known, that the present unhappy dispute has
arisen out of the following circumstances : [Here follows a detailed statement of their view of the case.]

Although the Legislature reverence the constitution of the
United States and its lawful authorities, yet there is a respect due
to the solemn and public acts, and to the honor and dignity of
our own state, and the unvarying assertion of her right, for a
period of thirty years, which right ought not to be relinquished,
Therefore,

Resolved by the Senate and House of Representatives of the
Commonwealth of Pennsylvania, &c.   That, as a member of the
Federal Union, the Legislature of Pennsylvania acknowledges the
supremacy, and will cheerfully submit to the authority of the
general government, as far as that authority is delegated by the
constitution of the United States.   But, whilst they yield to this
authority, when exercised within Constitutional limits, they trust
they will not be considered as acting hostile to the General Government, when, as *guardians of the State rights*, they can not permit an infringement of those rights, by an unconstitutional exercise of power in the United States' courts.

Resolved, That in a government like that of the United States,
where there are powers granted to the general government, and
rights reserved to the states, it is impossible, from the imperfec-
tions of language, so to define the limits of each, that difficulties
should not some times arise from a collision of powers : and it is
to be lamented, that no provision is made in the constitution for

determining disputes between the general and state governments by an impartial tribunal, when such cases occur.

Resolved, That from the construction the United States' courts give to their powers, the harmony of the states, if they resist encroachments on their rights, will frequently be interrupted ; and if to prevent this evil, they should, on all occasions yield to stretches of power, the reserved rights of the States will depend on the arbitrary power of the courts.

Resolved, That, should the independence of the states, as secured by the constitution, be destroyed, the liberties of the people in so extensive a country cannot long survive. To suffer the United States' courts to decide on STATE RIGHTS will, from a bias *in favor of power,* necessarily destroy the FEDERAL PART of our Government : And whenever the government of the United States becomes consolidated, we may learn from the history of nations what will be the event.

To prevent the balance between the general and state governments from being destroyed, and the harmony of the States from being interrupted,

Resolved, That our Senators in Congress be instructed, and our Representatives requested, to use their influence to procure an amendment to the Constitution of the United States, that an impartial tribunal may be established to determine disputes between the general and state governments ; and, that they be further instructed to use their endeavors, that in the meanwhile, such arrangements may be made, between the government of the Union and of this State, as will put an end to existing difficulties.

Resolved, That the Governor be requested to transmit a copy of these resolutions, to the Executive of the United States, to be laid before Congress, at their next session. And that he be authorized and directed to correspond with the President on the subject in controversy, and to agree to such arrangements as may be in the power of the executive to make, or that Congress may make, either by the appointment of commissioners or otherwise, for settling the difficulties between the two governments.

And, That the Governor be also requested to transmit a copy to the Executives of the several States in the Union, with a request, that they may be laid before their respective Legislatures.

[*Pamphlet Laws of Pennsylvania,* 1808–09, 200.]

24. Reply of the General Assembly of Virginia to Pennsylvania.

January 26, 1810.

The foregoing resolutions of Pennsylvania were not concurred in by a single State. On the contrary the Legislatures of at least eleven States passed resolutions of disapproval, as follows: New Hampshire, Massachusetts, Vermont, New Jersey, Maryland, Virginia, North Carolina, Georgia, Ohio, Kentucky, Tennessee. See *Journals of the Senate and House of Pennsylvania*, for 1809–1812; Ames, *Proposed Amendments*, 160, notes, 329. The most elaborate of these replies came from Virginia. It is of unusual interest owing to both the previous and subsequent action of Virginia relative to the jurisdiction of the Federal Government.

The committee, to whom was referred the communication of the governor of Pennsylvania, covering certain resolutions of the legislature of that state, proposing an amendment to the constitution of the United States, by the appointment of an impartial tribunal to decide disputes between the state and federal judiciary, have had the same under their consideration, and are of opinion that a tribunal is already provided by the constitution of the United States, *to wit:* the Supreme Court, more eminently qualified from their habits and duties, from the mode of their selection, and from the tenure of their offices, to decide the disputes aforesaid in an enlightened and impartial manner, than any other tribunal which could be erected.

The members of the Supreme Court are selected from those in the United States who are most celebrated for virtue and legal learning; not at the will of a singal individual, but by the concurrent wishes of the President and Senate of the United States, they will therefore have no local prejudices and partialities.

The duties they have to perform lead them necessarily to the most enlarged and accurate acquaintance with the jurisdiction of the federal and several state courts together, and with the admirable symmetry of our government.

The tenure of their offices enables them to pronounce the sound and correct opinions they may have formed, without fear, favor, or partiality.

The amendment to the constitution proposed by Pennsylvania seems to be founded upon the idea that the federal judiciary will, from a lust of power, enlarge their jurisdiction to the total annihilation of the jurisdiction of the state courts, that they will exercise their *will* instead of the *law* and the *constitution*. This argument, if it proves anything, would operate more strongly against the tribunal proposed to be created which promises so little, than against the Supreme Court, which for reasons given before had every thing connected with their appointment calculated to ensure confidence. What security have we, were the proposed amendments adopted, that this tribunal would not substitute their *will* and their *pleasure* in the place of *law* ?

The judiciary are the weakest of the three departments of government, and least dangerous to the political rights of the constitution ; they hold neither the *purse* nor the *sword*, and even to enforce their own judgments and decrees, must ultimately depend upon the executive arm. Should the federal judiciary, however, unmindful of their weakness, unmindful of the duty which they owe to themselves and their country, become corrupt, and transcend the limits of their jurisdiction, would the proposed amendment oppose even a probable barrier in such an improbable state of things? The creation of a tribunal, such as is proposed by Pennsylvania, so far as we are enabled to form an idea of it from a description given in the resolutions of the legislature of that state, would, in the opinion of your committee, tend rather to invite than prevent a collision between the federal and state courts. It might also become, in process of time, a serious and dangerous embarrassment to the operations of the general government.

Resolved therefore, That the legislature of this state do disapprove of the amendment to the constitution of the United States, proposed by the legislature of Pennsylvania.

Resolved also, That his excellency the governor be, and is hereby requested, to transmit forthwith a copy of the foregoing preamble and resolutions, to each of the senators and representatives of this state in Congress, and to the executive of the several states in the Union, with a request that the same may be laid before the legislatures thereof.

[*Acts of General Assembly of Virginia*, 1809–10, 102, 103.]

25. Extracts from the Preamble and Resolutions of the House of Representatives of Pennsylvania.

February 3, 1810.

Chagrined at the success of the Federal Courts, and disappointed with the replies of the other States to their proposal to amend the Constitution, both branches of the General Assembly of Pennsylvania, early in the year 1810, drew up elaborate reports and resolutions reviewing the questions at issue anew. Extracts from the Report and Resolutions of the House of Representatives follow. The Minority presented a long report sharply condemning the action of the State authorities and a series of resolutions in support of the jurisdiction of the Federal Government. This was offered as a substitute for the Majority report, but was rejected by a vote of 25 *yeas* to 67 *nays*. (*Journal of the House*, 1809–10, 403–424; *Amer. Register*, 1810, 113–136.) In the Senate a committee brought in an extensive report in justification of the position taken by the State, and resolutions renewing their proposal of a constitutional amendment for the establishment of a " disinterested tribunal " to determine disputes between the General and the State governments, and also recommending the reward of the members of the militia who had suffered conviction. (*Journal of the Senate*, 1809–10, 376–382.) Neither these resolutions nor those of the House were acted upon by the Senate. For *Text* and action thereon, cf. *Journal of the House*, 1809–10, 250–254, 402–426, 433–436; *Journal of the Senate*, 1809–10, 226–233.

* * * From this view of the subject, the committee are of opinion, that the constitution of the United States, has been violated by the decision of the judge, and the constitutional rights of the state invaded. The question then occurs, in what manner is a state to defend her rights against such invasion? It has already been observed, that the constitution of the United States guarantees to each state a republican form of government; that the powers not delegated to the United States, are reserved to the states respectively without entering into a detail of the rights reserved or not delegated, suffice it to say, that " the right of acquiring, possessing and protecting property is one." If this be not one of the powers not delegated, then indeed a state is in a worse and more degraded situation than the most obscure individual, whose property cannot be taken from him when fairly acquired, without his consent, even for publick use, without a compensation. In the case before us, all the constituted authorities of the state, have uniformly asserted their rights, and protested against every attempt to infringe them.

It may be asked, who is to decide the question? If it be alledged the state has not the right, it may justly be replied, the power invading it, has not. It is a case unprovided for in the constitution, and there is no common umpire. * * *

Resolved by the Senate and House of Representatives, That after most solemnly declaring their readiness, cheerfully to submit to all legal and constitutional decisions of the federal courts, they cannot but express their highest disapprobation of what they conceive to be the illegal and unconstitutional conduct of the same in the case of Gideon Olmstead. (59 *yeas* to 33 *nays.*)

Resolved, That the sovereignty and independence of the states, as guaranteed by the constitution of the United States, ought to be most zealously guarded, and every attempt to depreciate the value of those rights, and to consolidate these states into one general government, is hostile to the liberty and happiness of the people, and merits our most decided disapprobation. (88 to 2.)

Resolved, That the governor was justified in the efforts which he made to sustain the rights and sovereignty of the state, and the promptitude and fidelity with which he executed his legal and constitutional powers, under the act of April second, one thousand eight hundred and three, merits our highest approbation. (60 to 33.)

Resolved, That we highly approve of the conduct of our predecessors, in requesting the members of both houses of congress to use their best endeavours to have the constitution of the United States so amended, that an impartial tribunal be appointed to determine disputes between the general and state governments.

Resolved, That the governor be requested to transmit a copy of these resolutions, together with the foregoing statement, to each of the senators and representatives in congress from this state.

---

26. Resolutions of Pennsylvania against the Bank.

January 11, 1811.

The attempt to secure the renewal of the charter of the United States Bank in 1811, called out resolutions in opposition from the legislatures of Pennsylvania and Virginia. The following resolutions of the General Assembly of Pennsylvania are of especial interest in view of the state rights doctrines asserted in the Preamble. As first passed by the House the language of the

Preamble was even stronger, and closely followed the text of the first resolve of the Kentucky Resolutions of 1798, but it was amended by the Senate by a vote of 20 to 8 and agreed to by the House in the form given below.

References: Text given in *Pamphlet Laws of Penna.*, 1810–11, 268, 269, also in *Amer. State Papers, Finance*, II, 467. Text as passed by the House with action of the Senate, *Senate Journal of Penna.*, 1810–11, 92, 93, 104, 105. McMaster, III, 386–389; Adams, V, 207, 328–337; Schouler, II, 316.

The people of the United States by the adoption of the federal constitution established a general government for special purposes, reserving to themselves respectively, the rights and authorities not delegated in that instrument. To the compact thereby created, each state acceded in its character as a state, and is a party. The act of union thus entered into being to all intents and purposes a treaty between sovereign states, the general government by this treaty was not constituted the exclusive or final judge of the powers it was to exercise ; for if it were so to judge then its judgment and not the constitution would be the measure of its authority.

Should the general government in any of its departments violate the provisions of the constitution, it rests with the states, and with the people, to apply suitable remedies.

With these impressions, the legislature of Pennsylvania, ever solicitous to secure an administration of the federal and state governments, conformably to the true spirit of their respective constitutions, feel it their duty to express their sentiments upon an important subject now before congress, viz., the continuance or establishment of a bank. From a careful review of the powers vested in the general government, they have the most positive conviction that the authority to grant charters of incorporation, within the jurisdiction of any state without the consent thereof is not recognized in that instrument, either expressly, or by a warrantable implication ; Therefore,

Resolved, By the Senate and House of Representatives of the Commonwealth of Pennsylvania, in General Assembly met, That the senators of this state in the senate of the United States, be, and they are hereby instructed, and the representatives of this state in the house of representatives of the United States be, and they hereby are requested to use every exertion in their power, to prevent the charter of the bank of the United States from being renewed, or any other bank from being chartered by Congress, designed to have operation within the jurisdiction of any state, without first having obtained the consent of the legislature of such state.

Resolved, That the governor be, and he hereby is requested to forward a copy of the above preamble and resolution, to each of the senators and representatives of this state, in the Congress of the United States.

---

27. Resolutions of Virginia against the Bank.

January 22, 1811.

The following resolutions were disregarded by Senator Richard Brent, of Virginia, thereupon the General Assembly adopted a Report elaborately presenting an historical argument in favor of the doctrine of instructions and called upon Senator Brent to resign. *Acts of Virginia,* 1811-12, 143–152. Texts of following resolutions, *Acts of Virginia,* 1810–11, 121; also, *Amer. State Papers, Finance,* II, 467; *Annals,* 1810–11, 201.

The General Assembly of Virginia view with the most serious concern the late attempts which have been made to obtain from Congress a renewal of the charter incorporating the Bank of the United States. This assembly are deeply impressed with the conviction that the original grant of that charter was unconstitutional; that congress have no power whatever to renew it; and that the exercise of such a power would be not only unconstitutional, but a dangerous encroachment on the sovereignty of the states— Therefore,

Resolved, That the senators of this state in the Congress of the United States be instructed, and our representatives most earnestly requested, in the execution of their duties as faithful representatives of their country, to use their best efforts in opposing by every means in their power the renewal of the charter of the bank of the United States.

Massachusetts and the Militia Question.

1812-1814.

When war was declared against Great Britain, June 18, 1812, (*U. S. Stat. at Large,* II, 755) the Federalist minority issued an Address to their Constituents, protesting both against the war and the manner in which the declaration of war had been secured.   That this war was " a party and not a national war " and entered upon by the United States "as a divided people " was soon evident by the position taken by the authorities of several of the New England States, relative to the power of the Federal Government over the State Militia.   By authority of the President, General Dearborn, on June 22, addressed the Governors of Massachusetts and Connecticut, making requisition for certain detachments of their militia, for service in the defence of the coast, but did not include in the call any officer of a high rank.   Governor Strong, of Massachusetts, not considering the call warranted by the Constitution, did not comply with the requisition, for reasons set forth in his correspondence with the Secretary of War, and as later stated in his Speech to the Legislature. Renewed requisitions from General Dearborn, and the Secretary of War during July, finally led to the submission of the questions involved to the Supreme Judicial Court of the State.   An extract from their decision follows :

The attitude of Massachusetts and Connecticut was severely condemned by President Madison in his message of November 4, 1812.   (Richardson, *Messages and Papers of the Presidents*, I, 516.)   The question still remained unsettled when in the summer of 1814 the coast of Maine was invaded, Governor Strong at the request of General Dearborn, called out the militia, but as they were placed under the command of a general of the State instead of the United States, the administration refused to be responsible for their maintenance (Secretary of War Monroe to Strong, Sept. 17, 1814, *State Papers, Military Affairs*, I, 614), and left Massachusetts and the other New England States to defend themselves largely at their own cost.   It was this situation that immediately led to the issuing of the call for the Hartford Convention. (See *post*, Nos. 36, 37.)

In 1817 the State of Massachusetts presented its claim to the Federal Government for reimbursement of the expenses contracted in maintaining the defence of the coast, and finally after an agitation of thirteen years, and the renunciation by the Governor and both branches of the Legislature of the principles maintained by the former authorities of the State, by act of May 31, 1830 (May session, 1823, *Resolves of Mass.*, 1819–24, 634–636, 640, 641, 644, 645), Massachusetts was awarded about one-half of the amount of her claim. (*U. S. Stat. at Large*, IV, 428.)   In 1827 the Supreme Court of the United States in *Martin v. Mott* (12 *Wheaton*, 19) decided adversely in a case involving the principles and position taken by the authorities of the New England States in regard to the constitutional rights of the Federal Government over the Militia.

References : SOURCES.   *An* ADDRESS *of Members of the House of Representatives of the Congress of the United States: To their* CONSTITUENTS *on the subject of the* WAR *with Great Britain* (Boston, 1812); also in the *Annals*, 12 *Cong.*, 1 *sess.*, 2196–2221; *Niles' Register*, II, 309–315.   The Senate of the Mass. Legislature, which was Republican, issued an *Address to the People of the Commonwealth* (Boston, 1812, 8°, 28 pages); also in *Niles*, II, 308, 309; in which they " say with assurance, that a deep and deadly design is formed against our happy Union."   The House which was Federalist also issued *An*

Address to the People of Massachusetts (n. t. p., 1812, 8°, 14 pages); also in *Niles*, II, 417–419. The *Correspondence* between the Secretary of War, the Governor and United States military officers is given in the *Annals*, 12 *Cong.*, 2 *sess.*, *Appx.*, 1295–1304; *Amer. State Papers, Military Affairs*, I, 321–325, 607–608, 610–614; *Senate Doc.*, 18 *Cong.* 1 *sess.*, II, No. 43, 135, 137–139, 142–164. All the important documents in connection with the Mass. claim are to be found in the above, and in *Military Affairs*, III, 8–10, 104–108; IV, 293–295; *Resolves of Mass.*, 1828–31, 256–263; *Cong. Debate*, 1829–30, 357–359. GENERAL REFERENCES: Adams, VI, 305, 309, 399–402; VIII, 219–223, 272; Barry, *Mass.*, III, 379–390; Dwight, *Hartford Convention*, 233–275 in passim, 282–285; Hildreth, VI, 319–325, 372–374, 484–500, 531; McMaster, III, 543–546; IV, 231, 244–247; Schouler, II, 356, 422–424; Von Holst, I, 233–246, 259–260; Adams, *New Eng. Federalism;* Kent, *Commentaries* (13th ed.), I, 263–265; Story (5th ed.), II, 121–126; Winsor, *Memorial Hist. of Boston*, III, 211–215, 303–311.

----

28. Extracts from the Letter of Governor Strong of Massachusetts to Secretary of War Eustis.

August 5, 1812.

The following extracts, together with the Opinion of the Judges, present briefly the reasons for the refusal of Governor Strong to honor the call for the militia. The Governor's views are set forth more fully in his Speech to the General Court, October 14, 1812. (*Resolves of Mass.*, 1812–15, 75, 78; also extract in Dwight, 241-243.) The Federalist House in their Answer, expressed their "unqualified approbation of the Governor's course." (*Ibid.*, 82, 83.) The Republican Senate, in their Answer, dissented from the opinions of the Governor, and declared that "the jealousy with which your Excellency regards the authority of the National Administration might suggest an apprehension for the safety of the Union." (*Ibid.*, 86–88.)

* * * As an opinion generally prevailed, that the Governor had no authority to call the militia into actual service, unless one of the exigencies contemplated by the constitution exists,[1] I thought it expedient to call the council together, and, having laid before them your letter, and those I have received from General Dearborn, I requested their advice on the subject of them.

The Council advised "that they were unable from a view of the Constitution of the United States, and the letters aforesaid, to

---

[1] "Congress may provide for calling forth the militia to execute the laws of the Union, suppress insurrection, and repel invasion."

perceive that any exigency exists which can render it advisable to comply with the said requisition. But, as upon important ques tions of law, and upon solemn occasions, the Governor and Council have authority to require the opinion of the Justices of the Supreme Judicial Court, it is advisable to request the opinion of the Supreme Court upon the following questions, viz. :

" 1st. Whether the commanders in chief of the militia of the several states have a right to determine, whether any of the exigencies contemplated by the constitution of the United States exist ; so as to require them to place the militia, or any part of it, in the service of the United States, at the request of the President, to be commanded by him pursuant to acts of Congress?"

" 2nd. Whether, when either of the exigencies exist, authorizing the employing the militia in the service of the United States, the militia thus employed, can be lawfully commanded by any officer, but of the militia, except by the President of the United States?"

I enclose a copy of the answer given by the judges to these questions.   *   *   *   I am fully disposed to afford all the aid to the measures of the national government which the constitution requires of me, but, I presume it will not be expected, or desired, that I shall fail in the duty which I owe to the people of this state, who have confided their interests to my care.

[Senate Doc. 13 Cong. 3 sess. Report of Com. on Military Affairs, Feb. 28, 1815, 34-38.]

29. Extract from the Opinion of the Judges of Massachusetts on the Militia Question, 1812.[1]

On the construction of the Federal and State constitutions must depend the answers to the several questions proposed. As the militia of the several states may be employed in the service of the United States, for the three specific purposes of executing the laws of the Union, of suppressing insurrections, and of repelling invasions, the opinion of the judges is requested, whether the Commanders-in-Chief of the militia of the several states have a right to determine whether any of the exigencies aforesaid exist, so as to require them to place the militia, or any part of it, in the

---

[1] Signed by Judges Parsons, Sewall and Parker.

service of the United States, at the request of the President, to be commanded by him pursuant to acts of Congress.

It is the opinion of the undersigned, that this right is vested in the Commanders-in-Chief of the militia of the several states.

The Federal Constitution provides, that whenever either of these exigencies exist, the militia may be employed, pursuant to some act of Congress, in the service of the United States ; but no power is given, either to the President or to Congress, to determine that either of the said exigencies do in fact exist. As this power is not delegated to the United States by the Federal Constitution, nor prohibited by it to the states, it is reserved to the states, respectively ; and from the nature of the power, it must be exercised by those with whom the states have respectively entrusted the chief command of the militia.

It is the duty of these commanders to execute this important trust, agreeably to the laws of their several states, respectively, without reference to the laws or officers of the United States, in all cases, except those specially provided in the Federal Constitution. They must, therefore, determine whether either of the special cases exist, obliging them to relinquish the execution of this trust, and to render themselves and the militia subject to the command of the President. A different construction, giving to Congress the right to determine when these special cases exist, authorizing them to call forth the whole of the militia, and taking them from the Commanders-in-Chief of the several states, and subjecting them to the command of the President, would place all the militia, in effect, at the will of Congress, and produce a military consolidation of the states, without any constitutional remedy against the intentions of the people, when ratifying the Constitution. Indeed, since passing the act of Congress of February 28, 1795, chapter 101, vesting in the President the power of calling forth the militia when the exigencies mentioned in the Constitution shall exist, if the President has the power of determining when those exigencies exist, the militia in the several states is, in effect, at his command, and subject to his control.

No inconvenience can reasonably be presumed to result from the construction which vests in the Commanders in Chief of the militia, in the several states, the right of determining when the exigencies exist, obliging them to place the militia in the service of the United States.   These exigencies are of such a nature, that the existence of them can be easily ascertained by, or made known to, the Commanders in Chief of the militia ; and when ascertained, the public interest will produce prompt obedience to the acts of Congress.

Another question proposed to the consideration of the judges, is, whether, when either of the exigencies exist, authorizing the employing of the militia in the service of the United States, the militia thus employed can be lawfully commanded by any officer not of the militia, except by the President of the United States ?

* * * The officers of the militia are to be appointed by the states, and the President may exercise his command of the militia by officers of the militia, duly appointed ; but we know of no constitutional provision authorizing any officer of the army of the United States to command the militia, or authorizing any officer of the militia to command the army of the United States.   The Congress may provide laws for the government of the militia when in actual service ; but to extend this power to placing them under the command of an officer not of the militia, except the President, would render nugatory the provision that the militia are to have officers appointed by the states. * * *

[Senate Doc. 13 Cong. 3 sess.   Report of Com. on Military Affairs, Feb. 28, 1815, 38–42.]

30. Report and Resolutions of Connecticut on the Militia Question.

August 25, 1812.

Upon the receipt of General Dearborn's requisition, Governor Griswold convened the Council, June 29, 1812.   This body advised him not to comply with the requisition on grounds similar to those afterwards taken by the authorities of Massachusetts.   Upon the renewal of the requisition by the Federal authorities, Governor Griswold, on August 4, reconvened the Council, which body again recommended a non-compliance with the requisition, whereupon the Governor called the General Assembly in extra session on August 25, and in his message reviewed the situation.   The General Assembly, on the same day, adopted a *Report* and *Resolutions*, extracts from which follow, and also a *Declaration* containing a justification of their action.   In 1814 a similar controversy to that with Massachusetts arose between the State authorities and the Federal administration over the commanding officer of the State militia, when called into the Federal service.

References: Text, *Report of Committee, August 25, 1812, on that part of the Governor's Speech which relates to his correspondence with the Secretary of War.* (New Haven, 1812, 8°, 14 pages.)   Also given in *Niles*, III, 22–25.   *Message of Governor Griswold, Special Session, with documents accompanying the same.* (New Haven, 1812, 8°, 22 pages); also given in *Niles*, III, 4, 5.   The text of these and earlier messages of the Governor and action of Council are given in Dwight, *Hartford Convention*, 243–248, 259–267; *Proclamation* of August 6, 1812, announcing proceedings of Council is in *Niles*, II, 389.   Report of committee of Legislature on the conflict over the command of the militia, Oct., 1814, *Niles*, VII, sup., 106, 107.   For *Correspondence* of the Governor and the Federal authorities, see *Amer. State Papers, Military Affairs*, I, 325, 326, 608, 614–621; *Annals*, 12 *Cong.*, 2 *Sess.*, Appx., 1304–1310; *Report of Com. on Military Affairs, Feb.* 28, 1815, *State Papers*, 13 *Cong.*, 3 *sess.*, 18–22, 55–80.   For general references, see *ante* p. 56.

The committee consider it as of the highest importance, that no ground should be taken, on this subject, but that which is strictly constitutional, and that, being taken, it should be maintained at every hazard.

  * * * * * * *

It is very apparent that the claim set up by the administration of the government of the United States, is, that when a war has been declared to exist, between this and any foreign country, the militia of the several states are liable to be demanded, by the administration of the government of the United States, to enter their forts, and there remain, upon the presumption, that the enemy *may* invade the place or places, which they are ordered to garrison and defend.   And that for this purpose, they may be ordered to any part of the United States.

  * * * * * * *

If then the militia can be constitutionally required to man the garrison of the United States, they may continue to be so required, as long as the danger continues to exist; and to become, for all the purposes of carrying on the war, within the United States, standing troops of the United States.   And a declaration of war made by the administration of the government of the United States, and announced to the governors of the states, will substantially convert the militia of the states into such troops. Before it is agreed that the states have ceded such a power to the

United States the question ought to be examined with much attention.

On the fullest deliberation, your committee are not able to discover that the constitution of the United States justifies this claim.

The people of this state were among the first to adopt that constitution. They have been among the most prompt to satisfy all its lawful demands, and to give facility to its fair operations—they have enjoyed the benefits resulting from the union of the states; they have loved, and still love, and cherish *that* union, and will deeply regret, if any events shall occur to alienate their affection from it. They have a deep interest in its preservation, and are still disposed to yield a willing and prompt obedience to all the legitimate requirements of the constitution of the United States.

But it must not be forgotten, that the state of Connecticut is a FREE SOVEREIGN and INDEPENDENT state; that the United States are a *confederacy* of states; that we are a confederated and not a consolidated republic. The governor of this state is under a high and solemn obligation, " *to maintain the lawful rights and privileges thereof, as a sovereign, free and independent state,*" as he is " *to support the constitution of the United States,*" and the obligation to support the latter, imposes an additional obligation to support the former. The building cannot stand, if the pillars upon which it rests, are impaired or destroyed. The same constitution, which delegates powers to the general government, inhibits the exercise of powers, not delegated, and reserves those powers to the states respectively. The power to use the militia " to execute the laws, suppress insurrection and repel invasions," is granted to the general government. All other power over them is reserved to the states. And to add to their security, on the all important subject of their militia, the power of appointing their officers is *expressly* reserved. If then the administration of the general government demand the militia, when neither of the exigencies provided for by the constitution have occurred, or to be used *for purposes* not contemplated by that instrument, it would be not only the heighth of injustice to the militia, to be ordered into the service of the United States, to do such duty, but a violation of the constitution and laws of this state, and of the United States. Once employed in the service of the United States, the militia would become subject to the articles of war, and exposed to be punished with death, if they should leave a service, which by the constitution of their country, they are not bound to perform.

From an attentive consideration of the constitution and laws of the United States, it is evident to the Committee, that the militia of the several states are to be employed by the United States, for the purpose only of performing special services, in cases where no other military force could be conveniently had or properly exercised; and when those services are performed, they are to return to their several homes. The committee cannot believe, that it was ever intended that they should be liable, on demand of the president upon the governor of the state, to be ordered into the service of the United States, to assist in carrying on an offensive war. They can only be so employed, under an act of the legislature of the state, authorizing it. On the expediency of passing such a law, or adopting any measures which the war may render necessary, the committee do not consider it is as within their commission to decide.

If congress, or the president of the United States shall apply to this state, to furnish troops to assist in carrying on the war, the request will doubtless meet with the attention which it will merit.

The committee will only take the liberty to remark, that, should the manner in which the war is waged or prosecuted, induce the enemy to retaliate, by an actual invasion of any portion of our territory, or should we be threatened with invasion or attack from any enemies, the militia will always be prompt and zealous to defend their country.

The government of this state, as it ever has been, so it will continue to be, ready to comply with all constitutional requisitions of the general government. Faithful to itself and posterity, it will be faithful to the United States.

31. Rhode Island and the Militia Question.

October 6, 1812.

The following extract from the message of Governor William Jones to the General Assembly, October 6, 1812, gives the opinion of the Council of War upon the call for the militia made by the Federal authorities. For text see *Acts and Resolves of Rhode Island General Assembly, October,* 1812, 3–5; also in *Niles*, III, 179, 180. The action of the Governor and Council was approved at the same session, *Acts and Resolves*, 34. The Correspondence of the Governor and the Federal authorities and other documents for the period 1812–14, is in *Amer. State Papers, Military Affairs*, I, 608, 621, 622; *Report of Com. on Military Affairs, Feb.* 28, 1815, 13 *Cong.*, 3 *sess.*, *Senate Doc.*, 80–85. For subsequent action of the State, see *post*, No. 38.

[Upon the receipt of a letter from General Dearborn, on July 21, requesting him to order certain of the militia into the service of the United States, Governor Jones says,] I was induced to convene a council of war, and take their opinion of the measures most proper to adopt under these circumstances: * * * On the question whether the militia of this State can be withdrawn from the authority thereof, except in particular cases provided for by the constitution of the United States, they are unanimously of opinion, that they could not. On the second question, viz., when the militia are called for by the President of the United States, who is to be the judge whether those exigencies provided for by the constitution of the United States, exist or not? They were also unanimously of opinion that the executive of the State must, and of right ought to be judge. * * *

It is very much to be regretted that there should exist a difference of opinion between the President of the United States and the government of the individual States in any case, and particularly so as it respects the disposing of the detailed militia, when the nation is involved in war. Satisfied, however, that the principle adopted, and the course this State has pursued on that subject is not only perfectly in agreement with the letter, but with the spirit of the Constitution of the United States, I conceive an adherence thereunto indispensable; but should this General Assembly think the course erroneous, there is now an opportunity to correct it.

32. Vermont and the Militia Question.

1813–1814.

In 1813, Governor Martin Chittenden took a similar view of the constitutional relation of the state militia to the general government as that already adopted by the authorities of other New England States. In his speech to the Legislature, October 23, he outlined his position, as is given below. The majority of the Assembly adopted a report indorsing his views by a vote of 96 to 89, but 79 of the minority entered a protest on the Journal. (*Assembly Journal*, 1813, 137, 198.) By a Proclamation of November 10, the Governor commanded the recall of that portion of the militia which "has been ordered from our frontiers for the defence of a neighboring State, and has been placed under the command and at the disposal of an officer of the United States, out of the jurisdiction or control of the Executive of this State." The refusal of the troops to obey his orders, and the arrest of his representative, was followed by the introduction of a resolution in Congress instructing the prosecution of the Governor for treason. (*Annals of Cong.*, 1813–14, I, 859–861.) A counter resolution was presented in the Legislature of Massachusetts pledging the support of the State to the Governor and people of Vermont in their efforts to maintain their constitutional rights. (*Jour. of the House of Rep. of Mass.* (MS.), Jan. 14, 1814, No. 34, 173.) This led the Legislature of New Jersey, February 12, 1814, to adopt the following resolution: "*Resolved*, That the Legislature regards, with contempt and abhorrence, the ravings of an infuriated faction, either as issuing from a legislative body, a maniac governor, or discontented or ambitious demagogues; that the friends of our country and government may rest assured, the people of this State will meet internal insurection with the same promptitude they will the invasion of a cruel, vindictive and savage foe." (Niles' *Register*, VI, 11.) The Legislature of Pennsylvania, March 10, 1814, also adopted a Report and Resolutions condemning the action of the Governor and disapproving the proposed resolutions of Massachusetts as "evidently intended to intimidate" and "accompanied by a threat," and "calculated to add to the calamities of the war—the horrors of a civil war," and finally resolving "that they view with the utmost concern and disapprobation every attempt to screen from just punishment any individual or individuals, however elevated by station, who may violate the Constitution or laws of the United States, or who may directly adhere to or afford aid or comfort to the enemies of our beloved country." (*Amer. State Papers, Misc.*, II, 238, 239.) When the question of the command of the militia was raised in 1814, the Council of Vermont, when consulted by the Governor, unanimously resolved, October 28, 1814, that the "militia are to be commanded by officers appointed by the State, or by the President in person."

References: Text of Governor's Speech, is in *Records of the Governor and Council of the State of Vermont*, VI, 420; Proclamation of Nov. 10, 1813, *Ibid.*, 492; Reply of the Militia, *Ibid.*, 493, 494; Report and Resolves of the Council, Oct. 28, 1814, *Ibid*, 80, 85, 89, 92. The above documents are also in *Niles*, V, 181, 212, 230, 264, 423; VII, Sup. 99–105. See also, Adams, VII, 366, 367; VIII, 222; Hildreth, VI, 452, 453, 468; McMaster, IV, 226, 227.

Extract from Governor Chittenden's Speech. October 23, 1813.

The importance of the subject of the militia will not fail to claim your deliberate consideration. I have always considered this force peculiarly adapted and exclusively assigned for the ser-

vice and protection of the respective States ; excepting in cases
provided for by the national constitution, viz., *to execute the laws
of the Union, suppress insurrection, and repel invasions.* It never
could have been contemplated by the framers of our excellent
constitution, who, it appears, in the most cautious manner, guarded
the sovereignty of the States, or by the States, who adopted it,
that the whole body of the militia were, by any kind of magic, at
once to be transformed into a regular army for the purpose of
foreign conquest ; and it is to be regretted, that a construction
should have been given to the constitution, so peculiarly burdensome and oppressive to that important class of our fellow citizens.

---

33. Massachusetts on the Extension of Territorial Limits.

June 16, 1813.

The spring election of 1813 resulted in the Federalists securing control of
both branches of the General Court, as well as in the re-election of Governor
Strong.   The Governor in his *Speech* referred to territorial extension (*Resolves of Mass.* (1812–15), 231) and the House in its *Answer* considered the
effect of extension on the future influence of New England. (*Ibid.*, 238, 239.)
Josiah Quincy, who had opposed the admission of Louisiana, in a strong state
rights speech in Congress January 14, 1811, had declined a re-election to that
body, but accepted a seat in the State Senate, and at once took the lead in
opposing the policy of the Federal Government.   He was Chairman of the
Committee that drew up the Report and Resolutions relative to the extension
of Territory, extracts from which follow.   A Remonstrance against the war,
June 15, 1813, also contained a protest against the extension of territory.

References: The text of the *Report* and *Resolutions* is given in *Resolves of
Mass.* (1812–15), 310–318; also in *Niles*, IV, 285–287.   For the *Remonstrance* against the war, see *Resolves of Mass.*, 338, 339; also in *Amer. State
Papers, Misc.*, II, 210–214; and in *Niles*, IV, 297–301; the *Protest of the
Minority* is also included in last two references.   Quincy's speech in Con-
gress, cf. *Annals*, 11 Cong., III, 523–542; Johnston, *Amer. Orations* (ed.
1897), I, 180–204; Edmund Quincy, *Life of Josiah Quincy*, 205–218.   For
letter of Pickering on the resolutions, cf. *Ibid.*, 323, 324.   General references :
Of especial value, Quincy's *Quincy*, chs. XII, XIII; Adams, V, 325, 326;
VII, 64–66; Barry, *Mass.*, III, 398, 399; Hildreth, VI, 226–228, 426–429;
McMaster, III, 376–378; IV, 211–213; V, 408–411; Schouler, II, 314, 315,
420–422; Von Holst, I, 250–252.

The question touching the admission, into the Union, of states, created in territories, lying without the ancient limits of the United States, has been considered, by your Committee, in relation to constitutional principles and political consequences. By an Act of the Congress of the United States, passed the 8th day of April, 1812, entitled "an Act for the admission of the State of Louisiana into the Union and to extend the laws of the United States to the said State," the said State of Louisiana was admitted into the Union on an equal footing with the other States. This act was, in the opinion of your Committee, a manifest usurpation, by the Congress of the United States, of a power not granted to that body by the federal constitution. The State of Louisiana was formed, in *countries situated beyond the limits of the old United States;* according as those limits were established by the treaty of Paris, commonly called the Treaty of Peace, in the year 1783; and as they existed, at the time of the formation and adoption of the federal constitution. And the position which your Committee undertake to maintain is this, that the Constitution of the United States did not invest Congress with the power to admit into the Union, States *created in territories not included within the limits of the United States;* as they existed, at the peace of 1783, and at the formation and adoption of the Constitution.

* * * * * * * * *

Now the State of Louisiana lies *without those limits;* and on this distinction the whole question of constitutional right depends. The power, assumed by Congress, in passing this act for the admission of Louisiana, if acquiesced in, is plainly a power to admit new States into this Union, at their discretion, without limit of place or country. Not only new States may be carved, at will, out of the boundless regions of Louisiana, but the whole extent of South America, indeed of the globe, is a sphere, within which it may operate without check or control, and with no other limit than such as Congress may choose to impose on its own discretion. [Here follows a detailed examination of the Constitution in refutation of the constitutionality of annexation and admission of new States.]

Now it is very apparent to your Committee, that the power to admit States, created in territories, beyond the limits of the old United States is one of the most critical and important, whether we consider its nature, or its consequences. It is, in truth, nothing less than the power to create in foreign countries, new political sovereignties, and to divest the old United States of a proportion of their political sovereignty, in favor of such foreigner. It is a power, which, in the opinion of your Committee, no wise people ever would have delegated, and which, they are persuaded, the people of the United States, and certainly, the people of Massachusetts, never did delegate. The proportion of the political weight of each foreign State, composing this union, depends upon the number of the States, which have a voice under the compact. This number, the Constitution permits Congress to multiply, at pleasure, within the limits of the original States, observing, only, the expressed limitations, in the Constitution. To pass these limitations and admit States, beyond the ancient boundaries, is, in the opinion of your Committee, an usurpation, as dangerous as it is manifest, inasmuch as these exterior States, after being admitted on an equal footing with the original States, may, and as they multiply, certainly will become, in fact, the arbiters of the destinies of the nation ; by availing themselves of the contrariety of interests and views which in such a confederacy of States necessarily arise, they hold the balance among the respective parties and govern the States, constitutionally composing the Union, by throwing their weight into whatever scale is most conformable to the ambition or projects of such foreign States.

Your Committee cannot, therefore, but look with extreme regret and reprobation upon the admission of the territory of Louisiana to an equal footing with the original and constitutionally admitted States ; and they cannot but consider the principle, asserted by this admission, as an usurpation of power, portending the most serious consequences to the perpetuation of this Union and the liberties of the American people.[1]

Although the character of this usurpation and its ultimate consequences ought, naturally, to excite an extreme degree of alarm in this quarter of the country, as it indicates that new and unconstitutional arbiters, remote from our interests and ignorant of them, are admitted into the Union, yet the nature of the remedy is, in the opinion of your Committee, a subject of much more difficulty than the certainty of the mischief.

[1] For action of Massachusetts in 1804 and 1809 in consequence of the annexation of Louisiana, see *ante*, 27, and note.

*   *   *   *   *   *   *

Nevertheless, in the opinion of your Committee, the Legislature of Massachusetts owe it to themselves, to the people of this State and to future generations, to make an open and distinct avowal of their sentiments upon this topick, to the end that no sanction may appear to be derived from their silence; and also that other States may be led to consider this intrusion of a foreign State into our confederacy, under this usurped authority, in a constitutional point of view as well as in its consequences, and that, thereby, a concurrence of sentiment and a coincidence of councils may result; whence alone can be hoped a termination of this usurpation, and of the evils, which are, apparently, about to flow from it.

Your Committee, therefore, propose for the adoption of the Legislature, the following resolutions :—

Resolved, As the sense of this Legislature, that the admission into the Union of States created in countries not comprehended within the original limits of the United States, is not authorized by the letter or the spirit of the federal Constitution.

Resolved, That it is the interest and duty of the people of Massachusetts, to oppose the admission of such States into the Union, as a measure tending to the dissolution of the confederacy.

Resolved, That the Act passed the eighth day of April, 1812, entitled "an Act for the admission of the State of Louisiana into the Union and to extend the laws of the United States to the said State," is, in the opinion of this Legislature, a violation of the Constitution of the United States; and that the Senators of this State, in Congress, be instructed, and the Representatives thereof requested, to use their utmost endeavors to obtain a repeal of the same.

Resolved, That the Secretary of this Commonwealth be directed to transmit a copy of these Resolutions to each of the Senators and Representatives of this Commonwealth, in the Congress of the United States.

[Resolves of Massachusetts (1813), 310–318. Boston, 1813.]

34. The General Court of Massachusetts on the Embargo.

February 22, 1814.

Instead of heeding the Remonstrance of Massachusetts of June 15, 1813, the administration not only continued its previous policy towards the New England States, but added a new grievance through the enactment of a new and very stringent embargo law, December 17, 1813, (*U. S. Stat. at Large*, III, 88–93) which, it was charged, was aimed directly at New England. Upon the assembling of the General Court of Massachusetts at the opening of the year 1814, memorials and remonstrances from 38 towns poured in upon that body, as had been the case at the time of the embargo of 1808–09 (Cf. *ante*, 26–36), denouncing the war and praying for relief from the unbearable restrictions placed upon commerce (*Jour. of the House of Rep.* (MS.), May, 1813 to Feb., 1814, 174, 251, 260, 293). These were referred to a Joint Committee for consideration. On February 18 the Committee presented their report. It is sometimes known as "Lloyd's Report," from Wm. Lloyd, the Chairman of the Committee. The Report and Resolutions, extracts from which follow, were adopted by the House on the same day by a vote of 178 *yeas* to 43 *nays* (*Ibid.*, 348). It was debated in the Senate and finally passed, February 22, by a vote of 23 *yeas* to 8 *nays* (*Jour. of the Senate* (MS.), May, 1813 to Feb., 1814, 372, 386, 391). In compliance with the last of these resolves Governor Strong submitted these Resolutions, May 30. 1814, to the newly elected General Court, but the embargo and non-importation laws having been repealed the legislature refrained for the time being from calling the proposed convention. For subsequent action, see *post*, Nos. 36 and 37.

References: The text, printed by order of the Legislature, February 28, 1814, is in *Legislative Documents*, 1807–14, No. 19, 381–392; also in *Niles*, VI, 4–8. Governor's Speech and Replies of House and Senate, *Resolves of Mass.*, May 30, 1814; *Niles*, VI, 250, 251, 273–275; Adams, VIII, 1–15; Barry, *Mass.*, III, 401, 402; Hildreth, VI, 455, 456, 465–476, 484; McMaster, IV, 222–229; V, 411; Von Holst, I, 253–255.

* * * * * * The people, in their numerous memorials from all quarters of the commonwealth, appear to despair of obtaining redress from that government, which was established "To Promote the General Welfare." They see that the voice of the New England States, whose interests are common, is lost in the national Councils, and that the spirit of accommodation and regard to mutual safety and advantage, which produced the constitution and governed its early administration, have been sacrificed to the bitterness of party, and to the aggrandizement of one section of the union, at the expense of another.

*   *   *   *   *   *   *   *   *   *

Various are the forms in which these sentiments and feelings have been expressed to the legislature; but the tone and spirit, in all, are the same. They all discover an ardent attachment to the *Union of these States*, as the true source of security and happiness to all, and a reverence for the national constitution, as calculated in its spirit and principles to insure that Union, and establish that happiness: but they are all stamped with the melancholy conviction that the basis of that Union has been destroyed by a practical neglect of its principles; and that the durability of that Constitution has been endangered by a perversion and abuse of its powers.

* * * * * * * * * *

The memorialists have then enumerated the causes which have brought them to this unhappy conviction. They have seen a power grow up in the southern and western sections of the Union, by the admission and multiplication of states, not contemplated by the parties to the constitution, and not warranted by its principles; and they foresee an almost infinite progression in this system of creation, which threatens eventually to reduce the voice of New England, once powerful and effectual in the national councils, to the feeble expression of colonial complaints, unattended to and disregarded.

[Here follows an enumeration of the other acts of the Federal Government inimical to New England, from the laying of the embargo to the prohibition of "their *shore fishery* and coasting trade" "by an act more unfeeling and odious than the Boston port bill, which aroused the colonies into independence."]

This act is denounced by all the memorialists in the warmest and most energetic language as a gross and palpable violation of the principles of the Constitution; and they express decidedly their opinion, that it cannot be submitted to without a pusillanimous surrender of those rights and liberties, which their ancestors brought to these shores, which they fought and bled to maintain, and which we, their descendents, ought to be ready to defend, at the same expense and hazard, or forfeit the character of freemen.

With such a display of grievances, sufferings, and apprehensions before them, couched in terms of affecting eloquence, and breathing a spirit of firmness and resolution to procure by some means competent relief, your Committee cannot but be forcibly impressed. They believe in the existence of those grievances, and in the cause to which they have been ascribed. They believe that this war, so fertile in calamities, and so threatening in its consequences, has been waged with the worst possible views and carried on in the worst possible manner; forming a union of wickedness and weakness, which defies for a parallel the annals of the world. We believe, also, that its worst effects are yet to come; that loan upon loan, tax upon tax, and exaction upon exaction, must be imposed, until the comforts of the present, and the hopes of the rising generation are destroyed. An impoverished people will be an enslaved People. An army of sixty thousand men, become veteran by the time the war is ended, may be the instrument, as in former times, of destroying even the forms of Liberty; and will be as easy to establish a President for *life*, by their arms, as it has been for *four years* by intrigue. We tremble for the liberties of our Country! We think it the duty of the present generation, to stand between the next and despotism.

The Committee are of opinion that the late act laying an Embargo is unconstitutional, and void in divers of its provisions; not upon the narrow ground that the constitution has expressly prohibited such acts, but upon the more broad and liberal ground that the People never gave a power to Congress to enact them.

A direct prohibition would have weakened the argument against them, because it would have indicated an apprehension, that such power might be usurped.

A power to regulate Commerce is abused, when employed to destroy it; and a manifest and voluntary abuse of power sanctions the right of resistance, as much as a direct and palpable usurpation. The sovereignty reserved to the States, was reserved to protect the Citizens from acts of violence by the United States, as well as for purposes of domestic regulation. We spurn the idea that the free, sovereign and independent State of Massachusetts is reduced to a mere municipal corporation, without power to protect its people, and to defend them from oppression, from whatever quarter it comes. Whenever the national compact is violated, and the citizens of this state are oppressed by cruel and unauthorized laws, this legislature is bound to interpose[1] its power, and wrest from the oppressor his victim.

This is the spirit of our Union, and thus has it been explained by the very man, who now sets at defiance all the principles of his early political life.

The question, then, is not a question of power or right with this legislature, but of TIME AND EXPEDIENCY. The committee have deemed it to be their duty to stifle their feelings of indignation at the strides of despotism, which are visible under the guise of liberty, and the forms of Law, that they may dispassionately consider the various modes of relief, which have been suggested by some, or all of the memorialists, and report to the legislature the result of their deliberations. Three courses have been suggested by the memorialists.

1. That the legislature should remonstrate to Congress against the general course of its measures, and particularly against the embargo act.

2. That laws should be passed, tending directly to secure the Citizens of this Commonwealth in their persons, and property, and rights, and providing punishments for all such as should violate them.

3. That delegates should immediately be appointed by the Legislature to meet Delegates from such other States as shall elect any, for the purpose of devising proper measures to procure the united efforts of the commercial States, to obtain such amendments or explanations of the Constitution, as will secure them from future evils.

With respect to the first, the committee cannot recommend it.

It has been again, and again, resorted to, and with no other effect than to increase the evils complained of; and to subject to unjust reproaches and insinuations, a body, which ought never to be a suppliant to any power on earth.

With respect to the second, as far as it relates to acts of violence in the seizure of persons and property on land, without the formalities required by the constitution of this State, we be-

---

[1] A transcript from the Virginia Resolutions of 1798. Already by Act of Feb. 7, 1814, Massachusetts had prohibited the use of State jails for United States prisoners committed other than by judicial authority. Hildreth, VI, 469.

lieve that the provisions of our state and national constitutions, as well as the great principles of the common law are so plain, that no act of this Legislature can afford any additional security. And as to the prohibition of our fisheries and coasting trade, the Committee cannot, at this distressing juncture, recommend a remedy to be relied on so inadequate as would be afforded by the enaction of penal laws.

On the subject of a convention, the committee observe, that they entertain no doubt of the right of the Legislature to invite other states to a convention, and to join it themselves, for the great purposes of consulting for the general good, and of procuring amendments to the constitution, whenever they find that the practical construction given to it by the rulers, for the time being, is contrary to its true spirit and injurious to their immediate constituents. We know of no surer or better way to prevent that hostility to the Union, the result of oppression, which will eventually terminate in its downfall, than for the Wise and Good, of those States, which deem themselves oppressed, to assemble with delegated authority, and to propose, urge, and even insist upon such explicit declarations of power, or restriction, as will prevent the most hardy from any future attempts to oppress, under the color of the constitution. This was the mode proposed by *Mr. Madison* in answer to objections made, as to the tendency of the general Government, to usurp upon that of the States. And though he at a former period led the Legislature of Virginia into an opposition, without any justifiable cause ; yet it may be supposed that he and all others who understand the principles of our concurrent Sovereignty, will acknowledge the fitness and propriety of their asserting rights, which no people can ever relinquish.

But althongh the Committee are convinced of the right, and think the Legislature ought to vindicate it, of acting in concert with other States, in order to produce a powerful, and if possible an irresistable claim for such alterations, as will tend to preserve the Union, and restore violated privileges, yet they have considered that there are reasons which render it inexpedient at the present moment to exercise this power. Some of these reasons your Committee would suggest, that the memorialists may know that their pressing appeals are not postponed from any insensibility to them on the part of the Legislature. The Committee would here express their hope that the people of this Commonwealth, injured and oppressed as they have been, will as far as possible restrain their feelings of indignation, and patiently wait for the effectual interposition of the State Government for their relief; and the Committee doubt not that the real friends of peace will continue conscientiously to refrain from affording any voluntary aid or encouragement of this most disastrous war.

The Committee entertain no doubt that the sentiments and feelings expressed in the numerous memorials and remonstrances, which have been committed to them, are the genuine voice of a vast majority of the Citizens of this Commonwealth. But the Representatives who are soon to be returned for the next General Court, will come from the People, still more fully possessed of their views and wishes as to the all-important subject of obtaining, by further compact engrafted into the present constitution, a permanent security against future abuse of power; and of seeking effectual redress for the grievances and oppressions now endured. They will also assemble, better acquainted with the wishes and disposition of other States, suffering alike with this, to act in co-operation for these essential objects. In addition to this, some among our constituents indulge a hope of success from the negociation recently entered into for the *professed* purpose of restoring peace to our distracted and divided country.

       *   *   *   *   *   *   *   *

The return of peace would undoubtedly relieve the people from many of the burthens which they now suffer; but it is not to be forgotten, how the war was produced, how it has been conducted, how long its baleful consequences will continue, and how easily such evils may be again brought upon us, unless an effectual security be provided. Without war, experience has shown us, our commerce may be destroyed. Indeed there is now little hope that it will ever be restored, unless the people of Massachusetts and the other commercial States shall exert their united efforts in bringing back the constitution to its first principles.

Under these impressions the Committee beg leave to conclude by recommending the adoption of the following Resolutions. All which is respectfully submitted.

Resolved, That "the act laying an embargo on all Ships and vessels in the Ports and harbors of the United States," passed by the Congress of the United States on the 16th day of December, 1813, contains provisions not warranted by the Constitution of the United States, and violating the rights of the People of this Commonwealth.

Resolved, That the Inhabitants of the State of Massachusetts, have enjoyed, from its earliest settlement, the right of navigating from Port to Port within its limits and of fishing on its coasts ; that the free exercise and enjoyment of these Rights are essential to the comfort and subsistence of a numerous class of its citizens ; that the power of prohibiting to its Citizens the exercise of these rights was never delegated to the general government, and that all Laws passed by that Government, intended to have such an effect, are therefore unconstitutional and void.

Resolved, That the people of this commonwealth, "have a right to be secure from all unreasonable searches and seizures of their Persons, Houses, Papers, and all their Possessions ;" that all Laws rendering liable to seizure the property of a Citizen at the discretion of an Individual, without warrant from a Magistrate, issued on a complaint, supported on oath or affirmation, under the pretence that such property is "apparently on its way towards the territory of a foreign nation or the vicinity thereof," are arbitrary in their nature, tyrannical in their exercise, and subversive of the first principles of civil liberty.

Resolved, That the People of this Commonwealth, "have a right to be protected in the enjoyment of life, liberty, and property, according to standing Laws ;" and that all attempts to prohibit them in the enjoyment of this right by agents acting under Executive Instructions only, and armed with military force, are destructive of their freedom and altogether repugnant to the Constitution.

Resolved, That as the well grounded complaints of the People constitute a continued claim upon the Government, until their grievances are redressed, the several memorials and remonstrances referred to the Committee aforesaid be delivered to His Excellency the Governor, with a request that he or his successor in office would cause the same to be laid before the next General Court at an early day in their first Session.

[From manuscript in Mass. Archives.[1]]

[1] I am indebted to Miss L. House, Fellow in American History, University of Pennsylvania, for verifying the above text.

35. Connecticut on the Conscription Bill.

October Session, 1814.

Owing to the exigencies of the war, the administration in the fall of 1814 proposed the adoption of a conscription scheme, which was characterized by the oposition as grievously oppressive and unconstitutional. A bill, based upon the plan drawn by the Secretary of War, was introduced in Congress, and while still pending in the House of Representatives, the Legislature of Connecticut passed the following threatening resolutions. The conscription bill failed, but Congress adopted the Bill in regard to the Enlistment of Minors, December 10, 1814. (*U. S. Stat. at Large*, III, 146, 147.) In consequence of this act the Connecticut Legislature at the special session in January, 1815, passed *An Act to secure the rights of Parents, Masters and Guardians*, declaring the aforesaid act of Congress " repugnant to the spirit of the constitution of the United States, and an unauthorized interference with the laws and rights of this State," and requiring judges to discharge on *habeas corpus* all minors enlisted without the consent of their parents or guardians, subjecting to fine and imprisonment any person concerned in such enlistment who should remove any such minor out of the State. (*Public Statute Law of Connecticut*, Bk. II, ch. IV, 189, 190.) A similar law was enacted by Massachusetts, February 27, 1815. (*Laws of Mass.*, 1812–15, 640, 641.)

References: The text is found in the *Connecticut Courant*, Hartford, November 15, 1814; also in *Niles*, VII, Sup. 107, 108; Dwight, 336, 337. For general account, see Adams, VIII, 265–280; Dwight, 309–337; Hildredth, VI, 529–534; 554; McMaster, IV, 240–246; V, 412.

*   *   *   *   *   *   *   *   *   *

And whereas the principles of the plan and bill aforesaid, are, in the opinion of this assembly, not only intolerably burdensome and oppressive, but utterly subversive of the rights and liberties of the people of this state, and the freedom, sovereignty, and independence of the same, and inconsistent with the principles of the constitution of the United States.

And whereas it will become the imperious duty of the legislature of this state to exert themselves to ward off a blow so fatal to the liberties of a free people—

Resolved by this Assembly, That in case the plan and bill aforesaid, or any other bill on that subject, containing the principles aforesaid, shall be adopted, and assume the form of an act of Congress, the Governor of this state is hereby requested forthwith to convoke the General Assembly ; and, to avoid delay, he is hereby authorized and requested to issue his proclamation, requiring the attendance of the members thereof at such time and place as he may appoint, to the end that opportunity may be given to consider what measures may be adopted to secure and preserve the rights and liberties of the people of this state, and the freedom, sovereignty and independence of the same.

Massachusetts and the Call of the Hartford Convention.

October, 1814.

During the summer of 1814 New England, which hitherto had been spared by the British, was threatened with a general invasion, and the enemy actually occupied a portion of the Maine coast. The Federal Government still left New England to defend herself, and withheld supplies for the maintenance of the militia. In this crisis, Governor Strong, of Massachusetts, assembled the General Court in Special Session, October 5, 1814. That body acted promptly, passing an act authorizing the raising of a military corps of ten thousand men for the defence of the State (*Laws of Mass.*, 1812–15, 575–578), and adopting the Report and Resolutions of its Committee, recommending the assembling of a Convention of Delegates of the New England States, thus acting on the suggestion first proposed by the Joint Committee in their Report in the preceding February. (Cf. *Ante*, No. 34.) The minority in both the Senate and the House filed protests. Extracts from the Report and the Call for the Convention to be held in Hartford, December 15, 1814, follow.

References: Sources. The texts are in *Resolves of Mass.*, 1814, 567–571; also in *Niles*, VII, 149–153; the Circular Letter is in Dwight, 342, 343. For other documents including the Protests of the Minority of the Senate and of the House, cf. *Niles*, VII, 113, 114, 148–155, 180, 181. Report and Resolution of the General Assembly of Connecticut appointing seven delegates to the Convention is in Dwight, 344–350; also in *Niles*, VII, 164, 165. In the Connecticut Historical Society there are two contemporary prints of the same; the one, *To the Honorable the General Assembly, now in Session.* Large folio, broadside. (New Haven: Hudson and Woodward, 1814), attested in ink by Thomas Day, Secretary of State; the other, *Report | Of the Committee | To whom was referred His | Excellency's Speech*, etc. | Hudson & Woodward, Printers, | Church Street, New Haven.[1] | Octavo. pp. 8. The text of the report and resolutions of Rhode Island, which follow, are also found in *Niles*, VII, 180, 181. The report adopted by the Vermont Legislature, although Federalist, that it was inexpedient to accept the invitation, is given in *Assembly Journal* of 1814, 76, 84, 129; *Records of Governor and Council*, VI, 94, 463. Letter of Madison, on conduct of New England

----

[1] I am indebted to Mr. Albert C. Bates, Librarian, for these references.

States, Nov. 25, 1814, *Works*, II, 593. General references: Adams, VIII, 222–228; Dwight, 337–351; Hildreth, VI, 531–535; McMaster, IV, 246–248; Schouler, II, 424, 425; Von Holst, 258–262.

36. Extracts from the Report of the Committee of the General Court of Massachusetts, October 15, 1814.

[After reviewing the policy of the Federal Government toward the New England States, the report concludes :]

It is, therefore, with great concern that your Committee are obliged to declare their conviction that the Constitution of the United States, under the administration of the persons in power, has failed to secure to this Commonwealth, and as they believe, to the eastern section of this union, those equal rights and benefits which were the great objects of its formation, and which they cannot relinquish without ruin to themselves and posterity. These grievances justify and require vigorous, persevering and peaceable exertions, to unite those who realize the sufferings, and foresee the dangers of the country, in some system of measures, to obtain relief, for which the ordinary mode of procuring amendments to the constitution, affords no reasonable expectation, in season to prevent the completion of its ruin. The people, however, possess the means of certain redress ; and when their safety, which is the supreme law, is in question, these means should be promptly applied. The framers of the constitution made provision to amend defects, which were known to be incident to every human institution; and the provision itself was not less liable to be found defective upon experiment, than other parts of the instrument. When this deficiency becomes apparent, no reason can preclude the right of the whole people, who were parties to it, to adopt another ; and it is not a presumptuous expectation, that a spirit of equity and justice, enlightened by experience, would enable them to reconcile conflicting interests and obviate the principal causes of those dissentions, which unfit government for a state of peace and of war ; and so to amend the constitution, as to give vigor and duration to the union of the States. But as a proposition for such a convention from a single State, would, probably, be unsuccessful, and our dangers admit not of delay, it is recommended by the Committee, that in the first instance, a conference should be invited between those States, the affinity of whose interests is closest, and whose habits of intercourse, from their local situation and other causes, are most frequent, to the end, that, by a comparison of their sentiments and views, some mode of defence, suited to the circumstances and exigencies of those States, and measures for accelerating the return of public prosperity, may be devised ; and also to enable the delegates from those States, should they deem it expedient, to lay the foundation for a radical reform in the national compact, by inviting to a further convention, a deputation from all the States in the union. They therefore report the following Resolves, which are submitted :

* * * * * * *

Resolved, That twelve persons be appointed, as Delegates from this Commonwealth, to meet and confer with Delegates from the other States of New England, or any of them, upon the subjects of their public grievances and concerns, and upon the best means of preserving our resources and of defence against the enemy, and to advise and suggest for adoption by those respective States, such measures as they may deem expedient ; and also to take measures, if they shall think proper, for procuring a convention of Delegates from all the United States, in order to revise the Constitution thereof, and more effectually to secure the support and attachment of all the people, by placing all upon the basis of fair representation.

[*Resolves of Massachusetts,* 1814, 567–569. Boston, 1814.]

37. Call of the Convention.

Circular Letter to the Governors of the New England States on a Convention to be holden at Hartford, which his Excellency the Governor is requested to transmit.

17th October, 1814.

SIR,

Your Excellency will herewith receive certain resolutions of the Legislature of Massachusetts, which you are respectfully requested to take the earliest occasion to lay before the Legislature of your State, together with this letter, which is intended as an invitation to them to appoint Delegates, if they shall deem it expedient, to meet such others as may be appointed by this and other States at the time and place expressed in these resolutions.

The general objects of the proposed conference are first, to deliberate upon the dangers to which the Eastern section of the Union is exposed by the course of the war, and which there is too much reason to believe will thicken round them in its progress, and to devise, if practicable, means of security and defence, which may be consistent with the preservation of their resources from total ruin and adapted to their local situation, mutual relations and habits, and not repugnant to their obligations as members of the Union.

When convened for this object, which admits not of delay, it seems also expedient to submit to their consideration, the enquiry, whether the interests of these States demand that persevering endeavours be used by each of them to procure such amendments to be affected in the national constitution as may secure to them equal advantages; and whether, if in their judgment, this should be deemed impracticable under the existing provisions for amending that instrument, an experiment may be made without disadvantage to the nation, for obtaining a Convention from all the States in the Union, or such of them as may approve of the measure, with a view to obtain such amendment.

It cannot be necessary to anticipate objections to the measure which may arise from jealousy or fear. This Legislature is content, for its justification to repose upon the purity of its own motives, and upon the known attachment of its constituents to the national union, and to the rights and independence of their country.[1]

Read and accepted in both Houses, and thereupon

Resolved, That his Excellency the Governor be requested to transmit letters of the foregoing form, signed by the President of the Senate and Speaker of the House of Representatives, to the several Governors of the States of New Hampshire, Rhode Island, Connecticut, and Vermont, and also a copy of the resolutions to which it refers, with a request that the same may be laid before the Legislatures of their several States.

[*Resolves of Massachusetts*, 1814, 570, 571.]

[1] Signed by the President of the Senate and Speaker of the House.

38. Report and Resolutions of the Legislature of Rhode Island.

November 5, 1814.

The Legislature and the whole people of this State already but too well know how frequently and fruitlessly they have petitioned the Federal Government for some portion of those means of defence for which we have paid so dearly, and to which, by the Constitution, we are so fully entitled. Our most pressing petitions and representations to the head and various departments of the general government have often gone unanswered, sometimes have been answered by unmeaning professions and promises never performed, but generally by telling us to protect ourselves. The result is, that at this moment we have fewer means of defence, less show of protection afforded by that government, than we had ever at any period during a state of peace.

* * * * * * *

But while thus withdrawing from us all but the shadow of defence, and totally disregarding their duty and our just rights under the Constitution; that government is constantly demanding and taking from us those resources and revenues which, by the Constitution, we granted expressly to enable them to afford us that protection.

[Here follows an arraignment of the Federal Government for their neglect to defend their coast, declaring that:] for a long period we were left without any other evidence of the existence of a President or a government of the United States, than what we derived from the burthens imposed and the calamities brought upon us by them. And so perseveringly was this project against our rights pursued, that the President of the United States himself, in one of his public messages, openly, and with great chagrin, complained of the policy of the enemy in leaving this section of the country unassailed and unravaged. [The policy of the government in regard to the State militia is also severely censured.]

We are not alone in these calamities. Our sister States of the South have been almost equally oppressed and abused. They are beginning to assert their rights; and with us they will never suffer our common rights, under the constitution, to be prostrated by a government we have ourselves created.[1] Why should we dwell longer upon the unwarrantable treatment we receive, the unconstitutional attempts upon our constitutional rights. Our condition is stripped of all doubt and uncertainty. Our chief resources have been and still are to be taken as tribute ; but for our defence we are to look to ourselves.　　*　　*　　*

STATE OF RHODE ISLAND AND PROVIDENCE PLANTATIONS.

IN GENERAL ASSEMBLY, *October Session, A. D.* 1814.

Whereas, this General Assembly, having long witnessed, with regret and anxiety, the defenceless situation of this State, did, at their last session, request his Excellency the Governor to communicate with the Executives of our neighboring sister States upon the subject of our common defence by our mutual co-operation :[2] And whereas, those States, feeling equally with us the common misfortunes, and the necessity of united exertions ; have appointed, and invited us to appoint, Delegates to meet and confer upon our calamitous situation, and to devise and recommend wise and prudent measures for our common relief.

Resolved, That this General Assembly will appoint four Delegates from this State, to meet at Hartford, in the State of Connecticut, on the 15th day of December next, and confer with such Delegates as are or shall be appointed by other States upon the common dangers to which these States are exposed, upon the best means of co-operating for our mutual defence against the enemy, and upon the measures which it may be in the power of said States, consistently with their obligations, to adopt, to restore and secure to the people thereof their rights and privileges under the Constitution of the United States.

[Acts and Resolves of Rhode Island, October Session, 1814, 50–54.[3]]

[1] The Federalist Governor and House of Delegates of Maryland, during the year 1813 had repeatedly called attention to the defenceless condition of the State. Finally the House addressed a Memorial to Congress against the war. (*Amer. State Papers,* Misc. II, 231–233. See also *Niles,* IV, 219, 220; V, 260, 375–378; VII, 326–327.) It was communicated to Congress, Feb. 2, 1814, but a motion to print, after a sharp debate, was defeated in both Houses. *Annals,* 1813–14, 616–622, 1203–1228. For action of the House of Delegates, Dec. 17, 1814, on conscription bill, see McMaster, IV, 245.

[2] *Niles,* VII, 181.

[3] I am indebted to Mr. Clarence S. Brigham, Librarian of the Rhode Island Historical Society, for verifying the text of these resolutions.

39. Resolutions Adopted by the Hartford Convention.

January 4, 1815.

On December 15, 1814, twenty-six delegates from the States of Massachusetts, Connecticut and Rhode Island, the counties of Cheshire and Grafton in the State of New Hampshire, and the county of Windham in the State of Vermont, assembled in convention at Hartford. They continued in secret session until January 5, 1815. The result of their deliberations was embodied in a Report and Resolutions, which were immediately published. The Resolutions are given below. The General Court of Massachusetts, Jan. 27, 1815, passed resolutions approving of the proceedings of the Convention and for appointing Commissioners to proceed to the seat of the National Government to enter into negotiations with the Federal Authorities. (*Resolves of Mass.* (1812–1814), 590–592.) On Feb. 10, 1815, the General Court also adopted resolutions recommending the same amendments to the Federal Constitution as had been proposed by the Hartford Convention. (*Ibid.,* 615–617.) Similar action was also taken by Connecticut, and the resolutions of both States were presented to Congress. (Ames, *Proposed Amendments,* 46, 126, 180, 244, 264, 265, note, 269, 331, 332.) For reply of other States, see *post,* pp. 42–44. The news of peace rendered the mission of the Commissioners untimely, and discredited the whole movement. (*Report of the Commissioners of Mass. to Washington,* May 15, 1815, MS. in Mass. Archives, No. $\frac{50 32}{9}$.)

References: Text of Report and Resolutions in *The Proceedings of a Convention of Delegates, etc., convened at Hartford, December* 15, 1814. (Hartford, 1815.) A copy of this imprint, with the autograph signatures of the members, is in the Massachusetts Archives. The text is also found as follows: Pamphlet with same title, 3d ed. (Boston, 1815.) Appx. to *Resolves of Mass.,* 1812–15; Dwight, 352–379; *Niles,* VII, 305–313. The Journal is in Dwight, 383–398. The letter of Senator Pickering, and others, of March 3, 1815, in regard to laying the Amendments before Congress is in Mass. Archives, No. $\frac{50 32}{9}$. General References: Adams, VIII, ch. XI; Adams, *New England Federalism,* 81–90, 251–329; Hildreth, VI, 545–554; Lalor, I, 624–626; Lodge, *Cabot,* chs. XI–XIII; McMaster, IV, 248–252; *Niles,* VII (*cf.* Index); XXXIX, 434, 435; Quincy, *Quincy,* 356–358; Schouler, II, 425–429; Von Holst, I, 263–272. For additional bibliography, *cf.* Channing and Hart, *Guide,* § 173; MacDonald, *Documents,* 198.

THEREFORE RESOLVED,

That it be and hereby is recommended to the Legislatures of the several States represented in this Convention, to adopt all such measures as may be necessary effectually to protect the citizens of said States from the operation and effects of all acts which have been or may be passed by the Congress of the United

States, which shall contain provisions, subjecting the militia or other citizens to forcible drafts, conscriptions, or impressments, not authorized by the Constitution of the United States.

Resolved, That it be and hereby is recommended to the said Legislatures, to authorize an immediate and earnest application to be made to the Government of the United States, requesting their consent to some arrangement, whereby the said States may, separately or in concert, be empowered to assume upon themselves the defence of their territory against the enemy; and a reasonable portion of the taxes, collected within said States, may be paid into the respective treasuries thereof, and appropriated to the payment of the balance due said States, and to the future defence of the same. The amount so paid into the said treasuries to be credited, and the disbursements made as aforesaid to be charged to the United States.

Resolved, That it be, and it hereby is, recommended to the Legislatures of the aforesaid States, to pass laws (where it has not already been done) authorizing the Governours or Commanders in Chief of their militia to make detachments from the same, or to form voluntary corps, as shall be most convenient and conformable to their Constitutions, and to cause the same to be well armed, equipped and disciplined, and held in readiness for service; and upon the request of the Governour of either of the other States, to employ the whole of such detachment or corps, as well as the regular forces of the State, or such part thereof as may be required and can be spared consistently with the safety of the State, in assisting the State, making such request to repel any invasion thereof which shall be made or attempted by the publick enemy.

Resolved, That the following amendments of the Constitution of the United States, be recommended to the States represented as aforesaid, to be proposed by them for adoption by the State Legislatures, and in such cases as may be deemed expedient, by a Convention chosen by the people of each State.

And it is further recommended, that the said States shall persevere in their efforts to obtain such amendments, until the same shall be effected.

First. Representatives and direct taxes shall be apportioned among the several States which may be included within the union, according to their respective numbers of free persons, including those bound to serve for a term of years, and excluding Indians not taxed, and all other persons.

Second. No new State shall be admitted into the union by Congress in virtue of the power granted by the Constitution, without the concurrence of two thirds of both Houses.

Third. Congress shall not have power to lay any embargo on the ships or vessels of the citizens of the United States, in the ports or harbors thereof, for more than sixty days.

Fourth. Congress shall not have power, without the concurrence of two thirds of both Houses, to interdict the commercial intercourse between the United States and any foreign nation or the dependencies thereof.

Fifth. Congress shall not make or declare war, or authorize acts of hostility against any foreign nation, without the concurrence of two thirds of both Houses, except such acts of hostility be in defence of the territories of the United States, when actually invaded.

Sixth. No person who shall hereafter be naturalized, shall be eligible as a member of the Senate or House of Representatives of the United States, nor capable of holding any civil office under the authority of the United States.

Seventh. The same person shall not be elected President of the United States a second time; nor shall the President be elected from the same State two terms in succession.

Resolved, That if the application of these States to the government of the United States, recommended in a foregoing Resolution, should be unsuccessful, and peace should not be concluded, and the defence of these States should be neglected, as it has been since the commencement of the war, it will in the opinion of this Convention be expedient for the Legislatures of the several States to appoint Delegates to another Convention, to meet at Boston, in the State of Massachusetts, on the third Thursday of June next, with such powers and instructions as the exigency of a crisis so momentous may require.

Resolved, That the Hon. George Cabot, the Hon. Chauncey Goodrich, and the Hon. Daniel Lyman, or any two of them, be authorized to call another meeting of this Convention, to be holden in Boston, at any time before new Delegates shall be chosen, as recommended in the above Resolutions, if in their judgment the situation of the Country shall urgently require it.[1]

[*Proceedings of a Convention of Delegates, etc., convened at Hartford, December* 15, 1814, 25–27. Hartford, 1815.]

Replies of the States to the Hartford Convention Amendments.

These amendments as indorsed by the legislatures of Massachusetts and Connecticut did not even receive the approval of any of the other New England States, and the legislatures of the following nine States passed resolutions of disapproval: Vermont, New York, New Jersey, Pennsylvania, Virginia, North Carolina, Ohio, Tennessee and Louisiana. (For references, see Ames, *Proposed Amendments*, 46, note, 265, note, 332.) Most of the legislatures simply passed resolutions of non concurrence, but the legislatures of New York, New Jersey and Pennsylvania, accompanied their resolutions with interesting reports of disapproval. Extracts from the reports of New Jersey and New York follow. The very elaborate report of the Senate of Pennsylvania, written by a Federalist, is too long to be reprinted here, but is in *Senate Journal of Penna.*, 1814-15, 381–397; a digest of the report is given in *The Historical Register*, 1814, 131–136. A printed attested copy of this report was communicated to Massachusetts, and is in the Mass. Archives.

40. Reply of the Legislature of New Jersey.[2]

February 17, 1815.

HOUSE OF ASSEMBLY, *February* 10.

The committee to whom was referred the several propositions for the amendment of the Constitution of the United States, adopted by the general assembly of Connecticut, and at their request communicated to his excellency the governor, to be laid before the legislature of this state for their approbation and adoption, beg leave to report, that they have been induced by the untoward circumstances of the times, and the general aspect of our political affairs to consider the same, with a view rather to their general bearing, character and tendency, than to their several intrinsic merits. Under these impressions they are constrained to remark, that the leading purpose, the favorite master principle pervading all the propositions in question, is to reduce

[1] Signatures of the Delegates omitted.

[2] For message of Governor Pennington of Jan. 11, 1815, condemning the movement in the Eastern States, see *Niles*, VII, 108, 109.

within a narrower sphere the power and influence of the general government, and thereby to weaken its arm, at a time when, above all others, it requires to be strengthened. Their obvious tendency also is, to throw amongst the states of the union the apple of discord—to increase those jealousies and suspicions, which have been already too far excited, and to give new life, activity and nurture to those seeds of dissention and disunion which have been recently sown with an unsparing hand by insidious combinations and associations, all of them professing to promote the general good, but acting in direct opposition to their professions. The committee feel themselves impelled, therefore, by the strongest obligations of patriotism and duty, to recommend to the house, that each and all of the before mentioned seven propositions of amendment be most promptly and unqualifiedly rejected.

To which report the house of assembly agreed and thereupon,

Resolved, by the house of assembly of New Jersey, That the before mentioned seven propositions of amendment of the constitution of the United States be and the same are hereby rejected. [Agreed to by the Senate, February 17.]

[*Niles' Register*, VIII, 16.]

41. Extract from the Reply of the Legislature of New York.
April 17, 1815.

In the opinion of your committee, in order correctly to estimate the respect due to the resolutions referred to them, it is necessary to recur to the sources from whence they sprang ; and to the time and circumstances in which they originated. [Here follows an unfriendly summary of the work of the Hartford Convention and an inference as to its intentions.] From this convention, emanated the resolutions submitted to the consideration of your committee.

The enlightened patriots who formed the constitution of the United States, aware that confederated sovereignties are ever prone to factious combinations, wisely inserted a provision, " that no state should enter into any agreement or compact with another state." Yet in utter violation of this most explicit declaration of the constitution, was this convention called, these delegates appointed, and their proceedings approved by the states of Massachusetts and Connecticut. [Here follows a severe arraignment of the States of Massachusetts and Connecticut, and contrasts their conduct with that of New York.]

In the amendments proposed to the constitution, your committee can discover nothing inconsistent with the late conduct of the states by whom they are recommended. The effect of them, if adopted would be to create dissentions among the different members of the union, to enfeeble the national government, and to tempt all nations to encroach upon our rights. Your committee forbear to enter into a particular examination of the merits of these amendments, but they cannot but remark, that if the fifth, which requires the concurrence of two-thirds of both houses of congress to declare war, were adopted, no nation would ever fear our power. Recent experience has given us but too much reason to apprehend, that a portion of the people in the eastern section of the union are lost to a due sense of national honor. These combined with others, might put it out of the power of government to declare war, even if an insolent foe should plunder our commerce and kidnap our citizens. Your committee would further remark, that although an amendment is proposed, depriving certain states of a portion of their representation, in consideration of holding slaves, upon the ground that it is unequal in its operation ; yet nothing is suggested in favor of equalizing the representation in the senate, in which the states of Connecticut and Rhode Island are equally represented with this state, which contains four times as many as the former, and fourteen times as many as the latter.

Upon a considerate view of the whole subject, your committee are of opinion that as it becomes this honorable legislature, in the words of the father of his country, to " frown indignantly upon the first dawning of every attempt to alienate any portion of our country from the rest, or to enfeeble the sacred ties which now link together the various parts," that it would be proper to adopt the following resolution :

Resolved, That the seven several propositions of amendment to the constitution of the United States, in the words following, viz. [Here the resolutions are inserted] Be and the same are hereby rejected : and that his excellency the governor be requested to communicate information thereof, to the executive of the several states of the general government.

[*Niles' Register*, VIII, 99–101.]

THE RESERVED RIGHTS OF THE STATES
AND THE
JURISDICTION OF FEDERAL COURTS,
1819–1832.

---

42. Resolutions of Pennsylvania Against the Bank.

March 29, 1819.

The charter of the first Bank of the United States expired in 1811. All efforts to renew the same, or to create another bank, failed until April 10, 1816, when the act establishing the Bank of the United States of America was approved. (*U. S. Stat. at Large*, III, 266–277.) Hostility to a national bank soon reappeared, especially during the financial crisis of 1818–19. An unsuccessful effort was made in Congress to repeal its charter, and in several of the States the Legislatures determined to tax the branches of the Bank out of the State. (McMaster, III, 386–389; IV, 496, 497.) The action of Maryland led to the test case of *McCulloch v. Maryland* in 1819 (4 *Wheaton*, 316), in which the Supreme Court sustained the constitutionality of the Bank and its exemption from State taxation. In Pennsylvania, within which State the central office of the Bank was located, the Legislature again showed its hostility to a national bank [1] by adopting the resolution given below by a vote of 81 yeas to 4 nays in the House, and 14 yeas to 7 nays in the Senate.

References: Text, *Pamphlet Laws of Pennsylvania*, 1819, 289; also in *Laws of Pennsylvania*, VII, 673 (*Phila.*, 1822); *Annals of Congress*, 16 *Cong.*, 1 sess., 70, 102. The Legislative proceedings are given in *Journal of the House of Rep. of Penna.*, 1818-19, 200, 201, 341, 691, 692; *Journal of the Senate of Penna.*, 1818–19, 525. General references on the Act of 1816 and opposition to the Bank: Adams, VIII, 250, 251, 257–260; IX, 106,

---

[1] For action in 1811 see ante, pp. 52–54.

III, 116–118, 131; Hildreth, VI, 589–591, 650 654; McMaster, IV, 309–314, 495–508; Schouler, II, 447–449; III, 112–119; Von Holst, I, 387, 388. For additional references cf. MacDonald, *Documents*, 207; Channing and Hart's *Guide*, 356.

" That all power is inherent in the people, and all free governments are founded on their authority and instituted for their peace, safety and happiness," are the fundamental principles of republicanism.

To prevent the peace, safety and happiness of the people from being endangered, political orthodoxy teaches that they ought never to delegate a power which they can exercise with convenience themselves.

In proportion as the capital of a monied institution is increased, its branches extended and its direction removed from the body of the people, so also will be increased its power and inclination to do evil and to tyrannize ; therefore,

Resolved, That the following amendment be proposed to the Constitution of the United States, viz. : Congress shall make no law to erect or incorporate any bank or other monied institution, except within the District of Columbia, and every bank or other monied institution which shall be established by the authority of Congress shall, together with its branches and offices of discount and deposit, be confined to the District of Columbia.

Resolved, That our Senators and Representatives in Congress be requested to use their exertions to procure the adoption of the foregoing amendment.

Resolved, That the Governor be requested to transmit copies of the foregoing preamble, proposed amendment and resolutions to each of our Senators and Representatives in Congress, and also to transmit like copies to the executives of the several States, with a request that they lay the same before the Legislatures thereof, soliciting their co-operation in procuring the adoption of the foregoing amendment.

Replies of the States.

The invitation of the Legislature of Pennsylvania to the other States to co-operate with it in securing the adoption of the proposed amendment to the

Federal Constitution contained in the above resolutions brought out many
replies during the years 1819–1823. The amendment was approved of by the
Legislatures of Tennessee, Ohio, Indiana and Illinois, but disapproved of by
those of at least nine other States. (Ames, *Proposed Amendments*, 256, 336,
339.) The replies of South Carolina and New York follow. That of the
former is of especial interest in view of the strict construction attitude taken by
this State a few years later, while that of the latter is a fair statement of the
reason that led to the creation of the second Bank of the United States.
Other notable replies were those from Massachusetts and Georgia. The Legislature of Massachusetts maintained the utility and importance of the Bank,
declaring "that a bank limited in its operations to the District of Columbia
would be wholly inadequate to the exigencies of the national government."
(Resolutions of Jan. 31, 1820. *Resolves of Mass.*, 1819–24, 119, 120. Report
of indorsement, Jan. 17, 1823, *Ibid.*, 571, 572.) The resolutions of the General Assembly of Georgia declared that it was "not expedient to deny absolutely" the power of Congress to establish a bank, "although impressed with
the belief that the original grant of such power should be accompanied with a
resolution requiring the assent of each and every State to the location of the
said bank or any branches thereof within the limits of such State." (From
copy in *Journal of House of Rep. of Penna.*, 1822–23, 646, 647.)

---

43. Extract from the Reply of South Carolina.
December 12, 1821.

* * * Your committee are unanimously of opinion that as
Congress is constitutionally vested with the right to incorporate
a bank, it would be unwise and impolitic to restrict its operations
within such narrow limits as the District of Columbia. They
apprehend no danger from the exercise of the powers which the
people of the United States have confided to Congress, but
believe that in the exercise of these powers that body will render
them subservient to the great purposes of our national compact.
Your committee therefore beg leave to recommend to this House
the following resolution :

Resolved, That the Legislature of the State of South Carolina
do not concur in the amendment of the Constitution proposed
by Pennsylvania in the following words. [Here follow the text
of the amendment and a resolution for the transmission of their
reply to the other States.]

[*Acts and Resolutions of the General Assembly of South Carolina*, 1821,
69, 70. (Columbia, 1822.)]

44. Extract from the Reply of New York.

April 18, 1823.

*   *   *   *   *   *   *

The committee are aware of the advantages a national bank, with its branches established in the several States, under the laws of the Union, beyond the reach of the local authorities, may enjoy, to the injury of the State bank; nor have they disregarded the influence that may be exercised by such a powerful monied institution extending over the widespread union above the power and in no manner subject to the direction of the State governments, which seem to have alarmed (and in some measure to have iufluenced the proceedings of) the General Assembly of Pennsylvania. But when they take into consideration the extreme embarrassment of the National government during and immediately subsequent to the late war in its fiscal concerns, from which a national bank, with its branches spread over the Union, might have relieved it; the necessity that government was then under, of receiving its taxes and duties, in the depreciated paper of State banks, in no way subject to its control, and which had generally suspended specie payment, to the great loss of the National treasury, and the attending necessity of the government of opening accounts with, and making deposits in, from ninety to one hundred of these local institutions, the committee can not resist the conclusion that the dignity, the welfare, the prosperity and the permanency of that government (which is our pride and our admiration) forbid the adoption of the proposed amendment; and although it may be wished that the power now exercised by Congress in establishing a national bank, with branches in the several States, had been used with some limitation, subjecting them to such taxation in the respective States as the local banks were or might be subjected to, yet the committee unanimously have come to the conclusion that it would be unwise and impolitic to adopt the proposed amendment. [Here follow resolutions of non-concurrence and for transmission of the resolutions. Adopted without division in both Houses.]

[*House Journal of New York*, 1823, 826, 827, 937, 966; *Senate Journal*, 1823, 351, 361.]

45. Extracts from the Report and Resolutions of Ohio Relative to the Bank and the Powers of the Federal Judiciary.

January 3, 1821.

The hostility to the Bank also showed itself in Ohio. The General Assembly of that State, February 8, 1819, enacted a law placing a tax of $50,000 on each branch of the Bank of the United States that should be found within the State on and after the following 15th of September, and making express provision for enforcing the collection of the tax. (*Acts of Ohio*, XVII, 190–199.) This was done with the avowed purpose of compelling the Bank to cease doing business within the State. Notwithstanding the decision in the case of *McCulloch v. Maryland* (4 *Wheaton*, 316), rendered March 7, 1819, Osborn, the Auditor of the State of Ohio, determined to collect the tax from the two branches of the Bank, which had paid no attention to the act of the State. Disregarding the injunction issued by the Circuit Court of the United States, the Auditor's agents, acting under State warrants, forcibly seized the amount of the tax, $100,000, from the branch of the Bank at Chillicothe. The Bank thereupon instituted both civil and criminal suits against the parties in these proceedings. While one of the suits was still pending the General Assembly of Ohio assembled in December, 1820. It at once came to the support of the Auditor and his agents. A joint committee of both Houses presented on December 12 an exhaustive state rights argument, prepared by Charles Hammond, in defence of the position of the State in this controversy. This report and resolutions, extracts from which follow, were adopted with amendments by the House of Representatives December 28, 1820, and by the Senate January 3, 1821, after that body had receded from several amendments, the most important of which was one intended to make more stringent the recommendation relative to the withdrawal from the Bank of all privileges before the courts. The vote of the House of Representatives on the several resolutions is given in brackets after each of the resolves. The report and resolutions were communicated to both branches of Congress early in February, 1821, and after some objection were ordered printed. (*Annals of Congress*, 16 *Cong.*, 2 *sess.*, 257, 361, 1029.) The Ohio Legislature also followed out the recommendation of the report, and on January 29, 1821, passed *An Act to withdraw from the Bank of the United States the protection of the laws of this State in Certain Cases*. (*Acts of Ohio*, XIX, 108–110.) Attempts made in the session of 1821–22 to secure the repeal of the law levying the tax were defeated. (*Niles' Register*, XXI, 303, 342, 343.) Subsequently the Circuit Court gave a decision against Osborn, and March 19, 1824, the Supreme Court, in the case of *Osborn et al. v. the Bank of the United States* (9 *Wheaton*, 738), affirmed the decision in all its material points, and the restitution of the funds seized was finally effected.

References: The text of the Report and Resolutions is given in *Senate Docu-*

ments, 16 *Cong.*, 2 *sess.*, XII, No. 72, 35 pages. Also in *Executive Documents*, VI, No. 88; *Annals of Congress*, 1686–1714; as reported from the Joint Committee, *Journal of the House of Rep. of Ohio*, 1820–21, 98–132. Proceedings on the same, *Ibid.*, 188, 189, 192–195; *Journal of the Senate of Ohio*, 1820–21, 188, 189. Text of Resolutions only are given in *American State Papers, Miscellaneous*, II, 653, 654; *Niles*, XIX, 339–341. General references: Hildreth, VI, 680, 702; McMaster, IV, 497–504; V, 413; Schouler, III, 246; Story, *Commentaries*, §§ 1649–1655; *Const. History as seen in American Law*, 94–96; King, *Ohio*, 336–338. For contemporary account cf. *Niles*, XVII, 139, 310, 311; XIX, 65, 85, 129, 147, 227, 294, 310, 337, 346, 361, 449; XXI, 75, 76.

[The report opens with a review of the transactions in connection with the case of the Bank of the United States against the officers of the State in the United States Circuit Court.] The committee conceive that the proceeding in this case, by bill in chancery and injunction against the Auditor and Treasurer, is, to every substantial purpose, a process against the State. The Auditor and Treasurer are defendants in name and in form only, and can only be made and regarded as defendants to evade the provisions of the Constitution. From the view they have taken of the subject the conclusion seems inevitable that the Federal Courts have asserted a jurisdiction which a just construction of the Constitution does not warrant. And the committee conceive that to acquiesce in such an encroachment upon the privileges and authority of the State, without an effort to defend them, would be an act of treachery to the State itself, and to all the States that compose the American Union.

The committee are aware of the doctrine, that the Federal Courts are exclusively vested with jurisdiction to declare, in the last resort, the true interpretation of the Constitution of the United States. To this doctrine, in the latitude contended for, they never can give their assent.   *   *   *   *   *

By an express provision of the Constitution of the United States, a provision introduced purposely to effect that object, the States, in any controversies they may have with individuals, are placed beyond the jurisdiction of the Federal Courts. It would seem incontrovertible that the amendatory article [1] placed the States and the United States in a relation to each other different

---

[1] The XI amendment. See ante, p. 8.

from that in which they stood under the original Constitution. Different in this, that in all cases where the States could not be called to answer in the Federal Courts, these courts ceased to be a constitutional tribunal to investigate and determine their power and authority under the Constitution of the United States. The duty of the courts to declare the law terminated with their authority to execute it.

The committee conceive that such is the true, and that such is the settled construction of the Constitution; settled by an authority paramount to all others, and from which there can be no appeal, the authority of the people themselves.

So early as the year 1798 the States and the people were called to declare their opinions upon the question involving the relative rights and powers of the government of the United States. [Here follow extracts from the Kentucky and Virginia Resolutions of 1798.]

It cannot be forgotten that these resolves, and others connected with them, were occasioned by the acts of Congress, commonly called the alien and sedition laws, and by certain decisions in the Federal Circuit Courts, recognizing the obligatory force of the common law, as applicable to the federal jurisprudence.

The resolutions of Virginia were submitted to the Legislatures of the different States; Delaware, Rhode Island, Massachusetts; the Senate of New York, Connecticut, New Hampshire and Vermont returned answers to them,[1] strongly reprobating their principle, and all but Delaware and Connecticut, asserting that the federal judiciary were exclusively the expositors of the federal constitution. In the Virginia Legislature these answers were submitted to a committee, of which Mr. Madison was chairman, and in January, 1800, this committee made a report, which has ever since been consdered the true text-book of republican principles. In that report the claim that the federal judiciary is the exclusive expositor of the federal constitution is taken up and examined. [Here follow extracts from the Virginia report.]

The resolutions of Kentucky and Virginia, and of Massachusetts, Rhode Island, the Senate of New York, New Hampshire and Vermont, in reply, and the answers to these replies by the

[1] For these replies see ante, pp. 16–26.

Legislature of Virginia, were a direct and constitutional appeal to the States and the people upon the great question at issue. The appeal was decided by the presidential and other elections of 1800. The States and the people recognized and affirmed the doctrines of Kentucky and Virginia, by effecting a total change in the administration of the federal government. In the pardon of Callender, convicted under the sedition law, and in the remittance of his fines, the new administration unequivocally recognized the decision and the authority of the States and of the people. Thus has the question, whether the Federal Courts are the sole expositors of the Constitution of the United States in the last resort, or whether the States, "as in all other cases of compact among parties having no common judge," have an equal right to interpret that Constitution for themselves, where their sovereign rights are involved, been decided against the pretension of the federal judges, by the people themselves, the true source of all legitimate powers.[1]

In the opinion of the committee, the high authority of this precedent, as well as the clear right of the case, impose a duty upon the State from which it cannot shrink without dishonor. So long as one single constitutional effort can be made to save them, the State ought not to surrender its rights to the encroaching pretensions of the Circuit Court.

But justice should ever be held sacred. Pride and resentment are alike apologies for perseverance in error. If it were admitted that the proceedings of the Federal Court against the State, through its officers, are not warranted by the Constitution, still if the State has commenced in error it should abandon the controversy. Before, therefore, we determine upon the course we ought to pursue it is necessary to review and examine the ground upon which we stand. * * * The Constitution of the United States has distinctly expressed in what cases the taxing power of the State should be restrained. No maxim of legal construction is better settled and more universally acknowledged than that

---

[1] The assertion that the Virginia and Kentucky Resolutions were an issue in the election of 1800 does not appear to be substantiated by documentary evidence. See F. M. Anderson, *Contemporary Opinion of the Virginia and Kentucky Resolutions, American Historical Review*, V, 244.

express limitations of power, either in constitutions or in statutes, are distinct admissions that the power exists and may be exercised in every other case than those expressly limited. With a knowledge of these facts and doctrines in their minds, that a confidence in the power of the State to levy this tax should be almost universal is what every intelligent man would expect.

But after the law was enacted that levied the tax, and before the time of its taking effect, the Supreme Court of the United States, in the case of Maryland and McCulloch, decided that the States were debarred by the Constitution of the United States from assessing or levying any such tax. And upon the promulgation of this decision it is maintained, that it became the duty of the State and its officers to acquiesce, and treat the act of the Legislature as a dead letter. The committee have considered this position, and are not satisfied that it is a correct one.

* * * * * * *

It is not, however, either in theory or in practice, the necessary consequence of a decision of the Supreme Court, that all who claim rights of the same nature with those decided by the Court are required to acquiesce. There are cases in which the decisions of the tribunal have been followed by no effective consequences.

In the case of Marbury *vs.* Madison the Supreme Court of the United States decided that William Marbury was entitled to his commission as a justice of the peace for the District of Columbia; that the withholding of this commission by President Jefferson was violative of the legal vested right of Mr. Marbury. Notwithstanding this decision, Mr. Marbury never did obtain his commission; the person appointed in his place continued to act; his acts were admitted to be valid, and President Jefferson retained his standing in the estimation of the American people. The decison of the Supreme Court proved to be totally impotent and unavailing.

In the case of Fletcher *vs.* Peck the Supreme Court decided that the Yazoo purchasers from the State of Georgia were entitled to the lands. But the decision availed them nothing, unless a make-weight in effecting a compromise.

These two cases are evidence that in great questions of political rights and political powers a decision of the Supreme Court of the United States is not conclusive of the rights decided by it. If the United States stand justified in withholding a commission when the Court adjudged it to be the party's right; if the United States might, without reprehension, retain possession of the Yazoo lands after the Supreme Court decided that they were the property of the purchasers from Georgia, surely the State of Ohio ought not to be condemned because she did not abandon her solemn legislative acts as a dead letter upon the promulgation of an opinion of that tribunal. [Here follows a long argument in refutation of the principles maintained by the decision of the Federal Supreme Court in the case of McCulloch *vs.* Maryland. The report concludes with the following recommendations and resolutions :]

If an accommodation can be effected without prejudice to the right upon either side, it would seem to be desirable to all parties. With this view, as well as with a view to remove all improper impressions, the committee recommend that a proposition of compromise be made by law, making provision that upon the Bank discontinuing the suits now prosecuted against the public officers, and giving assurance that the branches shall be withdrawn, and only an agency left to settle its business, and collect its debts, the amount collected for tax shall be paid, without interest.

But the committee conceive that the General Assembly ought not to stop here. The reputation of the State has been assailed throughout the United States, and the nature of the controversy and her true course of conduct have alike been very much misunderstood. It behooves the General Assembly, even if a compromise be effected, to take measure for vindicating the character of the State, and also for awakening the attention of the separate States to the consequences that may result from the doctrines of the Federal Courts upon the questions that have arisen. And besides, as it is possible that the proposition of compromise may not be accepted, it is the duty of the General Assembly to take ulterior measures for asserting and maintaining the rights of the State by all constitutional means within their power.

In general, partial legislation is objectionable; but this is no ordinary case, and may therefore call for and warrant extraordinary measures. Since the exemptions claimed by the Bank are sustained upon the proposition that the power that created it must have the power to preserve it, there would seem to be a strict propriety in putting the creating power to the exercise of this preserving power, and thus ascertaining distinctly whether the executive and legislative departments of the government of the Union will recognize, sustain and enforce the doctrine of the judicial department.

For this purpose the committee recommend that provisions be made by law, forbidding the keepers of our jails from receiving into their custody any person committed at the suit of the Bank of the United States, or for any injury done to them; prohibiting our judicial officers from taking acknowledgments of conveyances where the Bank is a party, or when made for their use, and our recorders from receiving or recording such conveyances; forbidding our courts, justices of the peace, judges and grand juries from taking any cognizance of any wrong alleged to have been committed upon any species of property owned by the Bank, or upon any of its corporate rights or privileges, and prohibiting our notaries public from protesting any notes or bills held by the Bank or their agents or made payable to them.

The adoption of these measures will leave the Bank exclusively to the protection of the federal government, and its constitutional power to preserve it in the sense maintained by the Supreme Court may thus be fairly, peaceably and constitutionally tested. Congress must be called to provide a criminal code to punish wrongs committed upon it, and to devise a system of conveyance to enable it to receive and transmit estates, and being thus called to act, the National Legislature must be drawn to the serious consideration of a subject which the committee believe demands much more attention than it has excited. The measures proposed are peaceable and constitutional, conceived in no spirit of hostility to the government of the Union, but intended to bring fairly before the nation great and important questions, which must one day be discussed, and which may now be very safely investigated.

The committee conclude by recommending the adoption of the following resolutions:

Resolved, by the Great Assembly of the State of Ohio, That in respect to the powers of the governments of the several States that compose the American Union and the powers of the federal government, this General Assembly do recognize and approve the doctrines asserted by the Legislatures of Kentucky and Virginia in their resolutions of November and December, 1798, and January, 1800, and do consider that their principles have been recognized and adopted by a majority of the American people. [*Yeas* 59, *nays* 7.]

Resolved further, That this General Assembly do protest against the doctrines of the Federal Circuit Court, sitting in this State, avowed and maintained in their proceedings against the officers of the State upon account of their official acts, as being in direct violation of the 11th amendment to the Constitution of the United States. [*Yeas* 59, *nays* 7.]

Resolved further, That this General Assembly do assert and will maintain by all legal and constitutional means the rights of the States to tax the business and property of any private corporation of trade incorporated by the Congress of the United States and located to transact its corporate business within any State. [*Carried unanimously.*]

Resolved further, That the Bank of the United States is a private corporation of trade, the capital and business of which may be legally taxed in any State where they may be found. [*Yeas* 61, *nays* 4.]

Resolved further, That this General Assembly do protest against the doctrine that the political rights of the separate States that compose the American Union, and their powers as sovereign States, may be settled and determined in the Supreme Court of the United States, so as to conclude and bind them, in cases contrived between individuals, and where they are no one of them parties direct. [*Yeas* 64, *nays* 1.]

Resolved further, That the Governor transmit to the Governors of the several States a copy of the foregoing report and resolutions, to be laid before their respective Legislatures, with a request from the General Assembly that the Legislature of each State may express their opinion upon the matters therein contained. [*Carried unanimously.*]

Resolved further, That the Governor transmit a copy of the foregoing report and resolutions to the President of the United States and to the President of the Senate, and Speaker of the House of Representatives, to be laid before their respective Houses, that the principles upon which this State has and does proceed may be fairly and distinctly understood. [*Carried unanimously.*]

46. Reply of Massachusetts to Ohio.

February 7, 1822.

The foregoing Report and Resolutions of Ohio called out the following reply from the Legislature of Massachusetts. The text is given in *Resolves of Mass.,* 1819-24, 417-419; also in *Niles,* XXI, 404. A series of Resolves of a similar character were adopted by the House of Representatives of New Hampshire, June 28, 1821, by a vote of 172 *yeas* to 8 *nays,* but were indefinitely postponed by the Senate by a vote of 7 *yeas* to 5 *nays.* The text of these resolutions is printed in the *Journal of the Senate of New Hampshire,* 1821, 208-212; also in *Niles,* XX, 312, 313.

* * * The Supreme Court of the United States, the ultimate tribunal for the determination of all cases arising under the Constitution and laws of the Uuited States, have decided, after full argument upon all the questions raised, that the power to establish a bank is vested by the Constitution in Congress, and that its several branches are exempted from the taxing power of the States. The constitutional questions, then, having been thus solemnly determined in all the forms in which they can arise, the construction thus given to the Constitution appears to your committee to be final and binding upon the several States. If the operation of this is found to be injurious to the best welfare of the States, the remedy is to be found in an amendment to the Constitution. The Legislature of this State, however, is not called upon to sanction any such amendment, but to express its opinion upon the report and resolutions of the General Assembly of Ohio; but to comply with the request fully, holding, as your committee do, different opinions, would occupy this Legislature with the details of arguments better fitted for a judicial than a legislative body, and could hardly be justified by the sincere respect which is felt for the Legislature of the State of Ohio. Satisfied, as your committee are, with the construction which has been so often and so deliberately given to the Constitution, they do not perceive that any important end can be obtained by offering anything more than the result of their reflections, in the form of resolutions, which are herewith respectfully submitted to the consideration of the Legislature.

Resolved, By the Senate and House of Representatives, in General Court assembled, that in their opinion the power to establish a National Bank, with branches thereof in the several States, is vested by the Constitution in the Congress of the United States.

Second. *Resolved*, That the act of Congress, passed on the tenth day of April, in the year of our Lord one thousand eight hundred and sixteen, to incorporate the subscribers to the Bank of the United States, is a law made in pursuance of the Constitution of the United States.

Third. *Resolved*, That inasmuch as the Constitution of the United States, and the laws made in pursuance thereof, are the supreme law of the land, anything in the constitution or laws of any State to the contrary notwithstanding, the legislative acts of any State, so far as they prevent or defeat the operation of such laws, are void.

Fourth. *Resolved*, That the act of the Legislature of the State of Ohio levying a tax upon the branch of the National Bank established there, with the other measures proposed, would, if carried into effect, expel from the State such branch and defeat the operation of the law by virtue whereof it was established.

Fifth. *Resolved*, That as the judicial power of the United States extends to all cases arising in law and equity, under the Constitution and laws of the United States, it belongs to the judicial department to determine all cases arising from a conflict between the laws of the United States and the laws of a particular State.

Sixth. *Resolved*, That, in the opinion of this Legislature, the proceedings of the Circuit Court of the United States for the district of Ohio, against the officers of that State do not violate the eleventh amendment to the Constitution of the United States.

Seventh. *Resolved*, That the constitutional exercise and preservation of the judicial power of the United States is essential to the safety and prosperity of the Union, and that while this Legislature will be ever ready to afford its aid to any State against manifest usurpation or real encroachment upon its rights, it will also yield a reasonable confidence and support to all the departments of the National Government, so long as they continue in the rightful exercise of their constitutional powers.

Eighth. *Resolved*, That His Excellency the Governor be requested to transmit to the Governors of the several States of the Union, a copy of the foregoing report and resolutions.

47. Virginia on Jurisdiction of the Federal Courts.
February 19, 1821.

State sovereignty was aroused by the series of decisions of the Supreme Court of the United States, rendered during the years 1816–1824, asserting its jurisdiction and maintaining the powers of Congress. Virginia was especially prompt in condemning the principles asserted by the Court. Following the decision in the case of *McCulloch v. Maryland* (4 *Wheaton*, 316), in December, 1819, two different sets of resolutions, prefaced by long preambles protesting against the decision in this case, were introduced in the Legislature of Virginia. One of these suggested the procuring of an amendment to the Federal Constitution to establish a tribunal to decide cases in controversy between a State and the Federal Government, composed of representatives of both governments. (*Niles*, XVII, 310–314, 447.) Although neither of these resolutions were adopted at this time, the feeling of hostility to the Federal Court was further aroused by the case of *Cohen v. Virginia*, decided in 1821. (6 *Wheaton*, 264.) The writ issued by Chief Justice Marshall summoning the State authorities to appear before the Court in this case at once led to the renewed consideration of resolutions in the Legislature and to agitation in the press of the State. The report adopted by the House of Delegates, by a vote of 138 to 18, is printed in *Niles*, XX, 118–124. The resolutions of protest as finally adopted by both branches of the Legislature are given below. The following year resolutions proposing a series of amendments to the Constitution placing limitations upon the power and jurisdiction of the Federal Courts were defeated by a narrow margin in the Virginia House of Delegates. (*Niles*, XXI, 404.) The most noteworthy of the criticisms directed against these decisions, which appeared in the public press, were a series of articles written by Judge Roane of the Virginia Appellate Court, under the signature of "*Algernon Sidney*." His articles were published in the *Richmond Enquirer* in March, 1821. Of these Jefferson wrote: "I confess that they appeared to me to pulverize every word which had been delivered by Judge Marshall." (Letter of June 12, 1823; cf. *post.*) The correspondence of Jefferson during this period is filled with severe criticism upon the practices and opinions of the Federal

Judiciary. For his comments on the case of *Cohen v. Virginia* see his *Writings* (Ford ed.), X, 198-199, 226-232; *Works*, VII. 222, 223, 294-298; see also his expressions of alarm owing to the influence of the Judiciary, *Writings*, X, 140-143, 160, 161, 170, 177, 184, 189, 192, 200, 223, 224, 248, 259; *Works,* VII, 134, 192, 199, 216, 256, 278. For the more conservative views expressed by Madison in his correspondence with Judge Roane, Jefferson et al., see *Works*, III, 143-147, 217-222, 223, 224, 246, 291-293, 325-328; IV, 18, 47, 296, 297. For an account of the efforts made in Congress in 1821 to secure an amendment to the Constitution conferring upon the Senate appellate jurisdiction in certain cases see, Ames, *Proposed Amendments*, 161, 162; *Annals of Congress*, 17 *Cong.*, 1 *sess.*, 23-25, 68-92, 96-114. For comments on the case of Cohen v. Virginia see *Const. History as seen in Amer. Law*, 85-90; Landon, 312, 313; McMaster, V, 414. Van Santvoord's Chief Justices, 466-469.

*　　　*　　　*　　　*　　　*　　　*　　　*

Resolved, as the opinion of the General Assembly of Virginia, that the Supreme Court of the United States does not possess appellete jurisdiction in any case decided by a State court.

That, even if this appellate jurisdiction did exist in cases decided in a State court, between individuals, a State cannot be made a party defendant to any suit before a federal tribunal, commenced with a view to obtain a judgment against such State, or to reverse one obtained by it in a State court, or to any process or proceeding instituted in a Federal Court to correct or reverse a judgment entered in a State court for a penalty or punishment prescribed for the commission of any offence.

That a law passed by the Congress of the United States by virtue of that clause of the Constitution which gives to them the right of exclusive legislation over the District of Columbia has no greater force or effect out of the said District and within the limits of a State than the law of one State has within the limits of another State, or than a law of a State has within the District aforesaid.

Resolved, That the Supreme Court of the United States have no rightful authority under the Constitution to examine and correct the judgment for which the Commonwealth of Virginia has been " cited and admonished to be and appear at the Supreme Court of the United States," and that the General Assembly do hereby enter their most solemn protest against the jurisdiction of that Court over the matter.

[Acts of Virginia 1820-21, 142, 143. (Richmond, 1821.)]

Kentucky and the Federal Judiciary.

1821–1825.

During the period 1821 to 1825 the people of Kentucky were greatly exercised by the decisions of the Supreme Court of the United States, especially that in the case of *Green v. Biddle* (8 *Wheaton*, 1), declaring the Occupying Claimant Laws of 1797 and 1812 a violation of the 7th art. of the compact with Virginia of 1789, and hence unconstitutional as being contrary to the provisions of Art. I., Sect. 10, of the Federal Constitution, which prohibits any State from impairing the obligation of contract. After the decision of the Court, March 5, 1821, an application of Henry Clay for a rehearing was granted, and the case continued to the next term for argument. When the Legislature assembled in October it adopted a temperate report and resolutions, solemnly remonstrating against the adjudication in this case, authorizing the appointment of "commissioners to try and adjust matters with Virginia," and to oppose any decision of the Supreme Court that the laws in question were void. (*Acts of General Assembly of Ky.*, 1821, 456–469; cf. also *Niles*, XXI, 190, 191, 303, 404, 405.) During the following year the effort to effect an agreement with Virginia failed, by reason of the opposition in the Senate of that State. (Cf. Report of Commissioners of Kentucky, Henry Clay and John Rowan, *Journal of the Senate of Ky.*, 1823, 31–33; also Res. of Virginia, Feb. 18, 1823, *Acts of Virginia*, 1822–23, 121, 122.) Subsequently, Feb. 27, 1823, the Supreme Court handed down its decision, in confirmation of its previous position. An unsuccessful effort was made to secure a rehearing of the case by Judge Rowan, one of the commissioners for the State. (See his letter and petition, *Journal of the Senate of Ky.*, 1823, 35–59; Butler, *Kentucky*, 276–279.) This decision was called to the attention of the Assembly by Governor Adair, in the passage of his message given below. That body adopted a long and argumentative Report and Resolutions relative to this case, as well as to the decision of its own Court of Appeals on the Replevin and Endorsement Laws (*Acts of General Assembly of Ky.*, 1823–24, 488–516; *Jour. of the Senate of Ky.*, 1823–24, 189–220; see also *Niles*, XXV, 201, 275), and also an elaborate Remonstrance to Congress (*Acts of Ky.*, 520–527; *Journal of the Senate*, 288–297; *Executive Doc.*, 18 *Cong.*, 1 *sess.*, IV., No. 69). Extracts from these documents follow. Upon the receipt of this remonstrance attempts were made in Congress by the Senators and Representatives of Kentucky, aided by others, to require the concurrence of a greater number of judges than a majority in any opinion which involved the validity of a State law. Such a bill was reported favorably in the Senate, and the proposition was debated at length in both Houses in 1824. (*Annals of Cong.*, 18 *Cong.*, 1 *sess.*, 28, 38, 290, 574–577, 915, 916, 1291, 1428, 2514–2541, 2618–2620.) For summary of the history of this controversy see Butler, *History of Kentucky*, 266–279 [Louisville, 1834]; McMaster, V, 414–417; Sumner, *Jackson*, 122–129, 132–134.

48. Message of Governor John Adair of Kentucky.
November 4, 1823.

[After referring to the decision of the Supreme Court in this case he says:] Ours is a government founded on moral principles; its strongest support is in the affection of the people. Any judicial act that tends to alienate the minds, and consequently the affections, of large portions of the citizens; for instance, as in the present case, a whole State, by unhinging and overturning the course of legislation and adjudication acted on for years past, must in the same degree weaken the power and render less secure the stability of the government. I need not be told that the general government is authorized to use physical force to put down insurrection and enforce the execution of its laws. I know it; but I know, too, with equal certainty that the day when the government shall be compelled to resort to the bayonet, to compel a State to submit to its law, will not long precede an event of all others most to be deprecated.

I refer to these strong points, to show to what extent this principle may be carried. As to the immediate effects, the incalculable litigation and distress it may produce within this State, I leave it with the Legislature, who are better able to judge than myself. But the immediate effects and consequences of these decisions, on the property and pecuniary relations of the community, is not the view which most is to be apprehended. The principles they would establish, and the effects they would produce, sink much deeper, and would produce infinitely more permanent evils. They strike at the sovereignty of the State, and the right of the people to govern themselves. It is in this view that they have been contemplated, and justly excited the apprehensions of the most intelligent and sober-minded members of the community, and in this view the subject is committed to your most solemn consideration. In your wisdom the remedy is expected to be devised.

[*Journal of the Senate of Kentucky*, 1823, 10–12.]

49. Extract from Preamble and Resolutions of the Legislature.

December 29, 1823.

But why, it may be asked, were not the States, upon the formation of the Constitution of the United States, melted down and their existence abolished, if the doctrine be correct, that they can not suit their remedial system, by varying it, to the varied condition of society. If one unaltered and unalterable system of laws was destined to regulate, in perpetuity, the concerns of the people of the republics of America, * * * why the afflicting expenses of sustaining twenty-four different States, with the legislative, judiciary and executive machineries of sovereignty? Why, under this hypothesis, are they taunted with the *mock-lineaments*, contexture and aspect of sovereigns, when in *very deed*, they are dwarf vassals? Are the principles of Montesque vapid and illusory, and were the patriots who achieved the independence of the American States, and formed their respective constitutions and that of the United States, deluded into the erroneous belief that those principles were correct and had been verified by the experience of ages?

   *   *   *   *   *   *   *

Resolved by the Legislature of the Commonwealth of Kentucky, That they do hereby most solemnly protest, in the name and on the behalf of the good people of Kentucky, against the erroneous, injurious and degrading doctrines of the opinion of the Supreme Court of the United States, pronounced at the last session of that Court, in the case of Green and Biddle.

And it is further resolved, That this Legislature ought, as the first measure, to avoid the oppression and degradation inflicted by the opinion upon the State of Kentucky, to present to the Congress of the United States, a temperate but firm remonstrance against its doctrines, and therein to call upon the nation to guarantee to the State its co-equal sovereignty with the States which compose the Union, and also to request Congress therein, so to organize the Supreme Court of the United States that no constitutional question growing out of the Constitution of the United States, or the constitution of either of the States, involving

the validity of State laws, shall (not) be decided by said Court
unless two-thirds of all the members belonging to said Court shall
concur in such decision.[1]   And that a committee of two members
from the Senate and four from the House of Representatives be
appointed to prepare and report such remonstrance.

[*Acts of Kentucky*, 1823, 488–516 in passim.   Frankfort, 1824.]

50. Remonstrance of the Legislature of Kentucky.
January 7, 1824.

The Legislature of Kentucky feels itself constrained to remonstrate against the principle proclaimed by the Supreme Court of
the United States, at the last term of the Court, in the case of
Green, etc., *vs*. Biddle.   If it should be asked why the State of
Kentucky interferes with the decision of that Court in a case in
which she was not, and could not have been, a party, the answer
is because that Court has, in that case, most afflictingly interfered
with the great and essential rights of the State of Kentucky.

[Here follows a statement of the history and circumstances
leading to the passage of the Occupying Claimant Laws, and the
effect of the decision of the Court.]

The construction of the Court which thus disfranchises the
State of Kentucky, can neither exact the homage of the people
upon whom it acts, for the intellect employed in making it, nor
conciliate their patience under its humiliating and afflicting
effects.   If the same privative effects were attempted to be produced upon the individual and political rights of the people of
Kentucky, by a foreign armed force, and they were not to repel
it at every hazard, they would be denounced as a degenerate race,
unworthy of their patriotic sires, who assisted in achieving the
American Independence ; as a people unworthy of enjoying the
freedom they possessed.   In that case the United States, too,
would be bound, at whatever hazard, to vindicate the right of the
people of Kentucky to legislate over the territory of their State ;
to guarantee to them a republican *form of government*, which
includes the right insisted on.   And can it make any difference

[1] In Green v. Biddle three out of four judges sitting agreed in the opinion;
the other three judges of the Court were absent.

with the people of Kentucky, whether they are deprived of the right of regulating by law the territory which they inhabit, and the soil which they cultivate, by the Duke de Angoulème at the head of a French army,[1] or by the erroneous construction of three of the Judges of the Supreme Court of the United States? To them the privation of political and individual rights would be the same. In both instances they would have lost the power essential to freedom, to the right of self-government. In the former case their conscious humiliation would be less than in the latter, in proportion to the sturdiness of the resistance they would feel conscious of having made, and in proportion to the hope they might entertain of emancipating themselves by some happy effort of valor, and thereby regaining their rights; but in the latter case the tyrant code to which Kentucky is subjected by that decision, is inaccessible, perpetual, and incapable of being changed, beneficially or suitably, to the condition of Kentucky, by any power beneath the sun.

It cannot be denied, that the States, before the formation of the Constitution of the United States, possessed the power of legislating over the territory within their limits. It cannot be asserted, that a surrender of that power was made in that instrument, by the former to the latter, or that any restraint upon the exercise of that power by the States, is to be found in that Constitution. The 10th amendment to that instrument provides expressly, that " the powers not delegated (therein) to the United States, nor prohibited by it to the States, are reserved to the States respectively, or to the people."

The provision in that Constitution, for the formation of new States and their admission into the Union, evidently contemplates their possession of those powers essential to sovereignty, which were retained by the old States.

That the States of the Union should be sovereign, and co-equally so, seems to be not only contemplated, but enjoined by the Constitution of the United States.   *   *   *   *

The good of the *whole* requires equiponderance in the parts,

[1] The Duke of Angoulème had commanded the French army that had intervened in Spain in the preceding year (1823) as the agent of the " Holy Alliance."

and if that equilibrial power could be disturbed or destroyed by any one of the States, by paction with another, or otherwise, then would the *minor* control the *major*, and then would the chances against the perpetuity of the government of the United States be as twenty-four to one. *   *   *   *   *   *

[Referring to this decision of the Court they say:] But the injury inflicted upon the people, great and extensive as it is, and much as it is deplored, weighs but comparatively little with these remonstrants. It is the *principle* which that decision establishes at which they *shudder*, and with which they can never be reconciled. The people of Kentucky * * * can bear anything but degradation and disfranchisement. They can not bear to be construed out of their right of self-government; they value their freedom above everything else, and are as little inclined to be *reasoned* out of it as they would be to surrender it to *foreign force.* *   *   *   *   *   *   *   *   *

The power of local legislation was retained by the States, but it was retained to but little purpose if a central tribunal is to pass upon the laws enacted by the States. The power of legislation must be confided somewhere. It is of the essence of freedom that it should be exerted by those who are the subjects of the law; that the people who compose the society should enact the laws which the society needs. The possession or destitution of that power constitutes the *mighty difference* which exists between *freedom* and *slavery*. Kentucky claims to possess the power of legislating for itself; the decision denies her that power in relation to the most important subjects of its exercise, in relation to her own territory. The decision was given by three, a minority of the judges who composed that tribunal. There was a fourth judge on the bench; he dissented. Had the third agreed with the fourth, Kentucky had not been disfranchised; so that, in that particular case, the political destiny of a State was decided by a solitary judge. Can this appeal to the Congress, by the State of Kentucky, upon a subject in which she is so vitally interested, be unavailing? And has not the State a right to expect that her co-equal sovereignty with the other States of the Union will be guaranteed to her by that body? Has she not a right to expect that the Congress will, either by passing a law requiring, when any question shall come before that tribunal involving the validity of a law of any of the States, that a concurrence of at least *two-thirds* of all the judges shall be necessary to its vacation; or increasing the number of the judges, and thereby multiplying the chances of the States to escape the like calamities, and of this State to escape from its present thraldom, by exacting the exercise of more deliberation and an increased volume of intellect upon all such questions?

[*Acts of Kentucky*, 1823–24, 520-527 in passim.]

Kentucky and the Federal Judiciary (Continued).
1825-1826.

Congress having failed to take practical action on their remonstrance, the Legislature of Kentucky, January 12, 1825, adopted a new set of resolutions, calling upon their Senators and Representatives to support the passage of a law reorganizing the Supreme Court in conformity with their proposition of the previous year. In the preamble they declared that they " view the reports sent abroad, of their readiness to acquiesce in principles so monstrous, as groundless calumnies upon the State character, and upon the patriotism and firmness of the people, and calculated to aid in the prostration of State sovereignty, the main pillar of the Federal Union and American liberty." (*Acts of Ky.*, 1824–25, 281, 282.) Renewed efforts were made in Congress to secure the passage of the bill introduced in the previous session, but the measure failed. (*Cong. Debates*, 18 *Cong.*, 2 *sess.*, I, 365–370, 529–532.) The message of Governor Desha of November 7, 1825, called the attention of the Legislature to the subject anew, and also to the protection given to the Bank of the United States by the Federal Courts, and refers to the establishment of the new State Court of Appeals. (*Journal of the House of Rep. of Ky.*, 1825, 7 et seq.; *Niles*, XXIX, 219–224.) Extracts from this message are given below. In view of this message the House of Representatives passed resolutions calling upon the Governor to inform them of " the mode deemed most advisable in the opinion of the Executive to refuse obedience to the decisions and mandates of the Supreme Court of the United States, considered erroneous and unconstitutional, and whether, in the opinion of the Executive, it may be advisable to call forth the physical power of the State to resist the execution of the decisions of the Court, or in what manner the mandates of said Court should be met by disobedience." (*Niles*, XXIX, 228, 229.) When the Governor, however, came to the point of making specific recommendations, he counseled the House, in his response of Dec. 14, " to restrain their ardor and try yet a little while the pacific measures of an application to Congress." If, however, they are bent on " arraying the physical force of the country, then, I say, in their own wisdom may they look for the most advisable way of doing it, and on their own heads be the responsibility." (*Journals of the House of Rep. of Ky.*, 1825, 318.) There ensued a controversy of words between the House and the Governor, but argument seems to have been the limit of the resistance which either were prepared to take at this time. The Appellate Court of Kentucky refused to be bound by an opinion of the Supreme Court of the United States not concurred in by a majority of the whole Court. (*Bodley v. Gaither*, 3 *Monroe's Reports*, 58; *Niles*, XXIX, 245.) The difficulty was finally ended by a decision of the Supreme Court in 1831, in the case of *Hawkins et al. v. Barney's Lessees* (5 *Peters*, 457), affirming the constitutionality of the Act of Kentucky of Feb. 9, 1809, limiting the commencement of action against actual settlers within seven years of its passage. This controversy was intimately connected with the political contest between the "Old" and the "New" Court parties of 1824–26. (For account of same see Collins, *Historical Sketches of Ky*, 90–92, 102, 105; McMaster, V, 162–166, 416; Shaler, *Kentucky*, 176–183; Sumner, *Jackson*, 126–129, 132–134. For resolutions of Legislature see *Acts of Ky.*, 1823, 488–516; *Ibid.*, 1824–25, 221–239, 242–278; Messages of Governor, *Jour. of House of Rep.*, 1825, 7 et seq., 300–338.) As a result of these and other decisions of the Federal Judiciary renewed attempts were made in Congress in 1831 to restrict the jurisdiction of the Federal Courts, but the measures, although favorably reported, were defeated. (*Cong. Debates*, 620, 658–670, 730–740; *Appx.*, 77–86; *Niles*, XXXIX, 412–421; Landon, 315, 316.

51. Extract from Message of Governor Joseph Desha.
November 7, 1825.

The wrongs suffered by this State from the decision of the Supreme Court of the United States, declaring our occupants laws to be unconstitutional, have not been redressed. The remonstrance of a former General Assembly to the Congress of the United States has been considered by that body, in which many were found who acknowledged our wrongs, and the consequent duty of the general government to grant redress, but we have witnessed no practical result.

In the meantime the injurious decision is spreading its baneful influences.

* * * * * * *

I cannot too earnestly press upon you the propriety of again urging the consideration of this subject on Congress, and of availing yourselves of that occasion to remonstrate in strong terms against the power of making execution laws, lately exercised by the federal judges of this State, inviting their serious attention to the growing influence of the United States Bank, and requesting such a change in the charter of that corporation as will make it the duty of the directors to withdraw the branches located in any State upon the demand of the State Legislature.   *   *

When the general government encroaches upon the rights of the State, is it a safe principle to admit that a portion of the encroaching power shall have the right to determine finally whether an encroachment has been made or not?   In fact, most of the encroachments made by the general government flow through the Supreme Court itself, the very tribunal which claims to be the final arbiter of all such disputes.   What chance for justice have the States when the usurpers of their rights are made their judges?   Just as much as individuals when judged by their oppressors.   It is therefore believed to be the right, as it may hereafter become the duty of the State governments, to protect themselves from encroachments, and their citizens from oppression, by refusing obedience to the unconstitutional mandates of the federal judges.

Controversy with Georgia Relative to the Lands of the Creek Indians.

1825-1827.

The history of this controversy is so fully presented in the references cited below that it is only necessary to refer to the events immediately connected with the documents which follow.   In its efforts to satisfy Georgia by securing the lands of the Creeks, the United States government concluded the treaty of Indian Springs with a few of the Creek chiefs February 12, 1825.   (*U. S. Stat. at L.*, VII, 237–240.)   The rest of the Creeks disavowed the treaty, and put to death the leading chiefs who had signed it.   But Georgia had already taken steps to survey and occupy the country, although by the terms of this treaty the Creeks were given until September, 1826, to vacate the land.   President Adams sent a special agent to investigate the situation, and General Gaines to preserve peace among the Indians.   The Secretary of War, May 18, 1825, notified Governor Troup of Georgia that "the President expects . . . that the survey will be abandoned by Georgia till it can be done consistently with the provisions of the treaty."   (*Reports of House Committees*, 19 *Cong.*, 2 *sess.*, III, No. 98, 155–157; *Niles*, XXVIII, 317.)   Governor Troup replied

June 3, 1825, characterizing the President's request as "most extraordinary" and "unreasonable." "If the President believes that we will postpone the survey of the country to gratify the agent and the hostile Indians he deceives himself." (*Repts. of Com. o. c.*, 178; *Niles*, XXVIII, 318.) In a letter of June 15 to General Gaines, given below, Governor Troup made a similar declaration. (*Repts. of Com. o. c.*, 592–593; *Niles*, XXVIII, 393.) On this same date Governor Troup was notified "that the government of the United States will not be responsible for any consequences" which may result from the attempt to execute the survey. (*Repts. of Com. o. c.*, 225; *Niles*, XXVIII, 398.) Extracts from the Governor's replies to this notification follow, and will serve to present the attitude assumed by him in his voluminous correspondence with the United States government. In his message of November 8, 1825, Governor Troup presented the matter in controversy to the State Legislature (*Executive Doc.*, 19 *Cong.*, 2 *sess.*, IV, No. 59, 187–206; *Niles*, XXIX, 200–208), and that body endorsed his position. (*Acts of Georgia*, 1825, 204–209; *Repts. of Com. o. c.*, 840.) The United States government succeeded in making the treaty of Washington, January 24, 1826, which annulled the former treaty. (*U. S. Stat. at L.*, VII, 286–289.) Georgia, however, insisted on the validity of the treaty of Indian Springs as being more favorable. See the Resolutions of the Legislature which follow. (Message of Governor, Report and Resolutions of Nov. and Dec., 1826, are given in *Executive Doc. o. c.*, 5–22; *State Papers, Indian Affairs*, II, 728–734.) The Governor sent surveyors to run the boundary line into the Indian country, but the Indians forced them to desist, appealed to the President, who notified Troup that force would be used if necessary to prevent the survey (Letter of January 29, 1827, *State Papers, Indian Affairs*, II, 864), and laid the matter before Congress in a special message February 5, 1827. (*Richardson*, II, 370–373.) Troup returned a defiant answer, and called out the militia. (*Niles*, XXXII, 16.) His position was later endorsed by the Legislature in their report of December 24, 1827, given below. Congress was not prepared to give the President the support that the Legislature of Georgia did its Executive. Reports from special committees were discussed in both branches. The Senate adopted resolutions requesting the President "to continue his exertions to obtain for Georgia the lands within her limits." The House took no positive action. (*Cong. Debates*, 1826–27, 267–279, 498, 500, 935–938, 1029–1052, 1533–1541.) November 15, 1827, a treaty for the final cession of the lands within the State was concluded. (*U. S. Stat. at L.*, VII, 307–309.)

References: The documents relating to the controversy are given in *House Executive Documents*, 19 *Cong.*, 2 *sess.*, IV, No. 59, 404 pages; V, Nos. 76, 87; VI, No. 127; *Reports of House Committees*, III, No. 98, 846 pages; *American State Papers, Indian Affairs*, II; cf. Index, "*Georgia.*" Many of the documents are given in *Niles*, XXVIII, XXIX, XXXI, XXXII; cf. Index. Secondary works: Of prime importance are McMaster, V, 175–181; Von Holst, I, 433–448; cf. also Schouler, III, 370–373, 378–380; Sumner, *Jackson*, 174–178.

52. Extract from Letter of Governor Troup to General Gaines.

June 15, 1825.

SIR: I have this moment had the honor to receive your communication of the 14th inst., on the subject of the survey of the ceded country, and the running of the dividing line between Alabama and Georgia, and in which you request, that, in conformity with the expressed will of your Government, both the survey and the running of the line may be forborne, " until the period arrives at which the removal of the Indians is required."

It would give me great pleasure to comply with any request made by yourself or your Government. You would make none that did not to your apprehensions, seem reasonable and proper. As, however, there exists two independent parties to the question, each is permitted to decide for itself, and with all due deference to yours I must be permitted to say that my apprehension of the right and wrong leads me to the opposite conclusion— the conclusion to which the Legislature of Georgia, upon mature reflection, recently arrived by an almost unanimous voice, and which was made the foundation of my late communication to the Secretary of War, and my more recent one to you on the same subject.

I would deeply lament if any act, proceeding from myself, should cause the least embarrassment to yourself or your Government, especially considering the critical relations in which the United States stands to the Indians, and the great interest which the government of Georgia feels in their early and satisfactory adjustment, but it cannot be expected, by your Government, that important interests are to be surrendered, and rights deemed unquestionable abandoned by Georgia, because of any embarrassment which may arise in the intercourse and negotiations between the United States and the Indians. [Then follows his charge of the falsehood of the agent, upon which the instructions of the United States government were based.] On the part of the government of Georgia, the will of its highest constituted authority has been declared, upon the most solemn deliberation, that the line shall be run and the survey executed. It is for you, therefore, to bring it to the issue; it is for me only to repeat that, cost what it will the line will be run, and the survey effected. The government of Georgia will not retire from the position it occupies to gratify the Agent, or the hostile Indians, nor will it do so, I trust, because it knows that, in consequence of disobedience to an unlawful mandate, it may very soon be recorded that "Georgia was."

Suffer me to say, also, that your government has acted very precipitately and unadvisedly in this affair; after receiving notice of my intention to make the survey, it interposed no objection, though it had time to do so. A considerable interval elapsed, and it receives false information from the agent, upon which it issued its peremptory order. Soon after it receives further false information from the same agent, upon which it issues other orders, confirmatory of the first, and which you seem to consider final. 　　＊　　　＊　　　＊　　　＊　　　＊　　　＊

The suggestion you make in derogation of our claim to participate in the construction or execution of the treaty, giving to that suggestion its utmost force, is merely that we are not nominally parties to the treaty; whilst the answer to it is that we are party, in interest, deeper ten-fold than they who appear upon the paper, and that the paper in virtue of another paper to which we are parties, both nominally and in interest, passed a vested right of soil and of jurisdiction to Georgia, which none but the great Jehovah can divest.

[*Executive Documents*, 19 *Cong.*, 2 *sess.*, IV, No. 59, 236–238.]

53. Extract from Letter of Governor Troup to the War Department.

June 25, 1825.

Sir : I received this morning the note which, in the absence of the Secretary of War, the President of the United States directed you to address to me, and in which I am informed that "the project of surveying the lands ceded to the United States by the Creek nation of Indians, at the treaty of Indian Springs, before the expiration of the time specified by the 8th article of the treaty, for the removal of the Indians, will be wholly upon its (the government of Georgia) responsibility, and that the government (viz. : the government of the United States) will not in any manner be responsible for any consequences which may result from that measure." A very friendly admonition truly. * * * Nay more ; you repeat this order [forbidding the survey] to General Gaines, who is charged to promulgate it to the hostile Indians, so that whether there be anything obnoxious in the survey or not, they may seize it as a pretence, under the authority and with the support of the United States, to scalp and tomahawk our people as soon as we shall attempt that survey, and that in fact you adopt for the Indians gratuitously an imaginary wrong done to them, persuade them, even against their will, that it is a real one, and then leave them to indulge in unbridled fury the most tempestuous passions ; and this, I presume, is the meaning, in part, of the responsibilities which we are to incur if we disregard the mandate of the Government of the United States.

You will, therefore, in the absence of the Secretary of War, make known to the President that the Legislature, having, in concurrence with the expressed opinion of the Executive, come to the almost unanimous conclusion, that, by the treaty, the jurisdiction, together with the soil, passed to Georgia, and, in consequence thereof, authorized the Governor to cause the line to be run and the survey to be made. It becomes me, in candor, to state to the President, that the survey will be made, and in due time, and of which Major-General Gaines has already had sufficient notice.

Whilst in the execution of the decrees of our own constituted authorities, the Government of the United States will find nothing but frankness and magnanimity on our part, we may reasonably claim the observance, in like degree, of these noble qualities on theirs. When, therefore, certain responsibilities are spoken of in the communication of the President, we can rightfully inquire, what responsibilities? Georgia in the maintenance of her undoubted rights, fears no responsibilities ; yet it is well for Georgia to know them, so far as they are menaced by the United States. If it is intended that the Government of the United States will interpose its power to prevent the survey, the Government of Georgia cannot have too early or too distinct notice ; for how highly dishonorable would it be for the stronger party to avail itself of that power to surprise the weaker. If the government only means that, omitting its constitutional duty, it will not pacify the Indians, and make safe the frontier, whilst the officers of Georgia are in peaceful fulfilment of their instructions, connected with the survey, it is important to the Government of Georgia to know it; that, depending on itself for safety, it shall not depend in vain. But if the Government of the United States mean what is not even yet to be believed, that assuming, like their Agent, upon another not dissimilar occasion, an attitude of neutrality feigned and insincere, it will, like that Agent, harrow up the Indians to the commission of hostile and bloody deeds, then indeed the Government of Georgia should also know it, that it may guard and fence itself against the perfidy and treachery of false friends. In either event, however, the President of the United States may rest contented that the Government of Georgia cares for no responsibilities in the exercise of its right and the execution of its trust, but those which belong to conscience and to God, which, thanks to Him, is equally our God as the God of the United States.

[*Executive Documents*, 19 *Cong.*, 2 *sess.*, IV, No. 59, 267–269.]

54. Extract from Letter of Governor Troup to the Secretary of War.

August 15, 1825.

SIR : I have received your letter of the 21st ultimo, giving the desired explanation of the former one of the 15th day of June last, in which you wrote of undefined responsibilities which this Government must incur, if it attempted the survey of the lands acquired from the Creeks, and which results in the employment of the bayonet on your part, and of the tomahawk and scalping-knife on the part of the Indians, if the survey be attempted. I thank you for this explanation ; for whether your intent were good or evil, it equally became you to make it. You make known, at the same time, the resolution of the President, to refer the treaty to Congress, on the allegation that intrigue and treachery have been employed to procure it. This at once puts a stop to the survey, and you will inform the President that, until the will of the Legislature of Georgia is expressed, no measures will be taken to execute the survey.

The Executive of Georgia has no authority in the civil war with which the State is menaced to strike the first blow, nor has it the inclination to provoke it; that is left to those who have both the inclination and the authority, and who profess to love the Union best. The Legislature will, on their first meeting, decide what, in this respect, the rights and interests of the State demand. In the meantime, the right to make the survey is asserted, and the reference of the treaty to Congress, for revision, protested against without any qualification.   *   *   *

The Legislature of Georgia will, therefore, on its first meeting, [be advised] to resist any effort which may be made to wrest from the State the territory acquired by that treaty, and no matter by what authority that effort be made.   *   *   *   If the Legislature shall fail to vindicate that right, the responsibility will be theirs, not mine.

[*Executive Documents*, 19 *Cong.*, 2 *sess.*, IV, No. 59, 271-273.]

55. Resolutions of Georgia, on the Differences with the General Government Relative to the Treaties with the Creek Nation of Indians.

December 22, 1826.

Resolved, That Georgia owns exclusively the soil and jurisdiction of all the territory within her present chartered and conventional limits, and with the exception of the right to regulate commerce among the Indian tribes, claims the right to exercise, over any people, white or red, within those limits the authority of her laws, as she in her wisdom may think proper; and that she has never relinquished said right, either territorial or jurisdictional, to the General Government in any manner or by any instrument whatever, and the exercise of such right by the said last mentioned Government is illegal, unwarrantable and unjust.

Resolved, That threatening a State with an armed force, and actually attempting to carry said threats into execution, by stationing the military on its borders, whether the conduct of the State thus sought to be overawed be right or wrong, is contrary to the spirit and genius of our government, a fundamental principle of which is, that the military is subordinate to the civil authority; the former being the instrument of fatal necessity makes a resort to the latter always indispensable in the first instance; any other course is destructive of free government, subversive of State rights, and tending to the complete annihilation of State sovereignty.

Resolved, That the refusal to arrest and punish a military officer of the General Government, who had grossly violated a law of the land, in abusing and insulting the highest authorities of a State, is, as we conceive, an abuse of office, and if not properly atoned for, will and ought to leave this lasting reproach upon the nation, that even in a Republic the law affords no protection against the views of power, or the resentments of ambition.[1]

Resolved, That the retention of a civil officer in power, after earnest and repeated solicitations for his removal from a sovereign State, through its highest authorities, in which there was uncommon unanimity, and after, too, it was known to his Government that he was not only opposed to its own views, but was extremely inimical to the interests of the State in which he was placed, and highly insulting to her public functionaries, is an instance of contempt for the opinion of a State, and a disregard for the welfare of a large portion of the community, highly dangerous to the principles of representative government, where the public servant acts for the people, and not for himself; and where, as soon as he becomes obnoxious to their interests, he ought to be removed.[2]

Resolved, That the attempted abrogation of the treaty of the Indian Springs by the treaty of Washington, in so far as it divested

---

[1] This refers to General Gaines. A most undignified correspondence took place between Governor Troup and General Gaines. See *Executive Doc.,* 19 *Cong.,* 2 *sess.,* IV, No. 59, 247-253, 379-384; *Niles,* XXVIII, 396-398; XXIX, 47, 48. See Troup's correspondence with the President relative to Gaines, *Ex. Doc.,* 277-287; *Niles,* XXIX, 14-16.

[2] Report and Resolves of the Legislature, June 11, and of Dec. 22, 1825, called for the removal of Captain John Crowell, agent to the Creek Indians. *Acts of Georgia,* extra session, 1825, 35-45; annual session, 1825, 204-209; *Rept. of House Committees,* 19 *Cong.,* 2 *sess.,* III, No. 98, 188-196.

the State of Georgia of any right acquired under the former, is illegal and unconstitutional, and we feel the utmost confidence that, when the General Government comes to be informed that Georgia is deprived of lands to which she had an unquestionable claim by virtue of the first treaty, it will think with us in this regard ; and, actuated by its accustomed sense of justice, will take speedy steps to remove all obstructions to the full enjoyment of this, at present, contested right.

Resolved, That the assertion of the President, that we have no right to enter the Indian country within our own limits, for the purpose of ascertaining boundary, and effecting measures connected with the peaceable objects of internal improvement, without the consent of the Indians, is a doctrine which this State will not admit, and against which it does most solemnly *protest.* In this she has every confidence of the support of her sister States, especially those who have so long and so uninterruptedly enjoyed a similar right. And his solemn *protest* against any measure contemplated by the State to exert her right over this necessary and essential part of her sovereignty, is an instance of dictation and federal supremacy unwarranted by any grant of power to the General Government, and which we trust and believe the National Legislature will promptly disavow.

Resolved, That a separate copy of this report, with the documents necessary to support the facts therein detailed, be forwarded by his Excellency the Governor to our Senators and Representatives in Congress, to be by them respectively presented to each branch of Congress, with a request that they use their best exertions to have redressed the grievances of this State, in the various particulars to which this report has reference, and, for the future harmony of the States to request of that body to make an explicit declaration of the rights that belong to the National Government and those which belong to the State of Georgia, (and consequently to the other States,) resulting from the immediate difference of opinion specially enumerated in the foregoing report.

Resolved, That his Excellency the Governor be requested to forward also a copy of this report and the documents to the Governor of each State in the Union, with an earnest and respectful request that he lay the same before the Legislature of his

State; and they are hereby most affectionately and respectfully solicited to express to this State whether they are prepared to admit the foregoing principles, and the powers growing out of them as belonging to the General Government, and whether Georgia is bound and must submit to the treatment which she conceives she has most wrongfully sustained at the hands of the Executive Department of the General Government.

[*Acts of Georgia*, 1826, 234, 235. (Milledgeville, 1826.)]

56. Extract from Letter of Governor Troup to the Senators and Representatives of Georgia in Congress of the United States.

February 21, 1827.

I consider all questions of mere sovereignty as matter for negotiation between the States and the United States, until the competent tribunal shall be assigned by the Constitution itself for the adjustment of them.

I am not wanting in confidence in the Supreme Court of the United States in all cases falling within their acknowledged jurisdiction. As men I would not hesitate to refer our cause to their arbitration or umpirage. On an amicable issue made up between the United States and ourselves, we might have had no difficulty in referring it to them as judges, protesting at the same time against the jurisdiction, and saving our rights of sovereignty. If the United States will, with or without the consent of Georgia, make a question before the Supreme Court, it will be for the Government of Georgia ultimately to submit, or not, to the decision of that tribunal. But according to my limited conception, the Supreme Court is not made by the Constitution of the United States, the arbiter in controversies involving rights of sovereignty between the States and the United States.[1] The Senate of the United States may have so considered it, because it has been

[1] Governor Troup, in his message to the Legislature, November 7, 1826, said: "The government of either State is to be considered as an independent moral agent, having a conscience of its own, the arbiter within itself of right and wrong, to be influenced or controlled only by divine authority; and the conscience of this government has already passed definitively on the validity of the treaty of the Indian Springs." *State Papers, Indian Affairs*, II, 728.

proposed to make that honorable body itself the arbiter and umpire between them. The States cannot consent to refer to the Supreme Court, as of right and obligation, questions of sovereignty between them and the United States, because that Court, being of exclusive appointment by the Government of the United States, will make the United States the judge in their own cause ; this reason is equally applicable to a State tribunal. Hence, the difficulties likely to arise even by a resort to the civil process, and thus you will perceive how infinitely preferable it is to carry into effect immediately the measure contemplated by the instructions to the agent.

[*Niles' Register*, XXXII, 20.

---

57. Extract from Report of the Legislature of Georgia Commending the Course of Governor Troup.

December 24, 1827.

The Legislature cannot but conceive that it became the bounden duty of the Governor to consider the *whole transaction* as an invasion of our vested rights, offensive in its manner, and not warranted by any principle of justice, meriting that hearty defiance which belongs to a people peculiar for their submission to constitutioual authority, but equally remarkable for their opposition in every shape to tyranny and usurpation. And that he ought to have been prepared to resist the invasion of a " vested interest " as well in the unsettled territory acquired as in the heart of the oldest settlement of Georgia. Accordingly Governor Troup, in reply to the Secretary of War on the 17th of February last, declared that he felt it " to be his duty to resist to the utmost any military attack which the Government of the United States shall think proper to make on the territory, the People or the sovereignty of Georgia ; and all the measures necessary to the performance of this duty, according to our limited means, are in progress. From the first decisive act of hostility, you will be considered and treated as a public enemy, and with less repugnance, because you, to whom we might constitutionally have appealed, for our defence against invasions, are yourselves the invaders ; and what is more, the unblushing allies of the savages, whose cause

you have adopted." [1]   This course is altogether approved by the
committee, and what is extremely gratifying, seems to be justified
by most of our considerate sister States; and the replication of
the Governor, is the more satisfactory, because, unlike some
recreant threats that are made for *effect* and *intimidation*, it was
backed by a preparation so grave and determined, as to relieve it
from all suspicion of being *idle* or *unmeaning*.   *   *

[*Acts of Georgia*, 1827, 268–269.]

Controversy with Georgia Relative to the Jurisdiction Within the Territory of the Cherokee Nation.
1826-1831.

While the controversy over the lands of the Creeks was at its height the
government of Georgia gave renewed proof of its determination to secure also
the lands of the Cherokee Nation within the limits of the State.   The Legislature, December 4, 1826, passed resolutions calling on the President to conclude
a treaty with the Cherokees to extinguish their title to all these lands.   (*Acts
of Georgia*, 1826, 207, 208.)   The adoption of a written constitution by the
Cherokee Nation and their evident determination to remain permanently in
Georgia, led the next Legislature, December 27, 1827, to adopt a much more
aggressive report and resolutions, extracts from which follow.   (*House Executive Documents*, 20 *Cong.*, 1 *sess.*, III, No. 102; *Senate Doc.*, III, No. 88.)
The United States government being unable to induce the Cherokees to surrender the same, Georgia became impatient, and encouraged by President
Jackson's announcement of his Indian policy, (Message of Dec. 8, 1829,
Richardson, II, 457-459; cf. Resolutions of Georgia approving his policy,
Dec. 10, 1829, *Acts of Ga.*, 267-270,) proceeded to take more aggressive
measures for carrying out their previous declarations.   They supplemented
their earlier acts by passing, Dec. 19, 1829, a more comprehensive measure
annulling all laws and ordinances of the Cherokee Nation, and incorporating
the territory into five counties.   (*Acts of Georgia*, 1829, 98-101; *Senate Doc.*,
21 *Cong.*, 1 *sess.*, II, No. 98, 11-13; *Niles*, XXXVIII, 54, 328, 329.)   Judge
Clayton in an address to the Grand Jury of Clark County in the fall of 1830,
declared his purpose to enforce the act, and asserted that, " So far as I am
concerned, I only require the aid of public opinion and the arm of executive
authority, and no court on earth besides our own shall ever be troubled with
this question." (*Niles*, XXXIX, 99-101.)   The first case to raise the issue
of the legality of the jurisdiction of Georgia over this territory, grew out of the
trial and conviction, by the State Courts, of a Cherokee Indian, one George
Tassels, for the murder of another Indian.   Chief Justice Marshall of the Fed-

---

[1] *Executive Documents*, 19 *Cong.*, 2 *sess.*, VI, No. 127, 5; *Niles*, XXXIII, 16.

eral Supreme Court, on application, issued a writ of error, Dec. 12, 1830, citing the State authorities to appear before the Federal Court. Governor Gilmer submitted the same to the Legislature of the State, declaring his intention to disregard the writ, and that " any attempt to enforce such orders will be resisted with whatever force the laws have placed at my command." The Legislature supported his position in the resolutions given below. (A copy of the writ, the Governor's Message and the Resolutions of the Legislature are in *Niles*, XXXIX, 338.) The Court was defied, as Tassels was executed a few days later. (*Niles*, XXXIX, 353.) In the mean time, Congress having failed to grant their appeals for intervention, the Cherokee Nation had applied to the Supreme Court of the United States to restrain by injunction the execution of the above mentioned laws of Georgia within their territory. The attempt of their counsel, William Wirt, to get the Governor of Georgia to lay the whole question by agreement before the Supreme Court was ineffectual. (See correspondence of Wirt and Governor Gilmer, *Niles*, XXXIX, 58, 69–71; also Kennedy, *Life of Wirt*, II, 323.) The Supreme Court, while practically admitting the justice of the plea, dismissed the case for lack of jurisdiction. (Jan. 1831 : *Cherokee Nation v. The State of Georgia*, 5 *Peters*, 1.) The Indians issued an appeal to the People of the United States, May 21, 1831. (*Niles*, XL, 298.) For additional references see *post*, p. 129.

58. Resolutions of the Legislature Relative to the Cherokee Controversy.

December 27, 1827.

Your committee would recommend that one other, and the last, appeal be made to the General Government, with a view to open a negotiation with the Cherokee Indians upon this subject ; that the United States do instruct their commissioners to submit this report to the said Indians ; that if no such negotiation is opened, or if it is, and it proves to be unsuccessful, that, then, the next Legislature is recommended to take into consideration the propriety of using the most efficient measures for taking possession of, and extending our authority and laws over the whole of the lands in controversy. * * * * If the United States will not redeem her pledged honor ; and if the Indians continue to turn a deaf ear to the voice of reason and of friendship ; we now solemnly warn them of the consequence. The lands in question *belong* to Georgia—she *must* and she *will* have them. Influenced by the foregoing considerations, your committee beg leave to offer the following resolutions :

Resolved, That the United States, in failing to procure the lands in controversy " as early " as the same could be done upon " peaceable " and " reasonable terms " have palpably violated their contract with Georgia, and are now bound, at all hazards, and without regard to terms, to procure said lands for the use of Georgia.

Resolved, That the policy which has been pursued by the United States toward the Cherokee Indians, has not been in good faith toward Georgia ; and that, as all the difficulties which now exist to an extinguishment of the Indian title, have resulted from the acts of policy of the United States, it would be unjust and dishonorable in them to take shelter behind these difficulties.

Resolved, That all the lands appropriated and unappropriated, which lie within the conventional limits of Georgia, belong to her absolutely ; that the title is in her ; that the Indians are tenants at her will ; that she may, at any time she pleases, determine that tenancy by taking possession of the premises ; and that Georgia has the right to extend her authority and laws over the whole territory, and to coerce obedience to them, from all description of people, be they white, red, or black, who reside within her limits.

Resolved, That Georgia entertains for the General Government so high a regard, and is so solicitous to do no act that can disturb, or tend to disturb, the public tranquility, that she will not attempt to enforce her rights by violence, until all other means of redress fail.

Resolved, That to avoid a catastrophe which none would more sincerely deplore than ourselves, we make this solemn appeal to the President of the United States, that he take such steps as are usual, and as he may deem expedient and proper for the purpose of, and preparatory to, the holding of a treaty with the Cherokee Indians, the object of which shall be the extinguishment of their title to all the lands now in their possession within the limits of Georgia.

* * * * * * *

Resolved, That the late proceedings of the Cherokee Indians in framing a Constitution for their Nation,[1] and preparing to

[1] An abstract of the Cherokee Constitution is given in American Annual Register, 1829-30, 46, 47; also in Niles, XXXIII, 214, 346.

establish a Government independent of Georgia, is inconsistent with the rights of the said State, and therefore not recognized by this Government, and ought to be decidedly discountenanced by the General Government.

[*Acts of Georgia*, 1827, 248-250. (Milledgeville, 1828.)]

---

59. Resolutions of the Legislature Relative to the Case of George Tassels.

December 22, 1830.

Whereas, it appears by a communication, made by his Excellency the Governor, to this General Assembly, that the Chief Justice of the Supreme Court of the United States, has sanctioned a writ of error, and cited the State of Georgia, through her chief Magistrate, to appear before the Supreme Court of the United States to defend this State against said writ of error, at the instance of one George Tassels, recently convicted in Hall county, Superior Court, of the crime of murder. And whereas, the right to punish crimes, aganist the peace and good order of this state, in accordance with existing laws is an original and a necessary part of sovereignty which the State of Georgia has never parted with.

Be it therefore resolved by the Senate, and House of Representatives of the State of Georgia, in General Assembly met, That they view with feelings of the deepest regret, the interference by the Chief Justice of the Supreme Court of the United States, in the Administration of the criminal laws of this state, and that such an interference is a flagrant violation of her rights.

Resolved further, That his Excellency the Governor, be and he, and every officer of this State, is hereby requested and enjoined, to disregard any and every mandate and process that has been, or shall be served upon him or them, purporting to proceed from the Chief Justice, or any associate Justice of the Supreme Court of the United States, for the purpose of arresting the execution of any of the criminal laws of this State.

And be it further resolved, That his Excellency the Governor, be and he is hereby authorized and required, with all the force and means, placed at his command, by the Constitution and laws of this State, to resist and repel, any and every invasion, from whatever quarter, upon the administration of the criminal laws of this State.

Resolved, That the State of Georgia, will never so far compromise her sovereignty as an independent State, as to become a party to the case sought to be made before the Supreme Court of the United States, by the writ in question.

Resolved, That his Excellency the Governor, be and he is hereby, authorized, to communicate to the Sheriff of Hall countys by express, so much of the foregoing resolutions, and such order, as are necessary to insure the full execution of the laws, in the case of George Tassels, convicted of murder in Hall conuty.

[*Acts of Georgia*, 1830, 282, 283. (Milledgeville, 1831.)]

Controversy with Georgia over the Jurisdiction of the Cherokee Nation. (Continued.)

1831-1835.

Already in advance of the hearing of the case of the Cherokee Nation, the Legislature, December 22, 1830, had passed a new act to enforce their jurisdiction, which prohibited white persons residing within the territory inhabited by the Indians, without a license from the Governor, and the taking of an oath of loyalty to the State of Georgia. (*Acts of Georgia*, 1830, 114–117.) Samuel A. Worcester and several other missionaries, denying the jurisdiction of Georgia, refused obedience to this law. They were ultimately convicted and sentenced to four years imprisonment. (For contemporary accounts, records of their trial and other documents, see *Niles*, XL, 95, 132, 244–248, 296–298; XLI, 102, 174–176; *Amer. Annual Register*, 1831–32, Appx., 364–366). Worcester and his associates applied to the Supreme Court of the United States for a rehearing, and a writ was issued by Judge Baldwin, November 10, 1831, citing the authorities of Georgia to appear before the Court. (*Niles*, XLI, 313.) Governor Lumpkin laid the same before the Legislature, November 25, 1831, in the message which follows. The Legislature, December 26, approved of resolutions similar in language to those adopted in the case of Tassels. (*Acts of Georgia*, 1831, 259–261; *Niles*, XLI, 335, 336.) On the same day they approved also of an elaborate report in defence of the policy of the State in regard to the Indians and to the missionaries. (*Acts of Georgia*, 1831, 266–274; *Niles*, XLII, 58–60.) In January, 1832, the Supreme Court heard proceedings on the writ of error in the case of *Worcester v. Georgia*, and pronounced the claims of Georgia unjustified, and the law in question unconstitutional, and that Worcester sentence was null and void. (6 *Peters*,

515; *Niles*, XLII, 40–56.) The authorities of Georgia refused to recognize the decision of the Court or to release the missionaries. (*Niles*, XLII, 78; XLIII, 251.) A sharp debate was precipitated in Congress by the presentation of a petition in behalf of the missionaries by John Quincy Adams, March 5, 1832. (*Cong. Debates*, 1831–32, 2010–2036.) A year later, after Worcester had notified the Governor of Georgia that he had withdrawn his suit before the Supreme Court, he and his associates were released from prison by pardon of Gov. Lumpkin, January 4, 1833. (*Niles*, XLIII, 382, 383, 419; XLIV, 359, 360.) The Cherokee Indians during the period 1829–1835, repeatedly presented memorials to Congress for a " redress of their wrongs and for the protection of the United States." A large number of petitions in their behalf came from all parts of the country, but Congress favored the administration policy of the removal of all the Indian tribes to the west of the Mississippi river, and May 28, 1830, a bill authorizing this policy became a law. (*U. S. Stat. at L.*, IV, 411, 412.) Finally, December 29, 1835, the Cherokees agreed to a treaty relinquishing all their lands east of the Mississippi. (*U. S. Stat. at L.*, VII, 478–486.)

Additional references.—Among the many documents the following are the most important: Memorials of the Cherokees, *House Exec. Doc.*, 20 *Cong.*, 2 *sess.*, IV, No. 145; *Reports of House Com.*, 21 *Cong.*, 1 *sess.*, III, No. 311; *House Exec. Doc.*, 21 *Cong.*, 2 *sess.*, III, No. 57; *Ibid.*, 22 *Cong.*, 1 *sess.*, II, No. 45; *Ibid.*, 22 *Cong.*, 2 *sess.*, I, No. 2, pp. 39–40: *Senate Doc.*, 23 *Cong.*, 1 *sess.*, V, No. 386; *Ibid.*, 23 *Cong.*, 2 *sess.*, III, No. 71. Letter of S. A. Worcester, March 15, 1830, relative to the condition and civilization of the Cherokees, *Senate Doc.*, 21 *Cong.*, 1 *sess.*, II, No. 110, pp. 19–22. Speech of Clay et al., Feb. 4, 1835, *Cong. Debates*, 1834–35, 289–309; Speech of Webster, Oct. 12, 1832, *Works*, I, 268–276. Consult *Niles' Register*, XXXV–XLIV, " *Index;*" *American Annual Register*, 1825–1833, (8 vols.) "*Contents*," "*Georgia*," and "*Documents*." *State Papers, Indian Affairs*, II, 502–511, 526–529, 699 702. Secondary works: McMaster, V, 175–178, 181–183, 537–540; Von Holst, I, 448–458; Lalor, I, 390–394; Peck, *The Jacksonian Epoch*, 250–256; Greeley, *Amer. Conflict*, I, 105, 106; Sumner, *Jackson*, 178–182; Schouler, III, 478–480.

---

60. Message of Governor Lumpkin Relative to the Case of Worcester.

November 25, 1831.

[In communicating to the Legislature the writ from the Supreme Court of the United States, he writes :—] The obvious object of the proceedings to which this notice and these citations relate, is to call in question, and attempt to overthrow, that essential jurisdiction of the State, in criminal cases, which has been vested by our Constitution, in the superior courts of the several counties of the State.

My respect for the Supreme Court of the United States as a fundamental department of the federal government, induces me to indulge the earnest hope, that no mandate will ever proceed from that Court, attempting or intending to control one of the sovereign States of this Union, in the free exercise of its constitutional, criminal or civil jurisdiction. " The powers not delegated by the Constitution of the United States, nor prohibited by it to the States, are reserved to the States respectively." Such a control over our criminal jurisdiction, as these proceedings indicate, it is believed, has not been delegated to the United States, and consequently cannot be acquiesced in or submitted to.

Any attempt to infringe the evident right of a State to govern the entire population within its territorial limits, and to punish all offences committed against its laws, within those limits, (due regard being had to the cases expressly excepted by the Constitution of the United States), would be the usurpation of a power never granted by the States. Such an attempt, whenever made, will challenge the most determined resistance ; and if persevered in, will inevitably eventuate in the annihilation of our beloved Union.

In exercising the duties of that department of government, which devolve on me, I will disregard all unconstitutional requisitions, of whatever character or origin they may be ; and to the best of my abilities, will protect and defend the rights of the State, and use the means afforded to me, to maintain its laws and Constitution.

[*Niles' Register*, XLI, 313.]

Resolutions of Other States Relative to Georgia and and the Supreme Court.

Georgia's defiance of the Supreme Court in the case of Tassels, as well as the renewed attempt in Congress in 1831, to restrict the jurisdiction of the Federal Courts (cf. *Ante*, 112) led the Legislature of Massachusetts, March 14, 1831, to pass resolutions condemning the course of Georgia, asserting the jurisdiction of the Federal Courts and the duty of the President to enforce the Constitution and laws of the United States. (*Resolves of Mass.*, 1828–1831, 512, 513; *American Annual Register*, 1830–31, 316, 317.) These resolves were sent to other States, and were indorsed by the Legislature of Connecticut in the subjoined report and resolutions. In transmitting the same to the Legislature of Massachusetts, Jan. 9, 1832, Governor Levi Lincoln commented on the situation at length, noting that "the recent measures which have been proposed in some of our sister States, can be viewed only with alarm for the very existence of the Republic, . . . their inevitable tendency is to division and separation." (*Resolves of Mass.*, 1832, 50–52.) The Legislatures of Pennsylvania and New Jersey also passed in 1831 resolutions in support of the supremacy and integrity of the Federal Judiciary. (*Session Laws of Penna.*, 1830–31, 505; *Annual Register*, 1830–31, 336–339; *Ibid.*, 1831–32, 250.)

---

61. Report and Resolutions of Connecticut.
May Session, 1831.

Your committee have also had under consideration certain resolutions of the Legislature of the Commonwealth of Massachusetts, relative to the judicial power of the United States—a subject of sufficient importance to justify a more extended notice.

At a period when, in some portions of our country, a disposition is manifested to array the jealousies of the people against the judicial department of the government of the United States, when executive officers are instructed, in all the formality of legislative enactment, to disregard the legal precepts of the Supreme Court of the United States—it well becomes those who regard a dissolution of our Union as one of the most dreadful of political evils, to interpose a mild, but firm expression of their opinion. The people by their sovereign pleasure, created by the same act the executive, legislative and judicial departments of the federal government. The inefficiency of the old confederation to secure respect and obedience, taught them the necessity of so organizing the federal government, that it could lay its hands on individuals, and thus directly enforce the laws of the Union, and protect those acting under them from injury or interruption, by the laws of any one of the states. It was the force of external circumstances only that gave to the recommendations of the old congress the authority of laws. When the outward pressure was removed, the Union was practically dissolved, and anarchy ensued. Without the judicial department, the Congress of the United States would now be but an assemblage of embassadors, whose efficiency would begin and end in advisory consultations; the people would obey, or not, as their interests and feelings might dictate. The courts of the several states partake, too readily of local jealousies and excitements, to be entrusted with the final determination of questions involving the validity or construction of the federal laws; and questions of policy of much less importance than those that now agitate our country, would soon put an end to our ephemeral Union. The judicial department, therefore constitutes one of those peculiarities, which distinguish the present government from the old confederation—a co-ordinate branch—which, in the opinion of your committee, is absolutely necessary for the successful organization of our government.

It being one of the first principles of a republic, that the legislative and judicial departments be kept entirely distinct, the patriot has nothing to apprehend from the power or ambition of the courts. Speaking of the three great departments, an eminent civilian says, " the judiciary is next to nothing." It has indeed no power over the wealth or strength of the nation. It has neither force nor will, but merely judgment, and can not enforce even that, without the aid of the executive. * * * An independent judiciary is absolutely indispensable, for the protection of the people in their reserved rights, and for the preservation of every department of the government in its appropriate and destined action. It is indeed the great balance wheel of the Constitution; which from its own weakness needs, and its inestimable value deserves the constant care and vigilance of the community, to protect it from the attacks of the other departments of the government, both state and federal. * * *

Resolved, [Here follows quotation from Art. VI, § 2, of U. S. Const.]

Resolved, That we regard the judicial department of the government of the United States, as sacred in its origin, and invaluable in its purposes and objects, as either the executive or legislative departments; and we also regard the designs of any community, to destroy it, or to paralyze its influence, among the people of these states, as the manifestation of feelings, unfriendly to the permanent interests of our common country.

[From Copy in the *Journal of the House of Representatives of Pennsylvania*, 1831–32, II, 41–43.]

THE TARIFF AND NULLIFICATION, 1820–1833.

Tariff and Internal Improvements.

A reaction against the broad construction and nationalizing tendencies, which had characterized the policy of the dominant portion of the Democratic-Republican party in the period immediately following the close of the War of 1812–15, gradually began to show itself. First in the opposition to the United States Bank (see *ante*, pp, 89–103), and then to federal legislation relative to internal improvement and a protective tariff. The change in the attitude of the South from one of advocacy to that of opposition was very marked and significant. In Congress this change first became evident in connection with the internal improvement discussions, but after 1820 the hostility of the South to a protective tariff increasingly developed.

Opposition to the doctrine of broad construction led those who objected to a protective tariff on constitutional grounds to oppose also the other important feature of the so-called "American System," namely, national aid to internal improvement. This was necessary on ground of consistency, if for no other. It is not surprising therefore to find generally in the series of resolutions passed by the Southern States, during the period 1825–1832, condemnation of both the protective tariff and internal improvement acts. This was especially true to 1827. In fact, contemporary evidence indicates that more emphasis was placed upon the opposition to federal internal improvement measures than to the protective tariff bills prior to that date. In support of this statement may be cited the message of Governor Wilson of South Carolina in 1824, and that of Governor Tyler of Virginia in 1826, as also the correspondence of Jefferson and Madison for 1824–26, in all of which the subject of internal improvement measures is alone considered. After 1827 the tariff question came to the front and remained of chief importance during the remainder of the period. The close connection between the two subjects was pointed out at the time of Jackson's veto of the Maysville Road Bill, in 1830, by the Southern press and political leaders (*Niles*, XXXVIII, 319–321, 379; *post* p. 164), but the chief opposition continued to be directed against the protective tariff measures.

References: For monographic accounts of the tariff controversy see O. L. Elliott, *The Tariff Controversy in the United States*, Palo Alto, Cal., 1892; C. W. Harris, *The Sectional Struggle*, Phila., 1902 (full synopsis of the debates in Congress). F. W. Taussig, *Tariff History of the United States*, 17–24, 68–108. General References; The Tariff: Burgess, *Middle Period*, 10–12, 108–116, 157–163, 170–178; McMaster, IV, 490–494, 510–521; V, 229–267; Schouler, III, 173, 296–298, 382–385, 420–426, 468; Sumner, *Jackson*, 194–206; Von Holst, I, 396–400; Lalor, III, 859–864; Ballagh in *Amer. Hist. Assoc. Reports*, 1898, esp. 221–241. Internal Improvement: Burgess, 14–18, 116–122, 155, 157, 166–170; McMaster, IV, 410–415, 422–426; V, 147–150, 252, 263; Schouler, III, 247–254; 295, 296, 382–385, 480; Sumner, *Jackson*, 191–194; Von Holst, I, 389–396; Lalor, II, 568–571.

62. Report Adopted by the House of Representatives of South Carolina.

December, 1820.

The gradualness of the change in the attitude of the South on these questions is well illustrated by the growth of the opposition in the South Carolina Legislature, which was the first to officially denounce the constitutionality of the internal improvement and protective tariff acts. This is revealed in the documents for the years 1820–25, which follow. The first of these shows that in 1820, while a majority of the House of Representatives was opposed to the restrictive system on grounds of policy, they apparently conceded its constitutionality, and deprecated the memorializing of Congress. As the Journals of the General Assembly of South Carolina were not published until 1830, the text of this report is taken from *Niles*, XIX, 345, 346, and *Ibid.*, XLIII, 128. It is also given in the *Statutes at Large of South Carolina* (Thomas Cooper, editor), I, 226, 227 (Columbia, S. C., 1836), with acknowledgments to Niles. It does not appear to have passed the Senate, as Dr. Cooper states that it is not given in the Manuscript Journals or the published Pamphlet Laws.

The committee to whom was referred the preamble and resolutions submitted by the honorable member from Chesterfield,

(Pleasant May, esq.) on the subject of the Tariff proposed at the last session of congress. Respectfully Report:

That although your committee do, in common, they believe, with the great majority of their fellow-citizens, and particularly those in the Southern and Eastern States, entirely concur with the honorable member, so far as the general principles of political economy involved in the resolutions, are concerned: Although they most earnestly deprecate the restrictive system attempted to be forced upon the nation, as premature and pernicious—as a wretched expedient to repair the losses incurred in some commercial districts, by improvident and misdirected speculation: or as a still more unwarrantable project to make the most important interests of the country subservient to the most inconsiderable, and to compel those parts of the union which are *still* prosperous and flourishing, to contribute even by their utter ruin, to fill the coffers of a few monopolists in the others—

Yet when they reflect that the necessity at that time, universally felt, of regulating the commerce of the country by more enlarged and uniform principles was the first motive that induced the calling of a convention in '87 : When they consider that among the powers expressly given up by the states and vested in congress by the constitution, is this very one of enacting all laws relating to commerce :

Above all, when they advert to the consequences likely to result from the practice, unfortunately become too common, of arraying upon the questions of national policy, the states as *distinct and independent sovereignties* in opposition to, or, (what is much the same thing) with a view to exercise a control *over* the general government—Your committee feel it to be their indispensable duty to protest against a measure, of which they conceive the tendency to be so mischievous, and to recommend to the house, that, upon this, as on every other occasion, on which the general welfare of the republic is in question, they adhere to those wise, liberal and magnanimous principles by which this state has been hitherto so proudly distinguished.

In consideration of the above reasons, your Committee are of opinion that the preamble and resolutions referred to them be rejected.

South Carolina on the Powers of the Federal Government.

1824-1825.

Subsequent to the adoption of the preceding report, the question of the constitutionality of a protective tariff law had been clearly raised in Congress during the discussions preliminary to the passage of the act of 1824. In this
some of the South Carolina delegation led the way. (Mitchell, *Annals*, 17
Cong., 2 *sess.*, 1002; Hamilton, *Annals*, 18 *Cong.*, 1 *sess.*, II, 2207, 2208;
Hayne, *Ibid.*, I, 648, 649, also Barbour of Va., *Ibid.*, II, 1918–1920.) In
sympathy with this strict construction attitude, Governor Wilson called attention of the Legislature to the drift toward a "consolidated government," in
the subjoined passage taken from his annual message of December, 1824. It
is noteworthy that in proof of this he expressly refers to the internal improvement legislation of Congress, but fails to mention the tariff act of 1824. (Act
May 22, U. S. Stat. at L., IV, 25–30.) This would seem to indicate that up
to this time the internal improvement question was considered a more vital
issue than that of protection. Acting upon the Governor's suggestion the
Senate, Dec. 13, 1824, passed a series of resolves, which had been drawn by
Judge William Smith, denouncing as unconstitutional both the internal improvement and the protective tariff measures of the federal government, by a
vote of 30 to 13. (*Niles*, XXVII, 272, 338; *Ibid.*, XLIII, 128; *National
Intelligencer*, Dec. 24, 1824.) These were tabled in the House of Representatives, and a Report and Resolutions from the Select Committee were
adopted instead. The third, fourth and fifth resolves are notable, as they take
issue with the Senate, denying the right of the Legislature to question the acts
of the Federal Government. (*National Intelligencer*, Jan. 1, 1825; *Niles*,
XLIII, 128.) Extracts from this report and the resolutions follow. By the
next year the change in public opinion had so affected the House of Representatives that the same series of resolves which had received the approval of
the Senate the previous year were now introduced and passed by the House,
December 15, 1825, by a vote of 73 to 38. They were agreed to by the Sen-
ate on the following day, and were the first official condemnation by any State
Legislature of the internal improvement and protective tariff acts. (*Acts and
Resolutions of South Carolina*, 1825, 88, 89; *Statutes at Large* (Cooper ed.),
I, 228, 229; *Niles*, XXIX, 293; *Amer. Annual Register*, 1825–26, 342, 343.)
Contemporary works: Dr. Thomas Cooper published a pamphlet entitled *A
Tract on the Proposed Alteration of the Tariff submitted to the consideration
of the members from South Carolina in the ensuing Congress of 1823–4.*
Charleston, 1823. Reprinted Phila., 1824. 27 pages. Hayne's speech was
issued in pamphlet form. *Speech of Mr. Hayne against the Tariff Bill, April,
1824.* Charleston, 1824. 48 pages. For a recent study of South Carolina's
change of attitude cf. Houston, *Nullification in South Carolina*, esp. ch. IV.

63. Extract from Governor Wilson's Message to the Legislature, December, 1824.

There is one subject of deep and vital importance to the stability of the General and State Governments, to which I beg leave to invite your attention. Every friend of our present constitution, in its original purity, cannot but have witnessed the alarming extent to which the Federal Judiciary and Congress have gone toward establishing a great and consolidated government, subversive of the rights of the States and contravening the letter and spirit of the Constitution of the Union. The act of the last session of Congress appropriating money to make surveys,[1] is but an entering wedge which will be followed, no doubt by the expenditure of millions, unless the People apply the proper corrective, the day, I fear, is not far distant, when South Carolina shall be grievously assessed, to pay for the cutting of a canal across Cape Cod. None of the friends to the assumed powers of the General Government pretend to derive them from any specific grant of power in the Constitution, but claim them as implied, resulting or necessary to the common defence and general welfare. The construction contended for by them is an open violation of that which has heretofore universally been admitted the true rule for expounding all grants. It never for a moment entered into the imagination of the members of the convention that formed the union that they were surrendering the sovereignty and independence of the states. On the contrary, there was a universal sensitiveness on that point, which produced the section which declared all power not expressly granted to be reserved to the people or the states. Whenever we become a great consolidated nation, the day will soon arrive when we shall crumble into as many parts as there are cardinal points of the compass. It is our duty as public sentinels to give the alarm, in order that those who are friendly to the present constitution may preserve it in its original purity. The opinions of men in high office on this point should be known, that they may be properly appreciated by the people, who alone possess the corrective in their elective franchise.

[*National Intelligencer*, Dec. 13, 1824.]

---

[1] Act of April 30, 1824, *U. S. Stat. at L.*, IV, 22.

64. Extract from A Report and the Resolves of the House of Representatives of South Carolina, December, 1824.

Every citizen of these United States owes a double allegiance; namely to the government of the United States, and to the government of the individual State to which he may belong. He has no right to give an undue preference to either, to elevate or depress one at the expense of the other; but both, like his parents are equally entitled to his love and reverence. That man, therefore, who disseminates doctrines whose tendency is to give an unconstitutional preponderance to State, or United States' rights, must be regarded as inimical to the forms of government, under which we have hitherto so happily lived, and which the best men of our country have unceasingly prayed may be perpetual.

* * * * * * *

Resolved, That all power is inherent in the People; and governments are instituted for their welfare.

2. *Resolved*, That legislative representatives, are the limited agents or servants of the People, and not their sovereigns; and that they can legally do no act adverse to the interests of the People, or beyond the scope of their authority.

3. *Resolved*, That the People have conferred no power upon their State Legislature to impugn the Acts of the Federal Government or the decisions of the Supreme Court of the United States.[1]

4. *Resolved*, That any exercise of such a power by this state would be an act of usurpation.

5. *Resolved*, That the Representatives of the People in Congress are only responsible under God to the People themselves.

6. *Resolved*, That the People of this State are quite competent to the superintendence and control of the conduct of their

---

[1] Hon. Geo. McDuffie, of South Carolina, Feb. 5, 1824, delivered a speech in Congress relative to the distribution of powers, and in defence of implied powers. In it he said, "The Convention did not regard the State Governments as sentinels upon the watch-towers of freedom or in any respect more worthy of confidence than the General Government." The House of Representatives of his State evidently shared his views at this time, but both soon changed. (*Annals of Congress*, 18 *Cong.*, I *sess.*, 1372.)

Representatives in Congress as well as their Representatives in this Legislature.

7. *Resolved*, That the State Legislature has no power to propose amendments of the Constitution of the United States, but only to apply to Congress to call a Convention of the People for that purpose.

8. *Resolved*, That the liberty of the People of this Country will be seriously endangered, whenever they permit their servants in this Legislature or in Congress to use any power not delegated to them.

[*National Intelligencer*, January 1, 1825.]

65. South Carolina on Internal Improvements and the Tariff, December 16, 1825.

* * * Among those rights retained in this [the federal] constitution to the people, is, the unalienable right of remonstrating against any encroachments upon that constitution by the Congress of the United States, or any other officer belonging or acting under the General Government.

This right is not only retained and unalienable, but it is the birth right of every freeman. It belongs to him either in his individual or aggregate, his private or political capacity. To restrain it when respectfully exercised, would be to establish that odious doctrine of non resistance and perfect obedience.

The Committee therefore respectfully recommends to this House the adoption of the following Resolutions :—

1. *Resolved*, That Congress does not possess the power, under the constitution, to adopt a general system of internal improvement as a national measure.

2. *Resolved.* That a right to impose and collect taxes, does not authorize Congress to lay a tax for any other purposes than such as are necessarily embraced in the specific grants of power, and those necessarily implied therein.

3. *Resolved*, That Congress ought not to exercise a power granted for particular objects, to effect other objects, the right to effect which has never been conceded.

4. *Resolved*, That it is an unconstitutional exercise of power,

on the part of Congress, to tax the citizens of one State to make roads and canals for the citizens of another State.

5. *Resolved*, That it is an unconstitutional exercise of power, on the part of Congress, to lay duties to protect domestic manufactures.

[*Acts of South Carolina*, 1825, 88, 89.].

Resolves of Virginia.
1826-1827.

Virginia was the next State to declare against the broad construction policy. The correspondence of Jefferson and Madison for the years 1824–1826 reveal their especial concern in regard to the internal improvement legislation of the federal government. Shortly after President Adams' first message, in which he advocated a liberal internal improvement policy (Richardson, II, 311), Jefferson in a letter to Madison, of December 24, 1825, suggested the desirability of the Legislature of Virginia passing a new set of resolutions, following the precedent of 1798, declaring the obnoxious laws null and void, and he enclosed the draft of such a document, entitled " The Solemn Declaration and Protest of the Commonwealth of Virginia, on the principles of the Constitution of the United States of America, and on the violation of them." (Letter in Jefferson's *Works*, VII, 422–424; *Writings*, X, 348, 349; Draft of Protest, *Works*, IX, 496; *Writings*, X, 349–352; both in *Niles*, XXXVII, 79, 80.) Madison replied advising against this course. (*Works*, III, 511–514.) Jefferson in an interesting letter of Jan. 2, 1826, acquiesced, in view of the protest of South Carolina and of the fact that a proposed amendment expressly granting the power over internal improvement was before Congress, and that " opposition would come with more hope of success from any other State than from Virginia and South Carolina." (*Writings* X, 359.) For other interesting letters of the two ex-Presidents, see Jefferson's *Works*, VII, 336, 337, 426–428; *Writings*, X, 91, 299–301, 354–356, 358, 359; Madison's *Works*, III, 483, 506–510, 528–530. The amendment before Congress, like similar propositions in previous years, received little consideration. (Ames, *Proposed Amendments*, 261, 262.) The Legislature of Maryland, which was foremost in the advocacy of a national system of internal improvement, already in 1823 proposed an amendment to the Constitution to set at rest any doubt as to the power of Congress. (*Laws of Md.*, 1822–23, 140; *Annals*, 17 *Cong.*, 2 *sess.*, 698.) In reply to the resolves of South Carolina of December, 1825, denying this power, the Legislature, Jan. 14, 1826, adopted resolutions declaring that " Congress does possess the power under the Constitution, to adopt a general system of internal improvement." (*Laws of Maryland*, 1825–26, 236.)

In view of this situation the Legislature of Virginia, March 4, 1826, felt called upon to commit itself anew to the doctrine of 1798, and to record its condemnation of the obnoxious policy of the federal government in the resolutions given below. (*Acts of Virginia*, 1825-26, 114.) The final vote in the House on the preamble and resolutions was 120 yeas to 27 nays, and in the Senate 12 yeas to 8 nays. The text, vote and press comments are given in *Niles*, XXX, 38. At the opening of the next session of the Legislature, Governor John Tyler in his message of Dec. 4, 1826, in a rhetorical passage, pointed out "that more danger is to be apprehended to the State authorities by the exertion of the assumed power over roads and canals by the General Government than from almost any other source." (*Journal of House of Delegates*, 1826–27, 6 *et seq.;* also quoted in *Life of John Tyler*, 86, 87 [N. Y., 1844]; *National Intelligencer*, December 27, 1826.) This, together with the renewed efforts of the protectionists in Congress to secure an increased tariff (Jan. 17–March 4, 1827), led early in 1827, under the leadership of Mr. Giles, to the appointment of a Special Committee to inquire into the power and jurisdiction of the General Government. The Committee presented a long argumentative report, concluding with the subjoined resolutions. The vote of both branches is given in brackets after each resolve. The text is in the *Acts of Virginia*, 1826–27, 135, 136; the report, account of the debate and the vote, and other documents, are given in *Niles*, XXXII, 135-139, 167-170. Madison's letter of Feb. 7, 1827, commenting upon the proposed action of the Legislature is of interest. (*Works*, III, 551.)

66. Resolutions of Virginia, March 4th, 1826.

This General Assembly having carefully reviewed the resolutions of the sessions of 1798, and the report in support of them of 1799, and deeming the compact, on which they are a commentary, as unchanged in the powers which it delegates to the General Government, and the rights which are reserved to the States, doth now again " most solemnly declare a warm attachment to the union of the States, to maintain which, it pledges all its powers; and that for this end, it is their duty to watch over and oppose every infraction of those principles, which constitute the only basis of that Union, because, a faithful observance of them, can alone secure its existence and the public happiness:" "And doth further explicitly and peremptorily declare, that it views the powers of the Federal Government, as resulting from the compact to which the States are parties; as limited by the plain sense and intention of the instrument constituting that compact; as no farther valid than they are authorised by the grants enumerated in that compact; and that, in case of a deliberate, palpable and dangerous exercise of other powers, not granted by the said compact, the States who are parties thereto, have the right, and are in duty bound to interpose for arresting the progress of the evil, and for maintaining, within their respective limits, the authorities, rights and liberties appertaining to them."

In the opinion of this General Assembly, the principles here asserted, and the reasoning contained in the said report, apply with full force against the powers assumed by Congress, in the act imposing additional duties on foreign articles, for the promotion of American manufactures, and the acts directing surveys of routes for roads and canals, preparatory to a general system of internal improvement:

1. Be it therefore *Resolved*, That the imposition of taxes and duties, by the Congress of the United States, for the purpose of protecting and encouraging domestic manufactures, is an unconstitutional exercise of power, and is highly oppressive and partial in its operation. [House, 138 to 23; Senate, 12 to 9.]

2. *Resolved*, That the Congress of the United States does not possess the power, under the Constitution, to adopt a general system of internal improvement in the States, as a national measure. [House, 128 to 24; Senate, 15 to 6.]

3. *Resolved*, That the appropriation of money by the Congress of the United States, to construct roads and canals in the States is a violation of the Constitution. [House, 127 to 26; Senate, 12 to 8.]

[*Acts of Virginia*, 1825–26, 114.]

67. Resolutions of Virginia, March 6, 1827.

* * * The General Assembly of Virginia, actuated, as it always has been, by the most sincere disposition for the preservation of the Union of these States—believing that the Union can only be preserved, by keeping the General and State Governments within their respective spheres of action, as marked out by the Constitution of the United States—being also sincerely desirous that the General Government should be protected in the full and free exercise of all the specified powers granted to it by the Constitution of the United States—and being, at the same time, deeply impressed with a sense of its own duty, to preserve,

unimpaired, all the rights of the People and Government of this State, conferred upon it by the Constitution of the State, and of the United States—find itself reluctlantly constrained to enter its most solemn protest against the usurpations of the General Government as described in the report of its committee— Therefore,

1. *Resolved,* That this General Assembly, in behalf of the People and Government of this State, does, hereby, most solemnly protest against the claim or exercise of any power whatever, on the part of the General Government, to make internal improvements within the limits and jurisdiction of the several States, and particularly within the limits of the State of Virginia;—and also, against the claim or exercise of any power whatever, asserting or involving a jurisdiction over any part of the territory within the limits of this State, except over the objects and in the mode specified in the Constitution of the United States.   [House, 134 to 47 ; Senate, 15 to 7.]

2. *Resolved,* in like manner, that this General Assembly does hereby, most solemnly protest against any claim or exercise of power, whatever, on the part of the General Government, which serves to draw money from the inhabitants of this State, into the Treasury of the United States, and to disburse it for any object whatever, except for carrying into effect the grants of power to the General Government, contained in the Constitution of the United States.   [House, 159 to 19 ; Senate, 18 to 4.]

3. *Resolved,* in like manner, that this General Assembly does most solemnly protest against the claim or exercise of any power, whatever, on the part of the General Government, to protect domestic manufactures, the protection of manufactures not being amongst the grants of power to that Government, specified in the Constitution of the United States;—and also, against the operations of the act of Congress, passed May 22d, 1824, entitled, "An act to amend the several acts imposing duties on imports," generally called the tariff law, which vary the distribution of the proceeds of the labor of the community, in such a manner, as to transfer property from one portion of the United States to another and to take private property from the owner for the benefit of another person, not rendering public service ;—as unconstitu-

tional, unwise, unjust, unequal and oppressive. [House, 132 to
49 ; Senate, 14 to 8.]

[*Acts of Virginia*, 1826-27, 135, 136.]

---

68.   South Carolina and the Harrisburg Convention.
December 19, 1827.

The failure of the tariff bill of 1827, by the casting vote of Calhoun, led to
renewed efforts by the protectionists, which culminated in the Harrisburg
Convention of the Friends of Domestic Industry, which was in session July 30
to Aug. 3, 1827. It addressed a memorial to Congress, and through committees issued several addresses upon the commercial and economic conditions
of the country, with a view to influencing legislation in favor of protection.
(Minutes of Proceedings, *Niles*, XXXII, 388, 395; Memorial to Congress,
Ibid., 395-396; Addresses of Committees, *Ibid.*, XXXIII, 100-112, 123-128,
138-144, 149-160, 171-176, 188-192, 203-207.   See also *Amer. Annual
Reg.*, 1827-29, 39-41; Taussig, 82-85; McMaster, V, 245-247, 249-251;
Elliott, 239-242.)   The increased demands and activities of the protectionists
aroused emphatic protests from the South.   A popular agitation in South
Carolina, in which Dr. Cooper was prominent, found expression in the adoption of Memorials by citizens in various parts of the State addressed to the
State Legislature and to Congress. (*Niles* XXXIII, 26-32; McMaster, 247-
249 (Cooper's speech); Elliott, 244-249; Houston, chs. III and IV.)   These
condemned a protective tariff in strong language.   One such declared, " we
exist as a member of the Union *merely as an object of taxation*," and called
upon the State Legislature "to devise some means of freeing your fellow
citizens from a yoke too heavy to be borne."   Congress was warned that "the
inequalities and injustices of this state of things is becoming too glaring to
remain unnoticed, and the burthens it imposes on us is too *heavy to be borne
in silence any longer*." (*Niles*, XXXIII, 59, 60.)   Governor John Tayler, in
his message at the opening of the Legislature in November, 1827, called attention to the schemes of the Harrisburg Convention, and to the petitions and
remonstrances of the people. (*Ibid.*, 232.)   A Special Committee presented
an elaborate report and resolutions.   The former announced "that the period
has arrived when remonstrance is not only proper, but its neglect would be a
crime; seems to be the voice of South Carolina."   The resolutions follow.
The text of report and resolution are in *Acts of South Carolina*, 1827 28,
69-78; *House Doc.*, 20 Cong., 1 sess., 1827-28, III, *No.* 65; *Senate Doc.*, II,
No. 29; *Amer. State Papers, Finance*, V, 724-730; see also *Amer. Annual
Reg.*, 1827-29, I, pt. II, 136, 137; *Niles*, XXXIII, 275; McMaster, V, 252.

1. *Resolved*, That the Constitution of the United States is a
compact between the people of the different States with each

other, *as separate, independent sovereignties;*[1] and that for any
violation of the letter or spirit of that compact by the Congress
of the United States, it is not only the right of the *people*, but of
the *Legislatures*, who represent them to every extent not limited,
to remonstrate against violations of the fundamental compact.

2. *Resolved*, That the acts of Congress, known by the name of
Tariff Laws, the object of which is not the raising of revenues,
or the regulation of foreign commerce, but the promotion of
domestic manufactures, are violations of the Constitution in its
spirit, and ought to be repealed.

3. *Resolved*, That Congress has no power to construct roads
and canals in the States, for the purpose of internal improvement,
with or without the assent of the States in whose limits those
internal improvements are made ; the authority of Congress extending no further than to pass the *" necessary* and *proper* laws "
to carry into execution their enumerated powers.

4. *Resolved*, That the American Colonization Society is not
an object of national interest, and that Congress has no power in
any way to patronise, or direct appropriations for the benefit of
this or any other society.

5. *Resolved*, That our Senators in Congress be instructed, and
our Representatives requested, to continue to oppose every increase of the Tariff, *with a view to protect domestic manufactures,*
and all *appropriations to the purposes of internal improvements* of
the United States, and all *appropriations in favor of the Colonization Society*, or the *patronage of the same,* either directly or
indirectly, by the General Government. [Resolutions of transmission.]

[1] The report preceding the resolutions combats the view that the Federal
Constitution emanated from the people, as " one of the most dangerous doctrines that can be promulgated," and takes issue with the opinion of the U. S.
Supreme Court in the case of McCulloch *vs.* Maryland on this point. They
also declare " that collisions will sometimes arise between the States and Congress, when it would not only be unwise, but even unsafe, to submit questions
of disputed sovereignty to any judiciary tribunal;" " least of all ought the
States to consent to make the Supreme Court of the United States the arbiter
finally to decide points of vital importance to the States."

69. Extract from the Report of Georgia on the Tariff and Internal Improvements.

December 24, 1827.

Governor Troup in his message of Nov. 6, 1827, recommended the Legislature to adopt a "firm remonstrance" to Congress, and if this should be "unheeded" to address "the States having common interest with yourselves, and to suggest the expediency of concurring in a non-consumption agreement to be carried into effect by all the means which are constitutionally given to their respective legislatures." (*Niles*, XXXIII, 221, 222.) Acting upon the suggestion the Legislature adopted an argumentative report, presented by Judge Clayton, extracts from which follow. Text, *Acts of Georgia*, 1827, 203-214; *House Doc.*, 20 *Cong.*, 1 *sess.*, III, *No.* 120; *Amer. State Papers, Finance*, V, 852-857; *Niles*, XXXIII, 325-328; *Amer. Annual Reg.*, 1827-29, I, pt. II, 140.

The Committee are aware that it is assumed by the General Government, as expressed in the decisions of the Federal Court, that State Legislatures have no right to complain of its usurpations, however formidable or fatal. That the General Government is said to be " truly and emphatically a Government of the People," and, therefore, entirely out of the reach of representative bodies, whose sole duty it is to keep within the sphere of their own delegated trust. It would seem that, if even such a pretension were admissible, it should be considered no great breach of decorum, for a sovereign State, through its heighest known authority, to approach a Government it had contributed to establish, with a subject of complaint, especially, when it is perceived that much inferior bodies are patiently listened to, and listened to with effect. While manufacturing companies and self-created delegates, pretending to represent whole States, assemble for the purpose of directing the Congress what measures they must adopt, surely the Legislature of a State, without much violence to any known rule of modesty, may respectfully offer a counter remonstrance to such a growing temper of dictation. But it is not in this humble manner that your Committee would recommend the Legislature to prefer their just complaints to the General Government. They claim it as a right to remonstrate with that Government on all measues which they may conceive violative of the fundamental principles of its institutions. They affirm that those who create a delegated Government, have lawfully the power to restrain it within its proper bounds, and maintain the doctine asserted by Luther Martin, in his address to the Legislature of Maryland at the time of the adoption of the Federal Constitution, that " the proper constituents of the General Government are the States, and the States are to that Government what the People are to the States; that, this is entirely within the spirit and intention of the Federal Union."

[Here follows a lengthy argument in support of the view " ' that the terms of the grant, in the Federal Constitution, did not convey sovereign powers generally, but sovereign power limited to particular cases, and with *restrictive means* for executing such powers;' and further, that the powers ' were delegated, not by the People of United States at *large*, but by the People of the *respective States;* and that, therefore, it was a compact between the different *States;* ' " and that the Legislature is the guardian of the rights of the people from the encroachments of the General Government. This is supplemented by an elaborate argument in support of strict construction. The report concludes as follows :]

The Committee are fully sensible that every degree of moderation is due to the question, upon which they have founded the present serious complaint; but they owe it to truth and sincerity to say, that it is their decided opinion an increase of Tariff duties will and ought to be RESISTED by all legal and constitutional means, so as to avert the crying injustice of such an unconstituional measure.

They are constrained, too, to say, that this State ought to *oppose*, in every possible shape, the exercise of the power, on the part of the General Government, to encourage domestic manufactures or to promote internal improvement. They will not pretend, at present, to recommend the mode of OPPOSITION; but they will recommend the peaceable course of remonstrating with Congress on the subject, and of asking of that body to pause before it proceeds any further in measures that must inevitably destroy the affection of some of the States for the General Government. It will detract nothing from the firmness or wisdom of the Congress to listen to the voice of State Legislatures, while it is considering the memorials of *manufacturing companies.*

If to the contempt of *right*, there should be added the jealousy of *partiality*, it must be obvious to all that there will be an increased account of unmerited aggravation. How long a People shall be permitted to complain, or how much they can be made to suffer, has always been a matter of dangerous experiment or doubtful calculation; and knowledge, acquired under either issue, has never been without its certain and severe regrets. In conclusion your Committee recommend the following resolution:

Resolved, That His Excellency the Governor be, and he is, hereby requested to cause the foregoing report to be laid before Congress at its next session. And that he forward a copy of the same to each of the other States, to be laid before their respective Legisatures, for the concurrence of such as may approve of the principles therein avowed; and, as due notice to those who may dissent from the same, that Georgia as one of the contracting parties to the Federal Constitntion, and possessing equal rights with the other contracting party, will insist upon the construction of that instrument, contained in said REPORT, and will SUBMIT to no other.

---

70.   Extract from Report of North Carolina on the Tariff.

January, 1828.

Governor Burton, in his message of Nov. 21, 1827, referring to the exertion of South Carolina against the proposed increase in the tariff declares that "the dignity and interest of the State requires that North Carolina should not be silent." (*Niles*, XXXIII, 283.) The Legislature, acting upon this sugges-gestion, adopted the subjoined report. The text is given in *Exec. Doc.*, 20 *Cong.*, 1 *sess.*, III, *No.* 62; *Senate Doc.*, I, *No.* 30; *Amer. State Papers*, *Finance*, V, 721, 722. See McMaster, V, 251, 252.

The People of North Carolina * * * have seldom expressed a legislative opinion upon the measures of the General Government; being at all times, willing to give a full and fair opportunity to those charged with the management of public affairs, of being "judged by their measures." But a crisis has arisen in the political affairs of our country, which demands a prompt and decisive expression of public opinion. Under such circumstances, silence would be injustice to ourselves, and a want of candor to the other States of the Union.

The Committee are of opinion, that interests, either pecuniary or political, is the great point of union, from the smallest association up to the Confederacy of the United States; and that, whenever a system of policy is pursued by the General Government which strikes at the very foundation of the Union, it is the right of every member of the Confederacy to call their attention to the fundamental principles upon which the Government was formed; and if, they persist in measures ruinous in themselves, the question may fairly be discussed whether the checks and balances of the Government have not been overthrown; whether they have been instrumental in producing so onerous an effect; and whether the benefits of the Union are not more than counterbalanced by the evils.

The Committee will not assert that Congress have no power, under the Constitution, to lay duties on imports, which are intended to operate as a *protection* to manufactures; they maintain, however, that the *exercise* of such a power, as contemplated by the Woollens Bill, is a direct violation of the spirit of that instrument, and repugnant to the objects for which it was formed.

* * * It is conceded, that Congress have the express power to lay imposts; but it is maintained, that *that* power was given for the purpose of revenue, and revenue alone; and that any other use of the power is usurpation on the part of Congress.

*   *   *   *   *   *

Manufactures, in the United States, are not an object of *general* interest but of *local* interest; and yet they have received from the Government, not only a moderate and just encouragement, under the operation of a tariff of duties on imports, for purposes of revenue, but a protection by an enormous duty upon importations; which palsies every effort of the agriculturist, withers the product of his industry, and greatly impairs foreign commerce.

The Committee are of opinion, that the woollens bill, which received in the Congress of the United States, at its last session, so full and fair an investigation, is a measure, above all others which has ever occupied the attention of that enlightened body, calculated to produce an enormous tax on the agriculture of the

South, and to be destructive of revenue. They believe it to be a bill artfully designed for the advancement of the incorporated companies of New England, and admirably adapted to its end. They believe it fatal to the happiness, the morals, and the rights, of a large portion of our common country ; for it has its foundation in avarice, and consumes every patriotic feeling.

If such is the character and the operation of this measure, who can tell how long this Union can exist under it, and how soon may be realized the soul-chilling prediction, that " It is a rope of sand?"   *   *   *

71.   Remonstrance of Alabama.

January 15, 1828.

The following extract is the concluding passage of the Remonstrance, vigorously arraigning the Harrisburg Convention and the protectionists, adopted by the Legislature. The text is given in *Acts of Alabama*, 1827–28, 169–172; *Senate Doc.*, 20 *Cong.*, 1 *sess.*, III, *No.* 66; *House Exec. Doc.*, III, *No.* 113; *Amer. State Papers, Finance*, V, 848.

The allied powers of avarice, monopoly and ambition, through the Harrisburg Convention, and every subordinate channel of importunity at their command, call for a further subsidy on the labor of the South and Southwest, in the shape of a woolens bill, to pamper the gentlemen wool-growers and wool-carders of the Northeast ; and this, too at a time when agriculture is languishing and prostate, yielding a bare support to those who pursue it, and the mercantile and shipping interests partaking of the languor, and manufactures alone in a flourishing and prosperous condition. The interest least in need, thus urging, by the aid of such powerful political machinery, a further tribute from the interest least able to bear it, is surely sufficient to prove to Congress how vain and fruitless is the attempt to satisfy the inordinate cravings of the monopolist : one exaction leads to another, and every concession generates a new and more exorbitant demand.

When combinations, thus formidable, endeavor to throw the overgrown weight of the General Government upon the Southern and Southwestern States, dry up their commerce by sapping its foundation, degrade them from the proved equality of the Compact, into the humiliating condition of dependent tributaries to the greedy monopolists of the North and East—the victims would deserve the oppression, were they not promptly to interpose the most determined and unyielding resistance.

Let it not be again said, that, because the Southwest and South send no agents to beset the members of Congress, and have foreborne to petition or remonstrate in every village, or to call a counter-convention, that they are so recreant to duty as to acquiesce in the proposed oppression. On the contrary, let it be distinctly understood, that Alabama, in common with the Southern and Southwestern States, regards the power assumed by the General Government to control her internal concerns, by protecting duties, beyond the fair demands of the revenue, as a palpable usurpation of a power not given by the Constitution; and the proposed woollens bill, as a species of oppression little less than legalized pillage on the property of her citizens, to which she can never submit, until the constitutional means of resistance shall be exhausted.

72. Counter Resolutions.

1828.

Several of the Northern States either made reply to certain of the foregoing protests or passed resolutions favoring an increase of the tariff. Of the former class were the resolutions of Ohio, adopted Feb. 12, 1828, dissenting from the resolutions of South Carolina of 1827 (*Amer. State Papers, Finance*, V, 879), and of New Jersey, of March 4, 1828, in reply to South Carolina and Georgia, asserting the constitutionality of a protective tariff. (*Ibid.*, 964; *Laws of New Jersey*, 1827–28, 215.) Governor Lincoln, in transmitting the Georgia report to the Massachusetts Legislature, commented upon it as follows: "How far declarations thus threatening the very existence of the Confederacy are called for by any occasion, or in what better manner they can be met, than with a sad and reproving silence, I respectfully submit to your dispassionate consideration." "The concurrence of Massachusetts in the political doctrines avowed in the Report could not have been anticipated;—and the receipt of the documents may therefore the rather be regarded as notice to her of a determination not to submit to the construction of the Constitution, which probably *will be maintained here*, with a purpose as firm, if not in language, as ardent, as shall enforce the Resolves of the Sister State." (*Resolves of Mass.*, 1824–28, 679; *Niles*, XXXIV, 6.) Other resolutions favoring an increase in the protective tariff were passed in the winter of 1827–28 by the Legislatures of several States, typical of which are those of Pennsylvania (*Pamphlet Laws*, 1827–28, 496), Rhode Island, Indiana, Ohio and New York. (*Amer. State Papers, Finance*, V, 757, 873, 884; *Laws of Indiana*, 1827–28, 143; *Laws of New York*, 1828, 491.)

Remonstrance against the Tariff of 1828.

The passage of the "tariff of abominations" (Act of May 19, 1828, *U. S. Stat. at L.*, IV, 270–275) greatly increased the popular agitation in the South. During the summer and fall of 1828 it called out strong expressions of opposition, and even threats of resistance from political leaders, popular meetings and the press. (Examples of the same are given in *Niles*, XXXIV, 288–290, 300, 301, 339, 340, 351–356; XXXV, 14, 15, 203–208; *Amer. Annual Reg.*, 1829–1830, 62–65; see also McMaster, V, 255–262; Elliott, 245–249; Harris, 147–151.) The Governors of the Southern States, at the opening of the legislative session of 1828–29, condemned the new tariff act as unconstitutional and unjust, but counseled further remonstrance. (*Niles*, XXXV, 223, 260, 263, 273–279.) The Legislatures of South Carolina, Georgia, Alabama, Mississippi and Virginia voiced the popular feeling by adopting a notable series of protests and memorials. Several of these follow. Those of Alabama, of Jan. 29, 1829, are similar in tone to the others. They are given in the *Acts of Alabama*, 1828–29, 101, 102; *Senate Doc.*, 20 *Cong.*, 2 *sess*,, II, *No.* 103; *Amer. Annual Reg.*, I, pt. II, 147.

73. Resolutions of South Carolina.
December 20, 1828.

South Carolina again took the lead in the opposition. Following the advice of Governor Taylor (*Niles*, XXXV, 274, 275) the Legislature adopted, December 19, a report, the original of which had been drafted by John C. Calhoun, known as the "South Carolina Exposition," which was his first presentation of the doctrine of "nullification." (*S. C. Stat. at Large*, I, 247–273; Calhoun's *Works*, VI, 1–59.) The report concludes with a protest directed to Congress. This text is accessible, and is therefore not reprinted. (*Acts of South Carolina*, 1828, Appx., 17–19; *Stat. at L.*, I, 244, 245; *Senate Journal*, 20 *Cong.*, 2 *sess.*, 115–117; *Niles*, XXXV, 308–309; Elliott's *Debates*, IV, 380–382; MacDonald's *Documents*, 231–234. For history of, cf. Houston, 70–85; McMaster, V, 262–267; Sumner, *Jackson*, 207–219; Von Holst, *Calhoun*, ch. V.) On the following day, December 20, the Legislature also passed the following resolutions expressive of their opinion, which, together with their *Resolves of 1825 and 1827*, were to be sent to the other States. (*Acts of S. C.*, 1828, Appx., 9; *Stat. at L.*, I, 246; reprinted in *Senate Jour.*

of Penna., 1828–29, II, 500; Elliot, *Pamphlet*, 78.[1]) For various resolutions proposed, see *Pub. of Southern History Assoc.*, III, 212–220; *Niles*, XXXV, 304–310.

1. *Resolved*, That the opinion of this Legislature, on the subject of the assumed right of Congress to regulate duties on imports, for the purpose of encouraging domestic industry, as heretofore expressed in the various resolutions adopted in the years 1825 and 1827, is unchanged; and after the further aggression by the passage of the Tariff Act of 1828, this Legislature is restrained from the assertion of the sovereign rights of the state by the hope that the magnanimity and justice of the good people of the Union will effect the abandonment of a system, partial in its nature, unjust in its operation, and not within the powers delegated to Congress.

2. *Resolved*, That the measures to be pursued consequent on the perseverance in this system are purely questions of expediency, and not of allegiance; and that for the purpose of ascertaining the opinion and inviting the co-operation of other states, a copy of these and the resolutions heretofore adopted by this legislature, be transmitted to the Governor of the several states, with a request that they be laid before the several Legislatures to determine on such ulterior measures as they may think the occasion demands.

Georgia on the Tariff of 1828.

December 20, 1828.

Following the suggestion of Governor Forsyth, "to solemnly protest" against the obnoxious act to the Senate, and "to remonstrate in the strongest language with those States who have heretofore supported the wretched system"[2] (*Jour. of House of Rep. of Georgia*, 1828, 17–19; *Niles*, XXXV, 223), the Legislature adopted the following notable series of resolves under date of December 20, 1828: (1) Resolutions declaratory of State Rights in opposition to Federal legislation upon the tariff, internal improvement and slavery. *Acts of Georgia*, 1828, 174–177; *House Journal*, 20 Cong., 2 sess., 157–160; *Sen-*

---

[1] *Op. cit. ante*, p. 16. This pamphlet also contains extracts from some of the resolutions of other States, 76–79.

[2] Gov. Troup had suggested the same, Nov. 6, 1827. (*Niles*, XXXIII, 222.)

ate Doc., I, *No.* 42; *House Doc*, II, *No.* 70; MacDonald's *Documents*, 234–237. (2) Remonstrance to the Pro-Tariff States. *Acts of Ga.*, 1828, 177–183. This was in the nature of an appeal for the preservation of the Union, presenting an argument in favor of strict construction and against the constitutionality of the protective tariff. (3) Memorial to Anti-Tariff States. *Ibid.*, 183–192. The above are all reprinted in the *Senate Journal of Penna.*, 1828–29, II, 372–381, 502–511; *Acts of South Carolina*, 1829, 79–90; *S. C. Stat. at L.*, I, 274–291. (4) Protest to the Senate against the tariff of 1828. *Acts of Ga.*, 1828, 202, 203; *Exec. Doc.*, 20 *Cong.*, 2 *sess.*, I, *No.* 33; *Senate Jour.*, 70; *Niles*, XXXV, 291. Extracts from the last two of the series follow. The House also adopted a resolution, Dec. 17, 1828, authorizing the Governor, "in event of the failure of the present Congress to repeal or modify in compliance with the above protest, the tariff," to appoint nine delegates to meet in a convention of the Southern States "to deliberate upon and devise a suitable mode of resistance to that unjust, unconstitutional and oppressive law." (*Jour. House of Rep. of Ga.*, 1828, 312–315.) In the course of the next three years the Legislature adopted resolutions reaffirming its position, as follows: Dec. 19, 1829, *Acts of Ga*, 1829, 241–244; *Senate Doc.*, 21 *Cong.*, 1 *sess.*, I, *No.* 18; Dec. 23, 1830, *Acts of Ga.*, 1830, 256; *Niles*, XXXIX, 340; Dec. 27, 1831, reply to Delaware, *Acts of Ga.*, 1831, 312; *Niles*, XLI, 392.

74. Extract from Memorial of Georgia on the Subject of the late Tariff to the Anti-Tariff States, December 20, 1828.

[A summary of the principles of the opposition of the State of Georgia to the obnoxious tariff law of 1828, concluding with the following recommendations:]

We therefore, recommend to our sister states opposed to the recent tariff law, solemnly to protest to the Senate of the United States against that obnoxious law, to deprecate the abuse of limited powers, to accomplish ends capable of accomplishment by legitimate and prescribed means.

We recommend a remonstrance to the states in favor of the tariff, advising of its injurious tendency and operation to their sister states opposed to it, and insisting on the necessity of compromising sectional interests for the general good.

We recommend a policy for self-preservation; exhorting each state opposed to the tariff policy, to ward off its effects, by living as far as possible within itself.

We recommend a continued and strenuous exertion to defeat that general pernicious, and unconstitutional policy, contemplated and pursued by the advocates of the tariff.

Such means may restore federal legislation to the standard of constitutional correctness. Times, occasions and provocations, teach their proper lessons and expedients. Future measures will be dictated by expediency; the nature and tendency of injury will suggest the mode and measure of future resistance.

75. Protest of the Legislature of Georgia against the Tariff of 1828, December 20, 1828.

From a painful conviction, that a manifestation of the public sentiment, in the most imposing and impressive form, is called for by the present agitated state of the southern section of the Union, the General Assembly of the State of Georgia have deemed it their duty to adopt the novel expedient of addressing, in the name of the State, the Senate of the Congress of the United States.

In her sovereign character, the State of Georgia protests against the act of the last session of Congress, entitled "An act in alteration of the several acts imposing duties on imports," as deceptive in its title, fraudulent in its pretexts; oppressive in its exactions; partial and unjust in its operations; unconstitutional in its well-known objects; ruinous to commerce and agriculture —to secure a hateful monopoly to a combination of importunate manufacturers.

Demanding the repeal of an act, which has already disturbed the Union, endangered the public tranqnility, weakened the confidence of whole States in the Federal Government, and diminished the affection of large masses of the people to the Union itself, and the abandonment of the degrading system which considers the people incapable of wisely directing their own enterprise; which sets up the servants of the people, in Congress, as the exclusive judges of what pursuits are most advantageous and suitable for those by whom they were elected; the State of Georgia expects, that, in perpetual testimony thereof, this deliberate and solemn expression of her opinions, will be carefully preserved among the archives of the Senate; and, in justification of her character to the present generation and to posterity, if, unfortunately, Congress, disregarding this protest, and continuing to pervert powers granted for clearly defined and well understood purposes to effectuate objects never intended by the great parties by whom the Constitution was framed, to be entrusted to the controling guardianship of the Federal Government, should render necessary measures of a decisive character, for the protection of the people of the State, and the vindication of the Constitution of the United States.

76. Resolutions of Mississippi.

February 5, 1829.

In addition to the subjoined resolves the Legislature a year later, Feb. 5, 1830, adopted a new resolution concurring with the States of Georgia, South Carolina and Virginia in the soundness of the policy expressed in their different resolutions upon the subject of the Tariff, Colonization Society and Internal Improvement. (*Laws of Miss.*, 1830, 194.)

Resolved by the Senate and House of Representatives of the State of Mississippi, in General Assembly convened, That the Tariff of 1828 is contrary to the spirit of the Constitution of the United States; impolitic and oppressive in its operation on the Southern States, and ought to be resisted by all constitutional means.

And be it further resolved, That our Senators in Congress be instructed, and our Representatives requested, to use their best exertions to effect a revision or repeal of the present Tariff; and in the event of failing therein; to cause to be entered on the journals of each house of Congress their solemn protest. [Resolution of transmission to the several states.]

[*Laws of Mississippi*, 1829, 108, 109; also in *Journal of Penna. Senate*, 1829–30, 30.]

77. Resolutions of Virginia.

February 24, 1829.

Governor Giles in a special message of Feb. 8, 1828, and again in his annual message of Dec. 2, 1828, after expressing his opposition to the federal tariff act, committed the question as to what action the State should take to the Legislature. (*Niles*, XXXIII, 405; *Ibid.*, XXXV, 273, 274; *Amer. Annual Reg.*, 1827–29, 129–130.) That body adopted an elaborate report presenting the doctrine of strict construction as maintained by the State in its previous history, which concluded with the resolutions given below. The text of the report and resolutions are given in the *Acts of Virginia*, 1828-29, 159-170; *Senate Doc.*, 20 *Cong.*, 2 *sess.*, III, *No.* 105; reprinted in the *Journal of Senate of Penna.*, 1828-29, II, 522-534; and the *Acts of S. C.*, 1829, 71-79; *Stat. at L. of S. C.*, I, 292-302. The resolutions are also given in the *Amer. Annual Reg.*, 1827-29, 131. The vote of the House of Delegates is given in brackets after each resolve.

1. *Resolved*, as the opinion of this committee, That the Constitution of the United States, being a Federal Compact between sovereign States, in construing which no common arbiter is known, each State has the right to construe the Compact for itself· [Yeas 134, nays 68.]

2. *Resolved*, That in giving such construction in the opinion of this committee, each State should be guided, as Virginia has ever been, by a sense of forbearance and respect for the opinion of the other States, and by community of attachment to the Union, so far as the same may be consistent with self-preservation, and a determined purpose to preserve the purity of our Republican Institutions. [Yeas 166, nays 36.]

3. *Resolved*, That this General Assembly of Virginia, actuated by the desire of guarding the Constitution from all violation, anxious to preserve and perpetuate the Union, and to execute with fidelity the trust reposed in it by the people, as one of the high contracting parties, feels itself bound to declare, and it hereby most solemnly declares, its deliberate conviction, that the Acts of Congress, usually denominated the Tariff Laws, passed avowedly for the protection of Domestic Manufactures, are not authorized by the plain construction, true intent and meaning of the Constitution. [Yeas 126, nays 75.]

4. *Resolved*, also, That the said acts are partial in their operation, impolitic, and oppressive to a large portion of the people of the Union, and ought to be repealed. [Yeas 138, nays 62.]

[Resolutions of transmission.]

Counter Resolutions.

1830-32.

In reply to these anti-tariff manifestoes the Legislatures of several of the States adopted resolutions in support of the tariff of 1828. Those of Kentucky and Louisiana of 1830, and of Pennsylvania of 1831 are especially notable. References to additional resolutions of this character follow: Penna., Jan. 23, 1830, in support of constitutionality of tariff of 1828, *Laws of Penna.*, 1829–30, 406; Ohio, Feb. 22, 1830, *Senate Doc.*, 21 *Cong.*, 1 *sess.*, II, *No.* 90; Delaware, Jan. 12, 1831, tariff and internal improvement, *Ibid.*, 21 *Cong.*, 2 *sess.*, IV, *No.* 137; *Laws of Del.*, VIII, 105, both of concurrence with Penna.; New Jersey, tariff and internal improvement, *Amer. Annual Reg.*, 1831–32, 250; Penna., June 6, 1832, tariff and bank, *Senate Doc.*, 22 *Cong.*, 1 *sess.*, III, *No.* 161; *Niles*, XLI, 436; Connecticut, May session, 1832, *House Ex. Doc.*, 22 *Cong.*, 1 *sess.*, VI, *No.* 282; Vermont, Nov. 8, 1832, concurring with Penna. Res. of 1831, *Acts of Vermont*, 1832, 28–30; *Senate Doc.*, 22 *Cong.*, 2 *sess.*, I, *No.* 51.

---

78. Extract from Report of Kentucky in reply to South Carolina.

January 27, 1830.

The text is given in the *Acts of Kentucky*, 1829–30, 287–300; of the resolutions only in *Niles*, XXXVII, 428; *Amer. Annual Reg.*, 1829–30, 589.

The General Assembly of Kentucky cannot admit the right of a minority, either of the States or of the people, to set up their opinion not only in opposition, but to overrule that of the majority. And it cannot but view with regret and surprise, the assertion of the State of South Carolina:—" That the measures to be pursued, consequent on the perseverance in this system, are purely questions of expediency, and not of allegiance." The consequences of such a principle, if practically enforced, would be alarming in the extreme. Scarcely any important measure of the general government is ever adopted, to which one or more of the States are not opposed. If one State have a right to obstruct and defeat the execution of a law of Congress because it deems it unconstitutional, then every State has a similar right. When the dissatisfied State opposes to the Act of Congress its measures of obstruction, the alternative is presented, shall the act be enforced within the particular State, or be abandoned by Congress? If enforced, there is a civil war; if abandoned, without being repealed, a virtual dissolution of the Union. As the successful exercise of the power of resisting an act of Congress by one State, would naturally stimulate other States, disapproving other acts of that body, to similar resistance, the practical result would be, that Congress could adopt and enforce no measure whatever, to which any one of the twenty-four States might be opposed. It is in vain to say that the Tariff is characterized by the most enormous injustice. Who is to be the judge of that enormity? Who is to prescribe the limits of enormity, which will authorize resistance, and that which falls short of conferring that right? History and the nature of man demonstrate, that when his prejudices are aroused and his passions inflamed, it is not difficult to persuade him, that mild and equitable laws, are fraught with the most abominable injustice.

Nor can the State of South Carolina derive the smallest aid in sustaining its doctrine of resistance to the federal authority, from the manner in which the constitution was formed; whether it was the work of the people of the United States collectively, or is to be considered as a compact between sovereign States, or between the people of the several States with each other, there is, there can be, there ought to be, but one rule, which is, that the majority must govern.

Of course, the General Assembly does not mean to speak of, or to deny that there may be, acts of government, of such extreme oppression, as to justify, if there be no other remedy, an appeal to arms, when such cases unhappily—and it is fondly to be hoped they never will arise, they furnish their own laws; and it is the bounden duty of those who believe in the existence of such extreme oppression, to estimate well the probabilities and the perils of forcible resistance. The State of South Carolina is not supposed to have intended to assert, that the system of measures denominated the Tariff or the American system, present a just cause of civil war but that without producing civil war, that State may lawfully resist the execution of the system within its jurisdiction. It is, therefore, the ordinary rule of the federal government, and not the extraordinary cases referred to, which should form the subject of our present inquiry.

The right of the majority to govern flows from the fitness of things. It is the law of nature, because it is the dictate of reason, applied to human society. * * *

What is the voice of the majority in Congress, but the voice of the people, speaking by proxy? How absurd would it be, therefore, for the few to impeach the conduct of the many for an inconsiderable portion of the States to menace the subversion of the government, the dissolution of the Union, because the many demand the adoption of a measure, which, in the opinion of the few, militates against their interests? Previous to the war of eighteen hundred and twelve, a large proportion of the American people, indignant at the accumulated wrongs of the British Government, claimed at the hands of their representatives in Congress, a declaration of hostilities against England. It was an act of sovereignty, the exercise of which, the majority of the people had the constitutional right to demand, the minority that availed themselves of that occasion, to threaten the dismemberment of the Union, was regarded universally, as an unprincipled faction ; and the posture in which impartial history will present them to future times, ought ever to operate as an example to deter, rather than to be imitated. * * *

But the right of the majority to govern, clear as it is upon the grounds of reason and natural law, does not rest exclusively upon that ground. It is expressly secured by the Constitution of the United States in the creation of the Legislative power. By the fifth section of the first article of that instrument, it is provided, that "a majority of each (house) shall constitute a quorum to do business." In some instances indeed, a greater number than a bare majority is required ; but those exceptions, the result of precaution, like all exceptions, themselves prove the general rule.

The General Assembly of Kentucky cannot then agree with the State of South Carolina, that the perseverance of the General Government in the American system, leaves that State free to consider that the measures to be pursued, are " purely questions of expediency and not of allegiance." If the majority of the people of the United States in Congress assembled, adhere to that system, by abstaining from its repeal, neither the State of South

Carolina nor any other State in the Union, is at liberty to pass any act to defeat the system. That State and all other States, are bound by the terms of our constitutional union, to yield obedience to the system.

From the principles now advanced, there has been no deviation on the part of the General Assembly of Kentucky. At a former epoch, when certain acts passed by Congress, called the alien and sedition laws, which were believed to be unconstitutional by the General Assembly, it neither interposed nor threatened the adoption of any measures to defeat or obstruct their operation within the jurisdiction of Kentucky. It expressed, and expressed in very strong language, its disapprobation of them and its firm conviction that they were unconstitutional, and therefore void. There it stopped, and that is the limit which no state should pass, until it has formed the deliberate resolution of lighting up the torch of civil war. Every state, as well as every individual, has the incontestible right freely to form and to publish to the world, its opinion of any and of every act of the federal government. It may appeal to the reason of the people, enlighten their judgments, alarm their fears, and conciliate their support, to change federal rulers, or federal measures. But neither a state nor an individual can rightfully resist, by force, the execution of a law passed by Congress.

[Here follows a discussion of the constitutionality of internal improvement measures, denied by South Carolina, followed by a series of resolutions declaring the Tariff and Internal Improvement measure constitutional; and of transmission to the other states.]

---

79. Resolutions of Louisiana.

March 15, 1830.

These are of interest as recording the only dissenting voice among the planting States. Louisiana's attitude is explained by reason of her sugar interests. The text is given in *Acts of Louisiana*, 1830, 70–72; a copy in *Journal of Penna. House of Rep.*, 1830–31, II, 50, 51; and slightly changed in *Niles*, XXXVIII, 203.

Resolved by the senate and house of representatives of the

State of Louisiana, in general assembly convened, That the general assembly of their state do not concur in the views and sentiments expressed by the Resolutions of the Legislature of the State of Mississippi, relative to the Tariff of eighteen hundred and twenty-eight; that the legislature of this state does not perceive the unconstitutionality or impolicy of adopting such measures, nor has the state suffered any injury therefrom.

Resolved, That we concur in the resolutions of the legislature of the State of Vermont, by which they have declared the law of eighteen hundred and twenty-eight on the Tariff to be constitutional, expedient, and harmless to the southern states.

Resolved, That our senators in Congress be instructed and our representatives be requested, to accede to and support such measures as those contemplated by the law of eighteen hundred and twenty-eight on the Tariff.

[Resolution of transmission.]

80. Pennsylvania on the Powers of the Federal Government.

April 2, 1831.

By these resolutions the Legislature confirmed its previous endorsement of the tariff (1830), and joined other matters therewith, and the following year, June 1, 1832, again pronouced in favor of the tariff and the rechartering of the Bank. The resolves of 1831 were endorsed by New Jersey and Vermont (see *ante*, pp. 131, 158). The text of the following resolutions are in *Laws of Penna.*, 1830–31, 505, 506; *Amer. Annual Reg.*, 1830–31, 336–339; and as originally introduced in *Niles*, XL, 56, 69.

Resolved by the Senate and House of Representatives of the Commonwealth of Pennsylvania in General Assembly met, That as the sense of the Senate and House of Representatives of this Commonwealth, that the Constitution of the United States having proved itself by near half a century's experience a government beyond all others, capable of promoting rational liberty and the general welfare, it must be preserved.

Resolved, as the sense of the Senate and House of Representatives, that the Constitution of the United States, authorises acts of Congress to protect manufactures, and that the actual prosperity of the country attests the wisdom of such acts.

Resolved, as the sense of the Senate and House of Representatives, that any diminution of the protection now afforded to iron, would be impolitic and injudicious legislation.

Resolved, as the sense of the Senate and House of Representatives, that the Constitution of the United States authorises, and experience sanctions, the twenty-fifth section of the act of Congress, of September, one thousand seven hundred and eighty nine, and all others, empowering the federal judiciary to maintain the supreme laws.

Resolved, as the sense of the Senate and House of Representatives, that whereas the bank of the United States, has tended in a great degree, to maintain a sound and uniform currency, to facilitate the financial operations of the government, to regulate foreign and domestic exchange, and has been conducive to commercial prosperity, the legislature of Pennsylvania recommends a renewal of its charter, under such regulations and restrictions, as to the power of the respective states, as Congress may deem right and proper.

Resolved, as the sense of the Senate and House of Representatives, that as soon as the national debt shall be paid, the most equitable and just mode of disposing of the surplus funds which may remain in the treasury of the United States, after defraying the ordinary expenses of the government, and the payment of appropriations which may be made to objects of great national importance, will lay a distribution amongst the several states, in proportion to their representation in the Congress of the United States; and that the executive veto was properly exercised on the bill making an appropriation to the Maysville and Lexington Road.

Progress of Nullification in South Carolina and Resolutions of the Legislature.

1830.

While the citizens of South Carolina were unanimous in their opposition to the tariff law, they were not united in their support of the doctrine of nullification. As early as the fall of 1828 the " Friends of Union " began to organize, but did not prevent the adoption of the "exposition" of 1828. Hope of relief as a result of the election of Jackson for a time abated the excitement and postponed the issue. After an interval of a year, the theory of nullification was again brought to the front by Hayne in the great debate with Webster in the Senate in January, 1830. (*Cong. Debates*, 21 *Cong.*, 1 *sess.*, VI, *Pt.* I, 58–93; accessible reprints of extracts are in Elliot's *Debates*, IV, 496–519; MacDonald's *Documents*, 239–259; Johnson, *Amer. Orations*, I, 233–302; *Amer. Hist. Leaflets*, *No.* 30. For history of debate, Harris, 156–187; Houston, 86–96; Schouler, III, 482–491; McMaster, VI, ch. LIV; Thorpe, *U. S.*, II, 389–397.) Jackson's veto of the Maysville Road bill, May 27, 1830 (Richardson's, II, 483–493), for the moment seemed to reassure the South, and his action was hailed with enthusiastic praise.[1] Hayne declared "that it opened to the Southern States the first dawning of returning hope," and other prominent Southerners joined with him in the prediction that "the tariff will not long survive the death of internal improvement." (*Niles*, XXXVIII, 308–315, 319–321, 379.) With the opening of the summer there began in South Carolina a campaign for the calling of a convention to pronounce upon the question of nullification. "The State Rights and Union Party" opposed this project, and in their efforts they had the moral support of the President. (Letter of Jackson, Oct. 26, 1830, *Penna. Mag. of Hist.*, XII, 277.) The notable speeches of Hayne and Governor Miller in favor of, and that of Drayton and the address of Senator Smith against nullification, clearly defined the issue between the two parties. Smith, who had drawn the first anti-tariff resolutions of 1824, was defeated for re-election to the United States Senate by Miller. (*Niles*, XXXVIII, 375, 380; XXXIX, 117–119, 243–248, 250; Hunt, in *Pol. Sci. Quar.* VI, 232–247.) In the Legislature a bill for the calling a convention failed to receive the necessary two-thirds vote. (Senate, *yeas* 23, *nays* 12; House, *yeas*, 60, *nays* 56. *Niles*, XXXIX. 304, 330.) However, a series of resolutions on federal relations, consisting of the first four paragraphs of the Virginia resolutions and the first paragraph of the Kentucky resolutions of 1798, prefixed to the following resolve were reported. All were

---

[1] This veto had the effect of calling out new protests against internal improvement acts, or resolutions endorsing Jackson's position. The following are typical: Georgia, Dec. 22, 1830, *Acts of Ga.*, 1830, 256; *Ex. Doc.*, 21 *Cong.*, 2 *sess.*, II, *No.* 37; Dec. 24, 1832, approving Res. of Tenn., *House Ex. Doc.*, 22 *Cong.*, 2 *sess.*, II, *No.* 91; Maine, March 30, 1831, and of Tenn., Sept. 20, 1831, in *Jour. of Penna. House of Rep.*, 1831–32, II, 31–39, 673; New Hampshire, June 22, 1832, *Senate Doc.*, 22 *Cong.*, 2 *sess.*, I, *No.* 53. For counter replies, see *ante*, p. 158; also reply of Mass. to Tenn. and Ga., March 23, 1833, *Res. of Mass.*, 1832–34, 424–432.

adopted, Dec. 17, 1830. (*Acts of S. C.*, 1830, 59; *Stat. at L.*, I, 303, 304; *Niles*, XXXIX, 305; *Amer. Annual Reg.*, 1830-31, 253-255.) During the contest two letters of Madison's appeared denying that the resolutions of 1798 gave any sanction to the nullification doctrine. (*No. Amer. Review*, XXXI, 537-546 (1830); reprinted in *Works*, IV, 95-107; Elliot's *Debates*, IV, 600-608; *Niles*, XLIII, *sup.*, 25-28. For Governor Hamilton's comment see *Niles*, XL, 277; XLI, 101.) These resolutions of South Carolina, based on those of 1798, may be considered as their reply. For other letters of Madison for the years 1828-30, on the tariff and nullification, see *Works*, *esp.* III, 636-658, 663; IV, 5, 42-49, 61-66.

81. Extract from Resolutions of the Legislature, December 17, 1830.

Resolved, That the several acts of the Congress of the United States now of force, imposing duties upon imports, for the protection of domestic manufactures, have been and are, deliberate and highly dangerous and oppressive violations of the constitutional compact, and that whenever any State, which is suffering under this oppression, shall lose all reasonable hope of redress from the wisdom and justice of the Federal Government, it will be its right and duty to interpose, in its sovereign capacity, for the purpose of arresting the progress of the evil occasioned by the said unconstitutional acts.

Notes on the Tariff Controversy.

1831.

The tariff controversy in 1831 was marked in the country at large by the holding of general conventions by the Free Traders and the Protectionists. Both had in view the influencing of legislation. "The Free Trade Convention" was held at Philadelphia, Sept. 30-October 7. Some two hundred delegates from fifteen States were in attendance. It adopted an address and appointed a committee to draw up a memorial to Congress. Gallatin prepared the latter. His motion to strike out that portion of the address which declared a protective tariff unconstitutional was rejected 35 to 159. *The Journal of the Free Trade Convention, and their address to the People of the United States* (Phila., 1831, 75 pp.), contain the proceedings; given also in *Niles*, XLI, 105-107, 135-141, 156-158, 166. The Memorial is given in *Senate Doc.*, 22 *Cong.*, 1 *sess.*, I, *No.* 55; also in Taussig, *State Papers and Speeches on the Tariff*, 108-213 (Camb., 1892). "The Friends of Domestic Industry" assembled at New York, Oct. 26-Nov. 1. There were present nearly five hundred delegates from twelve States. They likewise issued an "Address to the People of the United States,' prepared various reports on different industries, and memorialized Congress. Their official publications were *Journal of the Proceedings of the Friends of Domestic Industry, Hezekiah Niles, Principal Secretary* (Baltimore, 1831, 44 pp.); *Reports of Committees and Memorial to Congress* (197 pp). The former is also published in *Niles*, XLI, 25, 180-192, 204-216; the latter forms the "*Addendum*" to *Niles*, Vol. XLI, 64 pp.

While the national agitation was taking place the local contest in South Carolina between the Unionists and the Nullificationists witnessed important developments. During the summer and fall Calhoun prepared a series of papers, restating and elaborating the nullification doctrine. The first of these, "*The Address on the Relation of the States and the Federal Government*," appeared in July. (*Works*, VI, 59-94; *Niles*, XL, 437-445; Jenkins' *Calhoun*, 161-187.) This was followed later by "*The Address to the People of South Carolina*" (*Works*, VI, 122-144) and "*The Report on Federal Relations*" (*Works*, VI, 94-123). Both were prepared for members of the Legislature. The contest between "The Union and the States Rights Party" and "The States Rights and Free Trade Party" was renewed. Both held rival celebrations on July 4 at Charleston. Certain portions of Jackson's letter in reply to an invitation to attend the dinner of the Union party called from the Legislature, when it assembled in December, the rejoinder given below. (Jackson's letter is given in *Niles*, XLI, 350, 351.) The report was adopted by a vote of 64 to 52 in the House, and 24 to 15 in the Senate. (*Legislative Proceedings of S. C.*, 1831, 60, 61, 68, 69.) The text is given in *Acts of S. C.*, 1831, 57-59; *Stat. at L.*, I, 305-308; extract in *Niles*, XLI, 334, 335; for report first adopted by the Senate, see *Ibid.*, 334, 335. The Legislature also adopted, Dec. 8, a resolution declaring that " on the tariff of protection and the rights of the states " "the opinion of the Legislature is unchanged." (*Acts of S. C.*, 1831, 28.) A "Memorial of the members of the Legislature opposed to Nullification," in favor of a reduction of the tariff, signed by sixty-one members of the minority, was presented to Congress. (*Senate Doc.*, 22 *Cong.*, 1 *sess.*, I, *No.* 34.) For other features of the local contest, see documents in *Niles*, XLI, 13, 65, 258, 259; Letters of Hayne and Hammond, 1830-34, *Amer. Hist. Rev.*, VI, 736-765; VII, 92-119; Correspondence of Calhoun, *Amer. Hist. Assoc. Rept.*, 1899, Vol. II. An unexcelled and almost unused source for tracing the activity of the Union Party are the papers of the Poinsett collection (MS.) in the Penna. Hist. Soc. Library. A selection from these is shortly to to be published, edited by Professor John B. McMaster. For secondary accounts consult Hunt, Article in *Pol. Sci. Quar.*, VI, 232-243; Houston, 98-104; Stille, *Life of Joel R. Poinsett*, in *Penna. Mag. of Hist.*, XII, esp. 257-279; *Amer. Annual Reg.*, 1831-32, 32-36; Lalor, II, 1050-1055; McMaster, VI, ch. LVI. Of contemporary pamphlets published in the interest of the Union movement the following are of interest: *The Tariff—Its True Character and Effect Practically Illustrated* (Charleston, 1830, 52 pp.); *National and State Rights Considered by the Hon. George McDuffie under the signature of One of the People*, etc. (Charleston, 1830,

40 pp.); a reprint of his article of 1821. The same was reprinted in a Phila. (2d) edition under the title, *Defence of a Liberal Construction of the Power of Congress*, etc. (Phila., June, 1832).

82.   Report of Legislature in Reply to Jackson's Letter of June 14, December 17, 1831.

[Commenting on the letter the Report declares:] The Committee, therefore, cannot but regard it, as the annunciation to the world by the President of the United States, that there is a plan of disorganization existing in South Carolina, against which, as chief executive of the United States, he has resolved to present an unsurmountable barrier.   *   *   *   The Committee finds it difficult to find language at once suitable to the occasion and the dignity of the House.

Is this Legislature to be schooled and rated by the President of the United States?

Is it to legislate under the sword of the Commander-in-Chief?

Is the will of one man to be substituted for deliberation—and the enactments of this body to be fashioned by an edict from a President, not only avowing a right to annul a law when passed, but practically assuming the right to interpose while it is yet under discussion?   The executive of a most limited government; the agent of an agency, but a part of a creature of the states, undertakes to prescribe a line of conduct to a free and sovereign State, under a denunciation of pains and penalties.   It cannot but be esteemed a signal instance of forebearance, calmly to enquire into this assumed power of the President over the States. Under no part of the Constitution, or penal law of Congress, known to the Committee, is the crime of disorganization recognized or made punishable.   It is to be lamented, that in denouncing a crime aud threatening punishment, the President had not used terms of more definite import.

If by the vague generality of the word disorganization be intended, as the context may perhaps indicate, that a plan of disunion existed in this State, it will be equally difficult to fix upon any constitutional or legal authority, or anything in the nature of our institutions, which imposes any duty or grants any power to the President to prevent it.   This is a confederacy of sovereign States, and each may withdraw from the confederacy when it chooses; such proceedings would neither be treason nor insurrection nor a violation of any portion of the Constitution. It is a right which is inherent in a sovereign State, and has not been delegated by the States of this Union. Whether assuming such an attitude might be cause of war on the part of the general government, may be questioned, but there can be no question that the President could not declare war. But the Committee deem it unnecessary to discuss a mere hypothetical question, the possible occurrence of which, if the President has contemplated it, is the result of his entire ignorance of the feelings and purposes of this State.

No one denies that it is his right and duty to see that the laws of the United States are faithfully executed and no portion of the Union will be more prompt to recognize the right, or to sustain and assist him in the duty, than the State of South Carolina—but at the same time, if in the deliberate judgment of the State, acting in her sovereign capacity, any enactment in Congress is decided to be in violation of the Constitution, and therefore no law—that judgment is paramount; and if the executive, or all the combined departments of the General Government, endeavor to enforce such enactment, it is by the law of tyrants, the exertion of brute force. If such a case should occur, which we pray a wise providence to avert, the State will throw herself on the protection of that providence, and if her destiny be slavery, she will not be mocked by the forms of a free government.

Resolved, That the letter of the President of the United States, to sundry citizens of this State, is an unauthorized interference in the affairs of this State: that the principles advanced in it are incompatible with the constitution, and subversive of the rights of the State—that the threatened course of executive conduct would, if acted upon, destroy the liberties of this country, and as a threat, is of dangerous precedent, highly repulsive to the feelings of a free people.

Resolved, That whilst we condemn the conduct of the President of the United States, when he is in error, we are willing to approve it, when, in our opinion, he is right; and that we regard with high gratification the sentiment expressed in his late message, that the Tariff ought to be reduced to the wants of the Government, and recognize in it the just response to the solemn resolutions of this Legislature.

---

83. Ordinance of Nullification of South Carolina.
November 24, 1832.

The revision of the tariff by the new law of July 14, 1832 (*U. S. Stat. at L.*, IV, 583–594), was not satisfactory to the South. (*Elliott*, 253–262; Harris, 201–229.) The South Carolina delegation in Congress at once issued an address to the people of that State, in which they declared as "their solemn and deliberate conviction that the protecting system must now be regarded as the settled policy of the country and that all hope of relief from Congress is irrevocably gone, they leave it with you, the sovereign power of the State, to determine whether the rights and liberties which you received as a precious inheritance from an illustrious ancestry shall be tamely surrendered without a struggle, or transmitted undiminished to your posterity." (*Niles*, XLII, 412–414.) The campaign for a State Convention at once opened. The Union Party in South Carolina attempted to defeat nullification by putting forward a project for a Southern Convention. (*Niles*, XLII, 350; XLIII, 66, 87, 88, 153, 175, 220–224.) The nullificationists were equally active. Mr. Calhoun, Aug. 28, contributed another exposition of nullification in his Letter to Governor Hamilton (*Works*, VI, 144–193; Jenkins, *Calhoun*, 195–232), and various addresses and resolutions were adopted by public meetings in support of this policy. (*Niles*, XLII, 426; XLIII, 56, 79.) As a result a Legislature favorable to calling a convention was elected. It assembled in special session Oct. 22. Governor Hamilton recommended a convention. (Message in *Niles*, XLIII, 173.) A bill for this purpose was at once enacted by a vote of 96 to 25 in the House and 31 to 13 in the Senate. (Text in *Acts of South Carolina*, 1834, *Appx.*, i, ii; *Niles*, XLIII, 152; *Amer. Annual Reg.*, 1830–31, 262, 263). The convention was in session at Columbia November 19–24. It appointed a committee, which prepared an elaborate exposition, approved of Addresses to the People of South Carolina and to the People of the United States, and November 24 adopted the Nullification Ordinance, which follows. *The Journal of the Convention* (Columbia, 1833), and the above are reprinted in *State Papers on Nullification*, 1–74, 293–320. (*Mass. Gen. Court, Misc. Doc.*, Boston, 1834.) The documents are also given in *S. C. Stat. at L.*, I, 312–354; *Niles*, XLIII, 219, 220, 231–239, 347, 348; *New York Assembly Doc.*, *No.* 3. The text of the Ordinance is given in MacDonald, 268; Preston, 300; *Amer. An. Reg.*, 1831–32, 263, 264. Calhoun prepared the draft of an Address to the People of the United States (*Works*, VI, 193–209), which was in part made use of in the address of the same title adopted by the convention.

An Ordinance

To Nullify Certain Acts of the Congress of the United States,
Purporting to be Laws, Laying Duties and Imposts on the
Importation of Foreign Commodities.

Whereas, the Congress of the United States, by various acts,
purporting to be acts laying duties and imposts on foreign imports, but in reality intended for the protection of domestic
manufactures, and the giving of bounties to classes and individuals
engaged in particular employments, at the expense and to the
injury and oppression of other classes and individuals, and by
wholly exempting from taxation certain foreign commodities,
such as are not produced or manufactured in the United States,
to afford a pretext for imposing higher and excessive duties on
articles similar to those intended to be protected, hath exceeded
its just powers under the Constitution, which confers on it no
authority to afford such protection, and hath violated the true
meaning and intent of the Constitution, which provides for equality
in imposing the burdens of taxation upon the several States and
portions of the Confederacy. *And whereas,* the said Congress,
exceeding its just power to impose taxes and collect revenue for
the purpose of effecting and accomplishing the specific objects
and purposes which the Constitution of the United States au-
thorizes it to effect and accomplish, hath raised and collected
unnecessary revenue, for objects unauthorized by the Constitution.—

We, therefore, the People of the State of South Carolina, in Conven-
tion assembled, do Declare and Ordain, and it is hereby Declared
and Ordained, That the several acts and parts of acts of the Congress of the United States, purporting to be laws for the imposing
of duties and imposts on the importation of foreign commodities,
and now having actual operation and effect within the United
States, and more especially an act entitled " an act in alteration
of the several acts imposing duties on imports," approved on
the nineteenth day of May, one thousand eight hundred and
twenty eight, and also, an act entitled " an act to alter and
amend the several acts imposing duties on imports," approved
on the fourteenth day of July, one thousand eight hundred and

thirty-two, are unauthorized by the Constitution of the United States, and violate the true meaning and intent thereof, and are null, void and no law, nor binding upon this State, its officers, or citizens; and all promises, contracts and obligations, made or entered into, or to be made or entered into, with purpose to secure the duties imposed by said acts, and all judicial proceedings which shall be hereafter had in affirmance thereof, are, and shall be held, utterly null and void.

And it is further Ordained, That it shall not be lawful for any of the constituted authorities, whether of this State, or of the United States, to enforce the payment of duties imposed by the said acts, within the limits of this State; but it shall be the duty of the Legislature to adopt such measures and pass such acts as may be necessary to give full effect to this Ordinance, and to prevent the enforcement and arrest the operation of the said acts and parts of acts of Congress of the United States within the limits of this State, from and after the first day of February next; and the duty of all other constituted authorities, and of all persons residing or being within the limits of this State, and they are hereby required and enjoined, to obey and give effect to this Ordinance, and such acts and measures of the Legislature as may be passed or adopted in obedience thereto.

And it is further Ordained, That in no case of law or equity, decided in the Courts of this State, wherein shall be drawn in question the authority of this Ordinance, or the validity of such act or acts of the Legislature as may be passed for the purpose of giving effect thereto, or the validity of the aforesaid acts of Congress, imposing duties, shall any appeal be taken or allowed to the Supreme Court of the United States; nor shall any copy of the record be permitted or allowed for that purpose; and if any such appeal shall be attempted to be taken, the Courts of this State shall proceed to execute and enforce their judgment, according to the laws and usages of the State, without reference to such attempted appeal, and the person or persons attempting to take such appeal may be dealt with as for a contempt of the Court.

And it is further Ordained, That all persons now holding any office of honor, profit or trust, civil or military, under this State, (members of the Legislature excepted) shall, within such time, and in such manner as the Legislature shall prescribe, take an oath, well and truly to obey, execute and enforce this Ordinance, and such act or acts of the Legislature as may be passed in pursuance thereof, according to the true intent and meaning of the same; and on the neglect or omission of any person or persons so to do, his or their office or offices shall be forthwith vacated, and shall be filled up as if such person or persons were dead or had resigned; and no person hereafter elected to any office of honor, profit or trust, civil or military, (members of the Legislature excepted) shall, until the Legislature shall otherwise provide and direct, enter on the execution of his office, or be in any respect competent to discharge the duties thereof, until he shall, in like manner, have taken a similar oath; and no juror shall be impannelled in any of the Courts of this State, in any cause in which shall be in question this Ordinance, or any act of the Legislature passed in pursuance thereof, unless he shall first, in addition to the usual oath, have taken an oath that he will well and truly obey, execute, and enforce this Ordinance, and such act or acts of the Legislature as may be passed to carry the same into operation and effect, according to the true intent and meaning thereof.

And we, the People of South Carolina, to the end that it may be fully understood by the Government of the United States, and the people of the co-States, that we are determined to maintain this, our Ordinance and Declaration, at every hazard, *Do further Declare*, that we will not submit to the application of force, on the part of the Federal Government, to reduce this State to obedience; but that we will consider the passage, by Congress, of any act authorizing the employment of a military or naval force against the State of South Carolina, her constituted authorities or citizens, or any act abolishing or closing the ports of this State, or any of them, or otherwise obstructing the free ingress of vessels to and from the said ports, or any other act, on the part of the Federal Government, to coerce the State, shut up her ports, destroy or harass her commerce, or to enforce the acts hereby declared to be null and void, otherwise than through the civil tribunals of the country, as inconsistent with the longer continuance of South Carolina in the Union; and that the People of this State will thenceforth hold themselves absolved from all further obligation to maintain or preserve their political connexion with the people of the other States, and will forthwith proceed to organize a separate Government, and to do all other acts and things which sovereign and independent States may of right do.

---

84. South Carolina's Reply to Jackson's Proclamation.

December 20, 1832.

The Legislature reassembled, Nov. 27, and speedily passed a series of Acts to carry the ordinance into effect. (For text of the same, and message of Governor Hamilton, and inaugural speech of Governor Hayne, see *Acts of S. C.*, 1832; *Legislative Proceedings*, 1832; *S. C. Stat. at L.*, I, 371-376; *Niles*, XLIII, 259, 260, 266, 267, 278, 279, 327, 328, 347, 348.) In view of the action of the State, President Jackson, Dec. 10, issued his notable Proclamation to the People of the State. (Text in *Senate Doc.*, 22 Cong., 2 sess., No. 30; reprinted in Richardson, II, 640-656; *Niles*, XLIII, 260-264; Elliot's *Debates*, IV, 582-592; MacDonald, 273-283.) *The Poinsett Papers* contain many letters of interest in this connection. Several of Jackson's letters to Poinsett are in *Penna. Mag. of History*, XII, 280 *et seq.* The following extract from an unpublished letter of Edward Livingston, Sec. of State, to Poinsett, dated Dec. 11, 1832, is important, in view of his connection with the proclamation;

"The Union party will be supported in their endeavors to preserve the Union, and one great object of the proclamation was to make them understand this.

Your situation personally is one of responsibility and danger, but your courage, prudence and energy are fully appreciated and will receive the admiration, as it deserves the gratitude of your country. Let me know the effect of the proclamation on the two parties of your state—it may encourage our friends, but I fear will not influence the conduct of the revolutionists; it will, I am sure, produce union in the other States, it was made argumentative for the purpose of enabling the people to judge for themselves on points on which they have been deceived by sophisms, and by the authority of names on [which] they have placed confidence, it was therefore judged necessary to [present the [1]] reasoning in plain language and to point the consequences [in words not] [fr]equently used in papers of this kind, but the occasion [was an] unusual one and a striking deviation from every day form was deemed necessary and proper.

A report will in a few days be made on the measures necessary for the col-

---

[1] Manuscript mutilated, words in brackets supplied.

lection of the revenue. This will be submitted to Congress and if they pass the necessary laws, I think your great men will soon be abandoned at least by their ——— adherents. This is a most important conjunction, if we return to order. The cause of free governments will receive additional strength from the failure to subvert them. If your mad men prevail, or even protract the struggle, the cause is lost for ever." [*Poinsett Papers*, MS., Vol. VII.]

The Legislature immediately replied to the President's Proclamation on Dec. 17 by authorizing the Governor to issue a counter proclamation and by passing the following resolutions. See *Acts of S. C.*, 1832, 29, 30, 38; *Legislative Proceedings*, 56-60; *S. C. Stat. at L.*, I, 355-357; *Exec. Doc.*, 22 *Cong.*, 2 *sess.*, I, *No.* 45; *Niles*, XLIII, 287, 288, 300. Governor Hayne's Proclamation of Dec. 21 is given in *Senate Doc.*, 22 *Cong.*, 2 *sess.*, *No.* 30, 78-92; *S. C. Stat. at L.*, I, 358-370; *Niles*, XLIII, 308-312. Historical works on nullification and compromise measures: Houston, chs. VII, VIII; Harris, ch. V; McMaster, VI, ch. LVI; Burgess, 178-189, 220-241; Thorpe, *Const. Hist. of U. S.*, II, 387-408; Schouler, III, 482-491; IV, 38-41, 86-111; Von Holst, I, ch. XII; Lalor, II, 1050-1055; Sumner, *Jackson*, 207-223, 277-291; Parton, *Jackson*, III, chs. XXXIII, XXXIV.

The Committee on federal relations, to which was referred the proclamation of the President of the United States, has had it under consideration, and recommend the adoption of the following resolutions:

Resolved, That the power vested by the Constitution and laws in the President of the United States, to issue his proclamation, does not authorize him in that mode, to interfere whenever he may think fit, in the affairs of the respective states, or that he should use it as a means of promulgating executive expositions of the Constitution, with the sanction of force thus superceding the action of other departments of the general government. [The vote, Senate, 25 to 5; House, no division.]

Resolved, That it is not competent to the President of the United States, to order by proclamation the constituted authorities of a state to repeal their legislation, and that the late attempt of the President to do so is unconstitutional, and manifests a disposition to arrogate and exercise a power utterly destructive of liberty. [Senate, 31 to 2; House, no division.]

Resolved, That the opinions of the President, in regard to the rights of the States, are erroneous and dangerous, leading not only to the establishment of a consolidated government in the stead of our free confederacy, but to the concentration of all powers in the chief executive. [Senate, 28 to 5 ; House, 87 to 14.]

Resolved, That the proclamation of the President is the more extraordinary, that he had silently, and as it is supposed, with entire approbation, witnessed our sister state of Georgia avow, act upon, and carry into effect, even to the taking of life, principles identical with those now denounced by him in South Carolina. [Senate, 30 to 3 ; House, 85 to 16.]

Resolved, That each state of the Union has the right, whenever it may deem such a course necessary for the preservation of its liberties or vital interests, to secede peaceably from the Union, and that there is no constitutional power in the general government, much less in the executive department, of that government, to retain by force such state in the Union. [Senate, 27 to 5 ; House, 94 to 7.]

Resolved, That the primary and paramount allegiance of the citizens of this state, native or adopted, is of right due to this state. [Senate, 27 to 5 ; House, 89 to 14.]

Resolved, That the declaration of the President of the United States in his said proclamation, of his personal feelings and relations towards the State of South Carolina, is rather an appeal to the loyalty of subjects, than to the patriotism of citizens, and is a blending of official and individual character, heretofore unknown in our state papers, and revolting to our conception of political propriety. [Senate, 28 to 5 ; House, no division.]

Resolved, That the undisguised indulgence of personal hostility in the said proclamation would be unworthy the animadversion of this legislature, but for the solemn and official form of the instrument which is made its vehicle. [Senate, 26 to 5 ; House, no division.]

Resolved, That the principles, doctrines and purposes, contained in the said proclamation are inconsistent with any just idea of a limited government, and subversive of the rights of the states and liberties of the people, and if submitted to in silence would lay a broad foundation for the establishment of monarchy. [Senate, 24 to 4 ; House no division.]

Resolved, That while this legislature has witnessed with sorrow such a relaxation of the spirit of our institutions, that a President of the United States dare venture upon this high handed measure, it regards with indignation the menaces which are directed against it, and the concentration of a standing army on our borders— that the state will repel force by force, and relying upon the blessings of God, will maintain its liberty at all hazards.

Resolved, That copies of these resolutions be sent to our members in Congress, to be laid before that body.

85. Call for a Convention of the States by South Carolina.

December 18, 1832.

The Legislature also adopted the following resolutions. The text is in *Acts of S. C.*, 1832, *Appx.* 28, 29; *Senate Jour.*, 22 *Cong.*, 2 *sess.*, 83; *House Ex. Doc.*, II, *No.* 59; *Niles*, XLIII, 300.

Whereas serious causes of discontent do exist among the States of this Union, from the exercise by Congress of powers not conferred or contemplated by the sovereign parties to the compact, therefore,

Resolved, That it is expedient that a Convention of the States be called as early as practicable to determine and consider such questions of disputed power, as have arisen between the States of the confederacy and the General Government.

Resolved, That the Governor be requested to transmit copies of this preamble and resolutions to the Governors of the Several States, with a request that the same be laid before the Legislatures of their respective States, and also to our Senators and Representatives in Congress, to be by them laid before Congress for consideration.

Reply to South Carolina's Call for a Convention.

1833.

The Legislatures of Delaware, Massachusetts and Ohio replied that it was inexpedient to hold such a convention. The text of the reply of Delaware, which follows, is found in *Senate Jour.*, 22 *Cong.*, 2 *sess.*, 157, 158; *Senate Doc.*, I, *No.* 66; *Niles*, XLIII, 422. The replies of Massachusetts and Ohio are given in *State Papers on Nullification*, 209, 244–257. Georgia proposed a Southern convention, and Alabama a convention to amend the Constitution, but at the same time condemned nullification. See *post*, pp. 179, 180; Ames, *Proposed Amendments*, 282.

86. Delaware on a Convention of the States, January 25, 1833.

Whereas certain resolutions, passed in December last by both branches of the Legislature of South Carolina, declaring " that it is expedient that a Convention of the States be called," etc., have been transmitted by the Executive of that State to the Governor of this, and by him laid before the General Assembly for an expression of its sentiments; Therefore,

Resolved, by the Senate and House of Representatives of the State of Delaware in General Assembly met, That the Constitution of the United States of America, which is a form of government established by the people of the United States of America, has expressly provided a tribunal in the Supreme Court of the United States, for the settlement of all controversies between the United States and the respective States, and of all controversies arising under that instrument itself.

Resolved, That the Constitution of the United States of America does not recognize any such tribunal or political assemblage as a Convention of the States, but has expressly provided for modes of amendment, if amendment be necessary, in the fifth article.   [Here follows the text of Article V.]   Any other mode must therefore be repugnant to its provisions.

Resolved, That such a Convention to propose amendments, when called by Congress, must be, in the nature of things, a Convention of the people from whom the Constitution derived its authority, and by whom alone it can be altered, and not a Convention of the States.

Resolved, That no such political assemblage as a Convention of the *States*, could take place as a *constituent* organ of Government; and that, if assembled, it could have no such power as that set forth by the resolutions of South Carolina, " to *consider* and *determine* such questions of disputed power as have arisen between the States of this Confederacy and the General Government."

Resolved, That it is not expedient for Congress to call " a Convention for proposing amendment " at this time. But that if any amendment be necessary, it comports with the views of the General Assembly of this State, that they should be proposed in the other mode provided by the Constitution—" by two-thirds of both Houses of Congress." [Resolutions of transmission.]

Replies of the Co-States.
1832-33.

The Legislatures of the several States adopted resolutions condemning the action of South Carolina, and the large majority also expressed their approval of the proclamation and action of the President. Maine alone of the Northern States condemned the tariff laws. New York, New Jersey, Pennsylvania, Maryland, Ohio and Kentucky declared expressly against the right of secession. The resolutions of Massachusetts, New York and Delaware were accompanied by elaborate reports discussing the nature of the Union. The resolutions of Maryland also dealt with the same. New Jersey, Delaware, Maryland and Kentucky declared that the Federal Supreme Court was the proper and only tribunal for the final settlement of controversies in relation to the Constitution and the laws of Congress. Condemnation by the Northern and Pro-Tariff States was to be expected, but even the other Southern States disapproved of the action of South Carolina. Official expression of opposition to the doctrine of nullification had not been lacking in several of the Southern States in the period 1828-31. (See *Niles,* XXXV, 263; XXXIX, 423; XLI, 272, 352.) The resolutions adopted by the Legislatures of several of the Southern and Anti-Tariff States, which follow, have been selected as being of especial interest and value. It will be noted that Georgia and Alabama suggested conventions, that Virginia and Alabama requested South Carolina to suspend her ordinance, and Congress to modify the tariff, and that Virginia disagreed with both the position of South Carolina and of the President, and voted to send a Commissioner to South Carolina.

The text of the replies of seventeen of the twenty-three Co-States to South Carolina are given in *State Papers on Nullification.* The resolves of two additional States, Kentucky and Tennessee, are in *Niles,* XLIII, 209, 220, 352; cf. also *Acts of Ky.,* 1833, 309-316; *Acts of Tenn.,* 1832; 55-57. Several of the above are in *House Ex. Doc.,* 22 Cong., 2 sess., Nos. 19, 67, 81, 90, 103, 114, 140, 141, 142; *Niles,* XLIII, 274, 299, 350-352, 383, 400, 422. See also *Pamphlet Laws* of the several States.

87. Georgia on a Southern Convention and
Nullification.

December 14, 1832.

Another set of resolutions making application for a convention to amend the Federal Constitution in thirteen particulars, and purporting to have passed the Legislature December 12, was sent to the other States and to Congress. It was entered upon the *Senate Jour.*, 22 *Cong.*, 2 *sess.*, 65, 66; also given in *State Papers on Nullification*, 238, 239. Replies of disapproval were adopted by Massachusetts, Connecticut and Mississippi. *Ibid.*, 258-267, 277-280, 286; Ames, *Prop. Amend.*, 282, 345. Later the Governor notified the several States that the above-mentioned resolutions had not been passed, but that the following, proposing a Southern convention, had been adopted instead. Letter of June 7, 1833, *Ibid.*, 269. For messages of Gov. Lumpkin and action of Legislature, see *Niles*, XLIII, 206-208, 251, 279, 280, 287.

WHEREAS, The Tariff Law of the last session of Congress has not satisfied the just expectation of the people of the Southern States : *whereas*, the recent attempt to provide a remedy for the evils which we suffer from the protective system, by a State Convention, not only will probably be abortive, but is likely, if persisted in, materially to disturb the public harmony, and lessen the moral force of the State : and, *whereas*, the resolutions adopted by the delegates of a minority of the people, and which are about to be submitted to the whole State for ratification, are in several respects of a most objectionable character, it becomes the duty of those who are the unquestionable representatives of the people of Georgia, to interpose for the purpose of tranquilizing the public mind, and concentrating the public will, by the recommendation of a course of policy, which, they trust, will obtain the general approbation of the community. Therefore,

Resolved, That if a Southern Convention be desirable, it is expedient for the State of Georgia, to invite the States of Virginia, North Carolina, South Carolina, Alabama, Tennessee, and Mississippi to concur with her in electing Delegates to a Convention, which shall take into consideration the Tariff system of the General Government, and devise and recommend the most effectual and proper mode of obtaining relief from the evils of that system. [Vote in House, 97 to 57.]

[Here follow provisions for a vote on the question of a Southern Convention and the details of the plan for its assembly, and resolutions condemning the action ot a certain Convention recently held in the State.[1]]

Resolved, That while we would provide a corrective for the possible continuance of those evils, of which we have so much reason to complain, we still hope that the regular operations of the General Government will supercede the necessity of any extraordinary measure on the part of the Southern people, and that we recognize the happiest augury of better things, in the growing certainty of the re-election of that illustrious patriot, Andrew Jackson.

Resolved, That we abhor the doctrine of Nullification as neither a peaceful, nor a constitutional remedy, but, on the contrary, as tending to civil commotion and disunion ; and while we deplore the rash and revolutionary measures, recently adopted by a Convention of the people of South Carolina, we deem it as paramount duty to warn our fellow citizens against the danger of adopting her mischievous policy.   [Vote in House, 102 to 51.]

[*State Papers on Nullification,* 271–274.]

88. Resolutions of Alabama Proposing a Convention.
January 12, 1833.

In addition to the following resolutions the Assembly also adopted another report, of the same date, recommending to Congress " a speedy modification of the tariff laws," the call of a Federal Convention, and to South Carolina to suspend the operation of her Ordinance, and " to abstain from the use of military power" to enforce the same, and to the government of the United States also to exercise moderation. *State Papers on Nullification,* 224, 225. The text of the subjoined resolutions is in *Ibid.,* 219–223; *Exec. Doc.,* 22 *Cong.,* 2 *sess.,* III, *No.* 141. None of the States responded to this suggestion for a convention. For Gov. Gayle's messages, cf. *Niles,* XLII, 352; XLIII, 220.

*   *   *   *   *   *   *

And now, at this fearful crisis, when one of our co-States has assumed the alarming attitude of declaring an act of Congress void within her limits, and the note of preparation is sounded to sustain this attitude by force, what shall Alabama do? Our

---

[1] An Anti-Tariff convention held at Milledgeville, November 12. Its proceedings are given in *Niles,* XLIII, 220–222, 230, 231.

answer is never to despair of our country. We believe that there is a vital energy, a living principle inherent in our institutions, and a sense of justice residing in the bosom of our fellow citizens, which, when properly appealed to, must succeed. We concede that our northern brethren believe that they are acting within the pale of the constitution, but can it be believed that they will, by insisting on the obnoxious duties, peril the union of these States, and make shipwreck of the last hope of mankind? Can any pecuniary benefit compensate for results like these? If blood be shed in this unhallowed contest, a wound will be inflicted which may never be healed: to confidence will succeed distrust, mutual recriminations, and mutual injuries; and the choicest blessings of Heaven, by the madness and folly of man, will be converted into the most deadly poison.

Deeply impressed with these views, we recommend the adoption of the following resolutions, which we are satisfied embody the opinions of our constituents, and, in their name, propose to our co-States a Federal Convention.

Be it resolved by the Senate and House of Representatives of the State of Alabama, in General Assembly convened, That, we consider the present tariff of duties unequal, unjust, oppressive, and against the spirit, true intent, and meaning of the constitution; that, if persevered in, its inevitable tendency will be to alienate the affections of the people of the Southern States from the General Government.

And be it further resolved, That we do not consider the tariff of 1832 as fastening upon the country the principle of protection; but that we receive it as the harbinger of better times—as a pledge that Congress will at no distant period, abandon the principle of protection altogether, and reduce the duties on imports to the actual wants of the Government, levying those duties on such articles as will operate most equally on all sections of the Union.

And be it further resolved, That nullification, which some of our southern brethren recommend as the constitutional remedy for the evils under which we labor, is unsound in theory and dangerous in practice; that as a remedy, it is unconstitutional and essentially revolutionary, leading in its consequences to anarchy and civil discord, and finally to the dissolution of the Union.

And be it further resolved, That we earnestly entreat the people of this State not to distrust the justice of the General Government, and to rest satisfied that, though long delayed, it will certainly be accorded to them. And above all things, to avoid those dangerous and unconstitutional remedies proposed for their imitation and adoption, no matter how specious their exterior, which may lead to bloodshed and disunion, and will certainly end in anarchy and civil discord. And, at the same time, we would most solemnly adjure the Congress of the United States, in the name of our common country, to abandon the exercise of those dubious and constructive powers claimed under the constitution, the assertion of which has produced jealousy, excitement, and dissatisfaction to the Government, and, if persevered in, will, in all human probability, dissolve this Union. By this means, and by this alone, can we be prevented from fulfilling our high destinies, and our onward march to greatness be arrested.

And be it further resolved, That as we have now, for the first time in the history of our country, presented to us the appalling spectacle of one of the States of this Union arraying herself against the General Government, and declaring sundry acts of Congress void and of no effect within her limits; presenting to Congress the alternative of repealing the obnoxious laws, or permitting her secession from the Union, and preparing by an armed force to sustain the position she has assumed; and as we cannot silently look on, and witness the failure of all the high raised hopes and just expectations of those patriots who cemented our liberty with their blood—Therefore, as a last resort, we recommend to our co-States the calling of a FEDERAL CONVENTION, to meet in the city of Washington, on the 1st of March, 1834, or at such other time and place as may be agreed on, which shall be authorized to devise and recommend some plan which will satisfy the discontents of the south, either by an explicit denial of the right of Congress to protect domestic industry by duties on imports laid for protection, or by defining and restricting the power aforesaid within certain prescribed limits, and making such other amendments and alterations in the constitution as time and experience have discovered to be necessary. [Resolutions of transmission.]

89. Resolves of North Carolina.

January 5, 1833.

Gov. Stokes' message is in *Niles*, XLIII, 219. The text of the resolutions is in *State Papers on Nullification*, 201, 202; *Niles*, XLIII, 351, 352. They passed by a vote of 47 to 7 in the Senate, and 98 to 22 in the House.

Resolved, That the General Assembly of the State of North Carolina doth entertain, and doth unequivocally express a warm attachment to the Constitution of the United States.

Resolved, That the General Assembly doth solemnly declare a devoted attachment to the Federal Union, believing that on its continuance depend the liberty, the peace and prosperity of the United States.

Resolved, That whatever diversity of opinion may prevail in this State, as to the constitutionality of the acts of Congress imposing duties on imports for protection, yet, it is believed, a large majority of the people think those acts unconstitutional; and they are united in the sentiment, that the existing Tariff is impolitic, unjust and oppressive; and they have urged, and will continue to urge its repeal.

Resolved, That the doctrine of Nullification as avowed by the State of South Carolina, and lately promulgated in an Ordinance, is revolutionary in its character, subversive of the Constitution of the United States and leads to a dissolution of the Union.

Resolved, That our Senators in Congress be instructed, and our representatives be requested to use all constitutional means in their power, to procure a peaceable adjustment of the existing controversy between the State of South Carolina and the General Government, and to produce a reconciliation between the contending parties. [Resolutions of transmission.]

90. Report and Resolves of Mississippi, January Session, 1833.

In relation to the Resolutions from the States of Maine, New Hampshire, and Pennsylvania, and that portion of the Message which points to the consideration, your Committee would express the belief that the sentiments of a majority of the people of this State in regard to the subjects to which they relate, are in accordance with those expressed by the General Assembly in the year

1829, declaring the Tariff of 1828, so far as it contemplated a system of protection, carried beyond the manufacture of such articles as are necessary to the national defence, to be "contrary to the spirit of the Constitution of the United States, impolitic and oppressive in its operation on the southern States, and should be resisted by all constitutional means." But fearful lest false inferences should be drawn from this expression of public opinion—inferences, calculated to induce a belief that this State is prepared to advocate and uphold the disorganizing doctrines, recently promulgated in South Carolina, your Committee deem it their duty to speak plainly, and to undeceive their Sister States in this respect. We are opposed to Nullification. We regard it as heresy, fatal to the existence of the Union. "It is resistance to law by force—it is disunion by force—it is civil war." Your Committee are constrained to express the opinion, that the State of South Carolina has acted with a reckless precipitancy, (originating, we would willingly believe, in delusion,) well calculated to detract from her former high character for wisdom in council, purity of patriotism, and a solicitous regard for the preservation of those fundamental principles, on which alone rest the peace, the prosperity and permanency of the Union. Your Committee deeply deplore the alarming crisis in our national affairs; they regret it the more as proceeding from the unwarrantable attitude assumed by a sister of the South, whose best interests are identified with our own. In the spirit of brethren of the same family, we would invoke them to pause—to hearken attentively to the paternal, yet ominous, warning of the Executive of the Union. We would conjure them to await patiently the gradual progress of public opinion; and to rely, with patriotic confidence, on the ultimate decision of the talented statesmen and pure patriots in the Congress of the United States. But they would also loudly proclaim, that this State owes a duty to the Union, above all minor considerations. That she prizes that Union less than liberty alone. That we heartily accord in the general political sentiments of the President of the United States, as expressed in his recent Proclamation; and that we stand firmly resolved, at whatever sacrifice of feeling, in all events, and at every hazard, to sustain him in enforcing the paramount laws of the land, and preserving the integrity of the Union—that Union, whose value we will never stop to calculate—holding it, as our fathers held it, precious above all price. Your Committee would therefore recommend the adoption of the following resolutions:

1. *Be it resolved by the Legislature of the State of Mississippi,* That, in the language of the father of his country, we will "indignantly frown upon the first dawning of every attempt to alienate any portion of our country from the rest, or to enfeeble the ties which link together its various parts."

2. *Resolved,* That the doctrine of Nullification is contrary to the letter and spirit of the Constitution, and in direct conflict with the welfare, safety and independence of every State in the Union; and to no one of them would its consequences be more deeply disastrous, more ruinous, than to the State of Mississippi —that State in which are concentrated our dearest interests— around which cling our most tender ties—the fair land of our nativity or adoption—the haven of our hopes, the home of our hearts.

3. *Resolved,* That we will, with heart and hand, sustain the President of the United States, in the full exercise of his legitimate powers, to restore peace and harmony to our distracted country, and to maintain, unsullied and unimpaired, the honor, the independence and integrity of the Union. [Resolutions of transmission.]

[*Laws of the State of Mississippi,* 1833, 246–248.]

91.   Resolves of Virginia.
January 26, 1833.

The text of the several messages of Gov. Floyd are given in *Niles,* XLII, 351; XLIII, 275, 379. For action of the Legislature, see *Ibid.,* 275, 276, 286. The text of the report is in *Ibid.,* 394–397; of the resolutions in *Acts of Virginia,* 1832–33, 201, 202; *State Papers on Nullification,* 195–197. For documents in connection with the mission of B. W. Leigh as Commissioner to South Carolina, see *Ibid.,* 323–337; *Niles,* XLIII, 397, 434, 435; XLIV, 71, 72. Report of Leigh upon his mission, *Calendar of Va. State Papers,* X, 584–586.

Whereas, the General Assembly of Virginia, actuated by an

ardent desire to preserve the peace and harmony of our common country—relying upon the sense of justice of the people of each and every State in the Union, as a sufficient pledge that their Representatives in Congress, will so modify the acts laying duties and imposts on the importation of foreign commodites, commonly called the Tariff Acts, that they will no longer furnish cause of complaint to the people of any particular State; believing, accordingly, that the people of South Carolina are mistaken in supposing that Congress will yield them no relief from the pressure of those acts, especially as the auspicious approach of the extinguishment of the public debt affords a just ground for the indulgence of a contrary expectation; and confident that they are too strongly attached to the union of the States, to resort to any proceedings which might dissolve or endanger it, whilst they have any fair hope of obtaining their object by more regular and peaceful measures; persuaded, also, that they will listen willingly and respectfully to the voice of Virginia, earnestly and affectionately requesting and entreating them to rescind or suspend their late Ordinance, and await the result of a combined and strenuous effort of the friends of union and peace, to affect an adjustment and reconciliation of all public differences now unhappily existing; regarding, moreover, an appeal to force on the part of the General Government, or on the part of the Government of South Carolina, as a measure which nothing but extreme necessity could justify or excuse in either; but, apprehensive at the same time, that if the present state of things is allowed to continue, acts of violence will occur, which may lead to consequences that all would deplore, cannot but deem it a solemn duty to interpose and mediate between the high contending parties, by the declaration of their opinions and wishes, which they trust that both will consider and respect. Therefore,

1. *Resolved, by the General Assembly, in the name and on behalf of the people of Virginia*, That the competent authorities of South Carolina be, and they are hereby earnestly and respectfully requested and entreated to rescind the Ordinance of the late Convention of that State, entitled "An Ordinance to Nullify certain Acts of the Congress of the United States, purporting to be laws laying duties and imposts on the importation of foreign

commodities;" or, at least to suspend its operation until the close of the first session of the next Congress,

2. *Resolved*, That the Congress of the United States be, and they are hereby earnestly and respectfully requested and entreated, so to modify the Acts laying duties and imposts on the importation of foreign commodities, commonly called the Tariff Acts, as to effect a gradual but speedy reduction of the resulting revenue of the General Government, to the standard of the necessary and proper expenditure for the support thereof.

3. *Resolved*, That the people of Virginia expect, and in the opinion of the General Assembly, the people of the other States have a right to expect, that the General Government, and the Government of South Carolina, and all persons acting under the authority of either, will carefully abstain from any and all acts whatever, which may be calculated to disturb the tranquility of the country, or endanger the existence of the Union.

AND WHEREAS, considering the opinions whlch have been advanced, and maintained by the Convention of South Carolina, in its late Ordinance and Addresses, on the one hand, and by the President of the United States, in his Proclamaton, bearing date the 10th day of December, 1832, on the other, the General Assembly deem it due to themselves, and the people whom they represent, to declare and make known their own views in relation to some of the important and interesting questions which these papers present.   Therefore,

4. *Resolved by the General Assembly*, That they continue to regard the doctrines of State Sovereignty and State Rights, as set forth in the Resolutions of 1798, and sustained by the Report thereon of 1799, as a true interpretation of the Constitution of the United States, and of the powers therein given to the General Government; but that they do not consider them as sanctioning the proceedings of South Carolina, indicated in her said Ordinance; nor as countenancing all the principles assumed by the President in his said Proclamation—many of which are in direct conflict with them.

5. *Resolved*, That this House will, by joint vote with the Senate, proceed on this day to elect a Commissioner, whose duty it shall be to proceed immediately to South Carolina, and commu-

nicate the foregoing Preamble and Resolutions to the Governor
of the State, with a request that they be communicated to the
Legislature of that State, or any Convention of its citizens, or
give them such other directions as in his judgment may be best
calculated to promote the objects which this Commonwealth
has in view; and that the said Commissioner be authorized to
express to the public authorities and people of our sister State,
in such manner as he may deem most expedient, our sincere
good will to our Sister State, and our anxious solicitude that the
kind and peaceful recommendations we have addressed to her,
may lead to an accommodation of all the difficulties between
that State and the General Government. [Resolutions of transmission.]

---

92.   South Carolina's Final Action.

March 18, 1833.

As South Carolina continued her preparations for resistance to force (see call
for volunteers, *Niles*, XLIII, 312), and the President showed his determination
to enforce the tariff laws in his special message of January 16, 1833, an armed
conflict seemed imminent as the critical date, February 1, drew near. Owing
to the failure of the other Southern States to support South Carolina, and the
indications that Congress would adopt a Force Bill, as well as the prospect of
a modification of the tariff, the leading nullificationists determined to avoid a
resort to force.   Accordingly, a meeting of citizens at Charleston, January 21,
informally suspended the nullification ordinance pending the action of Congress.
(*Niles*, XLIII, 380–382.)   At the solicitation of the Commissioner from Virginia,
B. W. Leigh, who presented the resolutions of the Legislature of that State,
the President of the Convention, James Hamilton, Jr., on February 13, issued
a call for the reassembling of that body on March 11.   Before the Convention
met, Congress, after a notable discussion, adopted both the Force Bill and the
Compromise Tariff Bill.   (For speeches of Webster and Calhoun of February
15 and 16, on nullification and the Force Bill, see *Cong. Debates*, 553–587,
750–774; Webster, *Works*, III, 448–505, Calhoun, *Works*, II, 197–309;
Johnson, *Amer. Orations*, I, 303–319.   The text of the Force Act is in *U. S.
Stat. at L.*, IV, 632–635; reprinted in MacDonald, 284–289.)   At the second
session of the South Carolina Convention the ordinance nullifying the tariff
laws was repealed March 15, but a new ordinance nullifying the " Force Bill "
was adopted March 18.   The text of the new ordinance, which follows, is
found in *S. C. Stat. at L.*, I, 400, 401; *Acts of S. C.*, 1834, *Appx.* ii.   *The
Journal of the second session of the Convention* (Columbus, 1833) is reprinted

in *State Papers on Nullification*, 321–375. The important documents are also given in *S. C. Stat. at L.*, I, 377–389. The correspondence of B. W. Leigh and the Reply of the Convention to Virginia are also contained in the above; see also *ante*, p. 185. For South Carolina's celebrations and comments upon the result of the controversy see *Niles*, XLIV, 58, 89, 107, 114, 126 128, 383; XLV, 23, 129. Gov. Hayne's message of congratulation of November 26, 1833, is in *Legislative Proceedings*, 1833, 1–8.

An Ordinance

To Nullify an Act of the Congress of the United States, entitled "An Act further to provide for the Collection of Duties on Imports," commonly called the Force Bill.

We, the People of the State of South Carolina in Convention assembled, do *Declare and Ordain*, that the Act of the Congress of the United States, entitled "An Act further to provide for the collection of duties on imports," approved the second day of March, 1833, is unauthorized by the Constitution of the United States, subversive of that Constitution, and destructive of public liberty; and that the same is, and shall be deemed, null and void, within the limits of this State; and it shall be the duty of the Legislature, at such time as they may deem expedient, to adopt such measures and pass such acts as may be necessary to prevent the enforcement thereof, and to inflict proper penalties on any person who shall do any act in execution or enforcement of the same within the limits of this State.

We do further Declare and Ordain, That the allegiance of the citizens of this State, while they continue such, is due to the said State; and that obedience only, and not allegiance, is due by them to any other power or authority, to whom a control over them has been, or may be delegated by the State; and the General Assembly of the said State is hereby empowered, from time to time, when they may deem it proper, to provide for the administration to the citizens and officers of the State, or such of the said officers as they may think fit, of suitable oaths or affirmations, binding them to the observance of such allegiance; and abjuring all other allegiance; and, also, to define what shall amount to a violation of their allegiance, and to provide the proper punishment for such violation.

The North-Eastern Boundary Controversy.

1831–32.

The States of Maine and Massachusetts were very much alarmed for fear that the recommendations of the King of Holland, arbitrator in the North Eastern boundary controversy, would be accepted. This would have deprived Maine of a considerable portion of the territory she claimed, and Massachusetts of the ownership of certain tracts of lands. Accordingly the Legislatures of both States passed resolutions protesting against the decision, and declaring that its acceptance would be null and void. The award was not accepted, and subsequently the boundary was determined by the Webster-Ashburton treaty (*Treaties and Conventions*, 432–438.) For other reports, resolves and additional documents, see *Resolves of Maine*, 1820–28, 659–797; *Ibid.*, 1829-35, 243–246, 449–500; *Resolves of Mass.*, 1832–35, 76–97; see also *Amer. An. Reg.*, 1826–27, 438–440; *Ibid.*, 1830–31, 306–316; *Ibid.*, 1831–32, 229–234; *Niles*, XLI, 227, 228; XLII, 100–104, 460–464; McMaster, V, 463–476; Thorpe, *Const. Hist. of Amer. People*, I, 340, 341, note.

93. Extract from Resolutions of the Legislature of the State of Maine, January 19, 1832.

Resolved, That the Constitution of the United States does not invest the General Government with unlimited and absolute powers, but confers only a special and modified sovereignty, without authority to cede to a foreign power any portion of territory belonging to a State, without its consent.

Resolved, "That if there is an attribute of State Sovereignty which is unqualified and undeniable, it is the right of jurisdiction to the utmost limits of State Territory; and if a single obligation under the Constitution rests upon the Confederacy, it is to guarantee the integrity of this territory to the quiet and undisturbed enjoyment of the States."

Resolved, That the doings of the King of Holland, on the subject of the boundary between the United States and Great Britain, are not a decision of the question submitted to the King of the Netherlands; and that his recommendation of a suitable or convenient line of boundary is not obligatory upon the parties to the submission.

Resolved, That this State protests against the adoption, by the Government of the United States, of the line of boundary recommended by the King of Holland as a suitable boundary between Great Britain and the United States; inasmuch as it

will be a violation of the rights of Maine,—rights acknowledged
and insisted upon by the General Government,—and will be a
precedent, which endangers the integrity, as well as the independence, of every State in the Union.

Resolved, That while the people of this State are disposed to
yield a ready obedience to the Constitution and laws of the
United States, they will never consent to surrender any portion
of their territory, on the recommendation of a Foreign Power.

[*Resolves of Maine*, 1829–35, 343.]

94. Extracts from Resolutions of Massachusetts, February 15, 1832.

Resolved, by the Senate and House of Representatives, in
General Court assembled, that the Government of the United
States possesses the constitutional right to ascertain and settle,
by negotiation with foreign powers, arbitration, or otherwise,
such parts of the boundary lines of the said States, as were left
doubtful by the Treaty of Peace of 1783, but that the said
Government does not possess the constitutional right to alter, by
negotiation with foreign powers, arbitration, or otherwise, the
boundary lines of the said States so far as the same were ascertained and settled by the said treaty, to the prejudice of the
territorial or other rights of any State, without the consent of
such State previously obtained. * * *

Resolved * * * that the Government of the United States,
in permitting the same to be made a question by the said Commissioners, and to be by them submitted to the arbitration of the
King of the Netherlands, without the consent of Massachusetts
and Maine previously obtained, exceeded its constitutional
powers, and that any decision which the said King might have
given upon said question, would have been entirely null and
void, for want of constitutional power in the Government of the
United States to make the submission.

* * * * * * *

Resolved, That the Government of the United States has no
constitutional right to cede any portion of the territory of the
States composing the Union to any foreign power, or to deprive
any State of any land, or other property without the consent of

such State, previously obtained; and that the adoption of the aforesaid new boundary line, recommended, as aforesaid, by the King of the Netherlands, without the consent, previously obtained, of the States of Massachusetts and Maine, would be a violation of the rights of jurisdiction and property, belonging respectively to the said States, and secured to them by the Federal Constitution; and that any act, purporting to have such effect, would be wholly null and void, and in no way obligatory upon the Government or People of either of the said States.

Resolved, That as the adoption, by the Government of the United States, of the aforesaid new boundary line, so recommended by the said King of the Netherlands, would deprive the Commonwealth of Massachusetts of large tracts of land, without equivalent, it is not expedient for the said Commonwealth to give consent thereto; and that the General Court hereby solemnly protest against such adoption, declaring, that any act, purporting to have such effect, will have been performed without the consent of the Commonwealth, and in violation of the rights thereof, as secured by the Federal Constitution, and will be consequently null and void and in no way obligatory upon the Government or people.

Resolved, That the General Court have received with satisfaction the communication made to them through His Excellency the Governor, from the Government of the State of Maine, of the proceedings of the said Government, upon this subject;— that they reciprocate the friendly sentiments, which have been expressed on this occasion, by that Government, and will readily and cheerfully coöperate with the State of Maine, in such measures as shall be best calculated to prevent the adoption, by the Government of the United States, of the new boundary line recommended, as aforesaid, by the King of the Netherlands.

* * * * * * *

[*Resolves of Mass.*, 1832–35, 92–97 *in passim.*]

SLAVERY AND THE CONSTITUTION, 1789–1845.

Early Resolutions on Slavery : Powers of Congress.

1790–1808.

The House of Representatives of the first Congress was called upon to define the powers vested in Congress relating to slavery. As this question became of such vital importance in the later struggle over slavery it seems desirable to note the first formal expression of opinion from an official source. The subjoined resolutions were adopted, March 23, 1790, by the Committee of the whole House, after an extended discussion, by a vote of 29 yeas to 25 nays, in place of the report of the special committee. *Annals, I Cong., 2 sess.*, 1413–1417, 1450–1474; *House Journal*, 168–181; Du Bois, *Suppression of the African Slave Trade*, ch. VIII; Schouler, I, 145–148; Wilson, *Rise and Fall of the Slave Power*, I, 60–67; Curtis, *Const. History*, II, 231–244.

Three years later Congress was led to exercise the power conferred upon it by the Constitution to pass the first Fugitive Slave Act, Feb. 12, 1793 (*Stat. at Large*, I, 302). See, McDougall, *Fugitive Slaves*, 16–19; Hildreth, IV, 406–440; Von Holst, I, 309–315; Wilson, I, ch. VI.

With the exception of the resolutions of Virginia, of 1800–1804, on colonization, referred to later, the only other phase of the slavery question which especially called out resolutions from the State legislatures during the early years was that of the abolition of the foreign slave trade. In the period 1804–'08 at least seven states, including North Carolina, Maryland and Tennessee proposed an amendment to the Constitution to abolish this trade, but this was deemed unnecessary, and the trade was prohibited by act of Congress, March 2, 1807, to go into effect on Jan. 1, 1808. (*Stat. at Large*, II, 426.) See Du Bois, ch. VIII; Ames, *Proposed Amendments*, 208, 209: Wilson, I, ch. VII.

---

95. The House of Representatives on the Powers of Congress.

March 23, 1790.

The Committee of the whole House, to whom was committed the report of the committee on memorials of the people called Quakers, and of the Pennsylvania Society for promoting the Abolition of Slavery, report the following amendments:

First. That the migration or importation of such persons as any of the States now existing shall think proper to admit, cannot be prohibited by Congress, prior to the year one thousand eight hundred and eight.

Secondly. That Congress have no authority to interfere in the emancipation of slaves, or in the treatment of them within any of the States; it remaining with the several States alone to provide any regulations therein, which humanity and true policy may require.

Thirdly. That Congress have authority to restrain the citizens of the United States from carrying on the African trade, for the purpose of supplying foreigners with slaves, and of providing, by proper regulations, for the humane treatment, during their passage, of slaves imported by the said citizens into the States admitting such importation.

Fourthly. That Congress have authority to prohibit foreigners from fitting out vessels in any port of the United States for transporting persons from Africa to any foreign port.[1]

[1] This resolution is the same as in the report of Special Committee.

96. Resolutions of Virginia on Colonization.

December 23, 1816.

As early as December 31, 1800, the Virginia House of Delegates, in consequence of a slave conspiracy authorized Governor Monroe to correspond with President Jefferson in regard to the purchase of lands " whither persons obnoxious to the laws and dangerous to the peace of society may be removed." This correspondence was laid before the legislature, and that body, on January 23, 1802, adopted resolutions in favor of the United States procuring a place without the limits of the country, preferably Africa or South America, for the colonization of free negroes. Again in December, 1804, other resolutions were passed favoring the setting apart a portion of Louisiana for this purpose. For text of these resolutions and the Monroe-Jefferson correspondence, see *American State Papers, Misc.*, I, 464–467; *Annals, 9 Cong., 2 sess.*, Appx., 994–1000. See also Jefferson's *Works*, V, 563; *Writings*, VIII, 103, 152, 161.

Here the matter rested until December 23, 1816, when the question was again raised by the subjoined resolutions of Virginia. (Vote of House, 137 to 9.) This movement was followed by the organization of the American Colonization Society at Washington a few days later. The objects of the society were shortly endorsed by Georgia, Dec. 19, 1817; Maryland, Jan. 26, 1818; Tennessee, in 1818, and Vermont, Nov. 5, 1819. Opposition to the movement did not appear until about 1824. (See *post*, p. 203.) Mercer's Report, 19 *Cong.*, 2 *sess., House Reports*, II, *No.* 101, contains the history of the society, extracts from its Reports and acts and resolutions of several of the states, 1817–27. See *Annual Reports of Amer. Col. Society*, 1818–; also *Memorial of the Semi-Centennial Anniversary of Amer. Col. Society* (1867), 65–78. The text of the Virginia resolutions is in *Acts of Virginia*, 1816–17, 200; *Niles*, XI, 275.

General references: Ballagh, *History of Slavery in Virginia*, 136, 137; McPherson in *Johns Hopkins Univ. Studies*, IX, 495–497; McMaster, IV, 557–563; V, 193–196; Schouler, II, 58, 129; III, 138–144; Von Holst, I, 329–333; Wilson, *Rise and Fall of Slave Power*, I, ch. XV.

WHEREAS the General Assembly of Virginia have repeatedly sought to obtain an asylum, beyond the limits of the United States, for such persons of colour, as had been, or might be emancipated under the laws of this commonwealth, but have hitherto found all their efforts, for the accomplishment of this desirable purpose, frustrated, either by the disturbed state of other nations, or domestic causes equally unpropitious to its success ;

They now avail themselves of a period, when peace has healed the wounds of humanity, and the principal nations of Europe have concurred, with the government of the United States, in abolishing the African slave trade, (a traffic which this commonwealth, both before and since the revolution, zealously sought to terminate,) to renew this effort, and do therefore resolve, that the executive be requested to correspond with the President of the United States, for the purpose of obtaining a territory upon the coast of Africa, or upon the shore of the North Pacific, or at some other place not within any of the States or territorial governments of the United States, to serve as an asylum for such persons of colour, as are now free, and may desire the same, and for those who may be hereafter emancipated, within this commonwealth ; and that the senators and representatives of this state in this congress of the United States be requested to exert their best efforts to aid the president of the United States in the attainment of the above object : *Provided*, that no contract or arrangement respecting such territory shall be obligatory on this commonwealth until ratified by the Legislature.

[*Acts of Virginia*, 1816, 200.]

The Missouri Contest.

1819–1820.

While the question of the admission of Missouri was still pending in Congress during the session of 1819–20, the legislatures of several of the northern states adopted resolutions against the admission of Missouri, except with the exclusion of slavery. Such resolutions were passed by Vermont, New Hampshire, Massachusetts, New York, New Jersey, Pennsylvania, Delaware, Ohio and Indiana. On the other hand, resolutions opposing any such restrictions were adopted by some of the southern states, including Maryland, Virginia and Kentucky. The Massachusetts and Virginia resolutions were each accompanied by a report containing the chief arguments advanced in support of their respective positions. The New Hampshire report (June, 1820) replied to that from Virginia. (*Niles*, XVIII, 337–340.) Examples of each class follow. For the text of others, see *Vermont Assembly Journal*, 1819, 109, 174, 212; *Records of Governor and Council of Vermont*, VI, 540; *Resolves of Massachusetts*, 1819–24, 147–151; *Journal of New York Assembly*, 1820, 115; *Laws of Pennsylvania*, VIII, 674; *Acts of Virginia*, 1819–20, 113–124; *Acts of Kentucky*, 1819–20, 989 990; *Senate Journal*, 16 Cong., 1 sess., 78–80, 113–

116, 124, 130, 131, 136. Several of the above are also given in *Niles*, XVII, 296, 334, 342-344, 395, 399, 400, 416; XVIII, 337-340; Greeley, *History of the Struggle of Slavery Extension and Restriction* (N. Y., 1856), 25-27; *National Intelligencer*, February 8, 1821; McMaster, IV, 577-579; Hildreth, VI, 687, 688.

General rererences: MacDonald, *Documents*, 219–226; Burgess, ch. IV; Greeley, *American Conflict*, I, ch. VII; Hildreth, VI, 661–712, *passim*; McMaster, IV, ch. XXXIX; Rhodes, I, 29–40; Schouler, III, 155–173, 178–186; Schurz, *Clay*, I, ch. VIII; Thorpe, *Constitutional History American People*, I, ch. X; Von Holst, I, ch. IX; Wilson, I, ch. XI, XII; Woodburn in *American Historical Association Reports*, 1893, 251–297; Jefferson's *Works*, VII, 158, 159, 194; *Writings*, X, 156–158, 172, 177, 178, 180; Madiscn's *Works*, III, 149–157, 167–169, 186, 187, 199; Monroe's *Writings*, VI, 114–116, 121, 160–162; Johnson, *American Orations* (Rev. Ed.), II, 33–101, 343–365; Channing and Hart, *Guide*, § 177.

------

97. Resolutions of Pennsylvania.

December 22, 1819.

* * * A measure was ardently supported in the last Congress of the United States, and will probably be as earnestly urged during the existing session of that body, which has a palpable tendency to impair the political relations of the several states ; which is calculated to mar the social happiness of the present, and future generations ; which, if adopted, would impede the march of humanity and freedom through the world, and would affix and perpetuate an odious stain upon the present race : a measure, in brief, which proposes to spread the crimes and cruelties of slavery, from the banks of the Mississippi to the shores of the Pacific.

When measures of this character are seriously advocated in the republican congress of America in the nineteenth century, the several states are invoked to the duty which they owe to the Deity, by the veneration which they entertain for the memory of the founders of the republic, and by a tender regard for posterity, to protest against its adoption, to refuse to covenant with crime, and to limit the range of an evil that already hangs in awful boding over so large a portion of the Union. * * *

If, indeed, the measure against which Pennsylvania considers it her duty to raise her voice, was calculated to abridge any of the rights guaranteed to the several states; if, odious as slavery is, it was proposed to hasten its extinction by means injurious to the states upon which it was unhappily entailed, Pennsylvania would be amongst the first to insist upon a sacred observance of the constitutional compact. But it cannot be pretended that the rights of any of the states are at all to be affected by the refusing to extend the mischiefs of human bondage over the boundless regions of the west, a territory which formed no part of the confederation at the adoption of the constitution; which has been but lately purchased from an European power by the people of the Union at large; which may or may not be admitted as a state into the Union at the discretion of Congress, which must establish a republican form of government, and no other; and whose climate affords none of the pretexts urged for resorting to the labor of natives of the torrid zone. Such a territory has no right, inherent or acquired, such as those states possessed which established the existing constitution. When that constitution was framed, in September, seventeen hundred and eighty seven, the concession that three fifths of the slaves in the states then existing should be represented in Congress, could not have been to embrace regions at that time held by a foreign power. On the contrary, so anxious were the Congress of that day to confine human bondage within its ancient home, that, on the thirteenth of July, seventeen hundred and eighty seven, that body unanimously declared that slavery or involuntary servitude should not exist in the extensive territories bounded by the Ohio, the Mississippi, Canada and the lakes. And in the ninth section of the first article of the constitution itself, the power of Congress to prohibit the migration of servile persons after the year eighteen hundred and eight, is expressly recognized; nor is there to be found in the statute book a single instance of the admission of a territory to the rank of a state, in which Congress have not adhered to the right vested in them by the constitution, to stipulate with the territory upon the conditions of such admission.

The Senate and House of Representatives of Pennsylvania, therefore, cannot but deprecate any departure from the humane and enlightened policy, pursued not only by the illustrious Congress of 1787, but by their successors, without exception. They are persuaded that, to open the fertile regions of the west to a servile race, would tend to increase their numbers beyond all past example, would open a new and steady market for the lawless venders of human flesh, and would render all schemes for obliterating this most foul blot upon the American character, useless and unavailing.

Under these convictions, and in the full persuasion that upon this topic there is but one opinion in Pennsylvania—

Resolved, by the Senate and House of Representatives of the Commonwealth of Pennsylvania, That the Senators and Representatives of this state in the Congress of the United States, be and they are hereby requested, to vote against the admission of any territory as a state into the Union, unless " the further introduction of slavery or involuntary servitude, except for the punishment of crimes, whereof the party shall have been duly convicted, shall be prohibited ; and all children born within the said territory, after its admission into the Union as a state, shall be free, but may be held to service until the age of twenty-five years."

[Resolution of transmission.]

[*Senate Journal,* 16 *Cong.,* 1 *sess.,* 78–80.]

---

98.   Resolutions of New Jersey.

January 24, 1820.

1. *They*[1] *do resolve and declare,* That the further admission of territories into the Union, without restriction of slavery, would, in their opinion, essentially impair the right of this and other existing states to equal representation in Congress, (a right at the foundation of the political compact,) inasmuch as such newly admitted slave holding state would be represented on the basis of their slave population ; a concession made at the formation of

---

[1] The representatives of the people of New Jersey, etc.

the constitution, in favor of the then existing states, but never stipulated for new states, nor to be inferred from any article or clause in that instrument.

2. *Resolved*, That, to admit the territory of Missouri as a state into the Union, without prohibiting slavery there, would, in the opinion of the representatives of the people of New Jersey aforesaid, be no less than to sanction this great political and moral evil, furnish the ready means of peopling a vast territory with slaves, and perpetuate all the dangers, crimes, and pernicious effects of domestic bondage.

3. *Resolved*, As the opinion of the representatives of the aforesaid, That, inasmuch as no territory has a right to be admitted into the Union but on the principles of the federal constitution, and only by a law of Congress consenting thereto on the part of the existing states, Congress may rightfully, and ought to refuse such law, unless upon reasonable and just conditions, assented to on the part of the people applying to become one of the states.

4. *Resolved*, In the opinion of the representatives aforesaid, That the article of the constitution which restrains Congress from prohibiting the migration or importation of slaves, until after the year eighteen hundred and eight, does, by necessary implication, admit the general power of Congress over the subject of slavery, and concedes to them the right to regulate and restrain such migration and importation after that time, into the existing or any newly to be created state.

5. *Resolved*, As the opinion of the representatives of the people of New Jersey aforesaid, That, inasmuch as Congress have a clear right to refuse the admission of a territory into the Union, by the terms of the constitution, they ought in the present case to exercise that absolute discretion, in order to preserve the political rights of the several existing states, and prevent the great national disgrace and multiplied mischiefs which must ensue from concedit, as a matter of right, in the immense territories yet to claim admission into the Union, beyond the Mississippi, that they may tolerate slavery.

[Resolution of transmission.]

[*Senate Journal*, 16 *Cong.*, 1 *sess.*, 113.]

99.   Resolutions of Virginia.

February 1, 1820.

The General Assembly of Virginia have beheld, with the deepest concern, the proceedings in congress, upon the petition of the people of Missouri to be admitted into the union.   They believe that the effort, which is now making, to impose upon the people, as one of the conditions of their admission, an unalterable inhibition of slavery, is forbidden, by good faith, by the constitution of the United States, and by considerations intimately connected with the tranquillity and welfare of the nation.   *   *   *
Entertaining these views of the obligation of the treaty, the principles of the constitution, and the character of the proposed measure ;—believing that the adoption of this measure would be an act of oppression to the people of Missouri, a breach of public faith, and a dangerous infraction of the constitution ;—believing, moreover, that it is eminently calculated to kindle the angriest passions ; to excite bitterness, jealousy and distrust among the states; to extinguish that spirit of concession, and destroy that mutual forbearance and fraternal affection which founded and have sustained our confederacy ;—sincerely attached to the union of these states, and the constitution which binds them together; —and anxious to avert the evils which threaten ;—the General Assembly has felt itself imperiously called upon to avow its opinions, and endeavor to give them effect.   Therefore,

Resolved, That, in the opinion of the General Assembly of Virginia, the people of Missouri have a right to demand, upon the faith of the treaty of 1803, that they shall be admitted into the union upon terms of equality with the other states.

That the congress of the United States have no right to impose upon the people of Missouri, as a condition of their admission into the union, the restriction which has been proposed in congress, or any other restriction not necessary to guarantee a republican form of government.

Resolved, That the senators from this state in the congress of the United States, be instructed, and the representatives requested, to use their best efforts in procuring the admission of the state of Missouri into the union, upon the principles contained in the foregoing resolutions, and in resisting any attempt which shall be made in congress, to impose conditions upon the people of Missouri, not warranted by the treaty of cession and the constitution of the United States. [Resolutions of transmission.]

[*Acts of Virginia*, 1819–20, 113, 123, 124.]

---

100. Vermont on the Missouri Constitution.

November 16, 1820.

The following resolutions were called out by the obnoxious clauses in the new constitution of Missouri, which led to a renewal of the contest in Congress in the session of 1820–21, and ended with a second compromise. The text is given in *Records of Governor and Council*, VI, 541–543; *Senate Journal*, 16 Cong., 2 sess., 50–54. For similar resolutions adopted by New York, Nov. 13, 1820, and by the Indiana House of Representatives Dec. 30, 1820, see *Niles*, XIX, 208; *National Intelligencer*, Feb. 8, 1821.

Resolved, That, in the opinion of this legislature, slavery, or involuntary servitude, in any of the United States, is a moral and political evil; and that its continuance can be justified by necessity alone.

That Congress has a right to inhibit any further introduction or extension of slavery, as one of the conditions upon which any new state shall be admitted into the Union.

Resolved, That this legislature views with regret and alarm, the attempt of the inhabitants of Missouri to obtain admission into the Union, as one of the United States, under a constitution which legalizes and secures the introduction and continuance of slavery ; and also contains provisions to prevent freemen of the United States from emigrating to, and settling in Missouri, on account of their origin, colour, and features. And that, in the opinion of this legislature, these principles, powers, and restrictions, contained in the reputed constitution of Missouri, are anti-republican, and repugnant to the constitution of the United States, and subversive of the unalienable rights of man.

Resolved, That the Senators from this state, in the Congress of the United States, be instructed, and the Representatives requested, to exert their influence, and use all legal means, to prevent the admission of Missouri, as a state, into the union of the United States, with those anti-republican features and powers in their constitution. [Resolution of transmission.]

---

101. Ohio on Emancipation and Colonization.

January 17, 1824.

The Ohio Legislature, by adopting the subjoined resolutions, revived the agitation of the colonization question. By June of 1825, eight other Northern States had indorsed the proposition (Pa., Vt., N. J., Del., Ill., Ind., Conn., Mass.), but six of the slave-holding states emphatically disapproved of the suggestion, viz.: Georgia, Dec. 7, 1824; South Carolina, Dec., 1824; Missouri, Jan. 22, 1825; Mississippi, Feb., 1825, and Jan. 23, 1826; Louisiana, Feb. 16, 1826, and Alabama, Jan. 1, 1827.

The text of several of these resolutions are given in *Papers of the Governor, Penna. Archives, 4th series*, V, 507, 555, 572, 580, 582, 602–604, 621, 643–645, and in the session laws of the above-mentioned States. See also McMaster, V. 204; W. H. Smith, *Political History of Slavery*, I, 23, 24.

"*Resolved* by the General Assembly of the State of Ohio ; That the consideration of a system providing for the gradual emancipation of the people of color, held in servitude in the United States, be recommended to the Legislatures of the several States of the American Union, and to the Congress of the United States.

Resolved, That in the opinion of the General Assembly a system of foreign colonization, with correspondent measures might be adopted that would in due time effect the entire emancipation of the slaves in our country without any violation of the national compact, or infringement of the rights of individuals ; by the passage of a law by the general government (with the consent of the slaveholding states) which should provide that all children or persons now held in slavery, born after the passage of such law, should be free at the age of twenty-one years (being supported during their minority by the persons claiming the service of their parents) providing they then consent to be transported to the intended place of colonization—Also—

Resolved, That it is expedient that such a system should be predicated upon the principle that the evil of slavery is a national one, and that the people and the states of this Union ought mutually to participate in the duties and burthens of removing it.

Resolved, That his Excellency, the Governor be requested to forward a copy of the foregoing Resolutions to his Excellency the Governor of each of the United States, requesting him to lay the same before the legislature thereof: and that his Excellency will also forward a like copy to each of our Senators and Representatives in Congress requesting their co-operation in all national measures having a tendency to effect the grand object embraced therein.

[*Laws of Ohio, Local,* 1824, 160.]

South Carolina's Reply to Ohio and the Federal Government.

In consequence of the disclosure of a negro plot at Charleston, in May, 1822, the Legislature passed, among other precautionary measures, the "Negro Seamen Act," Dec. 21, 1822. (*Acts of S. C.,* 1822, 11–14.) The enforcement of this law soon brought out protests from American masters. (*Annals,* 17 *Cong.,* 2 *sess.,* 1055; *Niles,* XXIV, 31, 32.) The test case of *Elkinson vs. Deliesseline* came before the U. S. District Court and Judge Wm. Johnson, a citizen of South Carolina, on August 7, 1823, held the law unconstitutional. (*Niles,* XXV, 12–16, 47.) But South Carolina refused to abide by this decision and continued to enforce the law. Soon complaints were lodged by the British Government at the State Department. (*Niles,* XXVII, 261, 262.) The Attorney-General, William Wirt, gave the opinion that the law was neither constitutional nor compatible with the rights of England under the treaty. (1 *Opinions Attorney-General,* 659; *Niles,* XXVII, 262, 263.) This protest, together with Wirt's opinion, were sent to Governor Wilson, of South Carolina, and by him transmitted to the legislature, Nov. 25, 1824 (Message in *Niles,* XXVII, 261.)

In the meantime the Legislature of Georgia, Dec. 22, 1823, suggested a remedy by proposing to so amend the Federal Constitution as to leave "the importation or ingress of any person of color" into a state wholly to the laws of each state. The Ohio proposition also came before the legislature at about this time. The above circumstance accounts in part for the character of Governor Wilson's Message, transmitting the Georgia proposition and the reply of the Senate to the Attorney-General's opinion and the Ohio proposal, which follow. The House refused to accept the Senate resolves and adopted a milder reply. The Georgia amendment, between 1824 and 1826, was approved by Missouri, Mississippi and Louisiana, and disapproved of by nine other states. (Ames, *Proposed Amendments*, 210, 339.)

Not only was this act enforced by South Carolina with impunity, especially against domestic vessels, Attorney-General Berrien, in 1830, having reversed Wirt's opinion (2 *Opinions Attorney-General*, 433), but all the other southern sea-board states adopted somewhat similar restrictions, while those of Florida and Alabama apparently were copied from the laws of South Carolina. (Florida, Act of 1832, Thompson's *Digest*, 546; Alabama, Act of 1831, Clay's *Digest*, 546.) The frictions growing out of the administration of these laws led to a renewal of the agitation in 1844. (See *post*, 237.)

General references: McMaster, V, 200–204, 417; Von Holst, III, 128, 129; Wilson, I, 576, 577. For account of the insurrection, see *Atlantic Monthly*, VII, 730–740.

---

102. Message of Governor John L. Wilson of South Carolina.

December 1, 1824.

In submitting this proposed amendment, I feel a confidence that I am submitting, what already attaches to each state in its sovereign and independent capacity. A few days since I had the honor of enclosing to you the remonstrance of the British minister, Mr. Canning, on a clause of a legislative act passed in South Carolina, entitled " an act for the better regulation and government of free negroes and persons of color, and for other purposes," together with the opinion of Mr. Wirt upon the same. A reference to the rule laid down by England, under similar circumstances, will, at once, prove that the deductions I drew in my communication, were well warranted by her own practice.

[He refers to the opinion of Solicitor General Lee, in 1791, in regard to the right of self-defence of a state in the case of Roman Catholics.]

There should be a spirit of concert and of action among the slave-holding states, and a determined resistance to any violation of their local institutions. The crisis seems to have arrived when we are called upon to protect ourselves. The president of the

United States, and his law adviser, so far from resisting the efforts of a foreign ministry, appear to be disposed, by an argument drawn from the overwhelming powers of the general government, to make us the passive instruments of a policy, at war, not only with our interests, but destructive also of our national existence. The evils of slavery have been visited upon us by the cupidity of those who are now the champions of universal emancipation. A firm determination to resist, at the threshold, every invasion of our domestic tranquillity, and to preserve our sovereignty and independence as a state, is earnestly recommended ; and, if an appeal to the first principles of the right of self-government be disregarded, and reason be successfully combatted by sophistry and error, there would be more glory in forming a rampart with our bodies on the confines of our territory, than to be the victims of a successful rebellion, or the slaves of a great consolidated government.

[*Niles*, XXVII, 263, 264.]

103. Resolutions of the Senate of South Carolina.

December, 1824.

Resolved, That the state of South Carolina is desirous of complying with any measure necessary to promote harmony between this state and the government of the United States and foreign nations, and will cheerfully comply in all cases which do not involve a surrender of the safety and inherent rights of the state.

Resolved, That the legislature of this state has carefully considered the documents transmitted by the president of the United States, being a correspondence with the British minister relative to a law, passed December, 1822, regulating free negroes and persons of color, and can yet perceive no departure from the duties and rights of this state, or of the United States, in that law.

Resolved, That the legislature sees, with profound regret, the alarming symptoms of an unconstitutional interference with her colored population, whose condition, as it existed at the establishment of the present constitution of the United States, is expressly recognized, (paragraph 3 of sec. 2, of art. 1), and distinctly guaranteed by that instrument.

Resolved, That it is as much the duty of the state to guard against insubordination or insurrection among our colored population, or to control and regulate any cause which might excite or produce it, as to guard against any other evil, political or physical, which might assail us. This duty is paramount to all *laws,* all *treaties,* all *constitutions.* It arises from the supreme and permanent law of nature, the law of self-preservation ; and will never, by this state, be renounced, compromised, controlled or participated with any power whatever.

*   *   *   *   *   *   *

Resolved, That this legislature, having received a very strange and ill-advised communication from the legislature of the state of Ohio, approves of the reply of the governor of Georgia to a similar communication, and will, on this subject, be ready to make common cause with the state of Georgia, and the other southern states similarly circumstanced in this respect.

Resolved, Therefore, that the legislature of South Carolina *protests* against any claims of right, of the United States, to interfere, in any manner whatever, with the domestic regulations and preservatory measures in respect to that part of her property which forms the colored population of the state, and which property they will not permit to be meddled with, or tampered with, or in and manner ordered, regulated, or controlled by any other power, foreign or domestic, than this legislature. [Vote 36 to 6.]

[*Niles,* XXVII,264.]

---

104.   Resolutions of House of Representatives of South Carolina.

December, 1824.

Resolved, That the legislature of South Carolina have received, with regret, the communication from the state of Ohio, as the discussions to which it invites them can lead to no result but to the unfriendly intemperance of conflicting interests and opinions.

Resolved, That the legislature of Ohio be informed that the people of this state will adhere to a system, descended to them from their ancestors, and now inseparably connected with their social and political existence.

Resolved, That the governor be requested to transmit a copy of the above resolutions to the governor of Ohio.

[*Niles,* XXVII, 292.]

---

105. Extract from the Message of Governor Troup of Georgia.

May 23, 1825.

The legislature of Georgia already Dec. 7, 1824, had expressed its disapproval of the Ohio proposition. Governor Troup, aroused by the bill proposed by Senator King in the Senate, Feb. 18, 1825, for the establishment of a fund from the sale of public lands to be used for aiding in the emancipation of slaves and their removal, as also in the removal of free persons of color from such states permitting it, for purposes of colonization (*Senate Journal,* 18 *Cong.,* 2 *sess.,* 171; *Niles,* XXVIII, 276, 277), and by the supposed argument of Att.-Gen'l Wirt, gave expression to the following belligerent language in his annual message (*Niles,* XXVIII, 240). Resolutions in keeping therewith were introduced into the House, but were not passed. (*Ibid.,* XXVIII, 271, 272.) The Governor sent a special message, June 7, on the same subject, in which he declared that, "The United States can choose between our enmity and our love." (*Ibid.,* 277.) Again in his message of Nov. 8, he refers to the resolutions from the northern states on the subject of emancipation in strong language. (*Ibid.,* XXIX, 207.) References: *Niles,* XXVIII, 274–277; McMaster, V, 205, 206; Von Holst, I, 439, 440; Phillips, *Georgia and State Rights, Amer. Hist. Assoc. Rept.* 1901, II, 158–160.

Since your last meeting, our feelings have been again outraged by officious and impertinent intermeddlings with our domestic concerns. Beside the resolution presented for the consideration of the Senate by Mr. King, of New York, it is understood that the Attorney General of the United States, who may be presumed to represent his Government faithfully, and to speak as its mouth piece, has recently maintained, before the Supreme Court,[1] doc-

---

[1] See evidence of the Judges refuting this charge. *Niles,* XXVIII, 347–349.

trines on this subject, which, if sanctioned by that tribunal, will make it quite easy for the Congress, by a short decree, to divest this entire interest, without cost to themselves of one dollar, or of one acre of public land.   This is the uniform practice of the Government of the United States; if it wishes a principle established which it dare not establish for itself, a case is made before the Supreme Court, and the principle once settled, the act of Congress follows of course.   Soon, very soon, therefore, the United States' Government, discarding the mask, will openly lend itself to a combination of fanatics for the destruction of every thing valuable in the Southern country ; one movement of the Congress unresisted by you, and all is lost.   Temporize no longer—make known your resolution that this subject shall not be touched by them, but at their peril; but for its sacred guaranty by the constitution, we never would have become parties to that instrument ; at this moment you would not make yourselves parties to any constitution without it ; of course you will not be a party to it, from the moment the General Government shall make that movement.

If this matter be an evil, it is our own—if it be a sin, we can implore the forgiveness of it—to remove it we ask not even their sympathy or assistance : it may be our physical weakness—it is our moral strength. * * * I entreat you, therefore, most earnestly, now that it is not too late, to step forth, and, having exhausted the argument, to stand by your arms.

(*Executive Doc.*, 19 *Cong.*, 2 *sess.*, IV, No. 59, pp. 69, 70.)

Resolutions on the Colonization Society.

1827-1832.

The agitation aroused by the various propositions for emancipation, and the renewed efforts of the American Colonization Society in 1827 to obtain national aid for its projects (*Exec. Doc.*, 19 *Cong.*, 2 *sess.*, IV, No. 64), and a favorable report from a Committee of the House of Representatives, March 3, 1827 (*House Reports*, II, No. 101), called out a new series of resolutions *pro* and *con*.   The legislatures of at least ten States, during 1827–1832 indorsed this policy. (1827, Ky., Tenn., Del., Vt.; 1828, Ohio; 1829, Ind., Penn.; 1830, Ind., Md.; 1831, Mass.; 1832, Md., New York.) This was met by emphatic protests from some of the slave-holding states, notably the following: South Carolina, December 19, 1827. *Ante*, p. 145; Georgia, December 27, 1827, *Acts of Georgia*, 1827, 194–200; *Senate Doc.*, 20 *Cong.*, 1 *sess.*, III, No. 81; *Exec. Doc.*, III, No. 126; Dec. 20, 1828, *Ante*, pp. 153, 154; MacDonald, 234; Missouri, Jan. 23, 1829, *Laws of Mo.*, 1828–29, 89–91; *Senate Doc.*, 20 *Cong.*, 2 *sess.*, II, No. 89. The Georgia and Missouri reports presented arguments against the constitutionality of the proposed aid.

Maryland replied to Georgia, 1830 (*Niles*, XXXVII, 428), but in 1832 suggested, if necessary, an amendment to the constitution. *Acts of Md.*, 1831–32. Res. No. 124; Ames, *Proposed Amend.*, 207, 345. Ohio by 1831 had become non-committal, and declared "it is premature and inexpedient to express an opinion."

References: For resolutions favoring the society, see *House Reports*, 21 *Cong.*, 1 *sess.*, III, No. 348, pp. 20–26; *Ante*, p. 195; McMaster, V, 206–208. For the attitude of the South see Weeks, *Anti-Slavery Sentiment in the South, Pub. of Southern History Assoc.*, II, 97, 100–103, 112–115, *post*, p. —. For opposition from abolitionists, Garrison, *Life of Garrison*, I, 289–304; Jay, *Misc. Writings on Slavery*, 1–124.

---

106.   Delaware in Favor of the Colonization Society.

February 8, 1827.

Be it resolved, by the Senate and House of Representatives of the State of Delaware, in General Assembly met, That it is requisite for our prosperity, and, (what is of more important concern,) essential to our safety, that measures should be taken for the removal, from this country, of the free negroes and free mulattoes.

Resolved, That this general assembly approve the objects of "the American colonization society" and consider that these objects deserve public support, and that they ought to be fostered and encouraged by the national government, and with the national funds.

Resolved, That the Senators of this State in Congress, be requested to approve and promote, in the councils of the nation, measures for removing from this country to Africa, the free coloured people who may be willing to emigrate.

[*Laws of Delaware*, 1827, 158.]

107.   Georgia on the Colonization Society.

December 28, 1827.

* * * At the establishment of the Colonization Society, whatever may have been intended or avowed as its object, your Committee believe that they can say with truth, that the general impression in the southern States as to that object was, that it was
limited to the removal beyond the United States of the then free
people of color and their descendants, and none others.   Under
this impression, it at once received the sanction and countenance
of many of the humane, the wise, and the patriotic among us.
Auxiliary societies were formed in our own State, and the numbers, the influence, and the resources of the Society, were daily
increased.   It is now ascertained that this impression was false ;
and its officers, and your Committee believe the Society itself,
now boldly and fearlessly avow, that its object is, and ever has
been, to remove the whole colored population of the Union to
another land ; and to effect this object, so wild, fanatical, and
destructive in itself, they ask, that the general fund, to which the
slave holding States have so largely contributed, should be appropriated for a purpose so especially ruinous to the prosperity,
importance, and political strength, of the southern States.

That the people of the south, at the time of the adoption of the
Constitution, considered not only the retention, but the increase
of the slave population, to be all-important to the welfare and
interest of their States, is manifest from a reservation in that instrument itself, which, it cannot be doubted, was inserted on their
express requisition.   * * * What was the motive of those
people in insisting upon the reservation of the right to make such
importation for twenty years ?   Unquestionably to increase that
species of population.   Why increase it ?   Because they believed
it to be essential to the improvement, welfare, and prosperity of
their section of the country ; and upon the numbers of which, by
another provision of the Constitution, the weight of the southern
States in the general council in part depended.   If such were the
motive, and what other could there have been for the insertion of
that reservation, can it be believed that those very people meant,

by another clause, to give to Congress the power to appropriate money out to the common fund to which they were so largely to contribute, for the purpose of again removing that very population, the right to increase which was so carefully reserved ; that they insisted upon retaining the right to import Africans, merely again, and in part at their own expense, to re-export them to the shore from whence they had been brought ! Yet such would be the effect of the constructive power contended for.

    *   *   *   *   *   *   *

Your committee cannot avoid reprobating the cold-blooded selfishness, or unthinking zeal, which actuates many of our fellow-citizens in other states, to an interference with our local concerns and domestic relations, totally unwarranted either by humanity or constitutional right. Such interference is becoming every day more determined and more alarming. It commenced with a few unthinking zealots, who formed themselves into abolition societies ; was seized upon by more cunning and designing men for political purposes ; and is now supported by more than one of the States, as it is evident from the amendments of the Con-stitution proposed by legislative bodies, and so frequently, and indeed insultingly presented for our approbation. The result of such interference, if persevered in, is awful and inevitable. The people of Georgia know and strongly feel the advantages of the federal Union. As members of that Union, they are proud of its greatness—as children born under that Union, they love it with filial affection—as parties of that Union, they will ever defend it from foes, internal or external ; but they cannot, and will not, even for the preservation of that Union, permit their rights to be assailed—they will not permit their property to be rendered worthless—they will not permit their wives and their children to be driven as wanderers into strange lands—they will not permit their country to be made waste and desolate, " by those who come among us under the cloak of a time-serving and hypocritical benevolence." But how is this increasing evil to be met and remedied? Nothing can be hoped from remonstrance — the judicial tribunals of the Union cannot reach it—our own Legis-lature can by no enactment prevent it. How, then, is this evil to be remedied? Only by a firm and determined union of the people and the States of the south, declaring, through their legislative bodies, in a voice which must be heard, that they are ready and willing to make any sacrifice, rather than submit longer to such ruinous interference ; and warning their enemies that they are unwittingly preparing a mine, which once exploded, will lay our much-loved country in one common ruin. Your committee hope that such a calamity is yet far distant, and that there is still remaining in the Congress of the Union sufficient discretion, intelligence, and patriotism, to avert it altogether. With that hope, they deem it unnecessary now to do more than to recommend the adoption of the following resolutions :

Resolved, by the Senate and House of Representatives of the State of Georgia, in General Assembly met, That the Congress of the United States have no constitutional power to appropriate moneys to aid the American Colonization Society, or for objects to effect which that Society was established; and that this Legislature, representing the feelings and will of the people, and the sovereignty of the State of Georgia; in the name and in behalf of the State of Georgia, denying the right, solemnly protest against the exercise or any attempt to exercise such unconstitutional power, by the Congress of the United States.

*   *   *   *   *   *   *

And be it further resolved, That a copy of the above report and resolutions be forwarded to the Governor of each slave-holding State of the Union, with a request that the same shall be laid before the respective Legislatures, asking their concurrence in such constitutional mode, as to them shall seem best, to prevent the exercise of such power by the Congress of the United States.

[*Senate Doc.,* 20 *Cong.,* 1 *sess.,* III, No. 81.]

The South on the Abolition Question.

1831-1839.

The activity of the new type of Abolitionists, especially after the establishment of "The Liberator," Jan. 1, 1831, and the excitement caused by the Nat.
Turner insurrection in Southampton County, Virginia, in Aug., 1831, combined to arouse general apprehension throughout the South. (For insurrection, see Higginson in *Atlantic Monthly*, VIII, 173–187; Williams, *History
of the Negro Race in America*, II, 85–92.) Already in the Virginia Constitutional Convention of 1829, the subject of emancipation and of slave representation had been discussed. (*Proceedings and Debates of the Virginia State
Convention of 1829-30, passim;* Thorpe, *Const. Hist. Amer. People*, I, chs.
xiv, xv, *passim.*) In view of the recent insurrection, the Virginia Legislature
of 1831–32, discussed gradual emancipation and colonization as remedies, and
the institution of slavery was severely condemned by several of the speakers.
(See speeches of Philip A. Bolling, Thomas Marshall, John A. Chandler,
Henry Berry, Thomas J. Randolph, and James M'Dowell, Jr., in the House of
Delegates. Each printed separately [Richmond, 1832]; *Niles*, XLIII, 23;
Wilson, I, ch. xiv; Curtis, II, 250–253; Von Holst, II, 90–95.) But a reac-
tion set in and no legislation of this character followed.

Gov. Floyd of Va. in his message, Dec. 6, 1831, charged the recent insurrection as being instigated by the Abolitionists. (*Niles*, XLI, 350, 351.) The
accusation was repeated in other states. See message of Governor of La.
(*Ibid.*, 314, 315.) Georgia appropriated $5,000 for the arrest and trial of the
editor of "The Liberator." (*Acts of Ga.*, 1831, 255. For similar action of
Miss. see *Niles*, XLIX, 39.) The Legislature of Alabama appears to have
been the first to adopt a report and resolutions, Jan. 21, 1832, relative "to
the suppression of publications of an incendiary nature in other States."
(*Act of Ala.*, 1831–32, 116, 117.)

The establishment of the American Anti-Slavery Society in 1833, the continued efforts of the Abolitionists to circulate their publications in the South,
and the increase in the number of petitions for the abolition of slavery in the
District of Columbia led to a general demand on the part of the South for the
suppression of abolition publications and societies. Already during the summer of 1835 the rifling of the mails at Charleston, S. C., and the remarkable
correspondence of Postmaster-General Kendall had aroused national interest.
(*Niles*, XLVIII, 447, 448; XLIX, 7–9.) President Jackson in his message
of Dec. 2, 1835, recommended legislation to prohibit the circulation through
the mails of incendiary publications. (Richardson, III, 175, 176.) A bill
reported by Calhoun was defeated in the Senate, apparently on constitutional
grounds by a vote of 25 to 19. (See Report and Speech of Calhoun, *Works*,
II, 509–533; V, 190–208.)

The Governors of several of the Southern States devoted a large part of their annual messages of 1835 to the Abolitionists.   For the celebrated message of Gov. McDuffie of S. C., see *Jour. of the General Assembly*, 1835, 4–10; reprinted in *Amer. Hist. Leaflets*, No. 10; Message of 1836, *Jour. of General Assembly*, 1836, 9–12; Gov. Gayle of Ala., *Jour. of Alabama House of Rep.*, 1835, 12–14; reprinted in *Gulf States Hist. Mag.*, II, 29–34; for documents in connection with the demand for the extradition of Robert G. Williams, editor of "The Emancipator," and the refusal of Gov. Marcy of N. Y., see *Ibid.*, 28, 29; *Niles*, XLIX, 290, 358–360; Messages of Govs. Schley of Ga., and Swain of N. C., are in *Niles*, XLIX, 187, 228.   The Legislatures of seven of the states during the session of 1835–36, adopted reports and resolutions vigorously protesting, and demanding Northern legislation.   Those of South Carolina, Dec. 16, are given as typical.   *Acts and Res. of S. C.*, 1835, 26–28; North Carolina, Dec. 19, *Acts of N. C. Sess. of 1835*, 119–121; Georgia, Dec. 22, *Acts of Ga.*, 1835, 297–300; Alabama, Jan. 9, *Acts of Ala.*, 1835–36, 174, 175; *Senate Doc.*, 24 *Cong.* 1 *sess.*, II, No. 124; Virginia, Feb. 16, *Acts of Va.*, 1835–36, 395, 396; *Senate Doc.*, III, No. 233; Mississippi, Feb. 27; *Laws of Mississippi*, Jan.–Feb., 1839, 101–103; Kentucky, March 1, *Acts of Ky.*, 1835–36, 683–686; *Senate Doc.*, III, No. 249.   The texts of all the above are in the *Jour. of the Senate of Penna.*, 1835–36, II; several are also in *Niles*, XLIX, 245, 309, 318, 319, 362, 363.   Later resolutions were passed by Louisiana, Feb. 20, 1837, *Acts of La.*, 1837, 18, 19, and by Missouri, Feb. 12, 1839, *Laws of Mo.*, 1838–39, 337, 338.   The former proposed "a convention composed of delegates of the slave-holding States," "to enquire into and determine on the best possible means to obtain 'peaceably if they can, forcibly if they must,' that respect for their institutions to which they are entitled by the positive enactments of the Federal compact, and by the stronger law of self-preservation."

General references: Channing and Hart, *Guide*, §§ 187, 188; Von Holst, II, ch. ii; Wilson, I, esp. chs. xiii, xiv, xxiv; Greeley, I, 107–117, 122–125; Burgess, ch. xi; McMaster, VI, ch. lvi; Schouler, IV, 203–224; Benton, *Thirty Years' View*, I, 576–588, 609, 610; Garrison, *Garrison*, I, chs. vii, viii, ix, xii, xiv; II, ch. ii; Schurz, *Clay*, II, 69–78; Von Holst, *Calhoun*, 134–150; Smith, I, 41–45; Jay, *Misc. Writings*, 125 *et seq.;* Hart, *Contemporaries*, III, Nos. 169, 174, 175, 180; Goodell, *Slavery and Anti-Slavery*, 413, 414; Bryant and Gay, *United States*, IV, ch. xiii.

108. Resolutions of South Carolina.

December 16, 1835.

* * * * * * * *

The present condition of the slave question in the states of this confederacy, presents one of the most extraordinary spectacles which, your committee will venture to assert, has ever challanged the notice of the civilized world. We see sovereign states united by a common league, in about one-half of which states the institution of slavery not only exists, but its legal existence is solemnly recognized and guaranteed by their compact of union. Yet in the face of this compact, and the clear and distinct admission that the non-slaveholding states have not the slightest right, either constitutionally or otherwise, to interfere with this institution, the most incendiary associations are tolerated or permitted to exist within their limits, the object and ends of which not only strike at the prosperity and happiness of eleven states in the confederacy, but at their very social existence.

Painful as it may be, it is impossible to disguise the fact, that this is a condition of things which cannot, in the long run, be permitted to exist. Every wise instinct of self-preservation forbids it. Let it be admitted, that the three millions of free white inhabitants in the slave-holding states are amply competent to hold in secure and pacific subjection the two millions of slaves, which, by the inscrutable dispensations of Providence, have been placed under our dominion. Let it be admitted, that, by reason of an efficient police and judicious internal legislation, we may render abortive the designs of the fanatic and incendiary within our own limits, and that the torrent of pamphlets and tracts which the abolition presses of the north are pouring forth with an inexhaustible copiousness, is arrested the moment it reaches our frontier. Are we to wait until our enemies have built up, by the grossest misrepresentations and falsehoods, a body of public opinion against us, which it would be almost impossible to resist, without separating ourselves from the social system of the rest of the civilized world? Or are we to sit down content, because from our own vigilance and courage the torch of the incendiary and the dagger of the midnight assassin may never be applied? This is impossible. No people can live in a state of perpetual excitement and apprehension, although real danger may be long deferred. Such a condition of the public mind is destructive of all social happiness, and consequently must prove essentially injurious to the prosperity of a community that has the weakness to suffer under a perpetual panic. This would be true, if the causes of this excitement proceeded from the external hostility of a foreign nation. But how infinitely interesting and momentous the consideration becomes, when they flow from the acts and doings of citizens of states, with whom we are not only in amity, but to whom we are bound by the strongest bonds of common union, which was framed to promote the happiness, peace, security, and protection of all.

We have, therefore, a claim on the governments of the non-slave-holding states, not only moral and social, but of indispensible constitutional obligation, that this nuisance shall be abated. They not only owe it to us, but they owe it to themselves, to that union, at whose shrine they have so often offered up the highest pledges by which man can plight his temporal faith. * * * *

Your committee are aware, that it has been said, that no legislation can be adapted to arrest the proceedings of the abolitionists by the non-slaveholding states, without violating the great principles of the liberty of the press. We consider that this objection rests on no just foundation. There is certainly some difference between the freedom of discussion, and the liberty to deluge a friendly and coterminous state with seditious and incendiary tracts, pamphlets and pictorial representations, calculated to excite a portion of its population to revolt, rapine and bloodshed. We would fain believe, that the northern liberty of the press, would never be construed into a liberty, to lay the south in ashes. Under a law honestly passed to meet this crime against society, and treason against the Union, the whole circumstances of the case, and the *quo animo* of the offender might be left to a jury to determine like any other criminal issue, and if we are to believe in the condition of public opinion, as recently exhibited in most of the non-slaveholding states, we are far from thinking that such legislation would be a mere dead letter.

South Carolina will not anticipate the crisis, which must be presented by a refusal on the part of the non-slaveholding states, to accord to us the protection of such legislation, or such other means, as they may select for the suppression of the evils of which we complain, for she will not doubt the good faith and amity of her sister states. She desires to live in peace and harmony in this Union. In the assertion of her rights and in preferring her claims to be secure in the enjoyment of her property, under the compact, she desires to act in entire concert with those states, whose interests are identical with her own. She is, however, prepared to do her duty to herself and posterity, under all and every possible conjuncture of circumstances.

In conclusion, your committee, desirous of making a matter of record, both of our rights, and the assertion of the just expectation that they will be respected by those who are united with us in the bonds of a common union, beg leave to offer the following resolutions, for the adoption of both branches of the Legislature.

1. *Resolved*, That the formation of the abolition societies, and the acts and doings of certain fanatics, calling themselves abolitionists, in the non-slaveholding states of this confederacy, are in direct violation of the obligations of the compact of union, dissocial, and incendiary in the extreme.

2. *Resolved*, That no state having a just regard for her own peace and security can acquiesce in a state of things by which such conspiracies are engendered within the limits of a friendly state, united to her by the bonds of a common league of political association, without either surrendering or compromitting her most essential rights.

3. *Resolved*, That the Legislature of South Carolina, having every confidence in the justice and friendship of the non-slaveholding states, announces to her co-states her confident expectation, and she earnestly requests that the governments of these states will promptly and effectually suppress all those associations within their respective limits, purporting to be abolition societies, and that they will make it highly penal to print, publish and distribute newspapers, pamphlets, tracts and pictorial representations calculated and having an obvious tendency to excite the slaves of the southern states to insurrection and revolt.

4. *Resolved*, That, regarding the domestic slavery of the southern states as a subject exclusively within the control of each of the said states, we shall consider every interference, by any other state or the general government, as a direct and unlawful interference, to be resisted at once, and under every possible circumstance.

5. *Resolved*, In order that a salutary negative may be put on the mischievous, and unfounded assumption of some of the abolitionists—the non-slaveholding states are requested to disclaim by legislative declaration, all right, either on the part of themselves or the government of the United States, to interfere in any manner with domestic slavery, either in the states, or in the territories where it exists.

6. *Resolved*, That we should consider the abolition of slavery in the District of Columbia, as a violation of the rights of the citizens of that District, derived from the implied conditions on which that territory was ceded to the general government, and as an usurpation to be at once resisted as nothing more than the commencement of a scheme of much more extensive and flagrant injustice.

7. *Resolved*, That the legislature of South Carolina, regards with decided approbation, the measures of security adopted by the Post Office Department of the United States, in relation to the transmission of incendiary tracts. But if this highly essential and protective policy, be counteracted by congress, and the United States mail becomes a vehicle for the transmission of the mischievous documents, with which it was recently freighted, we, in this contingency, expect that the Chief Magistrate of our state, will forthwith call the legislature together, that timely measures may be taken to prevent its traversing our territory. [Resolutions of transmission.]

[*Acts and Resolutions of South Carolina, Dec. 1835*, 26–28.]

Reply of the Northern States.

1836–1839.

The Governors of several of the Northern States commented favorably upon these resolutions, especially Governors Marcy, of New York, and Everett, of Mass., in their messages of January, 1836. (Greeley, I, 124; *Resolves of Mass.*, 1835–36, 296–298.) Gov. Ritner, of Pennsylvania, alone took an uncompromising stand for freedom of speech and the press. (*Papers of the Governor*, VI, 250, 290–292.) None of the states enacted the legislation desired, but a few passed resolutions similar to the following adopted by New York. See *Laws of Ohio, Local*, 1835–36, 657; *Reports and Resolutions of Maine*, 1836, 47–50; *Laws of New Hamp.*, 1836–37, 228, 229; *Laws of Ind.*, 1838–39, 353; *Senate Doc.*, 25 *Cong.*, 3 *sess.*, III, No. 209; *Niles*, LVI, 15, 66; LVII, 378. In contrast to these, Vermont, Nov. 16, 1836, asserted "that neither Congress nor the state governments have any constitutional right to abridge the full expression of opinions or the transmission of them through the public mail." *Acts of Vt.*, 1836, 44; *Niles*, LI, 210. Also see *post*, p. 221.

109. New York in Reply to the South.

May 23, 1836.

Resolved unanimously, That the views and sentiments contained in the late annual message of the governor of this state, recognizing the constitutional right of the several states of the union, to regulate and control within their own limits, the relations of master and slave, and to continue or abolish the same as the governments of those states may respectively deem consistent with their duty, safety and welfare, meet the full and cordial concurrence of this legislature.

Resolved, That the people of this state, by responding with unexampled unanimity, to those views and sentiments, and manifesting their determination to abstain from, and to discountenance those political agitations and public discussions of the subject of domestic slavery, which were calculated to produce an exciting, an improper and a pernicious influence within the limits of other states, have given to the Union stronger guarantees than law could furnish, and rendered present legislation upon the subject by their representatives unnecessary and inexpedient. [Resolution of transmission.]

[*Laws of New York*, 1836. 811, 812.]

Slavery in the District of Columbia and the Right of Petition.

1836–1844.

As early as Jan. 23, 1829, the legislature of Penna. had adopted resolutions for the passage of a law to abolish slavery in the District of Columbia (*Laws of Penna.*, 1828–29, 371, 372; *Niles*, XXXV, 363. Vote, House, 81 to 8; Senate, 24 to 4), and the New York Assembly had passed the measure in the same year. (Jay, 160, 215,) The subject was debated in Congress, in 1829, and the Committee on the District reported adversely. (*Debates of Cong.*, 20 *Cong.*, 2 *sess.*, 167, 175–187, 191; *Reports of Committees*, No. 60.) No further resolutions from the Northern States on this subject appear until the denial of the right in the resolutions of the Southern States in 1835–36. Ante, p. 214. Vermont led the way in reasserting this right of Congress in connection with her declaration on the freedom of the mails. Ante, p. 220.

The increase in the number of petitions on this subject finally led to both houses of Congress adopting rules or practices restricting the right of petition for the abolition of slavery during the period 1836–1844. These so-called " gag rules " not only caused a great increase in the petitions, but also called out resolutions from the legislatures of several of the Northern States protesting against the " gag rules," and either asserting the right or praying for the abolition of slavery in the District, as follows: 1837, Mass., Vt.; 1838, Mass., Ct., Vt.; 1839, Vt.: 1840, N. Y., Mass.; 1842 and 1843, Vt. *Acts of Vermont*, 1836, 53; *Ibid.*, 1837, 108; *Ibid.*, 1838, 23; *Ibid.*, 1839, 20; *Ibid.*, 1841, 33; *Ibid.*, 1842, 97; *Res. of Mass.*, 1835–38, 559, 560, 734–736, 742–743; *Ibid.*, 1839–42, 262, 264; *Res. and Private Acts of Conn.*, 1838, 24–26; *House Ex. Doc.*, 25 *Cong.*, 2 *sess.*, X, Nos. 408 and 415; *Laws of New York*, 1840, 349; *Niles*, LII, 87, 150; LIII, 296, 297, 324; LIV, 236; LV, 351. The resolutions of Mass. of 1837 and New York of 1840, as typical of this class, are given below.

Great excitement and an extended debate was caused by the presentation of the Vermont resolution in the Senate in Dec., 1837. See Calhoun's resolution and speech, *Cong. Globe*, 25 *Cong.*, 2 *sess.*, 39, 55, 107–109; *Works*, III, 140–202; also earlier speeches on abolition petitions and defence of slavery, *Works*, II, 465–490, 625–633. For the speech of Slade, of Vt., in the House, and " the secession " of the southern members, Dec. 20, 1837, see *Cong. Globe*, 41, 45, 46; Adams, *Memoirs*, IX, 450–455. The legislature of Louisiana adopted resolutions, Jan. 9, 1838, thanking " that portion of the southern delegation who withdrew from the floor of Congress rather than suffer in their presence a debate on the abolition of slavery in the south." *Acts of La.*, 1838, 14, 15. Ohio, Feb. 12, 1842, adopted resolutions censuring J. Q. Adams for presenting the Haverhill petition, but rescinded the same, Feb. 27, 1845. *Laws of Ohio*, 1841–42, 213; *Ibid.*, 1844–45, 444.

General References: Tremain, *Slavery in the District of Columbia*, ch. iv;

Von Holst, II, 235–291, 467–484; Wilson, I, chs. xxiii, xxv, xxvi, xxviii, xxx, *passim;* Greeley, I, 142–147; Burgess, 252–270; McMaster, VI, chs. lx; Schouler, IV, 224–229, 296–302, 423–427; Benton, I, 609–623; Morse, *J. Q. Adams,* 243–289; Von Holst, *Calhoun,* 165–180; Jenkins, *Calhoun,* 328–336, 379–385; Peck, *The Jacksonian Epoch,* 373–391; Lalor, III, 167–169; Jay, 347–351; 379–408; Bryant & Gay, IV, 339–340.

---

110. Resolutions of the Legislature of Massachusetts.

April 12, 1837.

Whereas, the house of representatives of the United States, in the month of January, in the year of our Lord one thousand eight hundred and thirty-seven, did adopt a resolution, whereby it was ordered that all petitions, memorials, resolutions, propositions or papers, relating in any way, or to any extent whatever, to the subject of slavery, or to the abolition of slavery, without being either printed or referred, should be laid upon the table, and that no further action whatever should be had thereon; and whereas, such a disposition of petitions, then or thereafter to be received, was a virtual denial of the right itself; and whereas, by the resolution aforesaid, which was adopted by a standing rule of the aforesaid house of representatives, the petitions of a large number of the people of this Commonwealth, praying for the removal of a great social, moral and political evil, have been slighted and contemned : therefore,

Resolved, That the resolution above named is an assumption of power and authority at variance with the spirit and intent of the constitution of the United States, and injurious to the cause of freedom and free institutions ; that it does violence to the inherent, absolute and inalienable rights of man ; and that it tends essentially to impair those fundamental principles of natural justice and natural law which are antecedent to any written constitutions of government, independent of them all, and essential to the security of freedom in a state.[1]

[1] The Massachusetts resolutions of March 21, 1840, characterized the practice of the Senate as " a procedure not less despotic, in effect, than the unconstitutional rule adopted by the House."

Resolved, That our senators and representatives in Congress, in maintaining and advocating the full right of petition, have entitled themselves to the cordial approbation of the people of this Commonwealth.

Resolved, That Congress, having exclusive legislation in the District of Columbia, possess the right to abolish slavery in the said District, and that its exercise should only be restrained by a regard to the public good.

[*Resolves of Massachusetts,* 1835–38, 559, 560.]

---

111. Resolutions of New York on the Rights of Petition.

February 16, 1840.

Resolved, That the vote and decision of the house of representatives of the United States, on the twenty-eighth day of January last, by which that house refused to receive thereafter, or in any manner act upon, any petition relating to slavery in the United States, are, in the opinion and judgment of this legislature, a denial of the common right of any and every citizen of this country to be heard by their representatives upon any and every subject upon which they may think proper respectfully to address them, and are, moreover, a violation of the common and natural right of every human being to address his prayers for aid to those who have the power to afford protection and relief; and an open and direct infringement of the constitution of the United States, and of the principles of the declaration of independence.

Resolved, That this legislature has seen with deep regret, that certain representatives from the state of New York, voted with the majority for the adoption of the rule of the house of representatives, by which the right of petition is denied, and without whose votes the rule aforesaid could not have been adopted.

[*Laws of New York,* 1840. 349.]

Annexation of Texas.

1837-1845.

The resolutions relating to the annexation of Texas fall into the two periods of this movement, namely, 1837–38 and 1841–45. In the first period the following Southern States passed resolutions in favor: Kentucky, Jan. 24, 1837; South Carolina, Dec. 19, 1837; Alabama, Dec. 25, 1837; Tennessee, Jan. 20, 1838, while several of the Northern States adopted resolutions against, viz: Vermont, Nov. 1, 1837, Oct. sess. 1838; Rhode Island, Oct. sess. 1837; Ohio, Feb. 23, 1838; Massachusetts, March 16, 1838; Michigan, April 2, 1838; Conn., May sess. 1838. Those of Vermont of 1837, Alabama and Mississippi, are given as typical of the two classes. With the revival of the movement in 1841–42, Vermont again led the opposition, in which it was joined in the years 1842–45 by the legislatures of Mass., Conn., Ohio, N. J., Del. and R. I., while Alabama, Tenn., Miss., S. C., Mo. and La., zealously advocated annexation, and this project received the endorsement of Maine, New Hampshire and Ill. Several of the legislatures repeatedly adopted resolutions in advocacy of their position. Those of South Carolina and Mass. follow.

An address warning the country of the revival of the project of annexation was issued March 3, 1843, by thirteen anti-slavery members of the 27th Congress. It quoted from a significant report of the legislature of Mississippi, given below.[1] (*Niles*, LXIV, 173, 174; Greeley, I, 157, 158.) For popular movement in favor of "Texas or Disunion," and a Southern Convention in parts of the South in 1844–45, see *Niles*, LXVI and LXVII Index under "*Southern Convention.*"

References: For text of resolutions see *Session Laws* of the several States, also the *Senate Doc.*, and the *House Exec. Doc.*, for the following Congresses, 25 *Cong.* 2 *sess.*, 27 *Cong.* 2 *sess.*, 28 *Cong.* 1 *sess.*, 28 *Cong.* 2 *sess.*, 29 *Cong.* 1 *sess. Niles*, LXVII, 278, 281, 282, 346, 371. Channing and Hart, *Guide*, § 193; MacDonald, 343–346; Von Holst, II, ch. vii; III, ch. iii; Wilson, I, chs. xlii–xlv; Greeley, I, 147–175; Burgess, chs. xiii, xv; Benton, II, chs. 24, 135, 138–142, 148; McMaster, VI, ch. lx; Schouler, IV, 303–307, 440–459, 476–487; Garrison, *Garrison*, III, ch. v; Tyler, *Tyler*, chs. ix–xii; Von Holst, *Calhoun*, ch. viii; Thorpe, *United States*, II, 415–420; Thorpe, *Amer. People*, I, 336–340, notes; Greeley, *Slavery Extension or Restriction*, 31–44; Rhodes, I, 75–85.

---

[1] This report has not been found in any official document. From the context it would appear to have been drawn in 1837–38; if so, it was not adopted by the legislature as no resolves on Texas are given in the *Laws of Miss.*, until Feb. 25, 1842. This report may have been prepared in 1842, but no report is published with these resolves. *Laws of Miss.*, 1842, 257; *Senate Doc.*, 27 *Cong.*, 2 *sess.*, IV, No. 277.

112. Resolution of Vermont.

November 1, 1837.

1. *Resolved by the Senate and House of Representatives,* That our Senators in Congress be instructed, and our Representatives be requested to use their influence in that body to prevent the annexation of Texas to the Union.

2. *Resolved,* That representing as we do the People of Vermont, we do, hereby, in their name, SOLEMNLY PROTEST against such annexation in any form.

3. *Resolved,* That as the Representatives of the People of Vermont, we do solemnly protest against the admission into this Union, of any State whose constitution tolerates domestic slavery.

4. *Resolved,* That Congress have full power by the constitution, to abolish slavery and the slave trade in the District of Columbia and in the Territories of the United States.

5. *Resolved,* That our Senators in Congress be instructed and our Representatives requested to present the foregoing Report and Resolutions to their respective Houses in Congress, and to use their influence to carry the same speedily into effect.

[*Acts of Vermont, Oct. Session,* 1837, 60.]

---

113. Report of the Legislature of Mississippi on Annexation of Texas.

Session of 1837.[1]

*   *   *   But we hasten to suggest the importance of the annexation of Texas to this republic upon grounds somewhat local in their complexion, but of an import infinitely grave and interesting to the people who inhabit the Southern portion of this confederacy, where it is known that a species of domestic slavery is tolerated and protected by law, whose existence is prohibited by the legal regulations of other states of this confederacy; which system of slavery is held by all, who are familiarly acquainted with its practical effects, *to be of highly beneficial influence to the country within whose limits it is permitted to exist.*

[1] See note ante, p. 224.

The Committee feel authorized to say that this system is cherished by our constitutents as *the very palladium of their prosperity and happiness ;* and, whatever ignorant fanatics may elsewhere conjecture, the Committee are fully assured, upon the most dilligent observation and reflection upon the subject, that *the south does not possess within her limits a blessing with which the affections of her people are so closely entwined and so completely enfibered,* and whose value is more highly appreciated, than that which we are now considering.   *   *   *

It may not be improper here to remark that, during the last session of Congress, when a Senator from Mississippi proposed the acknowledgment of Texan independence, it was found with few exceptions, *the members of that body were ready to take ground upon it as upon the subject of slavery itself.*   *   *   *

We sincerely hope there is enough good sense and genuine love of country among our fellow-countrymen of the Northern States *to secure us final justice on this subject;* yet we can not consider it safe or expedient for the people of the South to entirely disregard the efforts of the fanatics, and the efforts of such men as Webster [1], and others who countenance such dangerous doctrines.

The northern states have no interests of their own which require any special safeguards for their defense, save only their domestic manufacture ; and God knows they have already received protections from the government on a most liberal scale ; under which encouragement they have improved and flourished beyond example. *The South has very peculiar interests to preserve,*—interests already violently assailed and boldly threatened.

Your Committee are fully persuaded that this protection to her best interests will be afforded by the annexation of Texas; an equipoise of influence in the halls of Congress will be secured, which will furnish us a permanent guarantee of protection.

[*Niles' Register*, LXIV, 173, 174.]

---

[1] In a part of the report omitted reference had been made to Webster's speech in New York, March 15, 1837. See *Works*, I, 354-357.

114.   Preamble and Resolutions of Alabama.

December 25, 1837.

The General Assembly of the State of Alabama have witnessed, with feelings of deep mortification, the course pursued by a few citizens of the United States, in opposition to the admission of the republic of Texas into the Federal Union.

Professing, as we have, friendship for civil liberty, and a devotion to the holy cause of freedom in every clime, it was to have been hoped that no voice would be heard among us, to rebuke an application from Texas for admission into this boasted asylum from oppression.   *   *   *

As far as it can be brought to bear upon the question in a constitutional or political point of view, precedents are not wanting, if justice could require or yield to precedent, which will sustain fully the advocates of the annexation of Texas. We refer to the acquisition of Louisiana, during the administration of Mr. Jefferson, and to the still more recent annexation of Florida, during the administration of Mr. Monroe. The inhabitants of those countries were not admitted into the Union at their own solicitation, but without their formal consent ; they were purchased of their royal and imperial masters with our common treasure, and, together with their soil, their religion, their language, their household goods, were brought within the pale of our General Government. How different, in many respects, is the case with the republic of Texas? Upon the unanimous application of her brave and chivalrous citizens, who may be said to be " bone of our bone, and flesh of our flesh," she seeks, "without money and without price," from us, to obtain shelter and protection under the ample folds of our Federal banner. Is there, in the whole length and breadth of our land, a friend of liberty, a lover of justice, or even a mere philanthropist, who can hesitate for one moment in the decision of this question?

There are some, it is to be apprehended and regretted, who view this subject alone through the dim and deceptive medium of sectional party feelings. We cannot consent to be influenced by such sordid and circumscribed motives.   *   *   *

The solid and everlasting foundation on which our political fathers sought to establish justice, to insure domestic peace, to form a perfect Union of our States, and to perpetuate the blessings of liberty to themselves and their posterity, was a well-regulated balance of governmental and territorial power. Since the formation of the constitution, the northeast, the north, and the northwest have increased more rapidly in numerical power of States and population, then the south and southwest. It needs but a glance at the map to satisfy the most superficial observer, that an over-balance is produced by the extreme northeast, which as regards territory, would be happily corrected and couter-balanced by the annexation of Texas. And when it is recollected, too, that the very territory which it is now proposed to acquire, was once within the scope of a just claim of our General Government, extending to the Rio del Norte, and that it was bartered for a mess of porridge by a prime-mover of the present opposition to its re-acquisition,[1] there remains no pretext for a subterfuge, under which the adversaries of annexation can hope to disguise the covert designs which, there is much reason to fear, prompted the exchange of our claims in Texas for the unappropriated portions of Florida, consisting mainly of barren sands and poisonous everglades.   *   *   *

1. *Be it resolved by the Senate and House of Representatives of the State of Alabama in General Assembly convened,* That the overture on the part of the republic of Texas, for annexation to the United States of America, ought to be met by the Federal authorities in the most friendly manner, and should be accepted as soon as it can be done without a violation of our honor as a nation, or any principle of international law.

2. *And be it further resolved,* That our Senators in Congress be instructed, and our Representatives requested, to urge and sustain the foregoing views on all proper occasions.

[*Acts of Alabama,* 1837, 129–131.]

---

[1] This refers to John Quincy Adams, but the charge of course was groundless.

115. South Carolina Declares Annexation Essential.

December 18, 1844.

Resolved, That the State of South Carolina takes the deepest interest in the annexation of Texas to this Federal Union, because we believe it essential to preserve the peace and permanent independence of the Confederacy, and must result in advancing prosperity of the whole country.

Resolved, That collateral issues, which have arisen in the progress of the Texas negotiations, by the official communication of Lord Aberdeen to the Federal Government, dated December 26, 1843,[1] in which he announces that Great Britain desires, and is constantly exerting herself to procure the "general abolition of slavery throughout the world," are of such a nature as to make the annexation of Texas a vital and permanent question to the people of South Carolina.

Resolved, That we look with confidence to the recent election of a Republican President and Vice-President as giving us a guarantee that all the constitutional powers of the government will be exerted to secure the immediate annexation of that Republic.

[*Acts and Resolutions of South Carolina,* 1844, 187.]

Massachusetts' Opposition to the Annexation of Texas.

1843-1845.

The state of Massachusetts took a very prominent part in opposing the annexation project. It passed resolves March 17, 1843, March 15, 1844, Feb. 22, and March 26, 1845. (*Acts and Res. of Mass.,* 1843–45, 68, 319, 320, 558–599, 651–653.) The two series which are given below are of especial interest as presenting a view similar to that taken by the same state in opposition to the annexation of Louisiana in 1803, and again in 1811–13 (*Ante,* pp. 65–68), as well as for their strong assertion of state rights. A similar constitutional position was taken by the Legislatures of Vt., Ohio, Del. and Conn. at this same time, and Maryland declared that annexation by joint resolution would be a flagrant violation of the Constitution on the very day that measure was approved, March 1, 1845. (*Acts and Res. of Vt., Oct. sess.,* 1845, 36; *Laws of Ohio,* 1844–45, 437; *Laws of Del.,* 1845, 90, 91; *Res. and Private act of*

[1] See Calhoun's reply to this communication, *Works,* V, 333–339.

Conn., May sess., 1845, 21; *Laws of Md.,* 1844–45, Res. No. 25. See C. F. Adams, *Texas and the Mass. Resolutions.* An Anti-Texas Convention was held in Mass. Jan. 29, 1845, *Niles,* LXVII, 363–367; also another in the fall of 1845. *Ibid.,* LIX, 178; Wilson, I, 622, ch. xlv.

---

116.   Massachusetts on the Annexation of Texas.

March 15, 1844.

1. *Resolved,* That the power to unite an independent foreign state with the United States is not among the powers delegated to the general government by the constitution of the United States.

2. *Resolved,* That the Commonwealth of Massachusetts, faithful to the compact between the people of the United States, according to the plain meaning and intent in which it was understood and acceded to by them, is sincerely anxious for its preservation, but that it is determined, as it doubts not the other states are, to submit to undelegated powers in no body of men on earth;[1] That the project of the annexation of Texas, unless arrested on the threshhold, may tend to drive these states into a dissolution of the union, and will furnish new calumnies against republican governments of exposing the gross contradiction of a people professing to be free, and yet seeking to extend and perpetuate the subjection of their slaves.

[Resolutions of transmission.]

[*Acts and Resolves of Massachusetts,* 1844.   319.]

---

117.   Massachusetts Denies the Legality of the Admission of Texas.

March 26, 1845.

Whereas, The Commonwealth of Massachusetts has, through her Legislature, with great unanimity, in the years one thousand eight hundred and forty-three, and forty-four, and forty-five, solemnly and strenuously protested against the admission, by the federal government, of the foreign nation of Texas, as a State,

---

[1] Quoted from the Kentucky Resolutions of 1798.

into the Union, because the act would be in direct violation of the Constitution of the United States, and because it would perpetuate the slavery of a portion of mankind in America, and because it would extend the unequal rule of representation, by federal numbers, over a new region never within the contemplation of those who consented to its establishment, at the time of the formation of the Constitution : *and whereas,* the consent of the executive and legislative departments of the government of the United States has been given, by a resolution passed on the twenty-seventh day of February last, to the adoption of preliminary measures to accomplish this nefarious project : Therefore, be it

Resolved, That Massachusetts hereby refuses to acknowledge the act of the government of the United States, authorizing the admission of Texas, as a legal act, in any way binding her from using her utmost exertions in coöperation with other States, by every lawful and constitutional measure, to annual its conditions, and defeat its accomplishment.

Resolved, That the annexation of a large slaveholding territory, at the will of the government of the United States, with the declared intention of giving strength to the institution of domestic slavery in these states, is an alarming encroachment upon the rights of the freemen of the Union, a perversion of the principles of republican government, a deliberate assault upon the compromises of the Constitution, and demands the strenuous, united and persevering opposition of all persons, without distinction, who claim to be the friends of human liberty.

Resolved, That the right to hold men as slaves was conceded by the Constitution of the United States to be a matter exclusively belonging to those States in which that right was acknowledged, upon the understanding, however, that the power which it gives, should be exercised strictly within those limits, but now that it arrogates the control of millions of freemen living beyond them, and puts at hazard the predominance of the principles of liberty in America, it justifies the adoption on their part, of a systematic policy of counteraction, by lawful and constitutional means, even though that policy should ultimately bring on the downfall of slavery itself.

Resolved, That the Constitution of the United States was framed in order to protect a people of freemen, and perpetuate the blessings of liberty to them and posterity, and that Massachusetts will coöperate with any, or all, of the free States of the Union, in an honest endeavor, by lawful means, to restore it in every case where it has been perverted from the fulfillment of its original and noble purpose.

Resolved, That no territory hereafter applying to be admitted to the Union, as a State, should be admitted without a condition that domestic slavery should be utterly extinguished within its borders, and Massachusetts denies the validity of any compromise whatsoever, that may have been, or that hereafter may be, entered into by persons in the government of the Union, intended to preclude the future application of such a condition by the people acting through their representatives in the Congress of the United States.

[Resolutions of transmission.]

[*Acts and Resolves of Massachusetts*, 1843–1845. 651–653.]

Inter-State Controversies. Georgia—Maine and Virginia—New York.

1837–1843.

In two cases the refusal of the Governors of Northern States to honor requisitions from the executives of Southern States for persons charged with "slave-stealing" created great excitement and general protest in the South. The first, between Georgia and Maine, occurred in 1837, the second, between Virginia and New York, in 1839. For the correspondence of Governors Scheley of Ga., and Dunlap of Me., see *Senate Doc.*, 26 *Cong.*, 1 *sess.*, V, No. 273, *Niles*, LIII, 71, 72; LV, 356. The refusal of the Governor of Maine to comply with the requisition led the Legislature of Georgia, Dec. 25, 1837, to call upon the Legislature of Maine to redress the grievance. (*Acts of Ga.*, 1837, 282–287.) Their failure to do so led Georgia to adopt a memorial to Congress, Dec. 24, 1839, declaring that "To this generation has been reserved the humiliating spectacle of a sovereign State making herself a city of refuge for fugitive felons from her sister confederates." They pronounced the existing laws inadequate, and proposed amending them so as to require the Federal Judges and Marshals to cause the arrest and delivery of fugitives from

justice and service. (*Acts of Ga.*, 1839, 229–231; *Senate Jour.*, 26 *Cong.*, 1
sess., 235, 236; *Niles* LVIII, 27.) New Jersey expressed its view on the obligation to carry out the law, *Niles*, LVI, 215, *Acts of N. J.*, 1838–39, 242.

In the meantime a second controversy had arisen owing to the refusal of
Gov. Seward of N. Y., to honor the requisition from Virginia. (For Seward's
correspondence with Va., 1839–41, and messages see *Works*, II, 385, 390,
413, 449–516.) The Virginia Legislature thereupon adopted an elaborate report and resolutions, March 17, 1840, extracts from which follow. (*Acts of
Va.*, 1839–40, 155–169.) Seward declining to reverse his decision, and New
York having passed a law granting trial by jury to fugitive slaves, (*Laws of
N. Y.*, 1840, 174.) Virginia retaliated March 13, 1841, by passing an in-
spection law entitled, " An act to prevent citizens of New York from carrying
slaves out of the Commonwealth," etc. (*Acts of Va.*, 1840–41; 79–82). Her
Executive, Gov. Gilmer refused to surrender a forger to New York until
Seward would honor his requisition for the slave-stealers, thereupon the Leg-
islature of Va. condemned the action of the Governor and he resigned.
(*Ibid*, 157, 158; *Niles*, LX, 55, 68–70, 150–152.) The Whig Legislature of
New York sustained Seward, but April 11, 1842, the Legislature being
Democratic, passed resolutions in disapproval of his position (*Laws of N. Y.*,
1842, 419), which Seward refused to transmit. (*Works*, II, 432–435.)

These two controversies called out resolutions from the other Southern
States pledging their support to Georgia and Virginia in the maintenance of
their rights. Those of South Carolina and Mississippi are given as representative. South Carolina, Dec. 17, 1841, also passed an inspection law directed
against New York, similar to that of Virginia. (*Act of S. C.*, 1841, 149–
152; *Niles*, LXI, 372.) The resolutions of the other states were adopted as
follows: Alabama, Feb. 2, 1839, Sess. of 1840–41, Apr. 27, 1841, Feb. 14,
1843. *Acts of Ala.* 1838–39, 211; *ibid*, 1840–41, 199; *ibid*, April 1841, 19;
ibid, Dec. 1843, 225; Louisiana, March 16, 1842, *Acts of La.*, 1842, 288,
289; Maryland, Apr. 6, 1841, *Acts of Md.*, 1841, Res. No. 9; Missouri, Feb.
16, 1841, *Laws of Mo.*, 1840–41, 336,337; South Carolina, Dec. 17, 1841, *Rep.
and Res. of S. C.*, 1841, 44–49. See also *Senate Doc.*, 26 *Cong.* 2 *sess.*, II, No.
96, III, No. 127, *Niles*, LVII, 272; LXIX, 374, 404; LX, 90; LXI, 372;
LXII, 86, 112, 117. For correspondence of Seward growing out of another
controversy with Georgia, see *Works*, II, 519–546; *Niles*, LXI, 241.

General references: Channing and Hart, *Guide*, § 189; Wilson, I, 473–475;
Von Holst, II, 538–540; Smith, I, 50, 51; Bryant and Gay, IV, 340–342;
Seward's *Works*, I, lxiii–lxv; Seward's *Autobiography*, 437–439, 463, 464,
528–531; Bancroft, *Seward*, I, 101–105; Lathrop, *Seward*, 38–42. Cal-
houn's *Works*, III, 155, 156; Winthrop, *Addresses and Speeches*, I, 340–352;
Pierce, *Sumner*, II, 256–259.

118. South Carolina on the Georgia-Maine Controversy.

December 20, 1839.

* * * The facilities which the Federal Constitution affords to citizens of the United States, who are inimical to slavery, of abducting and inveigling slaves from their owners, and the temptation to embrace those facilities, which is suggested by such impunity, as the authorities of Maine have provided for her citizens, presents a conjuncture, which the least timid, and the most prudent amongst us, may well deem full of peril to the rights of the South.   Where [when] the safe-guards of the Federal Constitution shall have become ineffectual and illusory, then, indeed, will the period have arrived, when the states of the South must take care that their citizens sustain no detriment.   Let us tell our brethren of the North, mildly, but resolutely, that if they did introduce slaves amongst us against our remonstrance, they shall not remove them against our consent, and that whilst we will tolerate no impairment of our title to our property, in the Halls of the Federal Legislature, we will, also, permit no State to convert itself into a city of refuge, for those who invade it as felons.

Your Committee recommend the adoption of the following resolutions :

1. *Resolved*, That it is the duty, as well as the right of any State, to insist on a faithful observance of the Federal Constitution, by each State in the Union.

2. *Resolved*, That to define crimes and felonies, within its jurisdiction, is an incident to the sovereignty of each State, and that no other State can question the exercise of that right.

3. *Resolved*, That to demand the surrender and removal of fugitives from its justice, is, by the Constitution, a right, and the arrest and surrender a duty ; that the denial or impairment of this right, is inconsistent with the constitutional obligation of a State and subversive of the peace and good government of the other States.

4. *Resolved*, That the right has been impaired, if not denied,

by the authorities of Maine and that this State will never consent, that any State shall become an asylum for those, who are fugitives from the justice of other States.

5. *Resolved*, That this State will make common cause with any State of the Confederacy, in maintaining their just rights, under the guarantee of the Constitution of the United States, and should the obligations of that instrument be disregarded, by those whose duty it may be to enforce them, it will take counsel with its co-States of the Confederacy, having similar interests to protect, or similar injuries to redress, in devising and adopting such measures as will maintain, *at all hazards*, those rights—and that property, which the obligations of the compact of union, *cancelled* as they then will be as to us, have failed to enforce. [Resolutions of transmission.]

[*Reports and Resolutions of S. C.*, 1839, 86–91, *passim.*]

---

119. Virginia on the New York-Virginia Controversy.

March 17, 1840.

* * * The patience of the south has already been too severely taxed, and we once for all, without bravado or threat, in the language of a distinguished senator of New York, warn the non-slave-holding states " that they may find when it is too late that the patience of the south, however well founded upon principle, from repeated aggressions will become exhausted." * * *

1. *Resolved*, That the reasons assigned by the governor of New York for his refusal to surrender Peter Johnson, Edward Smith and Isaac Gansey as fugitives from justice, upon the demand of the executive of this state, are wholly unsatisfactory ; and that that refusal is a palpable and dangerous violation of the constitution and laws of the United States.

2. *Resolved*, That the course pursued by the executive of New York cannot be acquiesced in ; and if sanctioned by that state and persisted in, it will become the solemn duty of Virginia to adopt the most decisive and efficient measures for the protection of the

property of her citizens, and the maintenance of rights, which she can and will not, under any circumstances, surrender or abandon.

3. *Resolved,* That the governor of this state be authorized and requested to renew his correspondence with the executive of New York, requesting that that functionary will review the grounds taken by him ; and that he will urge the consideration of the subject upon the legislature of his state.

4. *Resolved,* That the governor of Virginia be requested to open a correspondence with the executive of each of the slave-holding states, requesting their co-operation in any necessary and proper measure of redress which Virginia may be forced to adopt. [Resolutions of transmission.]

[*Acts of Virginia,* 1839–40, 168, 169.]

---

120. Mississippi on the Rendition of Fugitives from Justice.

February 6, 1841.

Be it resolved by the Legislature of the state of Mississippi, That the right of the executive authority of one state to demand fugitives from justice of the executive authority of another state, and the duty of the latter to surrender such fugitives upon such demand, is a right secured by the terms of the federal compact, a right which cannot be denied without a palpable violation of the constitution, and a right which no state legislature can annul, evade or impair.

Be it further resolved, That the attempt of the governor and legislature of the state of Maine, and the governor of New York, to evade, impair and deny that right, is deemed by this legislature, an outrage upon the chartered rights of Virginia and Georgia, and a precedent full of danger to all the slave-holding states.

Be it further resolved, That this state will make common cause with any of her sister states whose rights have been or may here-after be invaded as aforesaid, in any mode or measure of resistance or redress necessary for their or our protection. [Resolutions of transmission.]

[Laws of Mississippi, 1841, 155, 156.]

Inter-State Controversies.   South Carolina and Massachusetts.

1839–1845.

The "Negro Seaman's Act" of South Carolina of 1822 (Ante, pp. 204–207), was superseded by a new law, Dec. 19, 1835. (Acts of S. C., 1835, 34–39; Greeley, I, 179, note.)   This act like the previous one led to complaints. The Mass. Legislature passed resolves, April 8, 1839 and March 3, 1842, protesting against it, and authorizing the Governor to take steps to secure the release of any of their citizens so imprisoned. (Acts and Res. of Mass., 1839–42, 105, 568; Niles, LVIII, 110; House Jour., 26 Cong. 1 sess., 786.) These protests were without avail, and in the meantime Louisiana, March 16, 1842, passed a similar law. (Acts of La., 1842, 308–318.)   The Mass. Legislature then determined to test the constitutionality of these acts, and accordingly adopted resolutions March 24, 1843 and March 16, 1844, authorizing the Governor to send agents to each of these states to institute legal proceedings to that end. (Acts and Res. of Mass., 1843–45, 81, 330.)   Acting under the second of these measures, Samuel Hoar proceeded to Charleston and Henry Hubbard to New Orleans. Mr. Hoar upon his arrival addressed Gov. Hammond of S. C., who informed the Legislature of his mission. That body shortly passed the subjoined resolutions for Mr. Hoar's expulsion from the state, and an act to prohibit and punish similar missions in the future. (Acts of S. C., 1844, 160, 292, 293; Niles, LXVII, 326, 327, 346, 347; Greeley, I, 181.)   For Mr. Hoar's report of his treatment see, Niles, LXVII, 315–317 : and for similar experience of Mr. Hubbard in La., ibid, 323, 346, 398, 399.   The earlier resolutions of Mass. had called out a reply from Georgia, Dec. 28, 1842, sharply rebuking Mass's. resolutions " as the sickley effusions of a wild and reckless fanaticism," and defending her own law of a similar nature. (Acts of Ga., 1842, 181.)   Maine also protested against these acts of the southern states, March 22, 1843. (Senate Doc., 28 Cong. 1 sess., IV, No. 245.)   The action of S. C., was endorsed and that of Mass. condemned by the Legislatures of Ark., Ga., Miss. and Ala., during 1845–46. (Acts of Ark., 1844–45, 163, Acts of Ga., 1845, 209–211, Senate Doc., 29 Cong., 1 sess., IV, 100; Laws of Miss., 1846, 542, 543; Acts of Ala., 1844–45, 214.)   Mr. Hoar's report was submitted to the Legislature of Mass., and on March 25, 1845, they adopted an elaborate report severely arraigning S. C. and recording a solemn protest. On the following day they passed resolutions condemning the action of S. C. and La., which made " an appeal to the Federal Courts for redress in such cases, an offense punishable as an infamous crime," and demanding from Congress protection for her absent citizens. (*Acts and Res. of Mass.*, 1843–45, 626–645, 648, 649, 681–685; *Niles*, LXVII, 314, 315, 394–398.) Congress took no action, and Mass., May 22, 1852, again protested against the sale of her citizens into slavery, this time in Texas. (*Acts and Res. of Mass.*, 1852–53, 307.) The new act of S. C. called out a protest from the British consul in 1850, but the Legislature refused to essentially change the law. (*Report and Res. of S. C.*, 1850, 242–245; *ibid*, 1851, 99–111. References: Greeley, I, 178–185; Von Holst, III, 131–139; Wilson, I, ch. xli.

---

121.   South Carolina on the Mission of Samuel Hoar.

December 5, 1844.

Resolved, That the right to exclude from their territories seditious persons, or others, whose presence may be dangerous to their peace, is essential to every independent State.

Resolved, That free negroes and persons of color are not citizens of the United States within the meaning of the Constitution, which confers upon the citizens of one State the privileges and immunities of citizens in the several States.

Resolved, That the emissary sent by the State of Massachusetts to the State of South Carolina, with the avowed purpose of interfering with her institutions, and disturbing her peace, is to be regarded in the character he has assumed, and to be treated accordingly.

Resolved, That his Excellency the Governor be requested to expel from our territory the said Agent, after due notice to depart, and that the Legislature will sustain the Executive authority in any measures it may adopt for the purpose aforesaid.

[*Reports and Resolutions of South Carolina*, 1844, 160.]

Replies to Massachusetts' Proposal to Abolish Representation for Slaves.

1843-1844.

The Democratic Legislature of Mass., March 23, 1843, proposed an amendment to the Federal Constitution to apportion representatives and direct taxes among the States according to their respective number of free persons. (*Acts and Res. of Mass.*, 1843-45, 79.) Its presentation to Congress called out "the most memorable debate ever entertained in the House," (Adams, *Memoirs*, XI, 455,) and resolutions of condemnation from Georgia, Dec. 25, 1843, and Alabama, Jan. 17, 1844. The next Legislature of Mass., the Whigs now being in control, indorsed the same amendment. This second resolution aroused still greater excitement and condemnation both in and out of Congress. The legislatures of Virginia, Kentucky, Alabama and Georgia during 1844-45 bitterly denounced the proposition and the state of Mass. The resolutions of Virginia are given below. Mass. replied to Virginia's accusation March 14, 1844, unanimously reaffirming its position and the right of amendment. (*Acts and Res. of Mass.*, 1843-44, 325-328, *Niles*, LXVI, 67.) References: For text of Resolutions and discussion in Congress, see, *Acts of Ga.*, 1843, 186; *ibid*, 1845, 206, 207; *Acts of Ala.*, 1843-44, 196; *ibid*, 1844-45, 211-214; *Acts of Va.*, 1843-44, 115; *Acts of Ky.*, 1844, 269, 270; *Senate Doc.*, 28 *Cong.*, I *sess.*, III, Nos. 106, 156; *ibid*, 29 *Cong.*, I *sess.*, IV, No. 101; *Cong. Globe*, 28 *Cong.*, I *sess.*, 64-66, 179-180, 243, 342, 360, 361; *Niles*, LXV, 349, 382; LXVI, 13, 31. Wilson I, 482-487; Ames, *Proposed Amend.*, 46-49, 352; Julian, *Life of Giddings*, 151-153.

---

122. Virginia Condemns Massachusetts' Proposed Amendment.

February 15, 1844.

* * * It is well known that the recognition and protection of the peculiar interests of the slaveholding states, by making the slaves a part of the basis of representation and taxation in the federal government, was a compromise upon which the federal union of the states was formed ; was acknowledged by Massachusetts, in convention, as the language of all America ; adopted in the federal convention by a vote almost unanimous ; and is essen-

tial to the peace, welfare and continuance of the slaveholding states in this Union. Therefore,

1. *Resolved unanimously by the general assembly of Virginia,* That we cannot regard these resolutions as, in truth, a proposition to amend the federal constitution, but virtually one to dissolve the Union.

2. That whilst we have forborne the expression of complaint at the disturbance of the peace and safety of the south by the agitation of the subject of our peculiar domestic institutions, by individuals and voluntary societies at the north, we regard this attack by the highest constitutional authority of a sister state, as in the highest degree unjust, unkind, faithless to the compromises of the constitution, and meriting the deepest condemnation of every patriot and friend of the Union.

3. That when we look back to those periods of our history when Massachusetts and Virginia co-operated so cordially, zealously and effectively in achieving our independence, and securing it by the adoption of our federal constitution, we cannot but regard this attack with increased regret and abhorrence.

4. That the governor of this commonwealth be and he is hereby requested to communicate copies of the foregoing preamble and resolutions to the governors of the several states, with the request that they may be laid before their respective legislatures; to the senators and representatives in congress from Virginia; and especially to return the original resolutions to the governor of Massachusetts.

[*Acts of Virginia,* 1843–44, 115.]

SLAVERY AND THE UNION, 1845–1861.

123. Massachusetts Against the Mexican War and Slavery.

April 26, 1847.

Resolutions condemning the policy of the administration in the war with Mexico were passed in the sessions of 1846–47 by Vermont, Rhode Island, Maryland and Massachusetts. The latter is given below as typical. A few of the northern legislatures favored the war, although opposing the extension of slavery, as appears in the resolves of New York and Michigan of Feb., 1847. Some of the Southern States defended the administration against these attacks, notably three series of resolutions of Alabama of the sessions of 1847–48, and the elaborate resolves of Mississippi of March 4, 1848.

References: 29 *Cong.*, 2 *sess.*, *Senate Doc.*, II, No. 97; III, Nos. 122, 207; *House Exec. Doc.*, IV, Nos. 81, 85; 30 *Cong.*, 1 *sess.*, *Senate Misc.*, No. 85; *Acts of Vt.*, Oct. sess., 1846, 48, 49; *Acts of Mich.*, 1847, 193–195; *Laws of New York*, 1847, 377; *Laws of Alabama*, 1847–48, 447, 448, 456, 457; *Laws of Miss.*, 1848, 524, 525; *Niles*, LXXI, 371; Von Holst, III, 239–255, 335–338.

Resolved, That the present war with Mexico had its primary origin in the unconstitutional annexation to the United States of the foreign State of Texas; that it was unconstitutionally commenced by the order of the President, to General Taylor, to take military possession of territory in dispute between the United States and Mexico, and in the occupation of Mexico; and that it is now waged by a powerful nation against a weak neighbor—unnecessarily and without just cause, at immense cost of treasure and life, for the dismemberment of Mexico, and for the conquest of a portion of her territory, from which slavery has already been excluded, with the triple object of extending slavery, of strengthening the slave power, and of obtaining the control of the Free States, under the Constitution of the United States.

Resolved, That such a war of conquest, so hateful in its objects, so wanton, unjust and unconstitutional in its origin and character, must be regarded as a war against freedom, against humanity, against justice, against the Union, against the Constitution, and against the free states; and that a regard for the true interests and highest honor of the country, not less than the impulses of Christian duty, should arouse all good citizens to join in efforts to arrest this war, and in every just way to aid the country to retire from the position of aggression which it now occupies toward a weak, distracted neighbor, and sister republic.

Resolved, That our attention is directed anew to the "wrong and enormity" of slavery, and to the tyranny and usurpation of the "slave power," as displayed in the history of our country, particularly in the annexation of Texas, and the present war with Mexico; and that we are impressed with the unalterable conviction, that a regard for the fair fame of our country, for the principles of morals, and for that righteousness which exalteth a nation, sanctions and requires all constitutional efforts for the destruction of the unjust influence of the slave power, and for the abolition of slavery within the limits of the United States.

[*Acts and Resolves of Massachusetts,* 1846–48, 541, 542.]

The Wilmot Proviso and Slavery in the Territories.

1846-1850.

The efforts to secure the adoption by Congress of the Wilmot Proviso in August, 1846, and in February, 1847, and the later contest to obtain the recognition of a similar principle in the organization of the government in the newly acquired territory, were instrumental in calling out resolutions during the period 1846–1850, from the legislatures of nearly all the States.   During the year 1847 all of the New England and Middle States, together with Ohio and Michigan passed resolutions favoring the Wilmot Proviso, while prior to the ratification of the treaty with Mexico, March 16, 1848, the legislatures of Virginia, Missouri, Alabama and Texas had vigorously opposed it.

An even larger number of resolutions were prompted by the discussion relative to the organization of the territories during the years 1848–1850.   The following States passed resolves; those in opposition to slavery extension were: 1848, New Hamp., Vt., New York, Ohio (2), Wis.; 1849, New Hamp., Vt. (2), Mass., R. I., Conn., New York, Ill., Mich., Wis.; 1850, Mass., R. I. (2), Conn., New York, New Jersey, Ind., Mich. (3), Wis.   Those in favor of the extension were: 1848, So. Carolina; 1849, Va., No. Carolina, So. Carolina, Florida, Missouri; 1850, Md., Va., Ga., Miss. (2), Texas.   Typical resolutions from both sections follow.

References: For the texts of the resolutions see *Session Laws* of the several States, also the following congressional documents: 29 *Cong.*, 2 *sess.*, *Senate Doc.*, Nos. 122, 149, 153, 207, 219; *House Exec. Doc.*, Nos. 73, 89, 101; 30 *Cong.*, 1 *sess.*, *Senate Misc.*, Nos. 15, 17; *House Misc.*, Nos. 2, 19, 27, 84, 85, 91, 96; 30 *Cong.*, 2 *sess.*, *Senate Misc.*, Nos. 38, 41, 48, 51, 61, 62; *House Misc.*, Nos. 6, 9, 10, 12, 34, 42, 56, 58, 62; 31 *Cong.*, 1 *sess.*, *Senate Misc.*, Nos. 24, 52, 108, 121; *House Misc.*, Nos. 3, 4, 5, 10, 22, 25.   General references: Channing and Hart, *Guide*, § 196; Von Holst, III, 284–327; Wilson, II, chs. ii, iii; Greeley, I, 187–198; Greeley, *Slavery Extension*, 44–52; Lalor, III, 1114–1117; Burgess, 334–359; Rhodes, I, 89–98; Schouler, IV, 543; V, 66–70, 95–99, 115–120; W. H. Smith, I, ch. iv; Thorpe, U. S. II, 418–425; Curtis, II, 257–259; Benton, II, 694–700; *Niles*, LXXIII, 44.

---

124. Pennsylvania Favors the Wilmot Proviso.

January 22, 1847.

The following resolves are typical of the early resolutions adopted by the Northern States, referred to above.   Some of these, as those of Ohio, Feb. 8, 1847, also included the exclusion of slavery from the Territory of Oregon. (*Local Laws of Ohio*, 1846–47, 214.)

Whereas, The existing war with Mexico may result in the acquisition of new territory to the Union ;

And whereas, Measures are now pending in Congress, having in view the appropriation of money and the conferring authority upon the treaty-making power to this end ; therefore,

Resolved by the Senate and House of Representatives of the Commonwealth of Pennsylvania in General Assembly met, That our Senators and our Representatives in Congress be requested to vote against any measure whatever, by which territory will accrue to the Union, unless, as a part of the fundamental law upon which any contract or treaty for this purpose is based, slavery or involuntary servitude, except for crime, shall be forever prohibited.

[Resolutions of transmission.]

[*Laws of Pennsylvania, 1847, 489, 490.*]

---

125. Virginia Against the Wilmot Proviso.

March 8, 1847.

After the adoption of the Wilmot Proviso the second time by the House of Representatives, Feb. 15, 1847, Calhoun, on Feb. 19, in connection with a speech in the Senate in which he denounced the Proviso and called upon the South to repudiate compromise and stand upon their rights, presented a set of resolutions containing the new doctrine that Congress can impose no restrictions on slavery in the Territories.[1] (*Works*, IV, 339–349; *Niles*, LXXI, 407, 408. See also his speech and proceedings at Charleston, March 9, 1847. *Works*, IV, 394, 395; *Niles*, LXXII, 39, 40, 73–75; and his letter to a member of the Alabama Legislature, Benton, II, 698–700.) These led to an acrimonious debate between Benton and Calhoun. (*Benton*, II, 696–698; Calhoun, *Works*, IV, 362–382; *Niles*, LXXII, 223, 225.) Calhoun's resolutions were not pressed to a vote, but the principles underlying them were generally adopted in the South and found expression in the resolutions of several of the Southern Legislatures. (*Ante*, p. 243.) The first of these, the Virginia resolutions, were adopted unanimously, March 8, 1847, and contained in the second resolve the assertion of this doctrine in very nearly the language of Calhoun's second resolution. These typical resolutions, known as the " Platform of the South," are given below. The Virginia Legislature re-enacted these

[1] The resolutions of Georgia of Dec. 22, 1835, had maintained the legality of slavery in all the Territories, but this view was not urged until Calhoun presented his resolutions. *Acts of Georgia*, 1835, 29.

resolutions with additions, Jan. 20, 1849. (*Acts of Virginia*, 1848–49, 257, 258; *Senate Misc.*, 30 *Cong.*, 2 *sess.*, I, No. 48; *House Misc.*, No. 56; *Niles*, LXXV, 73.)

The Legislature of Alabama, in Dec., 1847, not only asserted the same in strong language but also declared that the Constitution " does not authorize it [Congress] to deprive or to empower others to deprive, a citizen of any of the said States of his property whatever it may be, in any such territory, except for 'public use,' and upon making 'just compensation' therefor," and announced that it would " act in concert with and make common cause with the other slave-holding States, for the defence, in any manner that may be necessary, of the institution [slavery] aforesaid." (*Acts of Ala.*, 1847–48, 450, 451.) The Texas Legislature, March 18, 1848, affirmed the same doctrine and declared " we will never submit to a usurpation of power which robs us of our rights." (*House Misc.*, 30 *Cong.*, 1 *sess.*, No. 91. See also *Ibid.*, No. 27.) About this time the doctrine of " squatter sovereignty" was brought forward (Speech of Dickinson, Jan. 12, 1848, *Cong. Globe*, 30 *Cong.*, 1 *sess.*, 159, 160; see also his resolutions, *Ibid.*, 21; and the Cass-Nicholson letter, *Niles*, LXXIII, 293), which alarmed Calhoun and other Southern leaders who denounced it. Yancey, of Alabama, secured its condemnation by the Alabama Democratic Convention in the so-called " Alabama Platform of 1848." This was approved by the Democratic party in some of the other Southern States, but Yancey's resolution was rejected by the National Democratic Convention of 1848 by a vote of 36 to 216. (Du Bose, *Yancey*, 199–220; Brown, *The Lower South*, 131–133; *Niles*, LXXIII, 392; Von Holst, III, 351–365; Wilson, II, 133. For letter of Gov. Brown, of Miss., to Gov. Smith, of Va., on receipt of the Virginia resolutions, see *Niles*, LXXII, 178.)

Whereas a bill appropriating money to prosecute war or negotiate peace with the Republic of Mexico, has passed the house of representatives of the United States, with the following proviso attached thereto : "*Provided*, That as an express and fundamental condition to the acquisition of any territory from the Republic of Mexico by the United States, by virture of any treaty which may be negotiated between them, and to the use by the executive of the moneys herein appropriated, neither slavery nor involuntary servitude shall ever exist in any part of said territory, except for crime, whereof the party shall be first duly convicted." And this general assembly deeming this proviso to be destructive of the compromises of the constitution of the United States, and an attack on the dearest rights of the south, as well as a dangerous and alarming usurpation by the federal government : Therefore ;

1. *Be it resolved unanimously by the general assembly of Virginia*, That the government of the United States has no control, directly or indirectly, mediately or immediately, over the institution of slavery, and that in taking any such control, it transcends the limits of its legitimate functions by destroying the internal organization of the sovereignties who created it.

2. *Resolved unanimously*, That all territory which may be acquired by the arms of the United States, or yielded by treaty with any foreign power, belongs to the several states of this union, as their joint and common property, in which each and all have equal rights, and that the enactment by the federal government of any law which should directly or by its effects prevent the citizens of any state from emigrating with their property of whatever description into such territory would make a discrimination unwarranted by and in violation of the constitution and the rights of the states from which such citizens emigrated, and in derogation of that perfect equality that belongs to the several states as members of this Union, and would tend directly to subvert the Union itself.

3. *Resolved*, That if in disregard alike of the spirit and principles of the act of congress on the admission of the state of Missouri into the Union, generally known as the Missouri compromise, and of every consideration of justice, of constitutional right and of fraternal feeling, the fearful issue shall be forced upon the country, which must result from the adoption and attempted enforcement of the proviso aforesaid as an act of the general government, the people of Virginia can have no difficulty in choosing between the only alternatives that will then remain of abject submission to aggression and outrage on the one hand, or determined resistance on the other, at all hazards and to the last extremity.

4. *Resolved unanimously*, That the general assembly holds it to be the duty of every man in every section of this confederacy, if the Union is dear to him, to oppose the passage of any law for whatever purpose, by which territory to be acquired may be subject to such a restriction.

5. *Resolved unanimously*, That the passage of the above-men-

tioned proviso makes it the duty of every slaveholding state, and of all the citizens thereof, as they value their dearest privileges, their sovereignty, their independence, their rights of property, to take firm, united and concerted action in this emergency.

[Resolutions of transmission.]

[Acts of Virginia, 1846–47, 236.]

126. Vermont on Slavery in the Territories and District of Columbia

October Session, 1848.

During this period the Legislature of Vermont adopted annually radical resolutions in condemnation of slavery. Those following are typical and represent the extreme Northern position. So offensive were the resolves of Vermont of Nov. 3, 1846, and of New Hampshire of June 30, 1847, that the copies transmitted to Virginia were returned by direction of the Legislature of that State. (*Acts of Vt., Oct. sess.,* 1846, 48, 49; *Senate Doc.,* 29 *Cong.,* 2 *sess.,* II, No. 97; *House Exec. Doc.,* IV, No. 81; *Laws of New Hamp., June sess.,* 1847, 488; *Senate Misc.,* 30 *Cong.,* 1 *sess.,* No. 17; *Acts of Va.,* 1846–47. 236, 237; *Niles,* LXXI, 333.) Similarly the resolutions of Vermont of Nov, 12, 1849, were returned by the Legislatures of Virginia and Maryland. (*Acts of Vt., Oct. sess.,* 1849, 47, 48; *House Misc.,* 31 *Cong.,* 1 *sess.,* I, No. 4; *Acts of Va.,* 1849–50, 234; *Laws of Md.,* 1849–50, Res. No. 28. For debate in Congress on the printing of the Vt. Res., see *Globe,* 31 *Cong,* 1 *sess.,* 119–123, 133–137, 1390; *Appx.,* 52–54, 91–97. For list of resolutions on the Wilmot Proviso see *ante,* p. 243).

The denial of the principles of the Virginia Resolution by some of the other Northern States call for especial mention. Thus New Hampshire in its resolutions of Dec. 29, 1848, declared " We rest with hope and confidence upon the opinion of the eminent jurists and statesmen, representing all parties, who declare that slavery, as a mere local institution, cannot be transferred to territories now free, without the positive interference of Congress in its behalf." (*Laws of N. H.,* 1848, 711.) Michigan, Jan. 13, 1849, asserted the principle that "slavery cannot exist without positive laws authorizing its existence." (*House Misc.,* 31 *Cong.,* 1 *sess.,* No. 10.)

The latter part of the subjoined resolves of Vermont call attention to the renewal of the agitation for the abolition of slavery and the slave trade in the District of Columbia during the period 1846–1850. (See *ante,* p. 221.) The following States passed resolves, all demanding the extinction of both slavery and the slave trade in the District with the exception of those from New York and New Jersey which related only to the slave trade: 1846, N. H.; 1848, N. H.,

R. I., Vt.; 1849, N. Y., R. I., Wis., Mass., N. J., O., Mich., Conn., Vt.; 1850, N. Y., R. I., Conn. (2). The resolution of Rhode Island of the May sess., 1848, anticipated Vermont in suggesting the removal of the seat of government. (*Laws of N. H.*, 1846, 333; *Ibid.*, 1848, 712; *Acts of Vt., Oct. sess.,* 1848, 40; *Ibid., Oct. sess.,* 1849, 48; *Acts and Res. of Mass.,* 1849, 200; *Acts and Res. of R. I., May sess.,* 1848, 11; *Ibid., Jan. sess.,* 1850, 27; *Res. and Private Acts of Conn., May sess.,* 1849, 60–63; *Ibid., May sess.,* 1850, 141–143; *Laws of N. Y.,* 1849, 727; *Ibid.,* 1850, 816–818; *Acts of N. J.,* 1849, 334; *Local Laws of Ohio,* 1848–49, 396; *Acts and Res. of Wis.,* 1849, 172; 29 *Cong.,* 2 *sess., House Exec. Doc.,* No. 24; *Senate Doc.,* No. 155; 30 *Cong.* 2 *sess., House Misc.,* Nos. 6, 8, 62; *Senate Misc.,* Nos. 61, 62; 31 *Cong.,* 1 *sess., House Misc.,* Nos. 2, 3, 9, 22; *Senate Misc.,* Nos. 52, 121. For replies of the Southern States, see *post,* p. 253). For discussion in Cong., see esp. *Globe,* 30 *Cong.,* 2 *sess.,* 83, 84, 105–110, 211–216; *Ibid.,* 31 *Cong.,* 1 *sess.,* 79 *et seq ;* Julian, *Giddings,* 258–262, 365–390.

Resolved, by the Senate and House of Representatives, That we seek, in vain, to discover any foundation for human slavery in the divine, or natural law, or the law of nations ; that its origin in all cases may be traced to fraud or physical force, and that all local laws for its continuance or protection have been afterwards introduced by the slaveholders themselves to justify and perpetuate their usurpation.

Resolved, That Congress possesses and ought immediately to exercise the power to prohibit slavery in the territories of New Mexico and California ; and that without such prohibition and the strong arm of the general government to enforce its observance, there is great danger that it will obtain a foothold there, not only without the aid of the local laws, but against them ; thus adding a still darker stain upon our national honor, and subjecting the free States to the injustice of a still greater inequality in their representation in Congress.

Resolved, That our Senators in Congress be instructed, and our Representatives requested, to exert their efforts for the passage of a law abolishing slavery in the District of Columbia, and prohibiting the traffic in slaves between the States.

Resolved, That it is unbecoming the representatives of freemen maintaining the declaration that *liberty is inalienable* to legislate for the general welfare, while their eyes are insulted with the frequent spectacle of men, chained, shackled, and driven to market, or confined in pens awaiting buyers; and, whereas, slavery in the District of Columbia exerts a baneful influence upon the action of Congress, checking the freedom of debate, threatening the freedom of the press, and controlling the executive departments of Washington; therefore

Resolved, That unless slavery in that district be speedily abolished by the action of Congress, with the assent of the inhabitants, it is the duty of Congress to pass a law removing the seat of government into the territory of some free State, more central, and more convenient for the nation, where the representatives of the people may be more free to legislate for the general welfare.

[*Acts and Resolves of Vermont, October Sess.*, 1848, 40, 41.]

Demand for a New Fugitive Slave Law.

The boarder States being especially exposed to the loss of their slaves through their escape to the free States and to Canada were the first to seek relief. As early as 1817 Maryland applied to Congress for the passage of a new Fugitive Slave Law, and renewed her efforts during the next few years. In 1826 she complained of the laws of Penna. and Delaware again kidnapping (McDougall, 23, 24, 107, 108; Siebert, 295–302). Kentucky, during the years 1820–27, thrice requested the government to negotiate with Great Britain relative to the return of fugitive slaves in Canada (*Acts of Ky.*, 1820, 223; *Ibid.*, 1823, 487; *Ibid.*, 1826–27, 197). Negotiations were undertaken but without effect [1] (*Niles*, XXXV, 289–291; Siebert, 299; McDougall, 25).

Following the decision in the case of *Prigg vs. Penn* (16 *Peters*, 611) in 1842 the real agitation for a new fugitive slave law began. This decision led some of the free States to pass a new class of personal liberty laws which greatly interferred with the rendition of fugitive slaves. The growth of abolition sentiment also had resulted in several cases of forcible rescue. These circumstances led the legislature of Maryland, in the Dec. session 1843, to pass resolutions calling for law making the rescue of a runaway slave a criminal offence (*Senate Doc.*, 28 *Conn.*, 1 *sess.*, IV, No. 270). Kentucky, March 1, 1847, adopted similar resolutions, which were suggested by the attack on Francis Troutman by "an abolition mob" in Marshall, Mich. (*Acts of Ky.*, 1847, 385, 386; *Senate Misc.*, 30 *Cong.*, 1 *sess.*, No. 19). The Senate Committee on the Judiciary reported a bill for a new fugitive slave law, but it was only advanced to a second reading (*Senate Reports*, No. 12). Finally the legislature

---

[1] Missouri renewed the suggestion Jan. 25, 1847, *Senate Doc.*, 29 *Cong.*, 2 *sess.*, III, No. 150.

of Virginia adopted an elaborate report arraigning the Northern States for
their Personal Liberty Laws and suggesting radical amendments to the Fugitive Slave Law.   Extracts from this report follow.   Georgia also included the
failure to return fugitives among her grievances (see *post*, p. 260).   The legislature of New Hampshire replied to Virginia July 7, 1849, declaring her report overdrawn, and expressed " in language too broad for truth and far too
angry for that courtesy which ought to be observed between sovereign States,"
and declaring that both sections were open to censure for their acts (*Laws of
N. H., June sess.*, 1849, 874–876).   Such was the situation prior to the adoption of the second Fugitive Slave Act, Sept. 18, 1850.

General References: McDougall, *Fugitive Slaves*, chs. ii, v; Siebert, *Underground Railroad*, 245, 246, 259–261, 264–267, 337, 338; Rhodes, I, 125, 126;
Wilson, II, chs. v–vii; Smith, I, 68–73.

---

127. Extract from Report of Virginia on the Rendition of Fugitive Slaves.

February 7, 1849.

*   *   *   *   *   *   *   *

Look well at these solemn warnings, and then look at the actual
state of things in the sixtieth year of the constitution !   It is
simply and undeniably this : That the South is wholly without the
benefit of that solemn constitutional guaranty which was so
sacredly pledged to it at the formation of this Union.   Our condition is precisely in effect, that which it was under the articles
of the old confederation.   No citizen of the South can pass the
frontier of a non-slaveholding state and there exercise his undoubted constitutional right of seizing his fugitive slave, with a
view to take him before a judicial officer and there prove his
right of ownership, without imminent danger of being prosecuted
criminally as a kidnapper, or being sued in a civil action for false
imprisonment—imprisoned himself for want of bail, and subjected
in his defence to an expense exceeding the whole value of the
property claimed, or finally of being mobbed or being put to
death in a street fight by insane fanatics or brutal ruffians.   In
short, the condition of things is, that at this day very few of the
owners of fugitive slaves have the hardihood to pass the frontier
of a non-slaveholding state and exercise their undoubted, adjudi-

cated constitutional right of seizing the fugitive. In such a conjuncture as this, the committee would be false to their duty—they
would be false to their country, if they did not give utterance to
their deliberate conviction, that the continuance of this state of
things cannot be, and ought not to be much longer endured by
the South—be the consequences what they may.

In such a diseased state of opinion as prevails in the non-slaveholding states on the subject of Southern slavery, it may well be
imagined what the character of their local legislation must be.
Yet it is deemed by the committee their duty to present before
the country the actual state of that legislation, that the people of
this commonwealth and of the entire South may see how rapid
and complete has been its transition from a fraternal interest in
our welfare to a rank and embittered hostility to our institutions.
The legislation to be found upon this subject, on the statute books
of the non-slaveholding states, may be divided into two classes.
The first of which would embrace the legislation of those states,
which professing a seeming respect for the obligations of the constitution, do, under the pretext of conforming to its requisitions,
subject the slave owner to conditions utterly incompatible with
the recovery of his slaves.   *   *   *

But, in the maddening process which abolitionism has made in
the Northern states, this class of laws has fallen far behind the
spirit of the times, and has yielded to a new brood of statutes'
marked by deeper venom and a more determined hostility. And
in this class are embraced,

Second. The laws of those states which affect no concealment
of their hatred to Southern institutions, nor of their utter and
open contempt and defiance of the obligations of the federal
compact.

Of this class, which is now indeed the prevailing legislation of
almost the whole non-slaveholding states, an act passed by the
general assembly of the state of Vermont, on the 1st day of
November, 1843, may be cited as a fair illustration.[1]   [Here follows the text of this act.]

Laws of similar character and in almost the same language are

---

[1] _Acts and Res. of Vermont,_ 1843, 11.

to be found on the statute books of Massachusetts [1] and Rhode Island.[2]

But the state of Pennsylvania has gone a bowshot beyond all the rest in this new legislative war against the constitutional rights of the slaveholding states. An act was passed by the Legislature of that state on the third of March eighteen hundred and forty-seven, entitled "An act to prevent kidnapping, preserve the public peace, prohibit the exercise of certain powers heretofore exercised by judges, justices of the peace," etc.[3] * * *

But this disgusting and revolting exhibition of faithless and unconstitutional legislation must now be brought to a close. It may be sufficient to remark, that the same embittered feeling against the rights of the slaveholder, with more or less of intensity, now marks, almost without exception, the legislation of every non-slaveholding state of this Union. So far, therefore, as our rights depend upon the aid and co-operation of state officers and state legislation, we are wholly without remedy or relief.

*   *   *   *   *   *   *   *

Against such a current of popular feeling and prejudice as now prevails on this subject in the non-slaveholding states, it will, therefore, be difficult to legislate, so as to accomplish the full and perfect enforcement of our rights, at all times and under all circumstances. Still, much of the evil that now threatens to disturb the relations between the two great divisions of this confederacy, and to endanger the future peace and tranquillity of this nation, may be repressed by wise, energetic and judicious legislation upon the part of Congress. We, at least, shall have discharged our duty to our country, by pointing out, in an honest spirit, to that tribunal having cognizance of the subject, those remedies which may control and restrain the evil within the limits of a patient endurance. Upon Congress, if it shall refuse to adopt the suggestion herein set forth, or wiser or better remedies than those suggested, be the painful responsibility of the consequences that must inevitably follow. * * *

[*Acts of Virginia*, 1849–1850, 240–254 *passim.*]

[1] *Laws of Mass.*, 1843, 33.   [2] *Acts and Res. of R. I.*, 1848, 12.
[3] *Laws of Penna.*, 1847, 206.

Calling a Southern Convention.

The discussion over slavery was vigorously renewed in Congress in the session of 1848–49. Early in the session, December 23, 1848, a caucus of sixty-nine Southern Delegates was held. An "Address to the people of the Southern States" was finally issued January 22, 1849, originally drawn by Calhoun, but amended as adopted. It reviewed the grievances of the South and called for "unity among ourselves," to resist any application of the Wilmot Proviso. (Calhoun's *Works*, VI, 290–313; *Niles*, LXXV, 84–88; see for Berrien's proposed substitute, *Niles*, LXXV, 101–104, for minority address, *Ibid.*, 231–233. Calhoun's Correspondence on address, *Amer. Hist. Assoc. Rept.*, 1899, II, 761–763). General references: Von Holst, III, 417–423; Benton, II, 753–756; Schouler, V, 115–118; Rhodes, I, 104, 105; Smith, I, 107, 108. This address found a general response in the public opinion of the South, as the resolutions of several State legislatures and public meetings show. South Carolina already Dec. 15, 1848, had declared "that the time for discussion has passed, and that this General Assembly is prepared to coöperate with her sister States in resisting the application of the Wilmot Proviso * * * at any and all hazard." *Rept. and Res. of So. Car.*, 1848, 147; *Senate Misc.*, 30 *Cong.*, 2 sess., I, No. 51. Florida, Jan. 13, 1849, announced herself ready to join other States "for the defence of our rights, whether through a Southern Convention or otherwise," *Ibid.*, II., No. 58, Virginia, Jan. 20, 1849, re-enacted her resolves of 1847, and made provision for a special session of the legislature, should Congress pass the obnoxious laws. (*Ante.*, pp. 244, 245), *Ibid.*, I, No. 48; North Carolina, Jan. 27, 1849, after denouncing the restrictive legislation, suggested the extension of the Missouri compromise line to the new territory. *House Misc.*, 30 *Cong.*, 2 sess., No. 54; *Laws of No. Car.*, 1848–49, 237. Missouri, March 10, 1849, asserted that the conduct of the Northern States released the slave-holding States from the compromise of 1820, and declared its willingness "to coöperate with the slave holding States for mutual protection against Northern fanaticism." *Laws of Mo.*, 1848–49, 667; *Senate Misc.*, 31 *Cong.*, 1 sess., I, No. 24. See also Meigs, *Life of Benton*, 409–414. For resolution of a Charleston meeting, see *Niles*, LXXV, 191.

In the meantime in Congress on Feb. 24, 1849, occurred an important debate between Calhoun and Webster over the question of extending the Constitution to the Territories. (See *Cong. Globe*, 30 *Cong.*, 2 sess., *Appx.* 272–274; *Niles*, LXXV., 148–150; Webster's *Works*, V, 308; Curtis, *Webster*, II, 364–372; Benton, II, 713–715, 729–733; Von Holst, III, 443–455; for remarks on resolves in *Cong. Globe*, 30 *Cong.*, 2 sess., 440, 456). The session ended without any agreement in regard to the government of the Territories.

Calhoun, as a means of uniting and organizing the South in order either to compel concessions from the North or prepare for secession, directed his efforts to secure the assembling of a Southern Convention. (See his correspondence of April, 1849, to Feb., 1850. *Amer. Hist. Assoc. Repts.*, 1899, II, 764–782, in *passim ;* letters to him, *Ibid.*, II, 1102–04, 1135–39, 1204–12. Mississippi formally inaugurated the movement,[1] explicitly following Calhoun's suggestion. (Letter to C. S. Tarpley of Miss., July 9, 1849, *Cong. Globe*, 32 *Cong.*, I *sess.*, *Appx.* 52). The Southern State Convention assembled at Jackson in Oct., 1849. After reviewing the situation, it issued " An Address to the Southern States," inviting them to send delegates to a convention to be held at Nashville, June 3, 1850, " with the view and hope of arresting the course of aggression, and, if not practicable, then to concentrate the South in will, understanding, and action," and as the possible ultimate resort the calling of another " like regularly constituted convention of all the assailed States, to provide, in the last resort, for their separate welfare by the formation of a compact and a Union, that will afford protection to their liberties and rights." *Cong. Globe*, 31 *Cong.*, I *sess.*, 578.

The resolves of the Legislature of Miss., embodying those of the Jackson Convention are given below. *Laws of Miss.*, 1850, 521–526; *Senate Misc.*, 31 *Cong.*, I *sess.*, I, No. 110. Another set of resolves were adopted by the Miss. Legislature on the same date, referring the question of the admission of California to the Nashville Convention. *Laws of Miss.*, 1850, 526–528, *Cong. Globe*, 579. Both Senators Foote and Jefferson Davis defended in Congress the action of Mississippi in calling the Convention, when presenting the resolutions of the Legislature in the spring of 1850. *Cong. Globe*, 577–579, 941–944. See also article by J. W. Garner, " The First Struggle over Secession in Miss.," in *Miss. Hist. Soc. Pub.*, IV, 89–92; Claiborne, *Life and Correspondence of John A. Quitman*, II, 21–26; *Cong. Globe*, 32 *Cong.*, 2 *sess.*, *Appx.* 63, 174; Schouler, V, 153–157; Thorpe, *U. S.*, II, 440, 441.

During the winter of 1849–50, the movement for the Convention grew in popularity, owing to the strained situation in Congress, and nine of the Southern States accepted the invitation and chose delegates (See *Post*, p. 262). References for the action of several States are: So. Car., Dec. 19, 1849, *Repts. & Res. of So. Car.*, 1849, 312–314; Texas, Feb. 11, 1850, *Law of Texas*, 1850, 171; Ga., Feb. 6, 1850, *Acts of Ga.*, 1849–50, 418; Va., Feb. 12, 1850, *Acts of Va.*, 1849–50, 233, 234.

---

128. Mississippi Calls a Southern Convention.

March 6, 1850.

* * * We have arrived at a period in the political existence of our country, when the fears of the patriot and philanthropist may well be excited, lest the noblest fabric of constitutional gov-

---

[1] The primary meeting was held May 7, 1849.

ernment on earth may, ere long, be laid in ruins by the elements of discord, engendered by an unholy lust for power, and the fell spirit of fanaticism acting upon the minds of our brethren of the non-slave holding States, and that beneath its ruins will be forever burried the hopes of an admiring world for the political regeneration of the enslaved millions. The fact can no longer be disguised, that our brethren of the free States, so called, disregarding the compromises of the constitution—*compromises without which* it never would have received the sanction of the slaveholding States, are determined to pursue towards those States a course of policy, and to adopt a system of legislation by Congress, destructive of their best rights and most cherished domestic institutions. In vain have the citizens of the slave States appealed to their brethren of the free States, in a spirit of brotherly love and devotion to that constitution framed by our fathers and cemented by their blood, as a common shield and protection for the rights of all their descendants. In vain have they invoked the guarantees of that sacred instrument, as a barrier to the encroachments of their brethren upon their rights. The spirit of forebearance and concession, which has been for more than thirty years manifested and acted on by the slave-holding States, has but strengthened the determination of their Northern brethren, to fasten upon them a system of legislation in regard to their peculiar domestic relations, as fatal in its effects to their prosperity and happiness as members of the confederacy, as it is unjust and contrary to the principles and provisions of the constitution.

Slavery, as it exists in the Southern States, recognized and protected by the constitution of the United States, is a domestic relation, subject to be abolished or modified by the sovereign power alone of the States in which it prevails; it is not a moral or political evil, but an element of prosperity and happiness both to the master and slave.

Abolish slavery, and you convert the fair and blooming fields of the South into barren heaths; their high-souled and chivalrous proprietors into abject dependents—and the *now* happy and contented slaves into squalid and degraded objects of misery and wretchedness!

The Southern States have remonstrated and forborne until fore-bearance is no longer a virtue.—The time has arrived when, if they hope to preserve their existence as equal members of the confederacy, and to avert the calamities which their Northern brethren, actuated by an insatiate and maddening thirst for power would entail upon them, they must prepare to act—to act with resolution, firmness and unity of purpose, trusting to the right-eousness of their cause and the protection of the Almighty Ruler of the destinies of nations, who ever looks benignently upon the exertions of those, who contend for the prerogatives of freemen ; therefore, be it

Resolved by the Legislature of the State of Mississippi,

That they cordially approve of the action of the Southern State Convention, held at the city of Jackson, on the first Monday of October, 1849, and adopt the following resolutions of said body as declaratory of the opinions of this Legislature and of the people of the State of Mississippi.

1st. Resolved, That we continue to entertain a devoted and cherished attachment to the Union, but we desire to have it as it was formed, and not as an engine of oppression.

2nd. Resolved, That the institution of slavery in the Southern States is left, by the constitution, exclusively under the control of the States in which it exists, as a part of their domestic policy, which they, and they only, have the right to regulate, abolish or perpetuate, as they may severally judge expedient ; and that all attempts on the part of Congress, or others, to interfere with this subject, either directly or indirectly, are in violation of the con-stitution, dangerous to the rights and safety of the South, and ought to be promptly resisted.

3d. Resolved, That Congress has no power to pass any law abolishing slavery in the District of Columbia, or to prohibit the slave trade between the several States, or to prohibit the intro-duction of slavery into the territories of the United States, and that the passage by Congress of any such law, would not only be a dangerous violation of the constitution, but would afford evi-dence of a fixed and deliberate design, on the part of that body, to interfere with the institution of slavery in the States.

4th. Resolved, That we would regard the passage, by Congress, of the "Wilmot proviso," (which would, in effect, deprive the citizens of the slave-holding States of an equal participation in the territories acquired equally by their blood and treasure), as an unjust and insulting discrimination—to which these States cannot without political degradation, submit ; and to which this convention, representing the feelings and opinions of the people of Mississippi, solemnly declare they will not submit.

5th. Resolved, that the passage of the "Wilmot Proviso," or of any law abolishing slavery in the District of Columbia, by the Congress of the United States, would, of itself, be such a breach of the federal compact, as, in that event, will make it the duty, as it is the right, of the slave-holding States, to take care of their own safety, and to treat the non-slave-holding States as enemies to the slave-holding States and their domestic institutions.

6th. Resolved, That in view of the frequent and increasing evidence of the determination of the people of the non-slave-holding States, to disregard the guarantees of the constitution, and to agitate the subject of slavery, both in and out of Congress, avowedly for the purpose of effecting its abolition in the States ; and also, in view of the facts set forth in the late "Address of the Southern Members of Congress," this convention proclaims the deliberate conviction, that the time has arrived when the Southern States should take counsel together for their common safety, and that a convention of the slave-holding States should be held at Nashville, Tennessee, on the first Monday in June next, to devise and adopt some mode of resistance to these aggressions.

*   *   *   *   *   *   *   *

8th. Resolved, That it is the duty of the Congress of the United States to provide territorial organization and governments for all the territories acquired by the common blood and treasure of the citizens of the several States ; and to provide the means of enforcing in said territories, the guarantees of the constitution of the United States in reference to the property of citizens of any of the States removing to any of said territories with the same, without distinction or limitation.

[*9th.* Appropriating money to defray expense of delegates to Nashville Convention and for convening the legislature if the safety of the South requires the separate or united action of the slave-holding States.]

10th. Be it further resolved, That in the event of the passage by the Congress of the United States of any of the measures enumerated in the preceding resolutions, and such action therein by the Convention of the slave-holding States, to be held in Nashville on the first Monday of June next, as shall, in the opinion of the Legislature, render a Convention of the Legislature necessary for the assertion and defense of their sovereign and constitutional rights, the Governor is hereby authorized and required to issue writs of election to the several counties of the State for the choice of delegates to said Convention. * * *

[*11th* and *12th* Resolves made provision for election of twelve delegates to Nashville Convention and for their payment.]

13th. Be it further resolved, That the State of Mississippi will stand by and sustain her sister States of the South in whatever course of action may be determined on by the convention of slave-holding States, to be held at Nashville on the first Monday of June next.

[*Laws of Mississippi, January–March* 1850, 521–526, *in passim.*]

Resolves on the Proposed Compromise Measures.

The famous debate in Congress upon Clay's Compromise measures and the failure to reach any agreement during the spring, in addition to the movement for calling a Southern Convention, gave rise to other resolves relating to slavery, during the first half of the year 1850, emanating from both Southern and Northern States' legislatures. These not only reflect the opinion of the respective sections, but also reveal the acute fear of the disruption of the Union. The typical resolutions of Georgia and of Connecticut follow. The very strong report of Georgia is given in *Acts of Ga.,* 1849–50, 405–409; *House Jour. of Ga.,* 1849–50, 309–315; see also, Phillips, *Amer. Hist. Assoc. Report,* 1901, II, 161–164; Von Holst, IV, 8. The Legislature also passed an Act on the same day providing for the calling of a State Convention in the event contemplated in the resolutions. *Acts of Ga.,* 1849–50, 122. In addition Texas, Virginia and Mississippi passed resolves either pledging themselves "to make common cause with the sister States of the South in the defense of their constitutional rights " (Texas) or providing for calling a Southern or State Convention in the event of the enactment of the obnoxious laws. Maryland also condemned the proposed legislation. *Laws of Texas*, 1850, 93; *Acts of Va.*, 1849–50, 233; *Laws of Miss.*, 1850, 526–528; *Laws of Md.*, 1849–50, Res. No. 37. The sentiment in the two border States of Kentucky and Tennessee was strongly in favor of the perpetuity of the Union. See Message of Gov. Crittenden of Ky., Dec. 31, 1849; Coleman, *Crittenden*, I, 350–352; Res. of Tenn., *Acts of Tenn.*, 1849–50, 572; *Senate Misc.*, 31 *Cong.*, 1 *sess.*, I, No. 66.

On the other hand, the resolves of several of the Northern States legislatures expressed bitter opposition to the proposed compromise, but for exactly opposite reasons. They pledged, however, their adherence to the Union and the compromises of the Constitution. The resolves of Rhode Island (2), New York and Massachusetts, were similar to those of Connecticut.[1] New Jersey and Mich. (2), passed resolves favoring the preservation of the Union and apparently of the Compromise. The Conn. resolves reasserted the position taken at the May session, 1849. *Res. and Private Acts of Conn.*, *May session*, 1849, 60–73. For the two sets of Conn. resolves passed at the May session, 1850, see 31 *Cong.*, 1 *sess.*, *Senate Misc.*, I, No. 121, *House Misc.*, I, No. 22. See *ante.*, p. 243, also *Acts and Res. of R. I.*, *Jan. sess.*, 1850, 27; *Ibid.*, *May sess.*, 1850, 6; *Acts of New York*, 1850, 816; *Acts and Res. of Mass.*, 1849–51, 518; *Acts of Mich.*, 1850, 453; *Senate Misc.*, 31 *Cong.*, 1 *sess.*, I, Nos. 52, 78, 80, 94. For debate in Mass. Legislature see Wilson, II, ch. xxi.

General references on Compromise of 1850: Channing & Hart, *Guide*, § 197; MacDonald, 378; Calhoun, *Works*, IV, 535–578; Jenkins, *Calhoun*, 415–439; *Amer. Hist. Assoc. Report*, 1899, II, 785–787; Webster, *Works*, V, 324–366, 373–405, 412–438; Sewards, *Works*, I, 51–131; Benton, II, chs. 189, 190; Curtis, *Webster*, II, chs. xxxvi, xxxvii; Lodge, *Webster*, 299–322; Rhodes, I, chs. ii, iii; Von Holst, III, chs. xv, xvi; Nicolay and Hay, *Lincoln*, I, chs. xiii–xviii; Thorpe, *U. S.*, II, 431–455; Schouler, V, 153–173, 178–187, 196–201; Smith, *Pol. Hist. of Slavery*, I, 113–129; Greeley, *Slavery Extension*, 54–70; Schurz, *Clay*, II, ch. xxvi; Bancroft, *Seward*, I, ch. xv; Hart, *Chase*, 120–130; Stephens, *War between the States*, II, 176–240; Pierce, *Sumner*, III, chs. xxxiv, xxxv; Lalor, I, 552–554; Wilson, *Slave Power*, II, chs. xx–xxiv.

---

129. Resolutions of Georgia.

February 8, 1850.

Whereas, The people of the non-slaveholding States have commenced and are persisting in a system of encroachment upon the

---

[1] New York also opposed the claim of Texas to New Mexico.

Constitution and the rights of a portion of the people of this confederacy, which is alike unjust and dangerous to the peace and
perpetuity of our cherished nation ; be it

*1st. Resolved by the Senate and House of Representatives of the
State of Georgia in General Assembly convened,* That the Government of the United States is one of limited powers, and cannot
rightfully exercise any authority not conferred by the Constitution.

2d. Resolved, That the Constitution grants no power to Congress to prohibit the introduction of slavery into any territory
belonging to the United States.

3d. Resolved, That the several States of the Union acceded to
the confederacy upon terms of perfect equality, and that the rights,
privileges and immunities secured by the Constitution belong alike
to the people of each State.

4th. Resolved, That any and all territory acquired by the United
States, whether by discovery, purchase or conquest, belongs in
common to the people of each State, and thither the people of
each State and every State have a common right to emigrate with
any property they may possess, and that any restriction upon this
right which will operate in favor of the people of one section to
the exclusion of those of another is unjust, oppressive and unwarranted by the Constitution.

5th. Resolved, That slaves are recognized by the Constitution
as property, and that the Wilmot Proviso, whether applied to
any territory at any time heretofore acquired, or which may be
hereafter acquired, is unconstitutional.

6th. Resolved, That Congress has no power, either directly or
indirectly, to interfere with the existence of slavery in the District
of Columbia.

7th. Resolved, That the refusal on the part of the non-slaveholding States to deliver up fugitive slaves who have escaped to
said States, upon proper demand being made therefor, is a plain
and palpable violation of the letter of the Constitution and an
intolerable outrage upon Southern rights, and that it is the imperative duty of Congress to pass laws providing for the enforcement
of this provision of the Constitution by federal, judicial and
ministerial officers responsible to the Federal Government.

8th. Resolved, That in the event of the passage of the Wilmot Proviso by Congress, the abolition of slavery in the District of Columbia, the admission of California as a State in its present pretended organization, or the continued refusal of the non-slaveholding States to deliver up fugitive slaves as provided in the Constitution, it will become the immediate and imperative duty of the people of this State to meet in convention to take into consideration the mode and measure of redress.

9th. Resolved, That the people of Georgia entertain an ardent feeling of devotion to the union of these States, and that nothing short of a persistence in the present system of encroachment upon our rights by the non-slaveholding States can induce us to contemplate the possibility of a dissolution.

10th. Resolved, That his Excellency the Governor be requested to forward copies of these resolutions to each of our Senators and Representatives in Congress, to the Legislatures of the several States, except Vermont and Connecticut, and to the President of the United States.

[*Acts of Georgia,* 1849–50, 409, 410.]

130. Resolves of Connecticut.

May Session, 1850.

Resolved, That Congress has full constitutional power to prohibit slavery in the territories of the United States, by legislative enactment, and that it is the duty of Congress to pass, without unnecessary delay, such strict and positive laws as will effectually shut out slavery from every portion of their territories.

Resolved, That Congress has like full constitutional power to remove slavery, and the slave trade, from the District of Columbia, and that this power should be at once exercised for the immediate prohibition of the slave trade therein, and for the abolition of slavery, upon such terms of compensation to the slaveholders as may be just and reasonable.

Resolved, That in the name of the people of Connecticut, we do hereby solemnly reaffirm an unalterable attachment to the

Federal Union, and our inflexible determination to adhere to our national constitution, and abide by all its compromises, to the letter and spirit of the same; while with equal unalterable and inflexible purpose, deterred by no threats of disunion, we shall forever oppose any and every measure of compromise, by which any portion of the territory now belonging to, or which may hereafter be acquired by the United States, shall be given up to, or left unprotected against the encroachments of slavery.

Resolved, That the integrity and permanence of American power on the Pacific Ocean, the increase of our commerce and wealth, the extension of our institutions, and the cause of human freedom on this continent, require the immediate admission of California into this Union, with her present Constitution, and the boundaries therein defined, without any reference to any other question or measure whatever.

Resolved, That inasmuch as the legislation necessary to give effect to the clause of the Constitution of the United States, relating to the delivering up of fugitive slaves, is within the exclusive jurisdiction of Congress, we hold it to be the duty of that body to pass such laws only in regard thereto as will secure to all persons whose surrender may be claimed, as having escaped from labor or service in another State, the right of having the validity of such claim determined by a jury in the State where such claim shall be made.

[Resolutions of transmission.]

[*Res. and Private Acts of Conn. May sess.*, 1850, 141–143.]

---

131.   The Nashville Convention.

While Congress was still laboring with the Compromise measures, the delegates chosen by nine Southern States assembled in convention at Nashville, Tenn., June 3–12, 1850. The convention was composed of 175 delegates, divided among nine states, as follows: Va., 6, S. Car., 17, Ga., 4, Flor., 4, Ala., 22, Miss., 12, Tex., 1, Ark., 2, Tenn., 100, but each state delegation cast but one vote. *Jour. of the Convention*, 25–29. Judge Wm. L. Sharkey, of Miss., was chosen President, *Ibid.*, 23. In his opening address he declared that "the object of the originators of the convention was not to dissolve the Union." "It had not been called to prevent, but to perpetuate the Union." (*N. Y. Tribune*, June 4, 1850.)

An address to the people of the fourteen Southern States, prepared by R. B. Rhett, of S. C., was issued. It reviewed the slavery agitation in Congress and condemned the pending measures. *Journal*, 9–22. A set of thirteen resolutions, drawn by John A Campbell, of Ala., were unanimously adopted on June 10th, and on the following day fifteen additional resolutions were similarly agreed to. *Journal*, 57–64. These resolutions follow. A copy of the *Resolutions, Address and Journal of Proceedings of the Southern Convention. Held at Nashville, Tennessee, June 3d to 12th inclusive, in the Year 1850* [Nashville, 1850, Pp. 65], is in the Harvard University Library. The first thirteen resolves are given in Cluskey, *Political Text Book* (2d ed.), 595, 596; also portions in the *Cong. Globe*, 32 *Cong.*, 1 *sess*, *Appx.* 337.

A second session of the Convention assembled at Nashville, November 11–19, 1850. Judge Sharkey, having accepted the Compromise measures, which in the meantime had been adopted, refused to issue the call for this session. The Convention, accordingly, irregularly assembled and was poorly attended by the representatives of those Southerners who were still disaffected. Some 70 delegates were present from the seven following states: Ala., Fla., Ga., Miss., So. Car., Tenn. and Va. Ex-Governor Chas. J. Mac-Donald, of Ga., the Vice-President, presided. Resolutions offered by Miss. were adopted, Tenn. alone dissenting. These affirmed the right of a State to secede from the Union, denounced the acts of Congress as unjust, and recommended a general Congress of Southern States to maintain Southern rights and preserve the Union if possible. These are given in Cluskey, 596–598. Also the Tennessee resolutions submitted as a substitute, *Ibid.*, 598, 599. Reports of the Convention are given in the *Boston Journal* and the *New York Herald*, Nov. 13, 20, and *The New York Tribune*, Nov. 27, 1850. General references: Von Holst, III, 531–534, IV, 3, 4; Rhodes, I, 173, 174, 196; Benton, II, ch. 198; Du Bose, *Yancey*, 247–249; Wilson, II, 286, 287.

Resolves of the Southern Convention at Nashville.

June 10, 11, 1850.

1. *Resolved*, That the territories of the United States belong to the people of the several States of this Union as their common property. That the citizens of the several States have equal rights to migrate with their property to these territories, and are equally entitled to the protection of the federal government in the enjoyment of that property so long as the territories remain under the charge of that government.

2. *Resolved*, That Congress has no power to exclude from the territory of the United States any property lawfully held in the

States of the Union, and any acts which may be passed by Congress to effect this result is a plain violation of the Constitution of the United States.

3. *Resolved*, That it is the duty of Congress to provide governments for the territories, since the spirit of American Institutions forbids the maintenance of military governments in time of peace, and as all laws heretofore existing in territories once belonging to foreign powers which interfere with the full enjoyment of religion, the freedom of the press, the trial by jury, and all other rights of persons and property as secured or recognized in the Constitution of the United States, are necessarily void so soon as such territories become American territories, it is the duty of the federal government to make early provision for the enactment of those laws which may be expedient and necessary to secure to the inhabitants of and emigrants to such territories the full benefit of the constitutional rights we assert.

4. *Resolved*, That to protect property existing in the several States of the Union the people of these States invested the federal government with the powers of war and negotiation and of sustaining armies and navies, and prohibited to State authorities the exercise of the same powers. They made no discrimination in the protection to be afforded or the description of the property to be defended, nor was it allowed to the federal government to determine what should be held as property. Whatever the States deal with as property the federal government is bound to recognize and defend as such. Therefore it is the sense of this Convention that all acts of the federal government which tend to denationalize property of any description recognized in the Constitution and laws of the States, or that discriminate in the degree and efficiency of the protection to be afforded to it, or which weaken or destroy the title of any citizen upon American territories, are plain and palpable violations of the fundamental law under which it exists.

5. *Resolved*, That the slaveholding States cannot and will not submit to the enactment by Congress of any law imposing onerous conditions or restraints upon the rights of masters to remove with their property into the territories of the United States, or to any

law making discrimination in favor of the proprietors of other property against them.

6. *Resolved*, That it is the duty of the federal government plainly to recognize and firmly to maintain the equal rights of the citizens of the several States in the territories of the United States, and to repudiate the power to make a discrimination between the proprietors of different species of property in the federal legislation. The fulfilment of this duty by the federal government would greatly tend to restore the peace of the country and to allay the exasperation and excitement which now exists between the different sections of the Union. For it is the deliberate opinion of this Convention that the tolerance Congress has given to the notion that federal authority might be employed incidentally and indirectly to subvert or weaken the institution existing in the States confessedly beyond federal jurisdiction and control, is a main cause of the discord which menaces the existence of the Union, and which has well nigh destroyed the efficient action of the federal government itself.

7. *Resolved*, That the performance of this duty is required by the fundamental law of the Union. The equality of the people of the several States composing the Union cannot be disturbed without disturbing the frame of American institutions. This principle is violated in the denial to the citizens of the slaveholding States of power to enter into the territories with the property lawfully acquired in the States. The warfare against this right is a war upon the Constitution. The defenders of this right are the defenders of the Constitution. Those who deny or impair its exercise, are unfaithful to the Constitution, and if disunion follows the destruction of the right they are the disunionists.

8. *Resolved*, That the performance of its duties, upon the principle we declare, would enable Congress to remove the embarrassments in which the country is now involved. The vacant territories of the United States, no longer regarded as prizes for sectional rapacity and ambition, would be gradually occupied by inhabitants drawn to them by their interests and feelings. The institutions fitted to them would be naturally applied by governments formed on American ideas, and approved by the deliberate

choice of their constituents. The community would be educated and disciplined under a republican administration in habits of self government, and fitted for an association as a State, and to the enjoyment of a place in the confederacy. A community so formed and organized might well claim admission to the Union and none would dispute the validity of the claim.

9. *Resolved*, That a recognition of this principle would deprive the questions between Texas and the United States of their sectional character, and would leave them for adjustment without disturbance from sectional prejudices and passions, upon considerations of magnanimity and justice.

10. *Resolved*, That a recognition of this principle would infuse a spirit of conciliation in the discussion and adjustment of all subjects of sectional dispute, which would afford a guarantee of an early and satisfactory determination.

11. *Resolved*, That in the event a dominent majority shall refuse to recognize the great constitutional rights we assert, and shall continue to deny the obligations of the Federal Government to maintain them, it is the sense of this convention that the territories should be treated as property, and divided between the sections of the Union, so that the rights of both sections be adequately secured in their respective shares. That we are aware this course is open to grave objections, but we are ready to acquiesce in the adoption of the line of 36 deg. 30 min. north latitude, extending to the Pacific ocean, as an extreme concession, upon considerations of what is due to the stability of our institutions.

12. *Resolved*, That it is the opinion of this Convention that this controversy should be ended, either by a recognition of the constitutional rights of the Southern people, or by an equitable partition of the territories. That the spectacle of a confederacy of States, involved in quarrels over the fruits of a war in which the American arms were crowned with glory, is humiliating. That the incorporation of the Wilmot Proviso in the offer of settlement, a proposition which fourteen States regard as disparaging and dishonorable, is degrading to the country. A termination to this controversy by the disruption of the confederacy or

by the abandonment of the territories to prevent such a result, would be a climax to the shame which attaches to the controversy which it is the paramount duty of Congress to avoid.

13. *Resolved*, That this Convention will not conclude that Congress will adjourn without making an adjustment of this controversy, and in the condition in which the Convention finds the question before Congress, it does not feel at liberty to discuss the methods suitable for a resistance to measures not yet adopted, which might involve a dishonor to the Southern States.

[Resolves 14–18 support the territorial claims of Texas, and assert the obligation of the government to admit four new slaveholding States, in addition to the State of Texas, out of the remaining territory.]

19. *Resolved*, That the whole legislative power of the United States Government is derived from the Constitution and delegated to Congress, and cannot be increased or diminished but by an amendment to the Constitution.

20. *Resolved*, That the acquisition of territory by the United States, whether occupied or vacant, either by purchase, conquest or treaty, adds nothing to the legislative power of Congress, as granted and limited in the Constitution.

21. *Resolved*, That the adoption of a foreign law existing at the time, in territory purchased, ceded or granted, is the exercise of legislative power, and cannot be done unless the law is of such a character as might rightfully be enacted by Congress under the Constitution, without reference to its pre-existence as a foreign law.

22. *Resolved*, That the alleged principle of the law of nations, recognizing, to some extent, the perpetuation of foreign laws in existence within a territory at the time of its acquisition by purchase, conquest or treaty, *cannot*, under our Constitution and form of government, go to the extent of continuing in force, in such territory, any law that could not be directly enacted by Congress, by virtue of the powers of legislation delegated to it by the Constitution.

23. *Resolved*, That no power of doing any act or thing by any of the Departments of our Government can be based upon the

principles of any foreign law, or of the laws of nations, beyond what exists in such Department under the Constitution of the United States, without reference to such foreign law or the laws of nations.

24. *Resolved*, That slavery exists in the United States independent of the Constitution. That it is recognized by the Constitution in a three-fold aspect, first as property, second as a domestic relation of service or labor under the law of a State, and lastly as a basis of political power. And viewed in any or all of these lights, Congress has no power under the Constitution to create or destroy it anywhere; nor can such power be derived from foreign laws, conquest, cession, treaty or the laws of nations, nor from any other source but an amendment of the Constitution itself.

25. *Resolved*, That the Constitution confers no power upon Congress to regulate or prohibit the sale and transfer of slaves between the States.

26. *Resolved*, That the reception or consideration by Congress of resolutions, memorials or petitions, from the States in which domestic slavery does not exist, or from the people of the said States, in relation to the institution of slavery where it does exist, with a view of effecting its abolition, or to impair the rights of those interested in it, to its peaceful and secure enjoyment, is a gross abuse and an entire perversion of the right of petition as secured by the federal Constitution, and if persisted in must and will lead to the most dangerous and lamentable consequences; that the right of petition for a redress of grievances as provided for by the Constitution was designed to enable the citizens of the United States to manifest and make known to Congress the existence of evils under which they were suffering, whether affecting them personally, locally or generally, and to cause such evils to be redressed by the people and competent authority, but was never designed or intended as a means of inflicting injury on others or jeopardizing the peaceful and secure enjoyment of their rights, whether existing under the Constitution or under the sovereignty and authority of the several States.

27. *Resolved*, That it is the duty of Congress to provide effect-

ual means of executing the 2d section of the 4th article of the Constitution, relating to the restoration of fugitives from service or labor.

28. *Resolved,* That when this Convention adjourn, it adjourn to meet at Nashville, in the State of Tennessee, the 6th Monday after the adjournment of the present session of Congress, and that the Southern States be recommended to fill their delegations forthwith.

[*Resolutions, Address and Journal of the Southern Convention,* 3-8.]

Action of the Southern States on the Compromise. The Secession Movement Checked

1850-1852.

The adoption of the series of compromise measures by Congress, between Aug. 13 and Sept. 20, 1850, was acquiesced in by the majority of Southerners, [1] but in a few of the States their enactment at first gave an impetus to the movement for secession. Georgia was the first State to take official action. Close upon the adjournment of Congress, Gov. George W. Towne, in accordance with the Act of February 8, 1850 (*Acts of Ga.,* 1849, 122, Ante. p. 258) issued a proclamation on September 23, calling a convention of the people to meet December 10 (*New York Tribune,* Sept. 28, 1850). Ex-Gov. McDonald led the secessionists, but three Congressmen, Robert Toombs, Howell Cobb and Alexander H. Stephens supported the acceptance of the compromise and their influence prevailed. This convention adopted an elaborate report together with the subjoined resolutions by a vote of 237 to 19. These soon were celebrated as the " Georgia Platform." See *Journal of the State Convention,* Dec., 1850, 18, 19, 26, 27, 32. Extracts are given in Cluskey, 599, 600; Stephens, *War Between the States,* II, 676, 677.[2] General references: Article by Phillips, *Amer. Hist. Assoc. Report,* 1901, II, 163-167; *Cong. Globe,* 32 *Cong.,* 1 *sess., Appx.* 255-258, 319-322, 342-345; Stovall, *Life of Toombs,* chs. vi, vii; Johnson & Browne, *Stephens,* 258-260; Stephens, II, 234, 235; Von Holst, IV, 8, 9, 214, note; Coleman, *Crittenden,* I, 364-376; Harden, *Life of Troup, Appx.* xx.

The Georgia platform exerted great influence in the other Southern States.

---

[1] A protest signed by ten senators from Southern States, to the bill for the admission of California, which passed the Senate August 13, 1850, was presented the following day. Its reception was refused. *Cong. Globe,* 31 *Cong.,* 1 *sess.,* 1578-1580, 1588; Cluskey, 605, 606; Benton, II, 769-772.

[2] Stephens gives the 4th article without the amendment adopted.

In Alabama a Union Legislature and Governor were chosen, but the secessionists under the lead of Yancey organized a Southern Rights Association,
and held a convention in the spring of 1851. An attempt was made to adopt
the Georgia platform in the Legislature, but although it was approved by the
Senate, it was defeated in the House. Garrett, *Reminiscences of Public Men
in Alabama*, 544–548; DuBois, *Yancey*, 261, 262; Brown, *Alabama*, 210.

The Maryland Constitutional Convention, called to frame a new Constitution, unanimously adopted Dec. 10, 1850, a series of resolves on the Compromise, declaring their acquiescence, although the measures did not fully
meet the just demands of the South. Further, that the fugitive slave law "is
but a tardy and meagre measure of compliance with the clear, explicit and
imperative injunction of the Constitution," that " the repeal of that law or the
failure to enforce its provisions " would lead to "a dissolution of the Union."
From a copy in *Exec. Docs. of No. Car.*, 1850–51, I, No. 18. See also
Johns Hopkins Univ. Studies, XX, 415; for reply of Gov. Collier of Alabama, see *Debates of Md. Convention*, 1850, I, 384.

Tennessee repudiated the Southern Convention held in her capital, by
electing a Whig Governor and Legislature in 1851. The latter, Feb. 28, 1852,
adopted a set of strong resolutions, denying the constitutional rights of secession, although admitting that of revolution under certain circumstances, pledging their support to the President in all legal means in executing the laws,
and approving the Compromise measures. *Acts of Tenn.*, 1851–52, 719–721;
Phelan, *History of Tennessee*, 434–437.

In Mississippi and South Carolina the secessionists made a vigorous fight.
Gov. John A. Quitman, of Miss., was an avowed and active advocate of
secession. The State's delegation in Congress, with the exception of Senator
Foote, who supported the Compromise, advocated resistance. Gov. Quitman
issued a proclamation calling the legislature to meet in special session, Nov.
18, 1850, to take action on the situation (Claiborne, *Quitman*, II, 43). In
his message to the legislature, he zealously presented his views. (*Ibid*, 46–
51; *Globe*, 32 *Cong.*, 1 *sess.*, *Appx.* 336.) That body on Nov. 30, passed
resolutions censuring Foote (*Senate Misc.*, 31 *Cong.*, 2 *sess.*, No. 2), indorsed
the Governor's position and adopted his suggestion by calling a State Convention to assemble in Nov., 1851, to consider the state of federal relations.
There followed a bitter contest between the "Southern Rights Party" and
"The Union Party," for the election of delegates to the Convention, which
resulted in the triumph of the Union party, and in the choice of Foote as
Governor. Foote had been a candidate against Quitman, and after the
latter's withdrawal against Jefferson Davis.

The Convention was in session Nov. 10 to 17, 1851. It adopted resolutions
substantially in accord with the Georgia Platform with only three dissenting
votes. Among its resolves, the 4th declared "That in the opinion of this
Convention the asserted right of secession from the Union on the part of the
State or States is utterly unsanctioned by the Federal Constitution," etc. It

also rebuked the legislature for calling the Convention without first having submitted the question to the people. This reversed all that had been done by the secessionists and summarily checked the movement to break up the Union.[1]

References: For resolutions and other documents see *Journal of the Conventions of the State of Mississippi*, 19, 20, 27–30, 47, 48 [Jackson, 1851]. J. F. H. Claiborne, *Life and Correspondence of John A. Quitman*, II, 36–52, 133–143, 148–151; *Cong. Globe*, 32 *Cong.*, 1 *sess.*, 35, 36, 49–65, 282–285; *Appx.* 336–342, 355–359. See an excellent article by J. W. Garner, in *Miss. Hist. Soc. Pub.*, IV, 93–104; also, Reuben Davis, *Recollections of Mississippi and Mississippians*, 315–324; Jefferson Davis, *Rise and Fall of Confederate Government*, I, ch. iii; Von Holst, IV, 4–7, 29, 35, 36, 105, 106; Rhodes, I, 226, 227; Smith, I, 137, 138.

---

132. The Georgia Platform.

December, 1850.

To the end, therefore, that the position of this State may be clearly apprehended by her confederates of the South and of the North, and that she may be blameless of all future consequences.

Be it resolved by the people of Georgia in Convention assembled,
First, That we hold the American Union secondary in importance only to the rights and principles it was designed to perpetuate ; that past associations, present fruition, and future prospects, will bind us to it so long as it continues to be the safeguard of those rights and principles.

Secondly, That if the thirteen original parties to the contract bordering the Atlantic in the narrow belt, while their separate interests were in embryo, their peculiar tendencies scarcely developed, their revolutionary trial and triumphs still green in memory, found Union impossible without compromise, the thirty-one of this day may well yield somewhat, in the conflict of opinion and policy, to preserve that Union which has extended the sway of republican government over a vast wilderness, to another ocean, and proportionately advanced civilization and national greatness.

---

[1] For action of South Carolina and Virginia see *post*, 272–276. In the remaining states the Compromise was generally accepted.

Thirdly, That in this spirit, the State of Georgia has maturely considered the action of Congress embracing a series of measures for the admission of California into the Union ; the organization of territorial governments for Utah and New Mexico ; the establishment of a boundary between the latter and the State of Texas ; the suppression of the slave trade in the District of Columbia, and the extradition of fugitive slaves ; and (connected with them) the rejection of propositions to exclude slavery from the Mexican territories and abolish it in the District of Columbia, and whilst she does not wholly approve, will abide by it as a permanent adjustment of this sectional controversy.

Fourthly, That the State of Georgia, in the judgment of this Convention, will and ought to resist, even (as a last resort) to a disruption of every tie which binds her to the Union, any action of Congress, upon the subject of slavery in the District of Columbia, or in places subject to the jurisdiction of Congress, incompatible with the safety, domestic tranquility, the rights and the honor of the slave-holding States ; or any act suppressing the slave trade between the slave-holding States, or in any refusal to admit as a State any territory hereafter applying because of the existence of slavery therein ; or in any act prohibiting the introduction of slaves into the territories of Utah and New Mexico, or any act repealing or materially modifying the laws now in force for the recovery of fugitive slaves.

Fifthly, That it is the deliberate opinion of this Convention that upon the faithful execution of the *Fugitive Slave Law* by the proper authorities depends the preservation of our much loved Union.

[*Journal of the State Convention, Dec.* 1850, 18, 19, 26, 27, 32.]

---

133. South Carolina Asserts the Right of Secession.
1850–52.

Public opinion in South Carolina was almost unanimously in favor of secession, but soon it was divided over the question whether the State should secede immediately and alone, or await the coöperation of other States. Gov. Seabrook's correspondence with Gov. Quitman in the fall of 1850, presents the situation (Claiborne, *Quitman,* II, 36–40). Gov. Seabrook in his message to the Legislature of November 26, declared that " the time then has arrived to resume the exercise of the powers of self-protection," and he asserted the right of secession (*Jour. of the Senate of S. C.*, 1850, 25–30). The Legislature, acting on the suggestion of the Second Nashville Convention, for a Convention of the States vested with full powers, adopted an Act, December 20, 1850, inviting the other slave holding States to send delegates to such a Convention to assemble in Montgomery, Ala , January 2, 1852, and made provision for the appointment of their representatives. [1] The same Act providing for the holding of a state Convention at the call of the Governor, to consider the final action of the State. (*Act of S. C.*, Dec., 1850, 55–57.) Another Act of the same date appropriated $350,000 for the defence of the State. [2] (*Ibid.*, 57–59. For debate on secession in this Legislature see *Amer. Annual Cyclopædia*, 1861, 646.)

During the year 1851, the agitation over the question of immediate and independent action of South Carolina or coöperation with other States continued. In May the Southern Rights Association held a Convention, and adopted resolutions declaring that if necessary South Carolina would proceed " without the coöperation of other Southern States." (*New York Tribune*, May 13, 1851.) Gov. J. H. Means, in a letter to Gov. Quitman May 12, predicted that the next Legislature would call the Convention together and that body would take action for the State to secede. (Claiborne, *Quitman*, II, 133, 134.) The fall election of delegates to the proposed Southern Congress, however, was a defeat for the independent secessionists. Gov. Means gave expression to his disappointment in his annual message, Nov. 25, 1851. (*Senate Journal of So. Car.*, 1851, 19, 20.) But the radical party succeeded in securing the passage by the Legislature of an Act, Dec. 16, 1851, for the assembling of the State Convention in April, 1852. (*Acts of So. Car.*, 1851, 100.) The election of delegates to the Convention resulted in the choice of 114 coöperationists to 54 secessionists. (*Tribune Almanac*, 1852, 43.) The Convention assembled at Columbia and was in session April 26–30, 1852, 168 delegates were in attendance. Gov. Means was chosen President. The report of a special committee, presented by Langdon Cheeves, contained the subjoined Resolutions and Ordinance. They were adopted by a vote of 136 to 19. For text see the *Journal of the State Convention of South Carolina*, 18, 19. [Columbia, 1852.]

The collapse of the South Carolina secession movement at this time is explained by Gov. Means in his message of Nov. 23, 1852, as due to the strife

---

[1] The Virginia Legislature, March 29, 1851, adopted resolutions declining to send delegates to the proposed Convention and appealed to South Carolina not to secede. *Acts of Va.*, 1850–51, 201. (See *post*, 275.)

[2] A report accompanying an appropriation of $10,000 for the publication of the Calhoun Manuscripts, set forth the South Carolina Doctrine. *Reports and Res. of S. C.*, 1850, 152–155.

between the parties, the one urging separate action, and the other advocating coöperation. "The discussion of these conflicting opinions produced the bitterest party feeling. Amid the convulsive throes of this fierce strife, the question of our wrongs was almost forgotten. * * * "The members of the Convention determined to bury all bitter feelings which had generated by the late contest. * * * The principles which have ever been held dear amongst us, were not only reaffirmed but set forth in the solemn form of an Ordinance." The Governor then called attention to the violation of the fugitive slave law and predicted that "Further aggressions—which will surely come—will convince our Sister Southern States, that the institution upon which not only the prosperity of the South but Republicanism itself depends, is no longer safe in the Union. Then we may hope that they will rise in the majesty of their strength and spirit, and in conjunction with us, either force our rights to be respected in the Union or take our place as a Southern Confederacy amongst the nations of the earth." *Journal of the Senate of So. Car.*, 1852, 29, 30.

General references: Van Holst, IV, 30–35, 111–115, 214; Greeley, I, 211; Rhodes, I, 226; *DeBow's Review*, XXIX, 754, 755. Two important contemporary pamphlets favoring secession are, *The Southern States, Their Present Peril and Their Certain Remedy*, etc. [by John Townsend], Charleston, Sept., 1850, Pp. 31 (Advocated coöperation), and *The Position and Course of the South*, by William H. Trescot, Charleston, 1850, Pp. 20. For Senator Rhett's speech in Congress, Dec., 15, 16, 1851, avowing himself a secessionist, see *Cong. Globe, Appx.*, 32 *Cong.*, 1 *sess.*, 44–48, 61–65.

Resolved by the people of South Carolina in Convention assembled, That the frequent violations of the Constitution of the United States by the Federal Government, and its encroachments upon the reserved rights of the sovereign States of this Union, especially in the relation to slavery, amply justifies this State, so far as any duty or obligation to her confederates is involved, in dissolving at once all political connection with her co-States, and that she forbears the exercise of this manifest right of self-government from consideration of expediency only.

AN ORDINANCE *to declare the right of this State to secede from the Federal Union.*

We, the people of the State of South Carolina, in Convention assembled, do declare and ordain, and it is hereby declared and ordained, That South Carolina, in the exercise of her sovereign will, as an independent State, acceded to the Federal Union, known as the United States of America, and that in the exercise of the same sovereign will it is her right, without let, hindrance or molestation from any power whatsoever, to secede from the said Federal Union, and that for the sufficiency of the causes which may impel her to such separation she is responsible alone, under God, to the tribunal of public opinion among the nations of the earth.

---

134. Resolutions of Virginia Relative to the Action of South Carolina.

March 29, 1851.

Although the Virginia Legislature had passed strong resolutions against the Wilmot Proviso in 1847 and in 1849 (Ante, pp. 244, 253), and Feb. 12, 1850, had favored the calling of a Southern Convention, and in certain contingencies of a State Convention (Ante, p. 258), the State was now disposed to accept the Compromise measures, as the following resolutions of the Legislature show. The attempt to substitute a strong state rights resolution in the Senate received only three votes. *Senate Jour. of Va.*, 1851, 209. *Acts of Va.*, 1850-51, 200; Von Holst, IV, 31; Rhodes, I, 226.

Whereas, The legislature of the State of South Carolina has passed an act to provide for the appointment of delegates to the Southern Congress, " to be entrusted with full power and authority to deliberate with the view and intention of arresting further aggression, and if possible of restoring the constitutional rights of the South, and if not, to recommend due provision for their future safety and independence," which act has been formally communicated to this general assembly.

1. *Be it therefore resolved by the general assembly of Virginia*, That whilst this State deeply sympathizes with South Carolina in the feelings excited by the unwarrantable interference of certain of the non-slaveholding States with our common institutions, and whilst diversity of opinion exists among the people of this commonwealth in regard to the wisdom, justice and constitutionality of the measures of the late Congress of the United States, taken as a whole, and commonly known as the compromise measures, yet the legislature of Virginia deems it a duty to declare to her

sister State of South Carolina that the people of this State are unwilling to take any action in consequence of the same calculated
to destroy the integrity of this Union.

2. *Resolved*, That regarding the said acts of the Congress of
the United States, taken together, as an adjustment of the exciting questions to which they relate, and cherishing the hope that
if fairly executed they will restore to the country that harmony
and confidence which of late have been so unhappily disturbed,
the State of Virginia deems it unwise in the present condition of
the country to send delegates to the proposed Southern Congress.

3. *Resolved*, That Virginia earnestly and affectionately appeals
to her sister State of South Carolina to desist from any meditated
secession upon her part, which cannot but tend to the destruction
of the Union and the loss to all of the States of the benefits that
spring from it.

4. *Resolved*, That Virginia, believing the constitution of the
United States, if faithfully administered, provides adequate protection to the rights of all the States of this confederacy, and still
looking to that instrument for defence within the Union, warned
by the experience of the past, the dangers of the present, and the
hopes of the future, invokes all who live under it to adhere more
strictly to it and to preserve inviolate the safeguards which it
affords to the rights of individual States and the interests of sectional minorities.

5. *Resolved*, That all acts of legislation or combinations designed in any way injuriously to affect the institution of slavery,
deserve the most unqualified reprobation, are peculiarly offensive
to the Southern States, and must, if persisted in, inevitably defeat
the restoration of peaceful and harmonious sentiments in the
States.

Resolution of transmission.]

[*Acts of Virginia, 1850–51*, 201.]

The North on the Compromise.

1850-1852.

The majority of the people of the north also accepted the compromise. This is attested to not only by the attitude of the press and the action of public meetings (Rhodes, I, 194–196), but also by the resolve of State legislatures. Those of Delaware, Illinois, Iowa, New Hampshire in 1851, New Jersey and Connecticut in 1852, adopted resolutions in approval of the compromise. The resolves of Illinois are notable, for in addition to approving the compromise, they declare that the exercise of the power of Congress upon slavery in the territories is "unnecessary and inexpedient,[1] and they repealed the resolve of the preceding general assembly favoring the Wilmot Proviso. The resolves of Iowa, the only free state that had not previously favored the Wilmot Proviso, declared that "the Constitution of the United States is a compact, a fundamental treaty;" but those of New Jersey, which were unanimously adopted by the legislature, are of especial interest as a late assertion of the compact theory by a northern state, as well as because of the debate excited by its presentation in Congress. They are given below. (In the Senate, *Cong. Globe*, 32 *Cong.*, I *sess.*, 541–543; in the House, speech by Giddings, and reply by Stanley, *Globe*, 531–535, 541, 542; Julian, *Giddings*, 287–290.) All these resolutions explicitly approved of the new Fugitive Slave Law, even Connecticut, although the law was not in harmony with the demand of its resolves of 1850 (Ante, 262). For text of the above resolutions see *Laws of Del.*, 1851, 609–611; *Acts of Ill.*, 1851, 205–207; *Laws of New Hamp.*, *June sess.*, 1851, 1083; *Res. and Private Acts of Conn.*, *May sess.*, 1852, 10; *House Misc.*, 32 *Cong.*, I *sess.*, Nos. 13, 20, 65.

There was, however, some dissent. Vermont promptly reasserted its former position, condemning the new fugitive slave law.[2] *Acts and Res. of Vermont*, *Oct. sess.*, 1850, 53, 54. Ohio, also called for the repeal of the fugitive slave law, and the enactment of a new law giving to the fugitive "the benefit of every legal defence."[3] *Local Laws of Ohio*, 1850–51, 814.

---

[1] These were quoted by Stephen A. Douglas in his speech of July 9, 1858, as remaining "to this day a standing instruction to her senators." *Political Debates between Lincoln and Douglas*, 7. [Columbus, 1860.]

[2] Virginia declined to receive resolutions of the Vermont Legislature on the promotion of the peace of the world. (*Acts and Res. of Vt.*, 1850, 57), "until that body shall show itself careful of the peace of the Union, by conforming its enactments to the Constitution of the United States and the laws passed in pursuance thereof." (*Acts of Va.*, 1850–51, 202). This was doubtless prompted by the passing of a personal liberty Act by Vermont this same year. *Acts of Vt.*, 1850, 9.

[3] They also declared that the fugitive slave law "ought never to receive the voluntary co-operation of our people." Ohio it should also be mentioned, had

The rescue of certain fugitives and the opposition to the rendition of others during the year 1851, led President Fillmore in his annual message, Dec. 2, 1851, to condemn the same and pronounce the compromise measure a final settlement of the matter. (Richardson, V, 137–139.) Senator Foote of Miss., fresh from the victory in his State, introduced on the same day his "Finality Resolutions" (*Globe*, 12). This precipitated an acrimonius debate which lasted over two months. It was participated in chiefly by Southern Senators. The resolution was not brought to a vote in the Senate, but in the House a similar resolution prompted by the presentation of some of the State resolutions, especially those from New Jersey, was adopted April 5, 1852, by a vote of 103 to 74 (*Globe*, 978–983).

Charles Sumner, on August 26, 1852, in the Senate made an impassioned speech in support of a resolution in effect to repeal the fugitive slave law. This led to a bitter debate, but the proposition received but four votes in its favor. Sumner, *Works*, III, 73–75, 87–196; *Globe, Appx.*, 1102–1125; Johnston, *American Orations*, II, 268–340; Pierce, *Sumner*, III, 289–311; Storey, *Sumner*, ch. vi. Such was the situation on the eve of the Presidential campaign of 1852, in which both parties adopted the "finality plank." Rhodes, I, 243–277; Von Holst, IV, chs. iii, iv.

---

135.   New Jersey on the Compromise Measures.
January 30, 1852.

Whereas, The Constitution of the United States is a compact between the several States and forms the basis of our Federal Union ;

And whereas, The said States, through their representatives, in sovereign capacities as States, by adopting said Constitution, conceded only such powers to the general government as were necessary " to form a more perfect union, establish justice, insure domestic tranquillity, provide for the common defence, promote the general welfare and secure the blessings of liberty to themselves and posterity ;"

renewed the idea of colonization. In 1849 she suggested the setting off a part of the territory acquired from Mexico for " the oppressed people of color." In 1850 she advocated the maintenance of Liberia and the colonization of free blacks there. *Laws of Ohio*, 1848–49, 395; *Ibid.*, 1849–50, 714. Indiana and Conn. also passed resolves favoring African colonization. *Laws of Ind.*, 1850, 247; *Ibid.*, 1851, 202; *Ibid.*, 1852, 174; *Res. and Private Acts of Conn.*, May sess., 1852, 10.

And whereas, The questions which agitated the country and absorbed so large a portion of the time of the last session of the Congress of the United States—questions in their nature directly opposed to the spirit and compromise of the Constitution, calculated to destroy our domestic tranquility and dismember our glorious Union—were happily terminated by the Compromise measures, it is deemed the imperative duty of this legislature to express their sentiments in relation thereto ; therefore,

1. *Resolved,* That the Constitution of the United States was framed in the spirit of wisdom and compromise, is the bond of our Federal Union, and can only be preserved by a strict adherence to its express and implied powers ; that New Jersey, one of the original thirteen States, has always adhered to the Constitution and is unalienably attached to the Union, and that she will resist, to the extent of her ability, any infraction of that sacred instrument.

2. *Resolved,* That this legislature cordially approves the measures adopted by the last session of Congress, known as the "compromise measures," and that every patriot in every part of our widely extended country has cause to rejoice in the adoption of said measures, as a triumph of constitutional rights over a spirit of wild and disorganizing fanaticism.

3. *Resolved,* That New Jersey will abide by and sustain the Compromise measures, and that her senators in the senate of the United States be instructed, and our representatives in Congress be requested, to resist any change, alteration, or repeal thereof.

4. *Resolved,* That the fugitive slave law is in accordance with the stipulations of the Constitution of the United States, and in its provisions, carries out the spirit and letter of the Constitution in its compromises, upon which our Union is founded.

5. *Resolved,* That we approve of the patriotic stand taken by the Executive of the United States in declaring his determination to execute and enforce all laws constitutionally enacted, and that the people of New Jersey will sustain him in so doing.

[Resolution of transmission.]

[House Miscellaneous Doc., 32 *Cong.,* 1st *Sess.,* No. 13.]

136. Louisiana on the Cuban Situation.

March 16, 1854.

The following resolves are illustrative of the movement in the South in favor of the annexation of Cuba. This propaganda found expression this same year in the revival of fillibustering expeditions and in the promulgation of the Ostend Manifesto, October 18, 1854. Soulé, our Minister to Spain, came from Louisiana, and his influence may have led to the passage of these resolves.

References: For the Ostend Manifesto, *House Ex. Doc.*, 33 *Cong.*, 2 *sess.*, X, No. 93; MacDonald, 405–412; *Amer. Hist. Leaflets*, No. 2. For the history of the movement see Channing and Hart, *Guide*, § 199; Latané, *Diplomatic Relations of the U. S. and Spanish America*, 105–136; Callahan, *Cuba and International Relations*, chs. vii–ix; Snow, *Amer. Diplomacy*, 344–357; Webster in *Pol. Sci. Quar.*, VIII, 1; Curtis, *Buchanan*, II, chs. iv–vi; Rhodes, II, 34–44; Von Holst, IV, 253–256; V, ch. 1; Wilson, II, ch. xlvii.

Be it resolved by the Senate and House of Representatives of the State of Louisiana, in general assembly convened, That we view with regret and alarm the policy recently inaugurated by the government of Spain in the island of Cuba, the manifest object and effect of which must be the abolition of slavery in that colony, and the sacrifice of the white race, with its arts, commerce and civilization, to a barbarous and inferior race.

Resolved, That the consummation of this policy will exercise a most pernicious influence upon the institutions and interests, social, commercial and political, of the United States.

Resolved, That, in our judgment, the time has arrived when the Federal Government should adopt the most decisive and energetic measures to thwart and defeat a policy conceived in hatred to this Republic, and calculated to retard her progress and prosperity.

[*Senate Miscellaneous Documents,* 33 *Cong.*, 1 *sess.*, No. 63.]

The Kansas–Nebraska Bill.

1854.

On Jan. 4, 1854, Senator Douglas reported his bill for the territorial government of Nebraska. (*Senate Repts.*, 33 *Cong.*, 1 *sess.*, No. 15.) Jan. 16, Dixon of Ky., offered his amendment for the repeal of the slavery restriction provision of the Missouri Compromise Act. Thus forced, Douglas presented, Jan. 23, his substitute measure, the Kansas-Nebraska bill, embodying the Dixon proposition. On the following day, the *Appeal of the Independent Democrats in Congress to the People of the United States* was issued. (*Cong. Globe*, 33 *Cong.*, 1 *sess.*, I, 281; *Amer. Hist. Leaflets*, No. 17.) It met with a prompt response from the North. The press, public meetings, and several State legislatures, as they assembled, denounced the measure. On the day that Douglas opened the debate, Jan. 30, the resolutions of the Democratic legislature of Rhode Island were presented to Congress. Before the approval of the bill on May 30, (*U. S. Stat. at Large*, X, 277–289), at least four other States, namely, Mass., New York, Maine and Conn., (2) had adopted resolutions against it, while Georgia, Miss., Ill., and Cal. passed resolutions favoring the measure.[1] The resolutions of Georgia and Connecticut follow. For texts of the several resolves see: *Senate Miss.*, 33 *Cong.*, 1 *sess.*, Nos. 15, 16, 22, 24, 28, 40, 48, 62, 65; *House Misc.*, Nos. 10, 16, 20, 23, 30, 32, 77; *Acts of R. I., Jan. sess.*, 1854, 275; *Acts and Res. of Mass.*, 1854, 415; *Res. of Maine*, 1854, 102; *Res. and Private Acts of Conn., May sess.*, 1854, 123–127; *Acts of Ga.*, 1853–54, 590; *Laws of Miss.*, 1854, 585; *Statutes of Cal.*, 1854, 274.

General references: Channing and Hart's *Guide*, § 199; MacDonald, *Documents*, 395–405. *Cong. Globe*, 33 *Cong.*, 1 *sess.*, *Index; Senate Reports*, I, No. 15, Burgess, ch. xix; Curtis II, 259–265; Curtis, *Hist. of the Rep. Party*, I, 136–147; Greeley I, 224–235; Greeley, *Slavery Extension*, 71–89; Johnston, *Amer. Pol. History*, II, 141–159; Rhodes, I, 424–500; Schouler, V, 280–292; Smith, I, ch. vi; Von Holst, IV, chs. vi-viii; V, ch. i; Wilson, II, ch. xxx; Bancroft, *Seward*, I, ch. xviii; Dixon, *True History of the Missouri Compromise and its Repeal*, chs. xvii-xx; Hart, *Chase*, 133–148; Schuckers, *Chase*, 135–161; Nicolay and Hay, *Lincoln*, I, ch. xix; Julian, *Giddings*, 310–314; Pierce, *Sumner*, III, 347–361; Storey, *Sumner*, ch. vii; Sumner, *Works*, III, 336–352; Seward, *Works*, IV, 433–479; Johnston, *Amer. Orations*, III, 3–87; Stovall, *Toombs*, ch. ix; Davis, *Rise and Fall of the Confederacy*, I, ch. v; Stevens, *War between the States*, II, ch. xvii.

---

137.   Georgia in Support of Nebraska Bill.

February 20, 1854.

The State of Georgia, in solemn convention, having firmly fixed herself upon the principles of the compromise measures of 1850, relating to the subject of slavery in the Territories of the United

---

[1] An unusual effort was made to secure the approval of the Legislature of Illinois. The House adopted the resolutions by a vote of 36 to 22, the Senate by 14 to 8. *Illinois House Jour.*, 1854, 167. *Senate Jour.*, 21, 26, 49, 78–81. See Nicolay and Hay, *Lincoln*, I, 366–367.

States, as a final settlement of the agitation of that question, its withdrawal from the halls of Congress and the political arena, and its reference to the people of the Territories interested therein ; and distinctly recognizing in those compromise measures the doctrine that it is not competent for Congress to impose any restrictions, as to the existence of slavery among them, upon the citizens moving into and settling upon the Territories of the Union, acquired or to be hereafter acquired ; but that the question whether slavery shall or shall not form a part of their domestic institutions is for them alone to determine for themselves ; and her present Executive having reiterated and affirmed the same fixed policy in his inaugural address.

Be it resolved by the Senate and House of Representatives of the State of Georgia in General Assembly met, That the Legislature of Georgia, as the representatives of the people, speaking their will and expressing their feelings, have had their confidence strengthened in the settled determination of the great body of the Northern people, to carry out in good faith those principles, in the practical application of them to the bills reported by Mr. Douglas from the Committee on Territories in the United States Senate at the present session proposing the organization of a Territorial government for the Territory of Nebraska.

And be it further resolved, That our Senators in Congress be, and they are hereby, instructed, and our representatives requested, to vote for and support those principles, and to use all proper means within their power for carrying them out, either as applied to the government of the Territory of Nebraska or in any other bill for Territorial government which may come before them.

[Resolution of transmission.]

[*Acts of Georgia,* 1853–1854, 590.]

138. Connecticut Opposes the Kansas-Nebraska Bill.

May Session, 1854.

Whereas, a bill is now pending in the Congress of the United States for the organization of the Territories of Kansas and Nebraska, by which the eighth section of the act preparatory to the admission of Missouri, approved March 6, 1820, is declared inoperative and void :

1. *Resolved*, by this general assembly, That the form of the prohibition of slavery, in the act of 1820, as well as its incorporation in an act designed to be irrepealable, pledged the public faith, to the whole extent of the power of Congress so to do, against any repeal of the prohibition so enacted, and that the people of Connecticut have therefore relied upon the perpetuity of that enactment, with full confidence in the integrity and honor, both of the national government, and of those States which sustain the institution of slavery within their own jurisdiction.

2. *Resolved*, That in the name and in behalf of the people of this State, we protest against the proposed repeal of the prohibition of slavery in the act preparatory to the admission of Missouri, as a violation of the national faith, as destructive of mutual confidence between the States of this Union, as exposing the Union itself to imminent peril, and as inconsistent with the fundamental principles of natural justice.

3. *Resolved*, That we declare our fixed purpose never to consent to the legal or actual admission of slavery into the territory from which it was excluded by the act of 1820, or to the admission of slave-holding States from any portion of the same.

4. *Resolved*, That the attempt to extend slavery over a vast region from which it has been by law excluded with the consent of the slave-holding States ought to awaken the people of Connecticut to the agressive character of slavery as a political power, and to unite them in determined hostility to its extension, and to its existence wherever it comes constitutionally within the reach of federal legislation.

5. *Resolved*, That this general assembly hereby declares itself ready to co-operate with other States, in any legal and constitutional measures, which the existing crisis or its consequenses shall demand, for the preservation of our rights and in defence of liberty.

6. *Resolved*, That our senators in Congress be instructed, and our representatives be earnestly requested, to oppose, by all lawful means, and to the last extremity, the bill under consideration,

with the clause abrogating the prohibition of slavery, known as the Missouri compromise.

[Resolution of transmission.]

[*Resolutions and Private Acts of Connecticut, May Session,* 1854, 125–127.]

The Kansas-Nebraska Act and the Fugitive Slave Law.

1854–55.

The adoption of the Kansas–Nebraska Bill and the excitement aroused by the rendition of Anthony Burns in Boston at about the same time, led almost immediately to the adoption of new sets of resolutions by the legislatures of Conn. and Rhode Island, then in session. The Conn. resolves demanded the repeal of the Kansas–Nebraska Act, declaring that the compromises on slavery had been " repudiated and deprived of their moral force and authority." They announced " that the government having no more power to establish slavery than to establish a monarchy, should at once relieve itself from all responsibility for the existence of slavery, wherever it possesses constitutional power to legislate for its extinction." The Rhode Island resolves were similar, and expressed opposition to the further acquisition of territory. Both legislatures called for the amendment or repeal of the fugitive slave law. *Res. and Private Acts of Conn., May sess.,* 1854, 123–125; *Acts and Res. of R. I., June sess.,* 1854, 61–62; *House Misc.,* 33 *Cong.,* 1 *sess.,* Nos. 94, 96; *Senate Misc.,* No. 71.

The Anti-Nebraska men won notable victories in the election of 1854, and to show their opposition to the extension of slavery and the fugitive slave law, Rhode Island, Conn., Vermont, Mass.[1] and Mich. passed Personal Liberty Laws in 1854 or 1855. To meet these State laws, Senator Toucey reported from the Judiciary Committee in Feb., 1855, a bill designed to strengthen the fugitive slave act; Sumner's motion to repeal the act now secured nine votes; Toucey's bill passed the Senate, Feb. 23, by a vote of 29 to 9, but was not considered in the House (*Cong. Globe,* 33 *Cong.,* 2 *sess.,* 783, 902; *Appx.,* 211–

[1] This act was passed over Gov. Gardner's veto. *Acts of Mass.,* 1855, 924–929, 1009–1012. Gov. Gardner, Jan. 3, 1856, recommended the repeal of such portions of the law as may conflict with the Const. and the laws of the United States. *Acts of Mass.,* 1856–57, 302–304. This was not done until 1858, when the act was amended. *Ibid.,* 1858, 151. Gov. Andrew in his inaugural, Jan. 5, 1861, defended the constitutionality of the law in reply to the charges made by the South. *Ibid.,* 1860–61, 579–584. Cf. Hart, *Contemporaries,* IV, 93–96; Garrison, III, 414–417; Pearson, *Life of John A. Andrew,* 70–72, 79–92, 132–140, 165–167.

246; Pierce, *Sumner*, III, 374–385, 390–393, 410–412; Sumner's *Works*, III, 355 367, 435, 450, 529–547). Meanwhile the legislatures of Michigan, Maine, Mass. and New York (Jan.–Apr., 1855) were demanding the "immediate and unconditional repeal" of the fugitive slave law and the Kansas–Nebraska Act. On the other side, Arkansas adopted resolves in approval of the latter measure, while Illinois expressed its disapproval of "all efforts having for their object the disturbance of the compromise measure of 1850, including the fugitive slave law." The resolutions of Arkansas, noteworthy for their attack upon Ohio, and those of Michigan, one of the leading States in the organization of the Republican party, as also the radical resolves of Mass., follow. For the texts of the other resolutions, see: *Senate Misc.*, 33 Cong., 2 sess., No. 11; *Ibid.*, 34 Cong., 1 sess., Nos. 11, 18, 81; *House Misc.*, Nos. 41, 81, 115, 121; *Acts and Res. of Maine*, 1855, 261, 262; *Acts and Res. of Mass.*, 1854–55, 941, 942, 946, 947; *Acts of New York*, 1855, 1120–1122; *Private Laws of Ill.*, *Jan. sess.*, 1855, 744.

General references: Rhodes, I, 500–506; II, 45–78; Schouler, V, 293–296, 301–308; Von Holst, V, 51–70, 130–138; Wilson, II, chs. xxxi–xxxiv; Bancroft, *Seward*, I, ch. xix; Garrison, *Garrison*, III, chs. xiv, xv; Nicolay and Hay, *Lincoln*, I, chs. xx, xxi; Stanwood, chs. xix, xx; Macy, *Political Parties*, chs. xiii, xiv; Pierce, *Sumner*, III, 374–393; Sumner, *Works*, III, 355–423, 435–450; Adams, *Richard Henry Dana*, I, 265–282; McDougall, *Fugitive Slaves*, 43–49, 66–70, 127; Siebert, *Underground Railroad*, 326–333; Curtis, *Republican Party*, I, chs. vi, vii; Julian, *Political Recollections* 134–150.

---

139. Arkansas Approves of the Kansas-Nebraska Act.

January 19, 1855.

Whereas the right of property in slaves is expressly recognized by the constitution of the United States, and is, by virtue of such recognition, guaranteed against unfriendly action on behalf of the general government: And whereas each State of the Union, by the fact of being a party to the federal compact, is also a party to the recognition and guarantee aforesaid: And whereas the citizens of each State are, in consequence of such citizenship, under the most sacred obligation to conform to the terms and tenor of the compact to which their State is a party: Therefore—

1. *Be it resolved by the General Assembly of the State of Arkansas*, That the legislation of Congress repealing the mis-named "compromise" of eighteen hundred and twenty, and asserting the doctrine of non-interference with slavery, alike in States and

Territories, is in strict accordance with the constitution, and in itself just and expedient, and is for these reasons cordially approved by the people of Arkansas.

2. *Resolved*, That the opposition of northern States to the legislation above mentioned is at war with the letter and spirit of the constitution, is grossly violative of plighted faith, and is a traitorous blow aimed at the rights of the South and the perpetuity of the Union.[1]

3. *Resolved*, That the citizens of the State of Ohio have pursued a course peculiarly unjust and odious in their fanatical hostility to institutions for which they are not responsible, in their encouragement of known felons, and endorsement of repeated and shameless violations of law and decency, and in their establishment of abolition presses, and circulation of incendiary documents, urging a servile population to bloodshed and rapine ; and by reason of the premises, it is the duty and the interest of the people of Arkansas to discontinue all social and commercial relations with the citizens of said State, and the same is hereby earnestly recommended as a punishment of past outrages and a preventive of further aggressions.

[Resolution of transmission.]

[*House Misc. Documents*, 33 *Cong.* 2 *Sess.*, No. 26.]

140.   Michigan on the Slavery Question.

January 26, 1855

Whereas, Slavery is regarded, by the people of this State, as a great moral, social, and political evil, at war with the principles of the Declaration of Independence and the great object contemplated by our forefathers in establishing the Constitution of the

---

[1] The Legislature of New Hampshire replied to the above, July 14, 1855, controverting the same.—One of the resolves declared " That all threats of a dissolution of the Union coming from the slave States, unless they are permitted to regulate the policy of the general government on the subject of slavery, have lost all their terrors for the people of New Hampshire, and that they are resolved to demand and enforce their rights in every crisis, and at any sacrifice, consistently with honor and the constitution. *Laws of New Hamp.* June Sess. 1855, 1613-1615; *Senate Misc.*, 34 *Cong.* 1 *Sess.* No. 81.

United States, an impediment to the prosperity of our common country, and an element of domestic weakness and discord ; and

Whereas, The people of Michigan owe it to the early and prudent exercise of the power of Congress over the Territories of the United States, in applying the anti-slavery restriction contained in the ordinance of 1787, that she is not now a slave-holding State ; and

Whereas, The people have heretofore, through their legislature, repeatedly and earnestly remonstrated against the further extension of slavery in the national Territories ; and

Whereas, The violation, by Congress, of the compact of 1820 has released the people of this State from all obligation to respect Congressional compromises for the extension or perpetuation of slavery ; therefore

Resolved, By the Senate and House of Representatives of the State of Michigan, That we hold the said repeal, and the permission granted by said Territorial act to introduce slavery into said Territories, to be a violation of a mutual covenant between the free States and the slave-holding States of the Union, justified by no necessity, present or prospective ; injurious to the rights of the former, tending to interrupt the internal harmony of the country, and to frustrate the well known purpose of the framers of the Constitution, who, by gradual legislation, designed ultimately to put an end to slavery,

Resolved, That we are opposed to the further extension of slavery, or the recognition or the permission thereof, in any Territory now owned, or which may hereafter be acquired by the United States.

Resolved, That we hold it to be within the constitutional power of Congress to abolish slavery and the slave trade in all the Territories of the United States, including the District of Columbia, and that it is their duty, in view of the great and permanent interests of the Nation, to pass laws for its immediate suppression and extinction in all such Territories and in said District.

Resolved, That our Senators in Congress be, and they are hereby, instructed, and our representatives requested, to vote for and use their best exertions to procure the passage of an Act of Congress that shall prohibit the introduction or existence of slavery in any of the Territories of the United States, and especially in Kansas and Nebraska, and to introduce, without delay, a bill for this latter purpose.

Resolved, That the Act of Congress of 1850, known as the Fugitive Slave Law, was, in the opinion of the people of this State, an unnecessary measure ; that it contains provisions of doubtful constitutionality ; that the mode of proceeding under it is harsh, unjust, and repugnant to the moral sense of the people of the free States, cruel and despotic towards the person claimed as a fugitive, and that we are in favor of its immediate repeal ; therefore

Resolved, That our Senators in Congress be, and they are hereby, instructed, and our Representatives requested, to use their best exertions to procure the immediate repeal of the Act of 1850, known as the Fugitive Slave Law.

[Resolution of transmission.]

[Acts of Michigan, 1855, 483–485.]

----

141.   Massachusetts on the Fugitive Slave Law.

April 6. 1855.

Resolved, Inasmuch as there is neither any power granted to the general government in the Constitution of the United States for the enactment of any law by Congress for the return of alleged fugitive slaves, nor any prohibition therein to the States against the passage of laws upon that subject, that the fugitive slave act is a direct violation of the tenth article of amendments to the Constitution of the United States, which declares that " the powers not delegated to the United States by the Constitution, nor prohibited by it to the States, are reserved to the States respectively, or to the people."

Resolved, That our senators and representatives in Congress be requested to use all honorable means to secure the unconditional repeal of the fugitive slave act of eighteen hundred and fifty, which is hostile alike to the provisions of the national Constitution and to the dictates of the Christian religion, an infraction equally of " the supreme law of the land," and of the " higher law " of God in consonance therewith.

[Resolution of transmission.]

[Acts and Resolves of Massachusetts, 1854–1855, 946–947.]

The Disturbance in Kansas.

1855–1857.

Following the adoption of the Kansas-Nebraska Act there ensued a race between the emigrants from the free and the slave states to Kansas, with the object of securing the control of the territorial government. Beginning with July, 1854, some of the former were sent out by the Emigrant Aid Company of Massachusetts. (For its activity see Eli Thayer, *The Kansas Crusade;* Chas. Robinson, *The Kansas Conflict*, ch. ix.; *Kansas Hist. Col.*, VI, 90–96.) The invasion of Kansas by Missourians on the occasion both of the election of the Territorial delegate, Nov. 29, 1854, and of the election of the Territorial Legislature, March 30, 1855, gave the pro-slavery party the control of the government. This invasion at once met with the indignant protest of the Legislatures of New York, Massachusetts and Connecticut, and later of Vermont.[1] The typical resolutions of Massachusetts are given below.

The adoption of a slave code by the Territorial Legislature during the summer of 1855 (Text, Wilder, *Annals of Kansas*, 56–59), and the inauguration by the free-states men of a rival government under the Topeka Constitution during the fall and winter of 1855–56 (Text, etc., Wilder, 63–89; Greeley, *Slavery Extension*, 148–156), and their application to Congress for the admission of Kansas under this constitution, excited general interest. President Pierce sent a special message to Congress, Jan. 24, 1856, declaring the Topeka movement illegal and Feb. 11 he issued a proclamation against those engaged in it. (Richardson, V, 352–360; 390, 391.) The House, Jan. 26, adopted a resolution declaring that the Missouri Compromise ought to be restored, by a vote of 101 to 100. (*Globe*, 34 *Cong.*, 1 *sess.*, 300, 301.) A special committee of the Senate, Douglas chairman, made a report, March 12, condemning the Emigrant Aid Company and repudiating the Topeka movement. Collamer, of Vermont, dissented. (*Senate Repts.*, No. 34.) The House, March 19, provided for the appointment of a Committee of Investigation. (Howard report presented, July 2, *House Repts.*, No. 200; see also House Report on Topeka Const., *Ibid.*, No. 181; also *House Exec. Doc.*, Nos. 28, 66; *House Repts.*, Nos. 3, 275; *House Misc.*, No. 3.)

In the meantime, Robinson, Governor under the Topeka Const., appealed to the governors of New York, Rhode Island and Ohio. The Legislatures of Rhode Island and Ohio responded, and later in the spring of 1856 those of Connecticut, Massachusetts and New Hampshire condemned the course of the national administration and the pro-slavery party, and favored the admis-

---

[1] The resolves of Massachusetts and Connecticut were returned by South Carolina, those of Vermont by Georgia and Mississippi, either because their language was offensive or because of the state's failure to observe its constitutional obligations. *Jour. of S. C. House of Rep.*, 1855, 30; *Acts of S. C.*, 1855, 305; *Acts of Ga.*, 1855–56, 552; *Laws of Miss.*, 1856, 431.

sion of Kansas as a free state.[1] On the other hand, several of the southern legislatures early in 1856 passed resolves expressive of their views. Texas and Kentucky supported the Kansas Nebraska Act [2] and the enforcement of the Fugitive Slave Act.[3] Mississippi adopted the subjoined resolutions on the situation in Kansas and for the encouragement of emigration thereto; while Georgia, Jan. 17, 1856, voted in favor of aiding emigrants to Kansas with free passes on State railroads, and followed this by an act, March 4, 1856, empowering the calling of a state convention, if any of the contingencies contemplated in the resolutions of the Georgia Convention of Dec., 1850, should result, " to consider and determine upon the time and mode of resistance." (See *ante*, 271, 272.) Louisiana indorsed President Pierce's policy in regard to slavery.

The Kansas situation was still further aggravated by the destruction of Lawrence, May 21, and the assault upon Senator Sumner, May 22. (See *post*, 293.) Under the influence of these events the Democratic and Republican National Conventions assembled in June. (For platforms with reference to slavery and Kansas, see Stanwood, 267, 270.) Under the spur of the convention's declarations the Democratic Senate, July 2, approved a bill, based on Toombs' proposition, which provided for a vote on a new territorial convention and a new constitution, while the Republican House, on the following day, voted to admit Kansas immediately under the Topeka constitution. The session ended with the two houses in disagreement. The free state legislature was dispersed, July 4, 1856, by United States troops under orders of Gov. Shannon, and a renewal of the Civil War in Kansas ensued.

During the winter of 1856–57 the Legislatures of Iowa, Wisconsin, Ohio and Maine passed resolves in opposition to the extension of slavery, while

---

[1] The Maine Legislature, April 10, 1856, declared itself averse to the extension of slavery over the territories, but disapproved of the resolves of the previous legislature of March 17, 1855. *Ante*, p. 281; *Acts and Res. of Maine*, 1856, 366.

[2] Several resolves were introduced and discussed in the Alabama Legislature in the winter of 1855–56, repudiating the doctrine of popular sovereignty, showing the beginning of a change of view. *House Jour. of Ala.*, 1855, 438–440; 472–474.

[3] Texas declared that a repeal or material modification of the same " would be a great cause of alarm," and Kentucky that it " would greatly endanger the safety of the Union." The New York, Connecticut and Vermont resolves of 1855 and those of Ohio in 1856 had condemned the Fugitive Slave Law, and called for its repeal; Vermont declaring that a slave brought into a free state by the consent of his master thereby became free; Ohio, that the law was " inconsistent with and unwarranted by the Constitution of the United States, and repugnant to the plainest principles of justice and humanity."

Vermont,[1] Iowa and Connecticut favored the admission of Kansas as a free state, and Michigan desired Congress to declare " the so-called Kansas Code null and void."

The Southern Commercial Convention at Savannah, Dec., 1856, adopted resolutions declaratory of the equal rights of the South in the Territories, denouncing the efforts of the Emigrant Aid societies to force a hostile population on Kansas, and recommending counter emigration. *De Bow's Review,* XXII, 101.

References for the texts of the foregoing resolutions: *Acts of N. Y.,* 1855, 1120–1122; *Acts and Res. of Mass.,* 1854–55, 975; *Ibid.,* 1856–57, 286–287; *Res. and Private Acts of Conn., May sess.,* 1855, 164–166; *Ibid., May sess.,* 1856, 83–85; *Acts and Res. of Vt., Oct. sess.,* 1855, 89, 91; *Ibid., Oct. sess.,* 1856, 63, 105; *Acts and Res. of R. I., Jan. sess.,* 1856, 82–84; *Local Laws of Ohio,* 1855–56, 237, 247; *Acts of Ohio,* 1857, 298: *Acts and Res. of Maine,* 1856, 366; *Ibid.,* 1857, 58–60; *Acts of Iowa,* 1856–57, 453; *Acts of Mich.,* 1857, 480; *Acts of Wis.,* 1857, 138; *Acts of Ky.,* 1855–56, 136–138; *Laws of Miss.,* 1856, 434; *Acts of Ga.,* 1855–56, 107, 108, 553; *Acts of La.,* 1856, 12; *34 Cong., 1 sess., Senate Misc.,* Nos. 15, 17, 49, 58; *House Misc.,* Nos. 42, 90, 100, 101, 103, 112, 120, 122; *34 Cong. 3 sess., Senate Misc.,* Nos. 17, 48; *House Misc.,* Nos. 38, 49; *35 Cong., 1 sess., Senate Misc.,* No. 188.

Bibliography: Channing and Hart, *Guide* §§ 200, 201; MacDonald, 413–415; Special Works on Kansas; Blackmar, *Life of Charles Robinson,* 110–215; Chas. Robinson, *The Kansas Conflict,* chs. iv–xiv; Springs, *Kansas,* chs. iii–ix; Wilder, *Annals of Kansas,* 57–110 *in passim,* gives votes at elections, organization of conventions and texts of constitutions, etc.; *Kansas Hist. Collections,* esp. vol. III, for biographical sketches of the several governors, vols. IV and V for executive minutes and papers; Contemporary Accounts, E. E. Hale, *Kansas and Nebraska* [1854]; Sara Robinson, *Kansas* [1856]; Wm. Phillips, *Conquest of Kansas by Missouri and Her Allies* [1856]; J. H. Gihon, *Governor Geary and Kansas* [1857]. General references: Burgess, ch. xx; Curtis, *The Republican Party,* I, 238–243; Greeley, I, 236–245; Greeley, *Slavery Extension,* 89–164; Johnston, *Amer. Pol. Hist.,* II, 159–168; Rhodes, II, 78–87, 150–168, 189–220; Schouler, V, 320–333, 341–349, 357–359; Smith, I, 185–192, 227–229; Stanwood, *Hist. of the Presidency,* ch. xx; Von Holst, V, chs. iii, v, vi, viii; Wilson, II, chs. xxxv, xxxvii; Nicolay and Hay, *Lincoln,* I, chs. xxii–xxv; Bancroft, *Seward,* I, ch. xx; Seward, *Works,* IV, 479–573; John Sherman, *Recollections,* I, ch. v; Julian, *Giddings,* 320–334; Pierce, *Sumner,* III, 427–439.

---

[1] The Vermont Legislature also passed an act, Nov. 18, 1856, appropriating $20,000 for the relief of the poor in Kansas. *Acts and Res. of Vt.,* 1856, 3. It was repealed a year later. Gov. Gardner vetoed a similar act of the Massachusetts Legislature appropriating $100,000. *Acts and Res. of Mass.,* 1856–57, 759–765.

142.   Massachusetts on the Disturbance in Kansas.

May 21, 1855.

Whereas, The Territory of Kansas, on occasion of the first two elections therein, has been violently invaded by an armed mob from the neighboring State of Missouri, the persons composing the said mob not only claiming themselves, without the least shadow of right, to vote at the said elections, but by high-handed violence and threats of death, deterring the citizens of said territory from the exercise of their right of suffrage ; therefore,

Resolved, That we respectfully call upon the law-abiding citizens of Missouri, and upon the executive and legislature of that State, speedily to disavow this gross outrage perpetrated by some of their ill-advised citizens, and to take prompt measures to prevent its repetition by them.

Resolved, That we call upon the President of the United States to take instant and effectual measures for sustaining in Kansas the sovereignty of the people against the violence and incursions of mobs from Missouri.

Resolved, That this commonwealth is ready, if necessary, to aid with her whole power the governor of Kansas, and the people of that Territory, or of any other Territory or State, in support of constitutional rights, by whomsoever infringed.

[Resolution of transmission.]

[*Acts and Resolves of Massachusetts,* 1854–1855, 975].

143.   Mississippi on the Kansas Situation.

March 12, 1856.

Resolved, By the Legislature of the State of Mississippi, That we sympathize deeply with the friends of domestic slavery in the Territory of Kansas, in the struggle they are carrying on in resistance to the efforts made to expel slavery therefrom, and that we fully appreciate the importance to the influence and safety of the South, that Kansas should become a slaveholding State, and that therefore we recommend to the people of this State to take early and active measures to encourage emigration to that Territory, and by all lawful and proper means to strengthen the hands of the friends of Southern institutions therein.

[*Laws of Mississippi*, 1856, 434.]

The Assault upon Charles Sumner.

1856.

The most important episode connected with the Kansas debate in Congress in 1856 was the impassioned speech of Senator Charles Sumner of Massachusetts, on "The Crime Against Kansas," delivered on May 19 and 20. This was followed by the assault upon him by Representative Preston Brooks of South Carolina, in the Senate Chamber on May 22. An investigating committee of the House reported a resolution in favor of the expulsion of Brooks, but it failed to secure the necessary two-thirds vote. (121 yeas to 95 nays.) Brooks resigned but was immediately re-elected almost unanimously. The indignation of the North, especially of New England, was profound, and found expression not only in the speeches of its representatives in Congress, resolutions of public meetings and societies, but also in the official action of the Legislatures of five New England states, condemning the assault in vigorous language, as follows: Massachusetts, May 31; Connecticut, May session; Rhode Island, May session; New Hampshire, July 12, and Vermont, November 18. In addition the Massachusetts Legislature immediately expressed its approval of "Mr. Sumner's manliness and courage," "and his defense of human rights and free territory," and demanded of "the national Congress a prompt and strict investigation into the recent assault upon Senator Sumner, and the expulsion by the House of Representatives of Mr. Brooks, of South Carolina, and any other member concerned with him in said assault." Vermont also adopted resolutions approving Sumner's speech. The Rhode Island and New Hampshire resolves also condemned the nearly coincidental destruction of Lawrence on May 21. The resolves of Rhode Island follow.

For the texts of the resolves see, *Acts and Res. of Mass.*, 1856–57, 286–288, 292; *Acts of R. I.*, *May sess.*, 1856, 28; *Laws of New Hamp.*, *June sess.*, 1856, 1781–1783; *Acts and Res. of Vt.*, *Oct. sess.*, 1856, 106-108, 109; 34 *Cong.*, I *sess.*, Senate *Misc.*, Nos. 64, 66, 80; *House Misc.*, Nos. 117, 118, 119; *Cong. Globe, Appx.*, 630–632. For report of House Investigating Committee, see *House Repts.*, No. 182; *Cong. Globe*, II, 1348–1367; see also *Senate Repts.*, No. 191. Sumner's speech is given in his *Works*, IV, 127–256; *House Repts.*, No. 182, 87–142; Johnson, *Amer. Orations*, III, 88–120; Brooks' speech, *Ibid.*, 121-128; *Cong. Globe, Appx.*, 886. For contemporary opinion of the assault, both northern and southern, *cf.* Sumner, *Works, IV, Appx.*, 257–342. General references: Pierce, *Sumner*, III, ch. xl; Story, *Sumner*, chs. viii, ix; Rhodes, II, 130–150; Von Holst, V, 313-333; Wilson, II, ch. xxxvi; Nicolay and Hay, *Lincoln*, II, ch. iii.

144.   Rhode Island on the Recent Occurrences in Congress and in Kansas.

May Session, 1856.

Resolved, by this General Assembly, the Senate and House of Representatives concurring therein: That the recent assault on the person of a Senator from Massachusetts, on the floor of the Senate Chamber of the United States, by a representative from South Carolina, is an outrage, the commission of which in a civilized community, no provocation can justify, and the enormity of which no excuse can palliate; and that the people have a right to claim of their representatives that the authors and contrivers of an assault so brutal and so cowardly shall at once be expelled from the Congress of the nation.

Resolved, That the assault thus made on a Senator for words spoken in debate, and the conduct of those political friends of the offender who sought to prevent an investigation into the offense, show a deliberate attempt to stifle freedom of speech in the national councils, and deserve the indignant rebuke and the uncompromising opposition of all who love their freedom, and who wish to maintain it.

Resolved, That this outrage, in connection with the acts of violence just perpetrated in Kansas, admonish us that a determination exists on the part of those now wielding the power of the general government to crush the advocates and upholders of freedom in free territory by force, bloodshed and civil war; and that the perversion of the power delegated by a free people for the preservation of their freedom to purposes of injustice, tyranny and oppression, demands the union and active co-operation of all who deserve to enjoy the blessings of liberty for the purpose of placing the government in the hands of those who will conduct it with due regard to the rights of freemen and the liberties of the people.

[*Acts and Resolves of Rhode Island, May Sess.,* 1856, 28, 29.]

Resolutions on the Dred Scott Decision.

1857-1859

While the question of the status of slavery in Kansas was still pending and the public was in consequence greatly excited, the Supreme Court of the United States rendered its opinion, March 6, 1857, in the celebrated case of *Dred Scott vs. Sanford*. It was an attempt on the part of the majority of the court to settle the vexed question of territorial slavery. Chief Justice Taney rendered the decision of the majority of the court, but each of the eight associate justices delivered a separate opinion. Curtis and McLean held that the question was not strictly within the jurisdiction of the court. The decision of the majority was most acceptable to the South, but was denounced by the Republican party and their leaders as " extra judicial and possessing no binding force." It was recognized by the Republicans and Southern Democrats that it shattered the Douglas doctrine of popular sovereignty. This was clearly brought out by Lincoln in his joint debate with Douglas in the following year.

The following State Legislatures adopted resolutions condemning the decision: 1857, Maine, April 15; Ohio, April 16 and 17; Connecticut, May sess.; New Hampshire, June 27; Vermont, November 10; 1858, Massachusetts, March 27; Vermont, October sess.; 1859, Maine, April 4. Maine and Ohio also called for the reorganization of the court. The latter passed a separate set of resolves demanding that to the several states should be given " that just proportion of the judges of the Supreme Court to which they are entitled by population and business." The resolutions of Ohio and Connecticut follow.

For texts of the resolves see *Res. of Maine*, 1857, 60; *Ibid.*, 1859, 286; *Acts of Ohio*, 297, 301; *Laws of New Hamp.*, *June sess.*, 1857, 1925; *Ibid.*, 1859, 2140; *Acts and Res. of Vt.*, *Oct. sess.*, 1857, 83; *Ibid.*, 1858, 66–68; *Acts and Res. of Mass.*, 1858–59, 170; 35 *Cong.*, 1 *sess.*, *Senate Misc.*, Nos. 14, 188, 231; *House Misc.*, Nos. 31, 123.

Bibliography: Channing and Hart, *Guide*, § 202. Text of decision is in 19 *Howard*, 393–633; extracts from, in MacDonald, 416–435; *Am. Hist. Leaflets*, No. 23; Cluskey, 147–205; Contemporary discussions: T. H. Benton, *Historical and Legal Examination of the Case of Dred Scott;* S. A. Foot, *Examination of the Case of Dred Scott;* Gray and Lowell, *Legal Review of the Case of Dred Scott;* J. C. Hurd, *Law of Freedom and Bondage*, I, §§ 489–539; General references: Burgess, ch. xxi; Carson, *Supreme Court*, II, ch. xv; Curtis, II, 266–279; Curtis, *Republican Party*, 275–282; Greeley, I, ch. xviii; Johnson, *Amer. Pol. History*, II, ch. viii; Macy *Political Parties*, chs. xvi, xix; Nicolay and Hay, *Lincoln*, II, chs. iv, v, viii, ix; Rhodes, II, 249–271, 319–339; Thorpe, *Const. Hist. of U. S.*, II, 536–551; Tyler, *Memoirs of R. B. Taney*, 358–391; Von Holst, VI, ch. i; Wilson, II, ch. xxxix; for Seward charge against Buchanan, see *Works*, IV, 574–604; Bancroft, *Seward*, I, 436–439, 446–449; Lincoln speeches, Johnson, *Amer. Pol. Orations*, III, 154–194. See also *Political Debates between Lincoln and Douglas*.

145. Ohio on the Dred Scott Decision.

April 17, 1857.

Resolved, by the General Assembly of the State of Ohio,

1st. That this general assembly has observed with regret that, in the opinion lately pronounced by Chief Justice Taney in behalf of a majority of the supreme court of the United States in the case of Dred Scott against J. H. Sanford, occasion has been taken to promulgate extra-judicially certain doctrines concerning slavery, not less contradictory to well-known facts of history, than repugnant to the plain provisions of the Constitution, and subversive to the rights of free men and free states.

2d. That in the judgment of this general assembly, every free person, born within the limits of any state of this union, is a citizen thereof, and to deny to any such person the right of sueing in the courts of the United States, in those cases where that right is guaranteed by the Constitution to all citizens of the United States, is a palpable and unwarrantable violation of that sacred instrument.

3d. That the doctrine announced by the chief justice, in behalf a majority of the court, that the Federal Constitution regards slaves as mere property, and protects the claims of masters to slaves, to the same extent, and in the same manner as the rights of owners in property, foreshadows, if it does not include the doctrine, that masters may hold slaves as property within the limits of free states, during temporary visits, or for purposes of transit, to the practical consequences of which doctrine no free state can submit with honor.

4th. That the doctrine also announced in behalf of a majority of the court that there exists no power in the general government to exclude slavery from the territories of the United States, subverts the spirit of the Constitution, annuls the just authority of the United States over their own territories, and contradicts the uniform practice of the government.

5th. That the general assembly, in behalf of the people of Ohio, hereby solemnly protest against these doctrines, as destructive of personal liberty, of state's rights, of constitutional obligations, and of the union, and so, protesting, further declares its unalterable

convictions that in the Declaration of Independence the fathers of
the republic intended to assert the indestructible and equal rights
of all men, without any exception or reservation whatever, to life,
liberty, and the pursuit of happiness ; and in the Constitution, by
the comprehensive guaranty that no person shall be deprived
of life, liberty or property, without due process of law, designed
to secure these rights against all invasion by the federal government, and to make the establishment of slavery outside of slave
states a constitutional impossibility.

[Resolution of transmission.]

[*Acts of Ohio*, 1857, 301.]

146.   Connecticut on the Dred Scott Decision and Kansas.

May Session, 1857.

*   *   *   *   *

Resolved, That slavery, being contrary to the principles of natural right, founded upon injustice and fraud, at war with the
principles upon which our government is founded, injurious to
the growth and prosperity of the country, and a reproach to a
people professing to love liberty, ought never to receive the
national sanction ; that while we recognize it as a local institution
maintained by force of the law of the State where it exists, and
over which we have no control and for which we have no responsibility, it is our right and our duty to resist to the last every
attempt to extend it to the Territories of the republic.

Resolved, That the majority of the judges of the Supreme Court
of the United States, in a recent case of Dred Scott, in declaring
that a *free* negro of the African race, whose ancestors were brought
to this country and sold as slaves, is not a citizen within the
meaning of the Constitution of the United States, and is not entitled to sue in a court of the United States, and that no State can
make him such a citizen ; that Congress has no power to prohibit
slavery in the Territories, that every slave-owner may carry his
slaves into the Territories and hold them therein as slaves ; that the
Federal government recognizes slaves as property and pledges itself
to protect it in the Territories, and that the Missouri compromise

act was void, when such declarations or opinions were not necessary for the decision of the case before said court, have departed
from the usages which have heretofore governed our courts;
have volunteered opinions which are not law ; have given occasion
for the belief that they promulgated such opinions for partisan purposes, and thereby have lowered the dignity of said court, and
diminished the respect heretofore awarded to its decisions.

Resolved, That the resolutions of the general assembly of this
State, passed in 1849, declaring that Congress has full constitutional power to prohibit slavery in the Territories of the United
States by legislative enactment, that the people of Connecticut,
while abiding by the compromises of the Constitution, and aver-
ring their attachment to the Federal Union, are unalterably opposed
to the extension of slavery into free territory, and the further extension of its influence into the councils of the Federal government ; that in resisting the extension of slavery, we do not make
a sectional issue, nor oppose the interests of the people of the
South, express *now,* as then, the sentiments of the people of Connecticut.

Resolved, That the people of Connecticut deeply sympathize
with their brethren in the Territory of Kansas in their struggles
against the aggressions of slavery, and earnestly desire that they
may continue to resist, by all lawful means, until they shall make
Kansas a free State.

Resolved, That our Senators in Congress are hereby instructed,
and our Representatives in Congress are hereby earnestly requested, to vote always, and in every stage of the question, against
the admission of another slaveholding State into the Federal
Union.

[Resolution of transmission.]

[*Senate Misc., 35 Cong., 1 Sess.,* III, No. 188.]

The Struggle over the Lecompton Constitution.

1857–1858

The pro-slavery party in Kansas now determined to hold a constitutional convention. The question of its expediency having been voted upon favorably at the election in Oct., 1856, the Territorial Legislature passed a measure, Feb. 19, 1857, authorizing the election of delegates, June 15. Gov. Geary vetoed the bill, as it failed to provide for the submission of the proposed constitution to the voters, but it became a law. The convention assembled at Lecompton, Sept. 7, 1857, and shortly adjourned, reassembling Oct. 19 to Nov. 7. The constitution was submitted to the people for adoption, "with slavery" or "without slavery," on Dec. 21, but votes against the constitution itself were not counted. The free-states men, who objected to the Lecompton constitution, refrained from voting, and the constitution, "with slavery," received 6,143 votes to 589 "without slavery." The election of officers under the constitution was held Jan. 4, 1858. (Wilder, 115, 127, 128, 134–147, 155–157.) In the meantime Robert J. Walker, who had succeeded Geary as Governor in July, had incurred the enmity of the pro-slavery party by rejecting the votes cast by certain counties at the election for the Territorial Legislature in Oct., 1857, thus enabling the free-states party to gain the control of the Legislature. At an election on Jan. 4, 1858, the free-states men rejected the Lecompton constitution by a vote of 10,226 to 138 for "with slavery" and 23 for "without slavery." (Wilder, 151, 152, 153, 154, 160.) President Buchanan transmitted the Lecompton constitution to Congress in a special message, Feb. 2, 1858, recommending its acceptance. (Richardson, V, 471–481; *Senate Doc.,* 35 *Cong.,* I *sess.,* vii, No. 21.) A bill to admit Kansas under this constitution passed the Senate, March 23, 1858, but the House, April I, substituted a bill to resubmit the constitution to a popular vote. Finally the two Houses agreed to a compromise measure, called "The English Bill," approved May 4, but the people of Kansas, Aug. 2, rejected the proposed land ordinance by a vote of 11,300 to 1,788. (Richardson, V, 498–502; Wilder, 186–188.)

Meanwhile the various state Legislatures were passing resolutions relating to the issue. By the spring of 1858, Rhode Island, Iowa, Ohio, Michigan, Maine, New York, Massachusetts and Wisconsin adopted resolves in opposition to the Lecompton constitution, and later in the year New Hampshire and Vermont condemned the attempt to coerce Kansas to accept slavery. One of the two sets of resolves adopted by Maine follows. On the other hand, in the winter of 1857–58, the Mississippi and Alabama Legislatures condemned the course of Gov. Walker and called for his removal,[1] and Virginia, Alabama, Tennessee, Texas and California passed resolves favoring the admission of Kansas under the Lecompton constitution.[2] Alabama, Jan. 28, 1858, even

---

[1] For other expressions of disapproval see Rhodes, II, 275.

[2] Tennessee and California censured their Senators, John Bell and D. C.

provided for the call of a state convention in case Kansas was refused admission under this constitution, and Texas authorized the election of delegates to meet with those from the other Southern States whenever the executives of a majority of the slave-holding states should deem such a convention necessary.

While Congress was discussing the Lecompton constitution, the territorial legislature, now controlled by the free-states men, called a new constitutional convention, which drew up the Leavenworth constitution, March 2–Apr. 3, 1858. (Wilder, 163, 166, 168-182.) About 4,000 votes were cast for it May 18th, and Jan. 6, 1859, it was presented to Congress, but no important action was taken. Eventually another constitutional convention assembled July 5–29, 1859, and drafted the Wyandotte constitution, prohibiting slavery. It was ratified Oct. 4th by a vote of 10,421 to 5,530. Under this constitution Kansas was finally admitted as a state, Jan. 29, 1861. (Wilder, 198, 199, 204-222, 225, 254; *Kansas Hist. Col.*, I-II, 236-247.)

References to text of state resolves: *Acts and Res. of R. I., Jan. sess.*, 1858, 40; *Acts of Ohio*, 1858, 193; *Acts of Mich.*, 1858, 200; *Acts and Res. of Mass.*, 1858-59, 168; *Resolves of Maine*, 1858, 186, 188; *Acts of N. Y.*, 1858, 661; *Laws of Wis.*, 1858, 217; *Law of New Hamp., June sess.*, 1858, 2031; *Acts of Vt., Oct. sess.*, 1858, 66; *Laws of Miss.*, 1857, 136; *Acts of Va.*, 1857-58, 288; *Acts of Ala.*, 1857-58, 426, 434; *Acts of Tenn.*, 1857-58, 423; *Stat. of Cal.*, 1858, 353; 35 *Cong.*, I *sess., Senate Misc.*, Nos. 140, 147, 149, 160, 165, 194, 204, 206, 228, 232, 242; *House Misc.*, 37, 44, 60, 81, 95, 103, 104, 124, 125.

Bibliography: *Ante*, 291. For debate see *Cong. Globe*, 35 *Cong.*, I *sess.* Also *Senate Repts.*, No. 82; *House Repts.*, No. 377. The texts of the various constitutions and vote upon the same are given in Wilder, *Annals of Kansas*, 110-232 *in passim;* that of the Lecompton constitution also in the above reports, and in Poore, *Federal and State Consts.*, I, 598-613. General references: Blackmar, *Robinson*, 215-249; Robinson, *Kansas Conflict*, chs. xv, xvii; Spring, *Kansas*, chs. x-xii; Burgess, ch. xxi; Curtis, *Buchanan*, II, 194-210; Nicolay and Hay, *Lincoln*, II, chs. vi, vii; Rhodes, II, 237-240, 271-301; Smith, I, 249-256; Schouler, V, 382-385, 391-400; Thorpe, II, 526-535; Von Holst, VI, chs. ii, iv, v, vi *in passim;* Wilson, II, chs. xl, xli, xlii; Bancroft, *Seward*, I, ch. xxi; Seward, *Works*, IV, 604-618; Coleman, *Crittenden*, II, ch. viii; Julian, *Giddings*, 337-353.

Broderick respectively, for their course on the Kansas question and called for their resignation. In 1861 California expunged its former resolves. *Acts of Tenn.*, 1857-58, 423-424; *Stat. of Cal.*, 1859, 383; *Ibid.*, 1861, 670.

[1] The resolves also declared "That Alabama, in their judgment, will and ought to resist, even as a last resort, to a disruption of every tie which binds her to the Union, any action of Congress upon the subject of slavery in the District of Columbia."

147. Maine Condemns the President and the Lecompton Constitution.

March 16, 1858

Resolved, That the people of Maine are unalterable in their devotion to the Constitution and the Union, and demand of the national administration an immediate return to the principles on which the Constitution was framed, and by which alone the Union can be preserved.

Resolved, That the Missouri compromise was a solemn compact between the free and slave States; that its perfidious breach in eighteen hundred and fifty-four deserved, as it received, the universal condemnation of our legislature and people, without regard to party, and such remains the unchangeable conviction of the State.

Resolved, That the reign of the late territorial government in Kansas presents a record of villainy and violence unparalleled in modern history, unfolding a gigantic plot to force African slavery upon the freemen of that Territory by the barbarous and bloody edicts of a foreign legislature, sustained throughout by the administration, with its army and territorial judiciary.

Resolved, That the recent message of the President of the United States is a falsification of the history of Kansas, a libel upon the free people of that Territory, and a deep disgrace to the American name, and to the office once filled by Washington.

Resolved, That the President's confession that the late foreign territorial government in Kansas would have been overthrown by the people long before its annihilation in October, unless he had upheld the usurpation by military power, reveals the complicity of the administration in the execrable scheme of governing Kansas by a minority sustained by Federal bayonets, setting up a military despotism to " crush out" the free-State majority, and the sovereignty of the people ; and his estimate that a standing army of "at least two thousand regular troops" had been found necessary to maintain the equilibrium of parties in that Territory, measures the magnitude of the free State majority—so enormous as to equal in effective power " at least two thousand " of his best " troops."

Resolved, That the President's astounding assertion that "Kansas is at this moment as much a slave State as Georgia or South Carolina," is a monstrous heresy, the slave-power's latest commentary on the doctrine of popular sovereignty, and a suggestive example of the operation of the Kansas-Nebraska bill.

Resolved, That, since this is his interpretation of the Constitution and the law, the people of Maine demand of the President its practical recognition, by an immediate withdrawal of the federal army, the territorial governor, and the infamous judiciary, that the " State" of Kansas may be left, like " Georgia or South Carolina," to the government of " State" officers, and to the protection of a " State" militia.

Resolved, That the Lecompton constitution was conceived in fraud and brought forth in contemptuous defiance of the popular will and in mockery of the professions of the Kansas-Nebraska bill, by which alone the iniquity became possible. Maine enters her solemn and indignant protest against the stupendous swindle.

Resolved, That those members of Congress who, at the passage of the Kansas-Nebraska bill, professed a belief in its avowed principle of popular sovereignty, are now loudly called upon to vindicate the sincerity of their professions by repudiating the Lecompton constitution, in which that principle has been shamelessly betrayed.

Resolved, That if that constitution shall finally be forced upon Kansas against the solemn remonstrance of its people, then, in the opinion of this legislature, they will be justified in resisting it at all hazards and to the last extremity ; and, in so righteous a struggle, the people of Maine are ready to aid them, both by sympathy and action.

Resolved, That the people of Maine have just cause for gratitude and pride that they are now fully represented in both branches of Congress by men who, entertaining and maintaining sentiments and principles in harmony with an immense majority of their constituents, require no specific instructions from this legislature. While their past course meets our approval, it affords us the surest guarantee that they will, to the extent of their ability, strive to avert from our country the impending danger, by resisting to the end the attempted outrage of forcing upon the free people of Kansas a slavery constitution that they abhor, and in formation of which they have had no part.

[Resolutions of transmission.]

[*Resolves of Maine*, 1858, 186–188.]

148.   Wisconsin Defies the Federal Courts.

March 19, 1859.

On the eve of the Civil War, the State of Wisconsin, through her courts, her legislature and the action of her citizens, attempted to practically nullify the Fugitive Slave Law and obstruct the enforcement of the judgments of the Federal Courts. The facts are as follows: Sherman M. Booth, the editor of *The Wisconsin Free Democrat*, was held to trial before the United States District Court, on the charge of having aided in the forcible rescue of a fugitive slave, Joshua Glover, at Milwaukee, March 11, 1854. Before the session of the Court, Booth applied to Judge A. D. Smith, of the State Supreme Court, for a writ of habeas corpus. Smith took a pronounced state rights view and discharged Booth on the ground that the Fugitive Slave Law was "unconstitutional and void." The decision was affirmed by the Wisconsin Supreme Court. (3 *Wisconsin Reports*, 1–135.) In course of time Booth was indicted by the United States District Court, and in Jan., 1855, tried and convicted. The news of his conviction excited great indignation throughout the State, meetings were held in various places and resolutions condemning the Fugitive Slave Law and demanding the enactment of a personal liberty law, and even threatening resistance, were adopted. Again the State Supreme Court released Booth on a writ of habeas corpus. On application, Chief Justice Taney issued a writ of error commanding the State Court to make return of its judgment and proceedings for review by Dec., 1855, but the State Court disregarded it. Finally, in March, 1857, the United States Supreme Court assumed jurisdiction in the case by procuring certified copies of the proceedings, and at the December term, 1858, reviewed and reversed the decision of the Supreme Court of Wisconsin. (*Ableman vs. Booth*, 21 *Howard*, 506.)

As a result of the Glover affair the Legislature of Wisconsin had passed in 1857 a personal liberty law (*Laws of Wis.*, 1857, 12), and in view of the recent decision of the Federal Court, they adopted, March 19, 1859, the subjoined protest and declaration of defiance, based on extreme state sovereignty ground. (Vote in the Assembly, 47 to 37; in the Senate, 13 to 12. *Laws of Wis.*, 1859, 247, 248.) The voters followed this up the same year by electing Booth's attorney, Byron Paine, to the State Supreme Court on the state rights and anti-slavery issue. Although the State Courts refused to enforce the judgment, Booth was re-arrested by a United States Marshal, March 1,

1860. On August 1, he was rescued, but re-arrested, Oct. 8, and finally pardoned by Pres. Buchanan near the close of his administration.

References: See especially, Vroman Mason, *The Fugitive Slave Law in Wisconsin, with Reference to Nullification Sentiment, Proc. of State Hist. Soc. of Wis.*, 1895, 117–144; Tyler, *Life of R. B. Taney*, 392–400; Thwaites, *Story of Wisconsin*, 247–254; Siebert, *Underground Railroad*, 327–330; Wilson, II, 444–446.

Whereas, The Supreme Court of the United States has assumed appellate jurisdiction in the matter of the petition of Sherman M. Booth for a writ of habeas corpus, presented and prosecuted to final judgment in the Supreme Court of this State, and has, without process, or any of the forms recognized by law, assumed the power to reverse that judgment in a matter involving the personal liberty of the citizen, asserted by and adjusted to him by the regular course of judicial proceedings upon the great writ of liberty secured to the people of each State by the Constitution of the United States :

And, whereas, Such assumption of power and authority by the Supreme Court of the United States, to become the final arbiter of the liberty of the citizen, and to override and nullify the judgments of the state courts' declaration thereof, is in a direct conflict with that provision of the Constitution of the United States which secures to the people the benefits of the writ of habeas corpus : therefore,

Resolved, The Senate concurring, That we regard the action of the Supreme Court of the United States, in assuming jurisdiction in the case before mentioned, as an arbitrary act of power, unauthorized by the Constitution, and virtually superseding the benefit of the writ of habeas corpus and prostrating the rights and liberties of the people at the foot of unlimited power.

Resolved, That this assumption of jurisdiction by the federal judiciary, in the said case, and without process, is an act of undelegated power, and therefore without authority, void, and of no force.

Resolved, That the government, formed by the Constitution of the United States was not the exclusive or final judge of the extent of the powers delegated to itself; but that, as in all other cases of compact among parties having no common judge, each party has an equal right to judge for itself, as well of infractions as of the mode and measure of redress.[1]

Resolved, That the principle and construction contended for by the party which now rules in the councils of the nation, that the general government is the exclusive judge of the extent of the powers delegated to it, stop nothing short of despotism, since the *discretion* of those who administer the government, and not the *Constitution,* would be the measure of their powers ; that the several states which formed that instrument, being sovereign and independent, have the unquestionable right to judge of its infraction ; and that a *positive defiance* of those sovereignties, of all unauthorized acts done or attempted to be done under color of that instrument, is the rightful remedy.

[*General Laws of Wisconsin,* 1859, 247, 248.]

149. New York Denounces the Re-opening of the Slave Trade.

April 18, 1859.

The growing demand for slave labor in the cotton states led to a marked increase in the number of foreign slaves that were brought into the country contrary to law. Beginning about 1854 there was initiated a considerable movement in favor of legally re-opening the foreign slave trade. Governor Adams of South Carolina recommended it in his message of November, 1856 (Cluskey, 524), and in the several Southern Commercial Conventions held between 1855 and 1859 there was a strong element in its favor, which finally at the Vicksburg Convention in May, 1859, secured the adoption of a resolution by a vote of 40 to 19, declaring " that all laws, state or federal, prohibiting the African slave-trade, ought to be repealed." (*De Bow's Review,* xxvii, 99.) Leading southerners in Congress favored the movement during the same period

The following resolves of the New York Legislature were called out in opposition to this movement.[2] The Legislature of New Hampshire, June 28, 1859, also denounced the proposition, and again, July 4, 1860, declared : " That the virtual re-opening of the slave trade in violation of the law, is a species of nullification more dangerous to the Union and more degrading to the country

[1] Quoted from the Kentucky resolutions of 1798.

[2] The Legislature of South Carolina returned the resolutions. *Repts. and Res. of South Carolina,* 1859, 536.

than that nullification which formerly threatened to accomplish disunion by force." *Laws of New Hamp.*, 1859, 2140; *Ibid.*, 1860, 2298.

References: For proceedings of the commercial conventions and southern opinion see *De Bow's Review*, XXII, 91, 102, 216–224; XXIII, 309–319; XXIV, 473–491, 579–606; XXV, 121, 122, 166–185, 289, 308, 491–506; XXVI, 51–66; XXVII, 94–235; Cluskey, 585–595. General accounts, DuBois, *Suppression of the Slave Trade*, ch. xi; Rhodes, II, 241, 367–372, 481, 482; Von Holst, V, 484–490; VI, 313–324; VII, 262–266; Wilson, II, ch. xlviii.; Collins, *Domestic Slave Trade*, 54–60.

Resolved, That this Legislature, and the citizens of this State, look with surprise, mortification and detestation upon the virtual reopening, within the Federal Union, of the slave trade ; that against this invasion of our laws, our feelings, and the dictates of Christianity, we solemnly protest here, as we will protest elsewhere, and especially at the ballot-box ; that we call upon the citizens of this Union, to make common cause, in the name of religion, humanity, and as friends of principles underlying our system of government, to unite in bringing to immediate arrest and punishment, all persons engaged in the unlawful and wicked slave trade, and hereby instruct our senators and representatives in Congress to exert all lawful powers for the immediate suppression of the infamous traffic.

[Resolution of transmission.]

[*Laws of New York*, 1850, 1210.]

Resolutions on the Harper's Ferry Raid.

1859-60.

One manifestation of the excitement caused by the attack of John Brown on Harper's Ferry, Oct. 16, 1859, was the adoption of resolutions by several of the southern Legislatures. Georgia Nov. 14, 1859, was the first to condemn the attack and to commend the action of the federal and state authorities. (*Acts of Ga.*, 1859, 400.) Tennessee, in the resolutions which follow, denounced Seward and the Republican party as responsible for the outbreak. (*Acts of Tenn.*, 1859–60, 653–656.)

In response to the discussion of Federal relations by Gov. Wm. H. Gist, in his message of Nov. 29, 1859, prompted by the Harper's Ferry raid, (*Jour. of the Senate of S. C.*, 1859, 20–23,) the Legislature adopted the subjoined resolutions. (*Reports and Res. of S. C.*, 1859, 578, 579.) The invitation to a conference of Southern States was accepted by the Legislature of Miss. Feb. 10, 1860, which suggested that the convention should convene at Atlanta, on the first Monday in June. They also provided for sending a commissioner to Virginia to express their indignation at the outrage committed in the invasion of her soil and of their readiness to unite with her in repelling any assailment of her people and her rights. (*Laws of Miss.*, 1860, 566.) The Legislature of Alabama, Feb. 25, declared "that Alabama fully concur in affirming the right of any state to secede from the confederacy," and "that under no circumstances will she submit to the foul domination of a sectional northern party." They also made provision by law for the calling of a State convention in case of the election of a Republican President, however, if a convention of slave-holding states assembled they were to be represented. (*Acts of Ala.*, 1859-60, 685-687, 689, 690.) Following the example of South Carolina, Mississippi appropriated $150,000 and Alabama $200,000 for "military contingencies."

The Legislature of Virginia replied, March 8, 1860, to the invitation presented by the commissioners from South Carolina and Mississippi, Messrs. C. J. Memminger and P. B. Starke, declaring it in, their opinion, inexpedient to appoint deputies to the conference proposed," believing "that efficient cooperation " will be more safely obtained by direct legislative action of the several states. (*Acts of Va.*, 1859-60, 707.) The Tennessee Legislature, March 23, took a similar position. (*Acts of Tenn.*, 1859-60, 681.) Gov. Letcher of Va., in his message of Jan. 7, 1861, replied to the strictures upon Virginia, which had been uttered by the recent governor of South Carolina in his annual message of Nov. 1860, because of her action in declining the invitation to the conference. (*Virginia Documents*, 1861, No. 1, ix, x.)

References: For paper presented by C. J. Memminger of S. C., to the Virginia Legislature on the grievances of the South, see *De Bow's Review*, XXIX, 751-771. Report of Investigating Committee on the Invasion at Harper's Ferry, *Senate Rept.*, 36 *Cong.* 1 *sess.*, II, No. 278. General references, Channing and Hart, *Guide*, § 202; F. B. Sanborn, *Life and Letters of John Brown*, Articles by Sanborn, *Atlantic Monthly*, April 1872; March 1875; *The Critic*, XLVII, 349; Redpath, *Echoes* of *Harper's Ferry*; Greeley, I, ch. xx; Nicolay and Hay, *Lincoln* II, ch. xi; Rhodes, II, 384-416; Von Holst, VII, ch. i; Wilson, II, chs. xlv, xlvi; Bancroft, *Seward*, I, 495-499; Garrison, III, ch. xix.

150.   Tennessee on the Attack on Harper's Ferry.

December 2, 1859.

Therefore, Resolved by the General Assembly of the State of Tennessee, That we recognize in the recent outbreak at Harper's Ferry the natural prints of this treasonable, *" irrepressible conflict"* doctrine [1] put forth by the great head of the Black Republican party and echoed by his subordinates, and that it becomes the imperative duty of national men of all parties throughout the Union to announce to the world their sense of its infamy, and to unite in crushing out its authors as traitors to their country and as deadly enemies to the public peace, the rights of the States and the preservation of our Republican Institutions.

Resolved, That we record it as the sense of the Tennessee Legislature that the declarations of Mr. Seward that a respectable portion of the Southern people, under the head of such men as Cassius M. Clay and Francis P. Blair, will unite with the Black Republican party to prevent the extension of slavery, and will eventually *" rise up against slavery,"* as a libel upon the honor and loyalty of the Southern people, and will but serve to make them more watchful and exacting of their public servants in the National Councils.

Resolved, That it is the duty of our Representatives in Congress to recognize as enemies to the Union, and especially to the slave States, all who in any way favor or affiliate with this sectional Black Republican party, and that any action on their part which favors co-operation with the Black Republicans in organizing the House and thus placing the offices and important committees of that body under their control would be false to the sentiment of the people of Tennessee, an insult to their constituents and disgraceful to themselves.

Resolved, That we acknowledge our appreciation of the promptness with which the National Administation took steps to check the recent conspiracy before it obtained the huge dimensions of a revolution.

[*Public Acts of Tennessee, 1859–60, 653–656.*]

[1] Seward's speech at Rochester, N. Y., Oct. 25, 1858, *Works,* IV, 289–302; Johnston, *Amer. Orations,* III, 195–229.

151. South Carolina Proposes a Southern Convention.

December 22, 1859.

Whereas, The State of South Carolina, by her ordinance of A. D. 1852, affirmed her right to secede from the confederacy whenever the occasion should arise justifying her in her own judgment in taking that step, and in the resolutions adopted by her Convention declared that she forbore the immediate exercise of that right from considerations of expediency only ;[1] and,

Whereas, More than seven years have elapsed since that Convention adjourned, and in the intervening time the assaults upon the institution of slavery and upon the rights and equality of the Southern States have unceasingly continued with increasing violence and in new and more alarming forms ; be it therefore

1. *Resolved unanimously,* That the State of South Carolina, still deferring to her Southern sisters, nevertheless respectfully announces to them that it is the deliberate judgment of this General Assembly that the slave-holding States should immediately meet together to concert measures for united action.[2]

2. *Resolved unanimously,* That the foregoing preamble and resolutions be communicated by the Governor to all the slave-holding States, with the earnest request of this State that they will appoint deputies and adopt such measures as in their judgment will promote the said meeting.

3. *Resolved unanimously,* That a special Commissioner be appointed by his Excellency the Governor to communicate the foregoing preamble and resolutions to the State of Virginia, and to express to the authorities of that State the cordial sympathy of the people of South Carolina with the people of Virginia, and their earnest desire to unite with them in measures of common defence.

4. *Resolved unanimously,* That the State of South Carolina owes

---

[1] *Ante,* 272-275.

[2] This resolution as originally passed by the Senate declared " that in her judgment the safety and honor of the slave-holding States imperatively demand a speedy separation from the other States of the Confederacy, and earnestly invites the slave-holding States to inaugurate the movement of Southern separation, in which she pledges herself promptly to unite." *Senate Journal of S. C.,* 1859, 136, 168.

it to her own citizens to protect them and their property from every enemy, and that, for the purpose of military preparations for any emergency, the sum of one hundred thousand dollars ($100,000) be appropriated for military contingencies.

[*Reports and Resolutions of the General Assembly of South Carolina*, 1859, 578, 579.]

Inauguration of the Secession Movement.

1860

As is well known South Carolina led the way out of the Union. In anticipation of the election of Lincoln, Gov. Wm. H. Gist of South Carolina, Oct. 5, 1860, entered into secret correspondence with the Governors of several of the Southern States relative to secession. (For his letters and the replies, see, Nicolay and Hay, *Lincoln*, II, 306–314.) Gov. Gist, Oct. 12, issued a proclamation convening the Legislature of South Carolina in special session. (*S. C. House Jour.*, 1860, 10.) On receipt of the news of Lincoln's election the Legislature, Nov. 13, called a convention of the People of the State. (*Stat. at Large of S. C.*, XVI, 734.) This Convention, Dec. 20, 1860, adopted an ordinance of secession, (*Jour. of Convention*, 46, 47.) and on Dec. 24, issued *A Declaration of Causes which Induced her Secession from the Federal Union.* (*Jour. of Convention, Appx.*, 325–331; Moore, *Rebellion Record*, I, Docs. 3; McPherson, *Political History of the Rebellion*, 15, 16.)

Similarly the Governor of Mississippi called the Legislature of that State in special session, Nov. 19, 1860, and Nov. 29 that body adopted the act for calling a Convention to meet Jan. 7, 1861. On the following day, Nov. 30, they issued the subjoined *Declaration* justifying secession as the proper remedy for their grievances. This, the first official declaration of a Southern State in justification of secession, subsequent to the election of Lincoln, although less well known than that of the South Carolina Convention issued nearly a month later, is of especial interest as a severe arraingement of the Free-States for their hostility to slavery. For the subsequent *Declaration of Causes* issued by the Mississippi Convention, see *post.* 318. The Georgia Legislature, Dec. 19, 1860, replied promising coöperation, and in case of secession suggested that the "seceding States should form a Confederacy under a republican form of government." (*Acts of Ga.*, 1860, 238–240.)

References: For bibliography on Secession see *post.* 317; Campaign of 1860. The resolutions presented by the Alabama Delegates at the Charleston Convention, April 30, 1860, prior to their withdrawal, presents the position of the extreme southern wing of the Democratic party on slavery. See *Proceedings of Democratic National Convention held in 1860*, 56, 57. [Cleveland, 1860.] See also M. Halstead, *A History of the National Political Conven-*

tions of the Current Presidential Campaign, 68–74. [Columbus, 1860.]
Secondary works: Burgess, *Civil War*, ch. iii; Bancroft, *Seward*, I; ch.
xxiv ; Nicolay and Hay, *Lincoln*, II, chs. xiii–xxviii : Rhodes, II, ch. xi;
Smith, I, ch. x; Stanwood, ch. xxi; Von Holst, VII, chs. iii–vi.

---

152. Mississippi Justifies Secession.

November 30, 1860.

Whereas, The Constitutional Union was formed by the several
States in their separate sovereign capacity for the purpose of
mutual advantage and protection ;

That the several States are distinct sovereignties, whose supremacy is limited so far only as the same has been delegated by
voluntary compact to a Federal Government, and when it fails to
accomplish the ends for which it was established, the parties to
the compact have the right to resume, each State for itself, such
delegated powers ;

That the institution of slavery existed prior to the formation of
the Federal Constitution, and is recognized by its letter, and all
efforts to impair its value or lessen its duration by Congress, or
any of the free States, is a violation of the compact of Union and
is destructive of the ends for which it was ordained, but in defiance of the principles of the Union thus established, the people of
the Northern States have assumed a revolutionary position towards
the Southern States ;

That they have set at defiance that provision of the Constitution which was intended to secure domestic tranquillity among the
States and promote their general welfare, namely : " No person
held to service or labor in one State, under the laws thereof,
escaping into another, shall, in consequence of any law or regulation therein, be discharged from such service or labor, but shall
be delivered up on claim of the party to whom such service or
labor may be due ;"

That they have by voluntary associations, individual agencies
and State legislation interfered with slavery as it prevails in the
slave-holding States ;

That they have enticed our slaves from us, and by State inter-

vention obstructed and prevented their rendition under the fugitive slave law ; [1]

That they continue their system of agitation obviously for the
purpose of encouraging other slaves to escape from service, to
weaken the institution in the slave-holding States by rendering
the holding of such property insecure, and as a consequence its
ultimate abolition certain ;

That they claim the right and demand its execution by Congress to exclude slavery from the Territories, but claim the right
of protection for every species of property owned by themselves ;

That they declare in every manner in which public opinion is
expressed their unalterable determination to exclude from admit-
tance into the Union any new State that tolerates slavery in its
Constitution, and thereby force Congress to a condemnation of
that species of property ;

That they thus seek by an increase of abolition States " to
acquire two-thirds of both houses " for the purpose of preparing
an amendment to the Constitution of the United States, abolishing slavery in the States, and so continue the agitation that the
proposed amendment shall be ratified by the Legislatures of
three-fourths of the States ;

That they have in violation of the comity of all civilized nations,
and in violation of the comity established by the Constitution of
the United States, insulted and outraged our citizens when travel-
ling among them for pleasure, health or business, by taking their
servants and liberating the same, under the forms of State laws,
and subjecting their owners to degrading and ignominious punishment ;

That to encourage the stealing of our property they have put
at defiance that provision of the Constitution which declares that
fugitives from justice [escaping] into another State, on demand of
the Executive authority of that State from which he fled, shall
be delivered up ;

---

[1] The South Carolina Declaration of Causes emphasized this charge. *Jour.
of Convention of So. Car.*, 1860–61, *Appx.*, 329, 330; Rhodes, III, 147, 253;
Nicolay & Hay, *Lincoln*, III, ch. ii; *Ante*, 284, note 1.

That they have sought to create domestic discord in the Southern States by incendiary publications;

That they encouraged a hostile invasion of a Southern State to excite insurrection, murder and rapine;

That they have deprived Southern citizens of their property and continue an unfriendly agitation of their domestic institutions, claiming for themselves perfect immunity from external interference with their domestic policy;

We of the Southern States alone made an exception to that universal quiet;

That they have elected a majority of Electors for President and Vice-President on the ground that there exists an irreconcilable conflict between the two sections of the Confederacy in reference to their respective systems of labor and in pursuance of their hostility to us and our institutions, thus declaring to the civilized world that the powers of this Government are to be used for the dishonor and overthrow of the Southern section of this great Confederacy. Therefore,

Be it resolved by the Legislature of the State of Mississippi, That in the opinion of those who now constitute the said Legislature, the secession of each aggrieved State is the proper remedy for these injuries.

[*Laws of Mississippi,* 1860, 43-45.]

Coercion or Compromise.

1861.

President Buchanan, Jan. 8, 1861, sent a special message to Congress relative to secession which evinced a much bolder tone in regard to the preservation of the Union, than his message of Dec. 3, 1860. (Richardson, V, 626-639, 655-659.) On Jan. 6, Governor Letcher, in his message at the opening of the session of the Virginia Legislature, declared that an attempt by federal troops to march through Virginia in order to employ force against a Southern State would be regarded as invasion and repelled by force. (*Virginia Documents,* 1861, No. I, xxiii.) These views were indorsed by the Legislature on the following day in the subjoined resolution. (*Acts of Va.,* 1861, 337.) On the other hand, the Legislature of New York, Jan. 14, passed resolutions commending the President's special message and tendering "men and money" in support of the Union. The text of these resolutions follow. Similar resolutions were speedily passed by the Legislatures of Ohio, Maine, Wisconsin, Minnesota, Massachusetts, Pennsylvania, Michigan and Indiana. Ohio and Indiana, however, expressed themselves as opposed to all laws contrary to the constitution and laws of the United States and as averse to intermeddling with the internal affairs and domestic institutions of other states.

References for text of resolutions: *Laws of N. Y.*, 1861, 819, 820; *Acts of Ohio*, 1861, 175, 176; *Laws of Wis.*, 1861, 343–345; *Laws of Minn.*, 1861, 339–341; *Acts and Res. of Mass.*, 1860–61, 535, 585–591; *Laws of Penna.*, 1861, 725–727; *Acts of Mich.*, 1861, 579; *Laws of Ind.*, 1861, 188, 189; *House Misc. Docs.*, 36 *Cong.* 2 sess., Nos. 22, 24, 26, 33.

The New York resolutions provoked denunciatory replies from several of the Southern States, especially from the border states. Already, Tenn., Jan. 16, had suggested that negotiations should be entered into with the President and the authorities of each of the Southern States to prevent all movements tending to coercion or collision. (*Acts of Tenn.*, 1861, 45.) Two days later upon receipt of the New York resolves, they replied that whenever any attempt was made to coerce a sovereign state of the South, "the people of Tennessee . . . will as one man resist such invasion of the soil of the South at any hazard and to the last extremity." (*Ibid.*, 46.) Gov. Letcher of Virginia, in his message of Jan. 17, transmitting the New York resolutions, denounced the same in severe language, declaring that "an attempt at coercion can have no other effect than to exasperate the people threatened to be coerced. Blood shed in civil strife can only enrich the soil, that must speedily produce a harvest of woe." (*Journal of Va. House of Delegates, Extra Session*, 1861, 51, 52.) The Legislature voted to return the resolutions to New York with a request that no similar document be again sent to them. (*Ibid.*, 52.) Although, Jan. 19, the Legislature invited the other states to a Peace Conference, (*Acts of Va.*, 1860–61, 338, 339.) which later assembled, it adopted resolutions, Jan. 21, announcing that "if all efforts to reconcile the unhappy differences existing between the two sections of the country shall prove to be abortive, then . . . every consideration of honor and interest demand that Virginia shall unite her destiny with the slave-holding states of the South." (*Acts of Va.*, 1861, 337.)

The Georgia secession convention replied, Jan. 18, by authorizing the transmission to New York of a resolution approving the conduct of Gov. Brown in taking possession of Ft. Pulaski by Georgia troops. (*Journal of Convention*, 1861, 26.) Texas, Feb. 1, and Missouri, Feb. 21, declared that if coercion was attempted they would make common cause with "their southern brethren" in resisting "such unconstitutional violence and tyrannical usurpation of power." (Texas, copy in *Va. Docs.*, 1861, No. 33, p. 7; *Laws of Mo.*, 1860–61, 773.) Kentucky also condemned coercion as "tending to the destruction of our common country." (*Acts of Ky.*, 1861, 49.)

In addition to the Virginia resolutions for a peace conference, five other states suggested a convention of the states. Tennessee, Jan. 22, proposed a convention of the slave-holding states at Nashville, Feb. 4, "to digest and define a basis upon which, if possible, the Federal Union and the constitutional rights of the slave states may be perpetuated and preserved," to be followed by a constitutional convention of all the states at Richmond, "to revise and perfect" such plan. (*Acts of Tenn.*, 1861, 49–52; *House Misc.*, 36 *Cong.* 2 *sess.*, No. 27.) Kentucky, Jan. 25., New Jersey, Jan. 29, Ohio and Indiana in March, proposed the calling of a convention to amend the constitution. Delaware approved of the Crittenden amendments. (*Acts of Ky.*, 1861, 47; *House Misc.*, Nos. 21, 31; *Acts of Ohio*, 1861, 181; *Va. Docs.*, 1861, Nos. xxi, xxv, xlii; *Laws of Del.*, 1861, 191.)   Bibliography: Coercion; Nicolay and Hay, *Lincoln*, III, ch. xxv; Von Holst, VII, 270, 271, 441; McPherson, *Rebellion*, 5, 6; *Rebellion Record*, I, Docs. 21; Compromise Measures; Channing and Hart, *Guide*, § 207; *Cong. Globe* 36, *Cong.* 2 *sess.*, *Index*; *Journal of Senate Committee of Thirteen*; *Journal of House Committee of Thirty-three;* text of Crittenden Compromise, *Cong. Globe*, 114; Peace Conference Amendments, *Senate Misc. Docs.*, No. 20; Proposed XIII Amendment, *U. S. Stat. at L.*, XII, 251; also given in MacDonald, 438–446. General references: Ames, *Proposed Amendments*, 194–210; Bancroft in *Pol. Sci. Quar.*, VI, 401–423; Chittenden, *Report of the Debates and Proceedings of Peace Congress*; Report of Commissioners of Virginia to Peace Conference, *Virginia Docs.*, 1861, No. xxxviii; Coleman, *Life of Crittenden*, II, ch. xiii–xv; Curtis, *Buchanan*, II, ch. xxi; Davis, *Confed. Govt.*, I, Pt. III, ch. viii; Greeley, I, chs. xxiv, xxv; Nicolay and Hay, *Lincoln*, III, ch. xxvi–xxviii; III, chs. i, x–xv; Rhodes, III, chs. xiii, xiv; Smith, I, 328–347; Thorpe, II, ch. vi; Von Holst, VII, chs. ix–xi; Wilson, III, chs. vi–viii.

---

153.   Virginia Denounces the Coercion of a State.

January 8, 1861.

Resolved by the General Assembly of Virginia, That the Union being formed by the assent of the sovereign States respectively, and being consistent only with freedom and the republican institutions guaranteed to each, cannot and ought not to be maintained by force.

That the government of the Union has no power to declare or make war against any of the States which have been its constituent members.

Resolved, That when any one or more of the States has determined, or shall determine, under existing circumstances, to withdraw from the Union, we are unalterably opposed to any attempt on the part of the federal government to coerce the same into reunion or submission, and that we will resist the same by all the means in our power.

[*Acts of Virginia*, 1861, 337.]

154. New York Tenders Aid in Support of the Union.

January 14, 1861.

Whereas, Treason, as defined by the Constitution of the United States, exists in one or more of the States of this Confederacy, and

Whereas, The insurgent State of South Carolina, after seizing the postoffice, custom house, moneys and fortifications of the federal government, has, by firing into a vessel ordered by the government to convey troops and provisions to Fort Sumter, virtually declared war; *And whereas*, The forts and property of the United States government in Georgia, Alabama and Louisiana have been unlawfully seized with hostile intentions; *And whereas further*, Senators in Congress avow and maintain their treasonable acts; therefore,

Resolved, That the Legislature of New York, profoundly impressed with the value of the Union, and determined to preserve it unimpaired, hail with joy the recent firm, dignified and patriotic special message of the President of the United States, and that we tender to him, through the chief magistrate of our own State, whatever aid in men and money he may require to enable him to enforce the laws and uphold the authority of the federal government. And that in defence of " the more perfect Union," which has conferred prosperity and happiness upon the American people, renewing the pledge given and redeemed by our fathers, we are ready to devote " our fortunes, our lives and our sacred honor in upholding the Union and the Constitution."

Resolved, That the Union-loving representatives and citizens of Delaware, Maryland, Virginia, North Carolina, Kentucky, Missouri and Tennessee, who labor with devoted courage and patriotism to withhold their States from the vortex of secession, are entitled to the gratitude and admiration of the whole people.

[Resolutions of Transmission.]

[*Laws of New York*, 1861, 819, 820.]

Extension of the Secession Movement.

1861.

The resolutions adopted by the caucus of southern senators, Jan. 5, 1861, advising immediate secession were promptly acted upon by the gulf states. (Res. in Nicolay and Hay, *Lincoln*, III, 180.) Mississippi was the first to follow South Carolina out of the Union. (*Ante*, 310.) The convention assembled Jan. 7, and on the 9th, adopted after an hour's consideration, an ordinance of secession, by a vote of 84 to 15. *Journal of the Convention*, 1861, 16, 119, 120. *A Declaration of the Immediate Causes which Induce and Justify Secession*, was adopted by the convention without dissent, Jan. 28, *Journal*, 86-88. This declaration supplementary to the earlier one, issued by the Legislature (*Ante*, 311), is of especial interest not only by reason of the arraignment of the free states, but also because it reveals to what extent the people regarded their interests as identified with slavery.

References for the secession of Mississippi: T. H. Woods, The Miss. Secession Convention of 1860, in *Miss. Hist. Soc. Pub.*, VI, 91-104; J. Davis, *Confed. Govt.*, I, 220-229; R. Davis, *Recollections*, 390 ff ; Garner, *Reconstruction in Miss.*, 4-8; Nicolay and Hay, *Lincoln*, III, 183-185; Rhodes, III, 284; Cox, in *Atlantic Monthly*, LXIX, 382.

Dates and references for the ordinances of secession of the other states: Florida, Jan. 10. Copy of ordinance in Smith's *Debates of Alabama Convention*, 1861, *Appx.*, 417. Alabama, Jan. 11, Smith's *Debates*, 76, 77, 118; Address to the People, *Ibid.*, *Appx.*, 445-447; Georgia, Jan. 19, *Journal of the Convention*, 1861, 31, 32, 35; Report in justification of secession, drawn by Mr. Toombs, *Ibid.*, 104-113; Louisiana, Jan. 24, *Journal of the Convention*, 1861, 17, 18; Texas, Feb. 1, ratified by the people, Feb. 23, *Ordinances Passed by the State Convention*, 1861, 18, 19; Virginia, April 17, ratified May 23. *Ordinances Adopted by the Convention of Virginia, Appx. to Acts of Va.*, 1861, 3; Arkansas, May 6, *Rebellion Record*, I, 259, 260; North Carolina, May 20, *Journal of Convention*, 1861, 13-16; Tenn., May 7, by Legislature, ratified June 8, Appleton's *Annual Cyclopædia*, 1861, 680. Texts are also given in *Amer. History Leaflets*, No. 12; Moore, *Rebellion Records*, I, *Documents*; Appleton, *Annual Cyclopædia*, 1861. See also for documents McPherson, *Rebellion*, 2-47 *in passim*.

General references: Channing and Hart, *Guide*, § 206; *Annual Cyclopædia*, 1861, 696-708; Burgess, *Civil War*, ch. iv; Curtis, *Buchanan*, chs.

xv–xx; Davis, *Confed. Govt.*, I, 77–85, 199–226; Greeley, I, chs. xxii, xxvi, xxx; Johnston, II, ch. x; Morse, *Lincoln*, I, ch. vij; Nicolay and Hay, *Lincoln*, II, ch. xvii–xxv; III, ch. i, iii–xiii; Pollard, *Lost Cause*, ch. iv–v; Rhodes, III, ch. xiii, xv; Schouler, V, 468–491; VI, 1–49; Smith, I, 300–350; Stephens, *War Between the States*, II, xviii, xix, xxi; Thorpe, II, ch. v; Von Holst, VII, chs. vii, viii; Wilson, III, chs. i, iv–xli; Du Bose, *Yancey*, ch. xxiii, xxiv; Cleveland, *Stephens*, ch. vi, Speeches, *Ibid.*, 694–728; Stovall, *Toombs* ch. xx, Johnston, *Amer. Pol. Orations*, III, 230–322; *De Bow's Review*, vols. xxviii, xxix, *in passim*.

---

155. Mississippi on the Causes of Secession.

January 26, 1861.

A DECLARATION OF THE IMMEDIATE CAUSES WHICH INDUCE AND JUS-
TIFY THE SECESSION OF THE STATE OF MISSISSIPPI FROM THE
FEDERAL UNION.

In the momentous step which our State has taken of dissolving its connection with the government of which we so long formed a part, it is but just that we should declare the prominent reasons which have induced our course.

Our position is thoroughly identified with the institution of slavery—the greatest material interest of the world. Its labor supplies the product which constitutes by far the largest and most important portions of the commerce of the earth. These products are peculiar to the climate verging on the tropical regions, and by an imperious law of nature none but the black race can bear exposure to the tropical sun. These products have become necessities of the world, and a blow at slavery is a blow at commerce and civilization. That blow has been long aimed at the institution, and was at the point of reaching its consummation. There was no choice left us but submission to the mandates of abolition or a dissolution of the Union, whose principles had been subverted to work out our ruin.

That we do not overstate the dangers to our institutions a reference to a few unquestionable facts will sufficiently prove.

The hostility to this institution commenced before the adoption of the Constitution, and was manifested in the well-known Ordinance of 1787 in regard to the Northwestern Territory.

The feeling increased until in 1819–20 it deprived the South of more than half the vast territory acquired from France.

The same hostility dismembered Texas and seized upon all the territory acquired from Mexico.

It has grown until it denies the right of property in slaves, and refuses protection to that right on the high seas, in the Territories and wherever the government of the United States has jurisdiction.

It refuses the admission of new slave States into the Union, and seeks to extinguish it by confining it within its present limits, denying the power of expansion.

It tramples the original equality of the South under foot.

It has nullified the Fugitive Slave Law in almost every free State in the Union, and has utterly broken the compact which our fathers pledged their faith to maintain.

It advocates negro equality, socially and politically, and promotes insurrection and incendiarism in our midst.

It has enlisted the press, its pulpit and its schools against us until the whole popular mind of the North is excited and inflamed with prejudice.

It has made combinations and formed associations to carry out its schemes of emancipation in the States and wherever else slavery exists.

It seeks not to elevate or to support the slave, but to destroy his present condition without providing a better.

It has invaded a State, and invested with the honors of martyrdom the wretch whose purpose was to apply flames to our dwellings and the weapons of destruction to our lives.

It has broken every compact into which it has entered for our security.

It has given indubitable evidence of its design to ruin our agriculture, to prostrate our industrial pursuits and to destroy our social system.

It knows no relenting or hesitation in its purposes : it stops not in its march of aggression, and leaves us no room to hope for cessation or for pause.

It has recently obtained control of the Government by the prosecution of its unhallowed schemes, and destroyed the last expectation of living together in friendship and brotherhood.

Utter subjugation awaits us in the Union, if we should consent longer to remain in it.   It is not a matter of choice, but of necessity.   We must either submit to degradation and to loss of property worth four billions of money or we must secede from the Union framed by our fathers, to secure this as well as every other species of property.   For far less cause than this our fathers separated from the Crown of England.

Our decision is made. We follow in their footsteps. We embrace the alternative of separation, and for the reasons here stated, we resolve to maintain our rights with the full consciousness of the justice of our course and the undoubting belief of our ability to maintain it.

[*Journal of the State Convention*, 1861, 86–88.]